AN ERA OF GREATNESS

- A Statistical Analysis of the Records and Achievements.

- The Reasons Underlying the Success.

- Special Memories of the Players, Coaches, Media, and Opponents – 35 years later.

Team celebration after winning the first National Championship, January 1, 1971, Orange Bowl.* (17-12 over LSU)

Editor's Note regarding the author Johnny Rodgers:

- Born in Omaha, Nebraska in 1951 and still lives in Omaha;

- UNL's first Heisman Trophy winner (1972);

- Twice All-American at wingback, wide receiver and kick returner (1971-1972);

- Rookie of the Year in the CFL (1973);

- 4 years All-Pro with Montreal in the C.F.L. (1973-1976) (Most Valuable Player Runner-up 1974);

- 2 years with San Diego in the NFL (1977-1978);

- Graduated with two degrees from UNL;

- Husker Player of the Century;

- MVP in the history of the Big 8;

- College Football Hall of Fame (2000).

D1209142

TABLE OF CONTENTS

TABLE OF CONTENTS

FOREWORD
By Tom Osborne

The 1970 and 1971 seasons were great for Nebraska football. In those two years, we had a combined record of 24 wins, no losses, one tie, two conference championships and two national championships. These seasons catapulted Nebraska into the elite ranks of college football and accomplished something that many Nebraskans thought would never happen - Nebraska winning a national championship. To win one championship is unusual; to win back-to-back championships is extraordinary, and only a handful of teams have done that in the history of college football. In order for those two great seasons to occur, several key elements had to fall into place. I will analyze each of these factors as I recall them.

First, there was the coach. Bob Devaney had turned the Nebraska program around in 1962, after Nebraska had gone through more than twenty years of very mediocre football success. Bob inherited a losing team in 1962 and immediately turned it into a winner. That year he won nine games and lost two, en route to a victory over Miami in the now extinct Gotham Bowl, which was held in New York City. People in Nebraska were ecstatic over the turnaround and were quickly enamored by Bob's style. Bob had a great sense of humor, charisma, and confidence in his ability to win. He also brought with him a great group of coaches from the University of Wyoming. I was fortunate to have gone to the University of Nebraska in 1962, after having played in the National Football League, and I got a job with Bob as a graduate assistant in that first spring that he was at Nebraska. Therefore, I had an excellent vantage point to observe what transpired over the next few seasons. Bob's strength was people skills. He knew when to drive players, when to joke with them and when to relate to each one of them on a personal level. The experienced, cohesive coaching staff that he brought with him from Wyoming allowed Bob to hit the ground running. Unlike many coaches, he did not have to go through the growing pains of assembling a staff and creating a smooth organization. Bob's main asset was his optimism. There was never a game he entered that he did not think he was going to win. This optimism was something that had been lacking in previous coaching staffs and often times they had played a very cautious game that was designed not so much to win, but to avoid getting beaten badly.

Bob followed that successful first season at Nebraska with four consecutive Big Eight Conference Championships from 1963 to 1966. As a result, the players and the fans had great confidence in Bob and his coaching staff. And Bob certainly had the skills to take a team all the way to the top.

A second factor that went into those Championships in 1970 and 1971 was the fact that in the 1967 and 1968 seasons we did not continue the success that Bob had enjoyed in his early years at Nebraska. We only managed to win six games and lose four each year, falling far short of winning the conference championship. We did not go to a bowl game in either of those years and there were significant rumblings among the fans. Those who had previously been singing Bob Devaney praises were suddenly skeptics, and there was a petition circulated in Omaha after the 1968 season to fire Bob. The 1968 season was particularly difficult for those of us on the coaching staff, as we lost to Kansas State in Lincoln, 12-0, and ended the season in Norman, losing 47-0 to Oklahoma. The Oklahoma loss was devastating, and we were never in the game. After that game there was pressure on Bob to fire some assistant coaches and even a few folks were of the opinion that Bob Devaney was no longer the person who should lead the Nebraska program. It may seem strange that I mention those two 6-4 seasons as being key components to the success enjoyed in 1970 and 1971. However, if we didn't have those two rather bleak years, we would not have made some of the changes that bore fruit in the championship years. Bob indicated to his critics that he was not going to fire assistants to preserve his job; that if one person left we all left together. The loyalty that Bob showed his staff was something that all of us deeply appreciated. We all pulled together and redoubled our efforts to see to it that the Nebraska program did not disintegrate further. The changes that Bob made were as follows:

(a) With the four consecutive conference championships in the mid-60s, we had become somewhat complacent and our recruiting had fallen off. So, during 1967 and particularly in 1968 Bob and the coaching staff worked especially hard to attract good athletes, and we got some good players. Quarterbacks such as Jerry Tagge and Van Brownson made us very solid at quarterback. Johnny Rodgers was recruited out of Omaha and was undoubtedly the most electrifying player in college football during his 3-year career at Nebraska. Joe Orduna and Jeff Kinney made our running back core very solid. Defensive Linemen like John Dutton and Larry Jacobson were outstanding players at the collegiate and professional level. Jerry Murtaugh set records as a linebacker. Willie Harper and Rich Glover were great defensive players. Bob also made the decision that we needed an infusion of talent that was already well developed and asked me to go to California to recruit junior college players, and particularly those that could help shore up our offensive line. We were able to recruit Bob Newton, Keith Wortman, Carl Johnson and Dick Rupert from the junior colleges ranks. (Newton, Wortman and Carl Johnson all played professional football after college.) Also, we recruited Bob Terrio at linebacker and many other successful junior college players who contributed to our success during that period of time.

(b) After the 1968 season, Bob Devaney told me he felt we needed to make a major change in our offense. During his first several years at Nebraska, Bob had been running the unbalanced line, full house offense that he had learned at Michigan State under Duffy Dougherty. Bob thought that we possibly needed to look at some of the things that Oklahoma had done with Steve Owens running out of the I-formation. I studied Oklahoma films, and many other I-formation teams and we installed the I-formation as our base offense in 1969. We also put in a fairly extensive audible system that became very helpful. Furthermore, under Monte Kiffen's leadership, we also evolved into a very effective 5-2 defensive football team. The changes in offensive and defensive schemes seemed to be major factors in the resurgence of Nebraska football. However, X's and O's are never much good without the players, and the key thing was that our recruiting improved remarkably after those two bad years.

(c) Another factor that made a huge difference during that period of time was the installation of strength training and a conditioning program in the off-season. Prior to the 1969 season, we had very little in strength training and off-season conditioning. I talked to Boyd Epley, who was a member of the track team at that time. Boyd had become very interested in weight training and convinced me that we needed to implement some strength training in the football team. He asked me to approach Bob Devaney about the possibility of allowing him to introduce strength training to our players. At that time there was a genuine fear and mistrust amongst coaches about strength training. The general misconception was that it made you "muscle bound," and therefore most coaches avoided strength training and lifting like the plague. Boyd was persuasive and Bob was very receptive to changing because of the nosedive we had taken. Thus, our strength-training program was born. Boyd was intelligent and innovative, and he was able to stay ahead of the curve in strength training over the next thirty-plus years. Because of the strength training and off-season conditioning program Boyd developed, we were able to maximize the talent of our players. We were also able to take some walk-on players who were limited in size, speed or strength and turn them into good players within two or three years.

(d) The last element that figured into our turnaround and our two national championships had to do with some good fortune. A key play that I will always remember was a fourth down play in the Nebraska vs. Kansas game of 1969. Nebraska had opened the 1969 season with a loss to USC, had come back to beat Texas A&M and Minnesota, and then lost to Missouri. So, we started the season two and two. After the disastrous season we had in 1968, our confidence level was not very high. We were trailing Kansas 17-14 with only a few minutes left to play, and with the ball near mid-field we went for it on fourth down and long. We threw a pass to Jim McFarland, our outstanding tight end, but it was badly overthrown. A Kansas defensive back tackled Jim before the ball reached him and a pass interference was called, giving us a first down fairly deep in the Kansas territory. It was one of those calls that could have gone either way. The ball could have been ruled uncatchable or the interference call could have been made. The result was that we went on to score in the last few seconds and won by a score of 21-17. I can remember the Kansas coach Pepper Rogers being quite upset at the call and I could understand his point of view. The reason that particular play was so important was that it enabled us to win a key game that kept our conference championship hopes alive. We became stronger and stronger throughout the 1969 season, running off seven straight wins including a win over Georgia in the Sun Bowl. That left us with a very confident squad with great momentum going into the 1970 season. In 1970, we dominated every game with the exception of the hard fought 21-21 tie at Southern Cal early in the season. In that game we ran a number of trick plays which all seemed to work, and we were able to come out of the game deadlocked. That tie preserved the opportunity to go undefeated the rest of the way, which we did. We culminated the season with a win over LSU in the Orange Bowl, and it was after this game that good fortune again became apparent. We went into the bowl game ranked 3rd in the national polls on New Years Day, but the two teams ahead of us lost and late that night in Miami we suddenly found ourselves alone atop the polls as National Champions. We had a great year, but if either one of the teams ranked ahead of us had won, we would not have been chosen National Champions.

The 1971 season was not as precarious as the 1970 National Championship season. We were a very dominant team and had few challenges. Johnny Rodgers emerged as the most dangerous player in the game. He was outstanding as a punt returner, pass-receiver, kickoff return man, and ball carrier on counters and reverses. Jerry Tagge emerged as one of the premier quarterbacks in the country and Jeff Kinney had a great year at I-back. Our defense was one of the top defenses in the country and we were expected to be undefeated. We disappointed no one as we went through a 13 game schedule undefeated and soundly beat Alabama 38-6 in the Orange Bowl. The win over Alabama was so meaningful to many of us because it avenged two earlier bowl game defeats by Alabama, one of which cost us the National Championship in 1965. Bob Devaney had stood in Bear Bryant's shadow during previous years. But after the Orange Bowl game in 1971, with Nebraska and Alabama both undefeated and ranked one and two, Bob stood alone on top of the college football world, as we defeated Alabama soundly. All of us were tremendously pleased and proud of what he and the University of Nebraska team had accomplished.

As I think about the 1970 and 1971 teams, several memories stand out. Chief among them would be some of the most fantastic punt returns I have ever seen, as Johnny Rodgers continued to get us quick scores or great field position. I remember the growing confidence of the players as those seasons unfolded. Even during the hard fought game of the century against Oklahoma, which Nebraska won 35-31, it seemed as though the players never doubted that they would eventually wear Oklahoma down and win the game. The closeness of the players and the coaches is also a strong memory for me. There was a powerful camaraderie among all of those involved with those great teams and great loyalty to the coaching staff and to Bob Devaney among the players. It also seemed that it was a great age for college football since much of the commercialization that has developed in recent years had not yet occurred. I can't say that the game was totally innocent in those days. However, the idea of corporate sponsorships, multimillion-dollar coaching salaries and huge expenditures for facilities had not yet begun to occur. The emotion, the interest in the game and the excellence on the field was somehow more spontaneous and innocent. I will always have fond memories of those days and I continue to have great relationships with so many of the players who were involved in that great era of Nebraska football history.

Tom Osborne
Assistant UNL Coach (1962-1972)
Head Coach UNL (1973-1997)
College Football Hall of Fame (1998)

FOREWORD

By Don "Fox" Bryant

During the long years of exciting football at the University of Nebraska, there have been a number of three-year periods of excellence.

(1)   It appears first during the reign of Coach "Bummy" Booth when the newly-named Cornhuskers posted a 25-2-0 record (6-2-0 in 1901; 9-0-0 in 1902; 10-0-0 in 1903); (a .961 winning percentage).

(2)   "Jumbo" Stiehm rolled to a 23-0-1 three-year mark in 1913-14-15 (.979 winning percentage).

(3)   Fred Dawson had a 18-4-2 triple in 1921-22-23 (including two wins over Knute Rockne's Notre Dame Four Horsemen); (.792 winning percentage).

(4)   D.X. Bible's Huskers were 23-4-1 in 1931-32-33 (.850 winning percentage).

(5)   "Biff" Jones enjoyed a three-season string of 19-8-1 in 1939-40-41, including a berth in the 1941 Rose Bowl game.

(6)   Bob Devaney's resurgent Huskers were 29-4-0 in 1963-64-65 (.879 winning percentage).

(6)   Tom Osborne's 1982-83-84 teams were 34-4-0 (.895 winning percentage).

(8)   Tom Osborne's 1993-94-95 teams were 36-1-0, with two national championships. Tom also can point to a pair of great triples before he retired (36-2-0 in 1995-96-97; and 36-2-0 in 1994-95-96), if you want to split up his 60-3-0 record over his last 5 years (a .952 winning percentage).

Treasured memories all, but there was another three-year period in Nebraska football history that kept the fans across the nation sitting on the edge of their seats in expectation of another sensational play by Johnny Rodgers, the dazzling darter from Omaha who left Tech High School for a four-year journey to the Heisman Trophy presentation.

Johnny R – or Johnny "the Jet", aptly named by the Husker radio voice of Lyell Bremser at the conclusion of a punt return that opened the scoring in the famed 1971 "Game of the Century" at Oklahoma on Thanksgiving Day – herewith presents the spotlight on a three-year period (1970-1972), during which he played a huge role in Coach Bob Devaney's revitalization of Nebraska's football fortunes – three Big Eight championships and two national championships in a 33-2-2 run through college football (1970-71-72).

Impressive indeed, but any analysis of the "Johnny Rodgers Era," must also pay tribute to a fourth year, 1969, when Devaney's Cornhuskers shifted offensive gears and Johnny left Tech High to join the Nebraska freshman team, coached by Jim Ross. A former secondary coach with Devaney at Wyoming and NU, and a former high school Coach, Ross was quick to report that the Cornhuskers had recruited "a kid from Omaha that can play."

Play Johnny did during that 1969 season, leading the Freshman team to a 3-1-0 record. He also led the team in rushing (310 yards, 5.4 average and 4 TDs); receiving (11-186 and two TDs); scoring (6 TDs, 36 points); kickoff returns (for 102 and 25.3 average; and punt returns (12 for 217 and a 17.5 average).

Meanwhile, in 1969 Devaney's varsity – shaking off two successive 6-4 seasons – welcomed two quarter-backs (Van Brownson and Jerry Tagge) along with sophomore running back Jeff Kinney and Junior College tackle Bob Newton to a group of veterans. The running game perked up. The Huskers relied heavily on passing the ball to split end Guy Ingles and tight end Jim McFarland, and a stout defense. Nebraska lost the fourth game of the season to Mel Gray and the Missouri Tigers in Columbia, then launched a 32-game streak without a defeat. After a 44-14 thrashing of Oklahoma and a 45-6 Sun Bowl win over the Georgia Bulldogs, Devaney and the Huskers welcomed Johnny Rodgers to the 1970 varsity.

The 1969 Cornhuskers established a lift-off base for the 1970 team and Johnny Rodgers would play a major role in a new three-year gallop that would stun the nation – three Big Eight championships, three Orange Bowl championships and two national championships.

Now it's time to defer to The Jet, himself. Let Johnny, his teammatess, coaches, opponents and friends provide an exciting story of those unforgettable 1970-71-72 seasons. By the way, Johnny is still the most exciting player Old Fox has seen in a long life of watching football games – it seemed like every time he touched the ball, everyone got ready to stand up!

DON "FOX" BRYANT
Associate Athletics Director, Emeritus
University of Nebraska-Lincoln
August, 2006

Don "Fox" Bryant
Associate Athletics Director, Emeritus
University of Nebraska-Lincoln

INTRODUCTION
By Johnny Rodgers

This year is the thirty-fifth anniversary of the 1971 Oklahoma vs. Nebraska, Thanksgiving Day, "Game of the Century." This legendary game was first proclaimed as "The Game of the Decade" by President Nixon in a November 11th letter to coach Devaney. The game exceeded the pre-game hype as a record Owen Field crowd of 63,385 and an international television audience (the game was beamed by satellite to Europe and the Far East) saw what later was named the Greatest college football game ever played. In the end, Nebraska prevailed over their fiercest Big 8 Conference foe (35-31). Coach Chuck Fairbanks called Nebraska, "the most complete college team ever assembled." This "Game of the Century" with that stellar 1971 team has since stood the test of time and has been proclaimed by many as the best ever in college football.

Many people believe that this "Era of Greatness" started with the Game of the Century in `71. Others say the era started the year before with our first National Championship win over LSU (17-12). I believe the "Era of Greatness" actually started in 1969, when we beat Oklahoma (44-14) and then defeated Georgia in the Sun Bowl (45-6). The "Era of Greatness" label is appropriate given the incredible results. Starting with a win over Kansas in `69, we ran off a record of 31-0-1. We had 30 All-Conference players and 12 All-American honors, 30 NFL draftees, 4 Bowl wins, 4 Conference titles and two National Championships. That sounds like a Great Era to me. How about you?

This book is a compilation of the memories and stories from the players and coaches themselves, sprinkled with humor, heart felt convictions, values and morals that we learned as boys and which have endured as we've grown into our manhood, thirty five years later. Who were our leaders amongst the players and coaches? What were our challenges and goals? Who and what inspired us to trust each other with our lives, then and now? Many of these stories have brought tears of joy to my eyes. Others have thrown me to the floor laughing so hard I thought I was going to hurt myself. But most of all, these memories have brought a feeling of pride as I have interviewed my friends of yesterday, who are still friends today, and will definitely be friends tomorrow. I've learned and noticed that the most powerful and most lasting friendships are those we make in the early seasons of our lives. There is nothing like learning and winning together and helping each other be the best we can be. Old friends and teammates seem to make the best friends especially now that we are all getting older.

I also chose to include interviews with some of our opponents since greatness is determined by what we accomplish and by the quality of our opposition. UNL had some tough times in the 1967 and 1968 seasons. It was during those two years that coach Melton said fans were passing around a petition to try to get them all fired. "During that period we played so bad I started to sign the petition myself." Melton said. Oklahoma fought us like dogs on the field and beat us badly during that difficult two-year stretch. Yet, the coaches used those difficult times to strengthen our nerves and sharpen our skills. Oklahoma was our greatest antagonist but also our greatest helper. It wasn't the defeats we suffered from Oklahoma or the victories that kept our hearts pumping when we took the field against them. It was the competition with the best that set the stage for our "Era of Greatness." With Oklahoma, the competition was always like "buttered popcorn." We knew that the greater the challenges the more the glory in overcoming them. After all, if you want to be the best you have to beat the best. Oklahoma players, coaches and fans always represented themselves with class during that era. It is helpful, then, to choose the best of our opponents to include in this book and I interviewed coaches and players from Oklahoma, Missouri and Kansas State, all of whom played such a key role in UNL's rise to greatness.

Our memories are filled with great plays made by those of us who were privileged to handle the ball in the so-called "skilled" positions. Naturally I have included interviews with many of those familiar names. Yet, I've always said, "It's what's up front that counts." Those up front, whether it was our offensive or defensive line, make the first contact and often determine the outcome of the game. After all, you never get a second chance to make a first impression. They made a heck of a first impression on our opponents. Those guys were always about getting it done and getting it done now! With all due respect to every one involved, I believe all the starting linemen on both sides of the ball on the `70 and `71 teams deserve to be in the Nebraska Football Hall of Fame. They never lost a game during a time when the consensus opinion was that the Big Eight played the best football top to bottom of any conference in the country. They gave the first hit on every play. They made the holes for the running plays. They gave the passing plays time to develop. They were the best and that is no brag - just fact. I have included a number of interviews with these often-overlooked heroes in the trenches. Without them, there would be no "Era of Greatness."

Greatness is something that is developed through hard work, setting lofty goals, overcoming obstacles, building teamwork, performing under pressure, and being coachable. Greatness is a blend of values, talent and perseverance. Greatness is a unique blend of leadership and discipline. Greatness is something that each one of us should strive to attain. Although this book is about an "Era of Greatness" achieved on the college football field, within the interviews you will find the keys to lifelong greatness as voiced by the coaches and players of that era. You will find the values they hold and stories about that journey. You will find that greatness is not just for those that score the touchdowns but also for those who waited in reserve for their opportunity. You will find that greatness is not just something that is decreed following the game or the season but something that began years before. You will also find that greatness must begin inside before it is ever achieved outside.

In preparing for these interviews, I contemplated many questions. This book is just a small part of hundreds of hours of wonderful conversations with old teammates, coaches and opponents. I wish there was space to include them all. Editing the interviews was no easy task as there are so many great stories. I hope you enjoy reading them as much as I've enjoyed doing the interviews. This was truly an "Era of Greatness."

PURPOSES

The three purposes of this book are:

(1) To describe and elaborate upon the many records and achievements of the 1969-1972 UNL Teams within a national historical perspective;

(2) To analyze the reasons underlying the success and to explore how this remarkable record was accomplished – season by season – and to pay tribute to the coaches, players, support personnel, media, fans and opponents who made it possible.

(3) To update us all on the progress of many of these remarkable student/athletes and coaches and trainers to the present day (families, careers, community involvement, etc.) as explained in their own words and as they look back 35 years later and reminisce about their experiences and the values that they learned in playing for or against "Big Red" during this period.

We hope you enjoy this "trip down memory lane". "Go Huskers!"

1915

1965

ACKNOWLEDGEMENTS

A football team cannot function effectively without teamwork. Similarly, this book could not have been organized and written without the valuable assistance of the following team players. A "Big Red" thank you to each and every one .

(1) **Steve Pederson**, UNL Athletic Director; **Chris Anderson**, Associate Athletic Director for Communications; **Keith Mann**, Media Relations Director; **Pat Logsdon,** Assistant A. D. for Administration and **Vicki Cartwright,** Media Relations Adminstrative Assistant.

(2) **Hollie Shives** for her skills in computer research and her dedication over several hundred hours in transcribing the interviews and typing the book.

(3) The research, editing and proof reading of **Dr. Rene Hlavac, Gary Stevenson, Larry Myers, "Biz" Jordan, Dr. Eric Kagaruki, Ron Thorngren, Brad Thorngren, Eddie Belle and John Kinney.**

(4) **Becky Enholm** of Becky Enholm Advertising Art Co., Inc for her most professional services in the layout and graphics.

(5) **Lois Brinton** in the NU Photo Service Department for her invaluable knowledge in selecting photographs.

(6) **Loren Murfield**, my business and literary coach.

(7) **John Gottschalk**, CEO and Publisher, Omaha World-Herald; and The Photo Services Departments in the Libraries of the **Omaha World-Herald (Jeanne Hauser)** and the **Lincoln Journal Star (Denise Matulka).**

World-Herald photos are identified with an asterisk.
All Omaha World-Herald photos in this book have been reprinted with the prior written permission of the World Herald which retains sole and exclusive copyright interest to all such photos. All rights reserved.

(8) The Author gratefully acknowledges the assistance of The Knights of The Round Table, L.L.C., which generously allowed the use of portions of its book, Why We Care (2004), in this book and has provided research materials and permission to use them in this book.

9) Finally, the author salutes the patience, knowledge, memories, sense of humor and wisdom of all the **players, coaches, trainers,** and **media personnel** who patiently gave their time to be interviewed. You are the heart and soul of this book. You are the best.

AN ERA OF GREATNESS:
(1969 – 1972)

1969

Won 9, Lost 2, Tied 0
Big Eight Champion
Sun Bowl Champion

DATE	OPPONENT	AP RANK NU/OPP.		RESULT	
S 20	USC	/ 5	L	21-31	
S 27	Texas A&M		W	14-0	
O 4	**Minnesota**		W	**42-14**	
O 11	**Missouri**	20t/ 7	L	**7-17**	
O 18	Kansas		W	21-17	
O 25	Oklahoma State		W	13-3	
N 1	Colorado	/ 18	W	20-7	
N 8	Iowa State	20t/	W	17-3	
N 15	**Kansas State**	17 /	W	**10-7**	
N 22	**Oklahoma**	16 /	W	**44-14**	

SUN BOWL

D 20	Georgia	14 /	W	45-6

FINAL RANKING: 11th AP (post-bowl),
12th UPI (regular season)

1970

Won 11, Lost 0, Tied 1
National Champion
Big Eight Champion
Orange Bowl Champion

DATE	OPPONENT	AP RANK NU/OPP.		RESULT	
S 12	Wake Forest	9 /	W	36-12	
S 19	**USC**	**9 / 3**	T	**21-21**	
S 26	Army	8 /	W	28-0	
O 3	**Minnesota**	6 /	W	**35-10**	
O 10	Missouri	6 / 16	W	21-7	
O 17	**Kansas**	5 /	W	**41-20**	
O 24	Oklahoma State	4 /	W	65-31	
O 31	**Colorado**	4 /	W	**29-13**	
N 7	**Iowa State**	4 /	W	**54-29**	
N 14	Kansas State-HC	4 / 20	W	51-13	
N 21	Oklahoma	3 /	W	28-21	

ORANGE BOWL

J 1	Louisiana State	3 / 5	W	17-12

FINAL RANKING: 1st AP (post-bowl),
3rd UPI (regular season)

*Away games in bold.

White House reception with President Richard Nixon, January '72.

1971

Won 13, Lost 0, Tied 0
National Champion
Big Eight Champion
Orange Bowl Champion

DATE	OPPONENT	AP RANK NU/OPP.	RESULT
11	Oregon	2 /	W 34-7
18	Minnesota	1 /	W 35-7
25	Texas A&M	1 /	W 34-7
2	Utah State	1 /	W 42-6
9	**Missouri**	**1 /**	**W 36-0**
16	Kansas-HC	1 /	W 55-0
23	**Oklahoma State**	**1 /**	**W 41-13**
30	Colorado	1 / 9	W 31-7
6	Iowa State	1 /	W 37-0
13	**Kansas State**	**1 /**	**W 44-17**
25	**Oklahoma**	**1 / 2**	**W 35-31**
4	**Hawaii**	**1 /**	**W 45-3**

RANGE BOWL

| 1 | Alabama | 1 / 2 | W 38-6 |

FINAL RANKING: 1st AP
1st UPI

1972

Won 9, Lost 2, Tied 1
Big Eight Champion
Orange Bowl Champion

DATE	OPPONENT	AP RANK NU/OPP.	RESULT
S 9	**UCLA**	**1 /**	**L 17-20**
S 16	Texas A&M	1 /	W 34-7
S 23	**Army**	**9 /**	**W 77-7**
S 30	Minnesota	7 /	W 49-0
O 14	Missouri	6 /	W 62-0
O 21	**Kansas**	**5 /**	**W 56-0**
O 28	Oklahoma St.-HC	3 /	W 34-0
N 4	**Colorado**	**3 / 15**	**W 33-10**
N 11	**Iowa State**	**3 / 17**	**T 23-23**
N 18	Kansas State	5 /	W 59-7
N 23	Oklahoma	5 / 4	L 14-17

ORANGE BOWL

| J 1 | Notre Dame | 9 / 12 | W 40-6 |

FINAL RANKING: 4th AP (post-bowl),
9th UPI (regular season)

*Away games in bold

AN ERA OF GREATNESS: COACH BOB DEVANEY'S FINAL FOUR SEASONS (1969 - 1972)

*"We are going to win
and the future is now!"*

Coach Bob Devaney (1962),
before his first Spring practice at UNL

An "Era" is "a period of time marked by distinctive character and events." "Greatness" is defined as "unusually or comparatively large in size or dimension; notable, remarkable, exceptionally outstanding or highly significant."

"Greatness" over a period of years is increasingly rare in college team sports. Consecutive major championships, continuing national records and enduring streaks of excellence occur much less frequently and to fewer teams in national collegiate athletic history.

In contrast, the University of Nebraska football in the four-year era from 1969 through 1972 was one of those rare and exceptionally bright shining periods. "An Era of Greatness" describes and analyzes this brilliant four year period in NU history. Under the leadership of Head Coach Bob Devaney, NU football rose to new heights of greatness, and these four championship teams achieved and contributed to the following significant milestones in UNL and national college history:

(1)   **Two consecutive National Championships with undefeated teams** (1970-1971);

(2)   **Four consecutive Big Eight Conference Championships** (won or shared); Devaney won 8 out of 11 Conference titles from 1962-1972 (73%).

(3)   **Four consecutive Bowl Game victories** over perennial national powers Georgia, LSU, Alabama and Notre Dame. The average score was 35 - 7.5, a 4 touchdown differential. The 1969 Sun Bowl victory was the first step in an ensuing national record of 35 consecutive bowl games (1969-2003).

4)   **A 32-game undefeated streak**, starting with the 5th game of the 1969 season and extending to the first game of the 1972 season. This was the second longest undefeated streak in Husker history.

(a)   NU was also undefeated in 23 consecutive home games.

(5) **Won nearly 90% of their games** with a 48 game record of 42 wins, 4 losses and 2 ties (.895 winning percentage and 10.5 wins per year average). The average score in the 48 games was 35.4 - 10.4, a 25-point differential.

(a) The four losses were by an average of only 6.5 points against traditional college powers USC, UCLA, Oklahoma and Missouri, and each game was not decided until the 4th quarter.

(b) The 2 ties were both to ranked teams on their home fields (USC and Iowa State).

(c) The 42 wins were by an average score of 37.5 - 8.9, a four touchdown differential . More specifically, the margins of victory break down as follows.

1. **5 games by 3 to 7 points (12%)**

Kansas State `69	(10-7)
Oklahoma `70	(28-21)
Oklahoma `71	(35-31)
LSU `71	(17-12)
Kansas `69	(21-17)

2. **2 games by 8-13 points (5%)**

Colorado `69	(20-7)
Oklahoma State `69	(13-3)

3. **35 games by 14 or more points ("Blowout wins") (83%)**

(d) Over 44 games, from the 5th game of `69 through the 12th game of `72, the record was 40-2-2, (.932 winning percentage). The 2 losses were both by 3 points.

(e) Comparatively over the 4-year period, **NU's 42 wins and .895 winning percentage led the nation.** NU's **total wins (784) (1890-2005) ranks 3rd** in college history, and NU is gaining on Michigan and Notre Dame.

(6) Each of these teams won at least 9 games. This started an illustrious **streak of 33 consecutive seasons with at least 9-wins** (1969-2001), which is still a national record by a wide margin.

(7) The 4 winning seasons continued the streak (started in 1962 and ending in 2004) of **42 consecutive winning seasons.** This ranks 3rd all-time in college football history.

(8) The 1971 team has been ranked by many analysts as **the best individual team of all-time.**

(9) For added historical perspective, UNL was playing and defeating "Big Time" opposition:

(a) **The Big 8 Conference without question was the toughest conference in America** during that time period (Nebraska, Oklahoma, Colorado, Missouri, Oklahoma State, Kansas, Kansas State and Iowa State).

(1) Big 8 teams won 4 out of 6 National championships between 1970-1975 (two by Nebraska and two by Oklahoma).

(2) In 1971 the top 3 ranked teams in the nation all came from the Big 8 (#1 Nebraska, #2 Oklahoma, #3 Colorado). This will probably never happen again in college football.

(3) NU's record in the tough Big 8 was 25-2-1 (.911 winning percentage). This included 3 straight wins against Oklahoma (1969-1971) and two of the victories were on OU's field.

(b) **For it's non-conference games, NU played most of the national powers from all areas of the country:** USC, UCLA, to

Army, Texas A&M, Notre Dame, Minnesota, LSU, Alabama and Georgia. [Miami and Florida State had not yet risen to national prominence] These 9 powerful non-conference foes, plus Oklahoma, Colorado and Nebraska, have won a total of 45 National championships in the 70 year history of Associated Press Voting (1936-2005).

(c)   NU played 13 "ranked" teams (in Top 20 at time of the game) with a record of 9-2-2 (.769 winning %) and an average score of 27.6 - 14.6, a 13 point differential.

(10)   At his retirement after the 1972 season, **Coach Devaney was the winningest active college football coach in America**, and today he stands as the 11th winningest coach in college history with a .806 winning percentage (136-30-7). His record at UNL was 100-20-2 (.829 winning percentage). Devaney became enshrined in the College Football Hall of Fame. UNL and Stanford are tied for first in the total number of coaches (6) in the Hall of Fame.

(11)   **Fan support was unprecedented**, and each team played before sold-out audiences at home games. This continued a record started in 1962 and which is now **a continuing national record of sell-outs** over 44 straight seasons and 278 games (1962-2005).

(12)   **Individual honors** of players on these four teams included 37 All-Conference, 11 All-American, 1 Heisman Trophy, 2 Outland Trophies and 1 Lombardi Trophy. 29 players went on to play pro football in the NFL or CFL.

(13)   **The players also excelled academically**. Over 90% graduated from college and there were 3 Academic All-Americans and 16 Academic All-Conference. UNL currently has one of the highest graduation rates in America and **leads the nation in total Academic All-Americans** with 222.

(14)   **Finally, the Assistant Coaches were gifted and close-knit:** Cletus Fischer, John Melton, Jim Ross, Carl Selmer, Monte Kiffin, Warren Powers, Tom Osborne, Bill Myles, Jim Walden and Thunder Thornton. Powers went on to be a successful Head Coach at Washington State and Missouri. Jim Walden became head coach of Washington State and Carl Selmer at Miami. Kiffin became one of the best defensive coordinators in NFL history (with Super Bowl Champion Tampa Bay in 2002). Osborne later became UNL Head Coach for 25 years (1973-1997) and retired in 1997 as the 5th winningest coach in College History (.836) and with 3 National Championships (1994,1995,1997).

Only a few schools in college history have ever come close to achieving such a spectacular four-year record. No college has ever won three consecutive national championships, and only 8 schools have achieved the lofty level of greatness of **two consecutive titles:**

(a)	Nebraska (twice) . . .	(1970-1971; 1994-1995);
(b)	Oklahoma (twice). . .	(1955-1956; 1974-1975);
(c)	Alabama (twice) . . .	(1964-1965; 1978-1979);
(d)	Notre Dame . . .	(1946-1947);
(e)	Minnesota . . .	(1940-1941);
(f)	Texas . . .	(1969-1970);
(g)	Army . . .	(1944-1945);
(h)	Southern Cal (USC) . . .	(2003-2004).

In addition to tremendous talent, there was an exceptional teamwork, chemistry, espirit de corps and personal closeness among members of these teams. This will be revealed in great detail later in the book.

THE STATISTICS SPEAK FOR THEMSELVES:

The Final Four years: "An Era of Greatness" (1969-1972)	1969	1970	1971	1972	4 year Summary; Averages
(1) **Won/Loss Record**	9 - 2	11 - 0 - 1	13 - 0	9 - 2 - 1	42-4-2 .895 winning % 10.5 wins per year
(2) **National Ranking** (Associated Press)	11th	1st	1st	4th	1st ... twice Top 5 ... 3 of 4
(3) **Big 8 Conference Record**	1st - tie (6 - 1)	1st (7 - 0)	1st (7 - 0)	1st (5 - 1 - 1)	1st ... 4 years 25-2-1 (.911 winning %)
(4) **Bowl Game Record**	Sun: 45 - 6, Georgia	Orange: 17 -12, LSU	Orange: 38 - 6, Alabama	Orange: 40 - 6, Notre Dame	4 wins (35 - 7.5 average score)
(5) **Undefeated in 32 Consecutive Games**	7	12	13		32 straight games without defeat (1969-1972)
(6) **UNL Average Score**	28.2	33.5	38.2	40.9	35.4
(7) **Opponent's Average Score**	10.7	14.9	8.0	8.1	10.5 26 games where opponent held to 7 or less (54%)
(8) **Point Differential**	17.5	18.6	30.2	32.8	24.9

(9) The Big 8 was the Toughest Conference in the Nation. The Big 8 produced the National Champion 4 out of 6 years from 1970-1975 (UNL twice & Oklahoma twice); In 1971 the Top 3 Teams were all in the Big 8 (UNL, Oklahoma and Colorado).

COMPARATIVE AVERAGE SCORES SHOW A CONSISTENCY IN HOME AND AWAY GAMES

The Final Four Years: "An Era of Greatness" (1969 -1972)	Average UNL Score	Average Opponent Score Point	Average Point Differential
(1) **Total of 48 Games** ■ 42-4-2 ■ .895 winning %	35.4	10.4 7 points or less in 26 games (54%)	25.0
(2) **Home Games (26)** ■ (24-2-0) ■ (.923 winning %)	34.6	8.8	25.8
(3) **Road Games (22)** (Bowls and Opponent's field) ■ 18-2-2 ■ .864 Winning %	38.0	12.7	25.3
(4) **Bowl Games (4)** ■ 4-0-0 ■ .1000 winning %	35.0	7.5	27.5
(5) **Against Ranked Teams (13)** ■ 9-2-2 ■ .769 winning %	27.6	14.6	13.0

AN ERA OF GREATNESS: COACH BOB DEVANEY'S FINAL FOUR SEASONS (1969 - 1972)

THE ASSISTANT COACHES AND TRAINERS

"I was fortunate to have the best Assistant Coaches in the Nation."

Coach Bob Devaney,
(at his Retirement Party in 1973)

Mike Corgan

Cletus Fischer

Monte Kiffin

John Melton

Bill Myles

Tom Osborne

Warren Powers

Jim Ross

Carl Selmer

Bill "Thunder" Thornton

*"They call it coaching,
but it is teaching...
you show them the reasons
why it is so and you repeat
and repeat until
they know."*

Vince Lombardi (1967)
The greatest pro football
coach of all-time.

Jim Walden

Boyd Epley
Weights & Conditioning

Paul Schneider
Trainer

George Sullivan
Trainer

PLAYERS ON THE FOUR TEAMS
WHO WERE AWARDED SPECIAL HONORS AND RECOGNITION

ALL-CONFERENCE (37)

1969	Ken Geddes	MG
	Bob Liggett	DT
	Jim McFarland	TE
	Jerry Murtaugh	LB
	Dana Stephenson	DB
1970	Bill Kosch	DB
	Donnie McGhee	OG
	Jerry Murtaugh	LB
	Bob Newton	OT
	Joe Orduna	HB
	Ed Periard	MG
	Johnny Rodgers	HB
	Paul Rogers	PK
	Dave Walline	DT
1971	Jim Anderson	DB
	Joe Blahak	DB
	Rich Glover	MG
	Willie Harper	DE
	Larry Jacobson	DT
	Carl Johnson	OT
	Jeff Kinney	HB
	Bill Kosch	DB
	Johnny Rodgers	HB
	Dick Rupert	OG
	Jerry Tagge	QB
	Bob Terrio	LB
1972	Joe Blahak	DB
	Rich Glover	MG
	Willie Harper	DE
	Johnny Rodgers	WB
	Daryl White	OT
1973	Frosty Anderson	SE
	John Dutton	DT
	Steve Manstedt	DE
	Daryl White	OT
1974	Marvin Crenshaw	OT
	Dave Humm	QB

ALL-AMERICANS (11)

Jerry Murtaugh	Linebacker	(`70)
Bob Newton	Tackle	(`70)
Jeff Kinney	Halfback	(`71)
Larry Jacobson	Def. Tackle	(`71)
Jerry Tagge	Quarterback	(`71)
Rich Glover	Middle Guard	(`71-`72)
Willie Harper	Def. End	(`71-`72)
Johnny Rodgers	Wingback	(`71-`72)
Daryl White	Off. Tackle	(`72-`73)
John Dutton	Tackle	(`73)
Dave Humm	Quarterback	(`74)

Heisman Trophy
Johnny Rodgers (`72)

Outland Trophy
Larry Jacobson (`71)
Rich Glover (`72)

Lombardi Trophy
Rich Glover (`72)

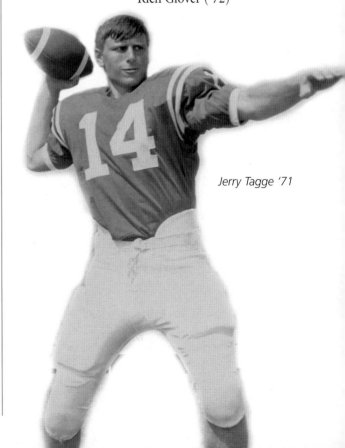

Jerry Tagge '71

ACADEMIC ALL-AMERICANS (3)

Randy Reeves	Def. Back	(`69)
Jeff Kinney	Halfback	(`71)
Larry Jacobson	Def. Tackle	(`71)

ACADEMIC ALL-CONFERENCE (16)

Larry Jacobson	Def. Tackle	(`69; `71)
Randy Reeves	Def. Back	(`69)
Paul Topliff	Tackle	(`69)
John Adkins	Def. End	(`70-`71)
Bill Kosch	Def. Back	(`70-`71)
Dave Walline	Def. Tackle	(`70)
Jim Anderson	Def. Back	(`71)
Woody Cox	Split End	(`71)
Jeff Kinney	Halfback	(`71)
Dave Mason	Linebacker	(`71-`72)
Dick Rupert	Guard	(`71)
Frosty Anderson	Back	(`72-`73)
Doug Dumler	Center	(`72)
Bill Janssen	Def. Tackle	(`72)

Rich Glover '72

PLAYERS WHO WERE DRAFTED AND/OR PLAYED PROFESSIONAL FOOTBALL (29)

1970	Ken Geddes	Linebacker	Detroit
	Mike Green	Running Back	San Diego
	Bob Liggett	Def. Tackle	Kansas City
	Glen Patterson	Center	Dallas
	Jim McFarland	Tight End	St. Louis
	Frank Patrick	Tight End	Green Bay
	Dana Stephenson	Def. Back	Chicago
	Mike Wynn	Def. End/Tackle	Oakland
1971:	Jerry Murtaugh	Linebacker	New England
	Bob Newton	Tackle	Chicago
	Joe Orduna	Running Back	San Francisco
	Paul Rogers	Kicker	Pittsburgh
	Dan Schneiss	Tight End	New England
1972:	Joe Blahak	Safety	Minnesota
	Van Brownson	Quarterback	Baltimore
	Rich Glover	Nose Guard	NY Giants
	Willie Harper	Linebacker	San Francisco
	Larry Jacobson	Def. Tackle	NY Giants
	Carl Johnson	Tackle	New Orleans
	Jeff Kinney	Running Back	Kansas City
	Johnny Rodgers	Receiver	Montreal
	Jerry Tagge	Quarterback	Green Bay
	Keith Wortman	Guard	Green Bay
1973:	John Dutton	Tackle	Dallas
	Daryl White	Off. Tackle	Detroit
1974:	Marvin Crenshaw	Off. Tackle	Pittsburgh
	Maury Damkroger	Fullback	New England
	Dave Humm	Quarterback	Oakland
	Steve Manstedt	Def. End	Washington

ALL-CONFERENCE PLAYERS

Frosty Anderson
1973

Jim Anderson
1971

Joe Blahak
1971-72

John Dutton
1973

Marvin Crenshaw
1974

Ken Geddes
1969

Rich Glover
1971-72

Willie Harper
1971-72

Dave Humm
1974

Larry Jacobson
1971

Carl Johnson
1971

Jeff Kinney
1971

Bill Kosch
1970-71

Bob Liggett
1969

Steve Manstedt
1973

ALL-CONFERENCE PLAYERS

Jim McFarland
1969

Donnie McGhee
1970

Jerry Murtaugh
1969-70

Bob Newton
1970

Joe Orduna
1970

Ed Periard
1970

Johnny Rodgers
1970-71-72

Paul Rogers
1970

Dick Rupert
1971

Dana Stephenson
1969

Jerry Tagge
1971

Bob Terrio
1971

Dave Walline
1970

Daryl White
1972-73

AN ERA OF GREATNESS: COACH BOB DEVANEY'S FINAL FOUR SEASONS (1969 - 1972)

The 1st National Championship
Guy Ingles makes a crucial catch.
Orange Bowl 1971 (NU 17 - LSU 12).

*"Many of UNL's teams in the early
20th Century were renowned and revered."*

Don "Fox" Bryant,
Why We Care p. 59 (2004)

During the time period from 1890 through 1940, the University of Nebraska became nationally known as a football powerhouse. NU traveled coast to coast by train and played most of the college powers. There were only 3 losing seasons. There were 6 undefeated seasons, 13 seasons with only one loss, and 18 seasons with only two losses. The winning percentage in 423 games was .731.

In the 38 years that NU played in a conference, NU dominated and won 24 Conference championships (63%). In 5 of the undefeated seasons, NU had a strong claim to the "mythical" national championship (1902, 1903, 1913, 1914 and 1915). The Associated Press did not start voting for an "official" national champion until 1936.

NU teams featured power running and strong defenses based upon overall team speed. 43% of all games were "shutouts" where the defense held the opponent to zero points. The offenses averaged 19 points, and the defenses allowed an incredible average of only 6.3 points scored by the opponents. Thus, the average point differential in the 423 games was two touchdowns. One writer in the 1920s described NU football teams as "The Mighty Mastodons of the Midwest."

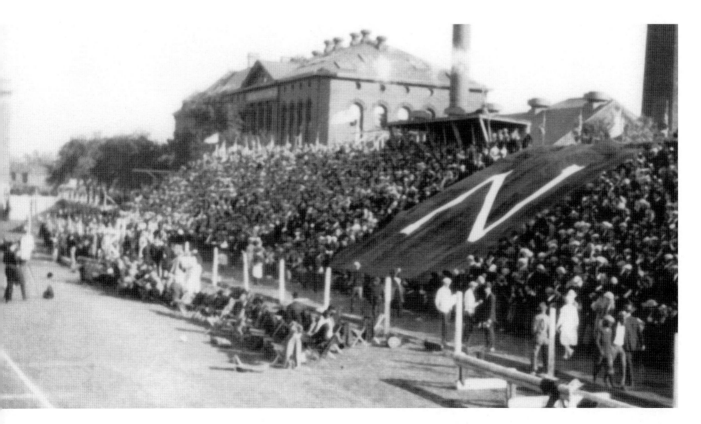

AN ERA OF GREATNESS: COACH BOB DEVANEY'S FINAL FOUR SEASONS (1969 - 1972)

THE STATISTICS
OF THE FIRST HALF CENTURY (1890 – 1940)

Let's examine the remarkable overall statistics of the 18 coaches who established such high standards for defense over a 51 year time span *(in descending order by "winning percentage)*:

COACH	YEARS	WON/LOST/TIED	WINNING PERCENTAGE	AVERAGE POINTS PER GAME	POINTS BY OPPONENT (PER GAME)	AVERAGE POINT DIFFERENTIAL
1. LANGDON FROTHINGHAM (1890)	1	2-0-0	.1000	14.0	0	14.0
2. JUMBO STIEHM (1911-15)	5	35-2-3	.913	27.9	4.1	23.8
3. BUMMY BOOTH (1900-05)	6	46-8-1	.845	23.7	3.9	19.8
4. FRED DAWSON (1921-24)	4	23-7-2	.750	24.7	6.0	18.7
5. DANA X. BIBLE (1929-36)	8	50-15-7	.743	14.2	6.7	7.5
6. EARNEST BEARG (1925-28)	4	23-7-3	.742	16.6	4.9	11.7
7. "KING" COLE (1907-10)	4	25-8-3	.736	22.7	7.0	15.7
8. "DOC" STEWART (1916-17)	2	11-4-0	.733	24.9	5.6	19.3
9. FIELDING YOST (1898)	1	8-3-0	.727	24.5	7.1	17.4
10. E.N. ROBINSON (1896-97)	2	11-4-1	.719	11.6	4.9	6.7
11. "BIFF" JONES (1937-40)	5	24-9-4	.686	12.1	7.6	4.5
12. FRANK CRAWFORD (1893-94)	2	9-4-1	.679	15.2	8.9	6.3
13. CHARLES THOMAS (1895)	1	6-3-0	.667	15.3	6.9	8.4
14. AMOS FOSTER (1906)	1	6-4-0	.600	16.4	7.3	9.1
15. T.U. LYMAN (1891)	1	2-2-0	.500	18	10	8
16. J.S. WILLIAMS (1892)	1	2-2-1	.500	4.2	8	-3.8
17. WILLIAM KLINE (1918)	1	2-3-1	.417	8.8	9.2	-0.4
18. EDWIN BRANCH (1899)	1	1-7-1	.167	5.4	18.2	-12.8
TOTALS:	51	423 GAMES (294-98-31)	.731	19	6.3	12.7

COACH "BUMMY" BOOTH'S 1902 TEAM
"THE MAGNIFICENT ELEVEN"

RECORD: 8-0-0

- Coach Walter "Bummy" Booth
- Played as an Independent (no conference)
- **Undefeated** and **unscored** upon in 32 consecutive quarters
- Defeated Minnesota away (6-0), Northwestern (12-0), Colorado away (10-0), Missouri away (12-0)
- Average Score in 8 games: 17.4 - 0
- A solid claim to be National Champion in 1902
- Individual stars: Johnny Bender, Maurice Benedict, John Westover, and Charles Borg

Coach Walter "Bummy" Booth *(1990 - 1905)*

- 2nd winningest coach in NU history (.845) (46 - 8 - 1)
- 24 consecutive wins (1901 -04)
- Average score in 55 games was 23.7 - 4
- Defense had shutouts in 37 of 55 games (67%)
- Retired in 1906 to practice Law in New York

"THE STIEHM ROLLERS"

1915 MISSOURI VALLEY CONFERENCE CHAMPION – A STRONG CLAIM TO BE NATIONAL CHAMPION

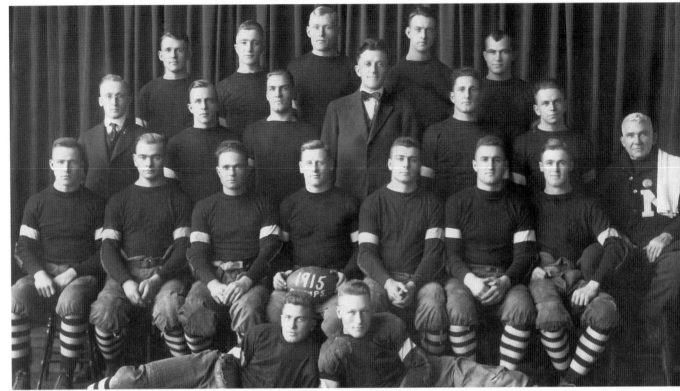

BACK ROW: Herbert Reese, Jimmy Gardner, Paul Halbersieben, Ellsworth Moser, Ed Kositzky.

THIRD ROW: Mgr. Guy Reed, John Cook, John Rassmussen, Coach E. O. Stiehm, Hugo Otapalik, Lum Doyle

SECOND ROW: Ted Riddell, Edson Shaw, E. L. Abbott, Capt. Dick Rutherford, Paul Shields, H. H. Corey, Guy Chamberlin

FRONT ROW: Joe Caley, P. W. Proctor

Coach Jumbo Stiehm

RECORD: 8-0-0 ("The Stiehm Rollers")

- Missouri Valley Conference champion
- Defeated Notre Dame (20-19); Notre Dame's only loss
- A strong claim to be National Champion
- Turned down invitation to the Rose Bowl
- Average score in 8 games: 34 - 4.9
  (29.1 point differential)
- All-Conference:
  Guy Chamberlin, back; H. H. Corey, tackle;
  Paul Shields, guard; E. L. Abbott, guard;
  Dick Rutherford, back
- All-American: Berlin "Guy" Chamberlin

Guy "The Champ" Chamberlin

- All-American Back/End (1915)
- College & Pro Football
  Hall of Fame

1922 TEAM
MISSOURI VALLEY CONFERENCE CHAMPIONS

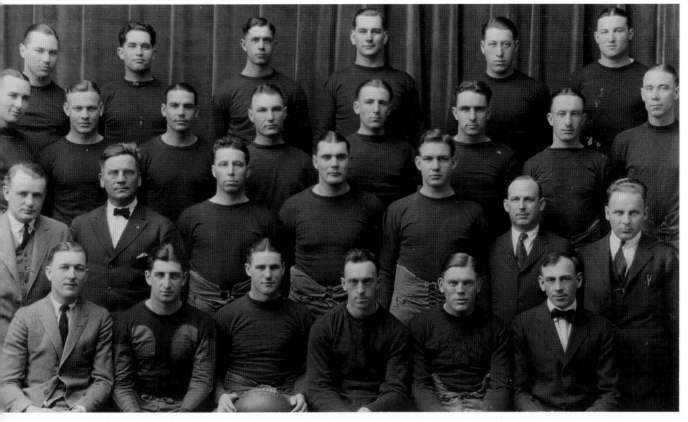

BACK ROW: Herb Dewitz, Ross McGlasson, Vern Lewellen, Joy Berquist, "Hank" Bassett, Dave Nobel.

THIRD ROW: Leo Scherer, "Sed" Hartman, George Klempke, Rufus Dewitz, Bryan Nixon, Eugene McAllister, George D. Hoy, Carl Peterson.

SECOND ROW: Coach Fred Dawson, Asst. Coach H. F. Schulte, Andy Schoeppel, "Bud" Weller, Adolph Wenke, Manager Tyson, Asst. Coach Bill Day.

FRONT ROW: Asst. Coach Clarence Swanson, "Bob" Russell, "Chick" Hartley, "Pete" Preston, Fred Thomsen, Asst. Coach Owen Frank.

Dave Noble scored 3 of the 4 touchdowns in NU's 2 wins over Notre Dame's Four Horsemen.

RECORD: 7-1-0

■ Coach Fred Dawson

■ Missouri Valley Conference Champions

■ Defeated Notre Dame (14-6), Oklahoma (39-7), Missouri (48-0)

■ Only loss to Syracuse (6-9) cost a claim to the National title

■ All-Conference: Leo Scherer (end), Bub Weller (tackle),
Adolph Wenke (tackle), Joy Berquist (guard),
Glen Preston (back), Dave Noble (back),
Chick Hartley (back)

■ Average score in 8 games: 35-4 (31 point differential)

1928 MISSOURI VALLEY CHAMPIONS
COACH ERNEST BEARG

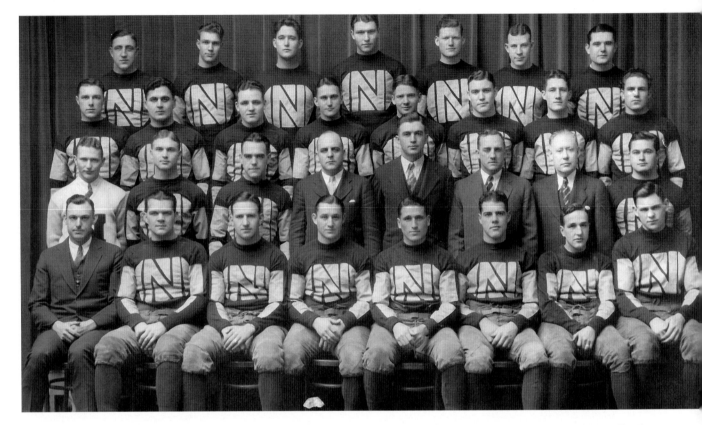

BACK ROW: Raymond Richards, Clifford Morgan, Marion Broadstone, George Ray, Ralph Jeffries, Walter Drath, Fay Russell.

THIRD ROW: Adolph Lewandowski, Elmer Greenberg, Clair Sloan, Harold Peaker, Robert Young, Claude Rowley, Frank Prucka, Harold Fraham.

SECOND ROW: Manager Marshall Keyes, Willard Witte, Clark McBride, Asst. Coaches B. F. Oakes and J. R. Rhodes, Asst. Coach Charles T. Black, Trainer M. J. McLean, Dan McMullen.

FRONT ROW: Head Coach Ernest E. Bearg, Leroy Lucas, Ted James, Captain Edward Howell, Captain Elmer Holm, Merle Zuver, George Farley, Glen Munn.

N.U. star Fullback "Blue" Howell

RECORD: 7-1-1

- Coach Ernest Bearg
- Undefeated Big Six Champion
- Defeated Syracuse (7-6) and tied Pittsburgh (0-0)
- Only loss to Army (3-13) at West Point denied a claim to the National Title
- Average score in 9 games: 16 - 3.4 (12.6 point differential)
- 5 shutouts by the defense
- All Conference: Marion Broadstone, tackle; Dan McMullen, guard; Ted James, center; Clair Sloan, back; Blue Howell, back; Clifford Ashburn, end; Glen Munn, tackle; Lafayette Russell, back
- All-American: Dan McMullen

1933 BIG SIX CHAMPIONS
COACH DANA X. BIBLE

BACK ROW: Mehring, Williams, Masterson, Thompson, Copple, Milne, Wilson, Hubka.
FOURTH ROW: Uptegrove, Meier, Jones, O'Brien, Sauer, Kilborne, Boswell.
THIRD ROW: Mead, Justice, Reese, Heldt, Skewes, Parsons, Pflum, Roby.
SECOND ROW: Cockburn, LaNoue, Benson, Keriakedes, Bishop, DeBus, Miller.
FRONT ROW: Assistant Coach Schulte, Assistant Coach Browne, Coach Bible, Trainer M. J. ''Doc'' McLean, Team Physician Dr. Deppen, Manager Clemmons.

Husker great George Sauer
All-American back (1933)

RECORD: 7-1-0

- Coach Dana X. Bible
- Undefeated Big Six Champion
- Defeated Texas, Iowa and Oregon State
- The only loss at Pittsburgh (0 - 6) cost a claim to the National Championship
- Average score in 9 games: 15 - 2.1 (12.9 point differential)
- 6 shutouts by the defense
- All-Conference: Lee Penny, end; Bruce Kilbourne, end; Gail O'Brien, tackle; Warren DeBus, guard; Frank Meier, center; George Sauer, back; Bernie Masterson, back; Hubert Boswell, back; Clair Bishop, guard
- All American: George Sauer

THE 1940 ROSE BOWL TEAM
UNDEFEATED BIG SIX CHAMPION – COACH "BIFF" JONES

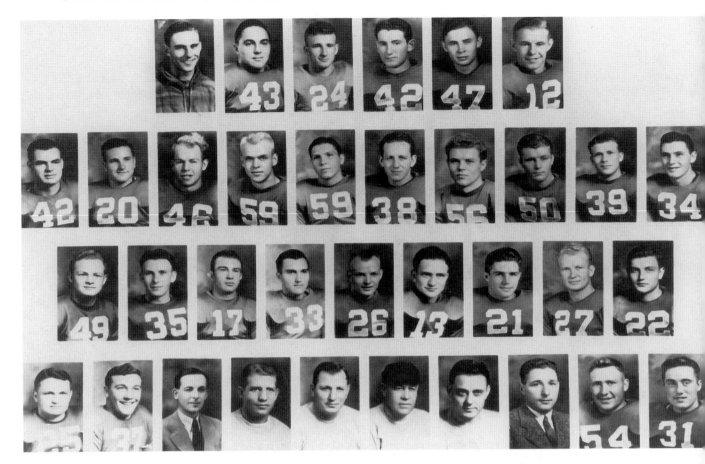

BACK ROW: Unknown, Leonard Muskin, Robert Cooper, Dale Bradley, George Abel, Jerry Kathol.
THIRD ROW: Howard Kelly, Fred Meier, Bunker, Allen Zikmund, Vic Schleich, Vike Francis, Robert Bonahoom,
              Fred Preston, Wayne Blue, Clarence Herndon.
SECOND ROW: Robert Burruss, Robert Kahler, Ed Schwartzkopf, Forrest Behm, Theos Thompson, Roy Petsch,
              George Knight, Walter Luther, Warren Alfson.
FRONT ROW: Herman Rohrig, Harry Hopp, Dr. Deppen, Glen Presnell, Link Lyman, Biff Jones (Head Coach),
              H. W. Browne, Elwyn Dees, Royal Kahler, Raymond Prochaska.

*Vike Francis scores NU's 1st
touchdown in '41 Rose Bowl*

RECORD: 8-2-0

- Coach "Biff" Jones
- Undefeated Big Six Champion
- Defeated Pittsburgh (9-7) and Indiana (13-7)
- Away losses to Minnesota (7-13) and Stanford (13-21) in the Rose Bowl
  (Minnesota and Stanford finished 1st and 2nd in AP Poll)
- Rose Bowl ('41) was first Bowl game for NU
  (NU had turned down a 1915 invitation to the Rose Bowl)
- Behm and Alfson All-Americans
- Average score in 10 games: 19.3 - 7.5 (11.8 point differential)

World War II (1941-1945) disrupted most college athletic programs. Nebraska already had one of the smallest population pools (and recruiting bases). NU did not have a R.O.T.C. program and thus Nebraska players could not continue football and receive military training at the same time in Nebraska. During the War years and afterwards Nebraska also was not able to continue getting high quality head coaches.

As a result, NU's record over these 21 years declined to 73 wins, 125 losses and 4 ties (.367 winning percentage).

There were 17 losing seasons, 3 winning seasons and one season at 5-5. Nebraska won no conference championships, but was 2nd four times and 3rd four times. NU was nationally ranked only one time (17th in 1950).

Nonetheless, fan support remained firm and loyal. There were major upsets of top ranked teams such as Army, Penn State, Minnesota, Missouri, Oklahoma and Texas. Attendance at home games was consistent, and the fans yearned for a return to the glory days when NU was a national power. They were ready for a new head coach to lead them to the promised land.

Memorial Stadium (1952) 35,000 Fans.

AN ERA OF GREATNESS: COACH BOB DEVANEY'S FINAL FOUR SEASONS (1969 - 1972)

A COMPARISON OF THE RECORDS
OF THE COACHES IN ERA TWO:

There were eight coaches during the 21 years.

YEARS	COACH	RECORD	AVERAGE POINTS SCORED	AVERAGE POINTS ALLOWED	POINT DIFFERENTIAL	SHUTOUTS BY DEFENSE
(1) 1 (1941)	Biff Jones	4-5-0	10.3	8.9	1.4	2
(2) 1 (1942)	Glenn Presnell	3-7-0	5.5	15.8	-10.3	2
(3) 2 (43-44)	Adolph J. Lewandowski Lewandowski	4-12-0 (.250)	9.3	30.0	-20.7	0
(4) 2 (45/48)	George "Potsy" Clark	6-13-0 (.316)	14.6	24.8	-10.2	3
(5) 2 (46-47)	Bernie Masterson	5-13-0 (.278)	13.2	19.5	- 6.3	2
(6) 7 (49-55)	Bill Glassford	31-35-3 (.471)	16.7	19.0	- 2.3	6
(7) 1 (1956)	Pete Elliot	4-6	12.5	10.6	1.9	0
(8) 5 (57-61)	Bill Jennings	15-34-1 (.310)	10.7	17.9	- 7.2	2

A. Highpoints: Major Victories During Era Two

1942 ...	7-0	Oklahoma
1949 ...	25-14	Colorado
1950 ...	32-26	Minnesota
	19-0	Penn State
	40-34	Missouri
1952 ...	28-13	Oregon (at Eugene)
1953 ...	20-16	Miami
1954 ...	27-7	Oregon State
	20-6	Colorado (at Boulder)
	25-19	Missouri
1956 ...	15-14	Missouri
1958 ...	14-7	Penn State
1959 ...	32-12	Minnesota
	7-6	Oregon State
	25-21	Oklahoma
	14-12	Colorado
1960 ...	14-13	Texas
	14-9	Army
	14-7	Oklahoma
1961 ...	21-14	Oklahoma (at Norman)

B. Fan Loyalty Continued Throughout The Period

Fan support continued. The camaraderie and the joy of competition were still alive and well. Being realistic, NU fans did not "expect" to win every game, but the "hope" was always there – that if they played well, the team "could" win any specific game. And sometimes this happened.

The average home attendance at Memorial Stadium shows consistent fan support:

AVERAGE ATTENDANCE PER GAME	COACH	
1946 ... 31,500	Masterson	(3-6-0)
1950 ... 34,800	Glassford	(6-2-1)
	Bobby Reynolds' sensational sophomore season	
1953 ... 33,800	Glassford	(3-6-1)
1956 ... 31,700	Elliot	(4-6-0)
1961 ... 30,300	Jennings final season	(3-6-1)

COACH BILL GLASSFORD
AND THE 1950 CORNHUSKER TEAM

UNIVERSITY OF NEBRASKA FOOTBALL 1950

BACK ROW: George Paynich, Joe Ponseigo, Richard Regier, Herman Kinlage, Wayne Handshy, Keith Fiene, Nick Adduci, Paul Grimm, Bob Mullen, Dick Goeglein, Verl Scott, Walter Spellman, Herb Reese, Louis Lehman.

FOURTH ROW: Kay Curtis, Ed Hussman, Dick Goll, Louis Roper, Ken Schroeder, Rich Novak, Tony Winey, Tom Harper.

THIRD ROW: Student Manager Robert Tritsch, Francis Nagle, Jim Godfrey, Hyle Thibault, Ted Britt, Larry Carney, Bob Reynolds, Carl Brassee, Jim Sommers.

SECOND ROW: Ron Clark, George Prochaska, Jim Levendusky, Don Boll, Frank Simon, William Maxe, William Wingender, Frank Meyer.

FRONT ROW: Jack Carroll, Don Bloom, William Mueller, Arthur Bauer, Don Strasheim, Rex Hoy, Joe McGill, Gerald Ferguson.

RECORD: 6-2-1

- ■ Coach Bill Glassford
- ■ 2nd to National Champion Oklahoma in Big Seven Conference
- ■ Defeated Minnesota (32-26) and Penn State (19-0)
- ■ NU's first winning season in 10 years
- ■ Ranked 17th in nation
- ■ Bobby Reynolds All-American halfback
- ■ Average score in 9 games: 34 - 24 (10 point differential)

Bobby Reynolds
All-American '50 – "Mr. Touchdown"

STARS FROM THE 1940s – 1950s

John Bordogna
- 1953 All-Big 7 Quarterback

Charlie Bryant
- 1954 All-Big 7 Guard

Willy Greenlaw
- 1955 All-Big 7 Back

Pat Fischer
- Nebraska Football Hall of Fame
- 17 years in the NFL setting many records (1961-'77)

Rex Fischer
- 1955 All-Big 7 Back
- Nebraska Football Hall of Fame
- M.D. UNL '59

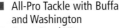

Ron McDole
- NFL 18 years (1961-78)
- All-Pro Tackle with Buffalo and Washington
- Super Bowl VI

Jon McWilliams
- 1955 All-Big 7 End

Jerry Minnick
- 1953 All-American Tackle

Fran Nagle
- 1950 All-Big 7 Quarterback

Tom "Train Wreck" Novak
- 1949 All-American Center
- All-Conference 4 years

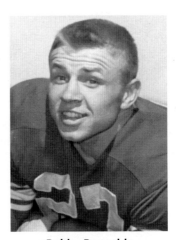

Bobby Reynolds
- 1950 All-American Halfback

Charlie Toogood
- 1949-50 All-Big 7 Tackle
- NFL 7 years (Rams, Cardinals)

"Robert S. Devaney . . . rescued Nebraska's football program from the depths of depression that lasted from 1940 until his arrival in Lincoln in 1962. A jovial and impish Irishman who left a Michigan high school career to apprentice with Duffy Daugherty at Michigan State before winning big at Wyoming, Devaney launched a football revival that would be the envy of Billy Graham's staff."

Don "Fox" Bryant
UNL Sports Information Director Emeritus
"Tales from the Nebraska Sidelines" (p. 31)

Bob Devaney was a standout end at Alma College in Michigan. He then coached high school football and was eventually hired as an assistant Coach by Duffy Daugherty at Michigan State.

Devaney became head coach at Wyoming in 1957, and he immediately made a successful impact. Wyoming won 4 of 5 Big Sky Conference Titles (1957-1961) and his overall

record was 35-10-2 (a .750 winning percentage). Devaney had proven that he was a winner and could build championship teams.

Starting in 1962, Coach Devaney changed NU football forever. He breathed new life into the players and the people in the State of Nebraska.

He won immediately. His record in his first five seasons (1962-1966) showed success:

(1)   4 out of 5 Big 8 Championships
(2)   5 consecutive Bowl games
(3)   Top 10 ranking 4 out of 5 seasons
(4)   .855 winning percentage (47-8-0)

Nebraska was back in the "Big Time" and was a contender for the National Championship. And in 2 seasons NU had a chance for the national title which was denied in 1963 by a loss to Air Force (13-17) and in 1965 with a loss to Alabama in the Orange Bowl (28-39). Devaney had a taste of playing for the national title.

"In 1962, NU hired Coach Devaney for $17,000 a year. That was the best investment ever made by the State of Nebraska."

Coach John Melton (2006)

AN ERA OF GREATNESS: COACH BOB DEVANEY'S FINAL FOUR SEASONS (1969 - 1972)

DEVANEY'S FIRST FIVE YEARS

"A Resurgence to New Heights of Excellence" (1962-1966)	1962	1963	1964	1965	1966	5 Year Summary; Averages
(1) **Won/Loss Record**	9 - 2	10 - 1	9 - 2	10 - 1	9 - 2	47 - 8 .855 winning %
(2) **National Ranking** (Associated Press)	none	5th	6th	5th	6th	Top 5 – Twice Top 10 – 4 Times
(3) **Big 8 Conference**	3rd (5 - 2)	1st (7 - 0)	1st (6 - 0)	1st (7 - 0)	1st (6 - 1)	1st ...80%
(4) **Bowl Games**	**Gotham** 36-24 Miami	**Orange** 13-7 Auburn	**Cotton** 7-10 Arkansas	**Orange** 28-29 Alabama	**Sugar** 7-34 Alabama	2 – 3 (40%)
(5) **UNL Average Score**	26.6	33.9	24.4	30.7	20.3	24.4
(6) **Opponent's Average Score**	12.8	9.4	7.7	11.7	9.8	9.4
(7) **Average Point Differential**	13.8	24.5	16.7	19.0	10.5	15.0

Coach Devaney enjoys a moment of tranquility.

EARLY DEVANEY
1963 BIG 8 AND ORANGE BOWL CHAMPIONS

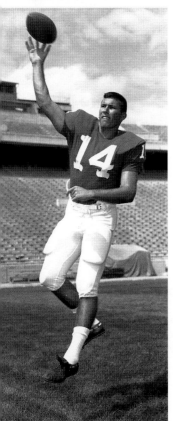

**UNIVERSITY OF NEBRASKA FOOTBALL 1963
BIG EIGHT CHAMPIONS/ORANGE BOWL CHAMPIONS**

BACK ROW: Larry Kramer, Walter Barnes, Freeman White, John Strohmeyer, Lloyd Voss, Dennis Claridge (co-captain), John Kirby (co-captain), Henry Woods, Larry Tomlinson, Kent McCloughan.

FOURTH ROW: Bruce Smith, Joe McNulty, Gene Young, Bobby Hohn, Lyle Sittler, Duncan Drum, Willie Paschall, Tony Jeter, John Dervin.

THIRD ROW: Rudy Johnson, Doug Tucker, Charles Doepke, Dick Callahan, Dave Theisen, Mike Kennedy, Ron Griesse, Bob Jones.

SECOND ROW: Maynard Smidt, Ted Vactor, Willie Ross, Ron Michka, Bill Haug, Bernie McGinn, Fred Duda.

FRONT ROW: Monte Kiffin, Coach Jim Ross, Coach Carl Selmer, Head Coach Bob Devaney, Coach Mike Corgan, Coach George Kelly, Bob Brown.

RECORD: 10-1-0

- Undefeated Big Eight Champion
- Orange Bowl Champion (NU 13 – Auburn 7)
  (NU's first Major Bowl Victory)
- Only loss to Air Force (13 - 17) cost a claim to the National Title
- Average score in 11 games: 24.8 - 10.5 (14.3 differential)
- All-Americans: Bob Brown, Larry Kramer
- All-Big 8 Conference: Dennis Claridge, quarterback;
                           Lloyd Voss, tackle; Bob Brown, guard

Dennis Claridge

■ All Big 8 Quarterback (1963)
■ Academic All-American

THE 1965 TEAM
BIG 8 CHAMPIONS

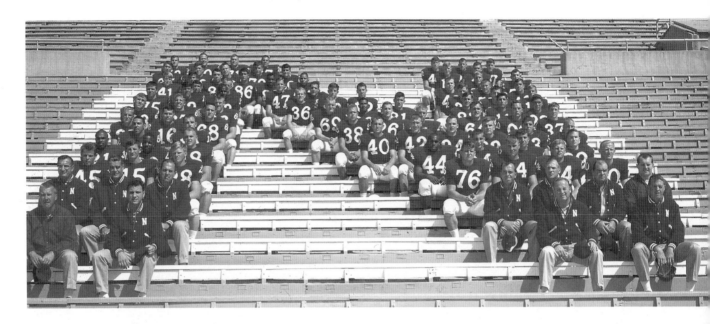

BACK ROW:	Bob Hill, Dick Czap, Jerry Wilks, Walt Barnes, Pete Tatman, Ron Kirkland, Stan Grell
ELEVENTH ROW:	Jim Gatziolis, Jerry Murphy, Lou Narish, Larry Hansen, Jim Osbery, Wayne Weber, Unknown
TENTH ROW:	George Buckler, Marv Mueller, Bill Haug, Ivan Zimmer, Freeman White, Tony Jeter, Rick Hoasch, Jim Unrath
NINTH ROW:	Paul Camastro, Craig Beck, Bob Weinman, Joe Unis, Len Janik, Duncan Drum, Mike Worley
EIGHTH ROW:	Bob Trucher, Carel Stith, Jim Brown, Larry Wachholtz, Mick Zeigler, Ernie Sigler, Miles Kimmel, Ed Hansen, Bill Neitleman
SEVENTH ROW:	Lynn Senkbeil, LaVerne Allers, Wayne Meylan, Mike Kennedy, Langston Coleman, Roger Kudrna, Tom Smith, Al Fierro, Steve Zemko
SIXTH ROW:	Dennis Thorell, Schindel, Leonard Canarsky, Rich Haasch, Ron Poggemeyer, Kaye Carstens, Jim McCord, Bill Startzer, Dennis Morrison
FIFTH ROW:	Jerry Patton, Mike Rudd, Ken Brunk, Al Kuehl, Dan Delaney, Dennis Richnotsky, Barry Alvarez, Paul Critchlow
FOURTH ROW:	Harry Wilson, Ben Gregory, Dennis Carlson, Charlie Winters, Tom Pappes, Rick Coleman, Larry Casey
THIRD ROW:	Frank Solich, Bob Churchich, Bill Johnson, Gary Brichacek, John Shromeyer, Kelly Peterson, Fred Duda
SECOND ROW:	John Melton, Jim Ross, Carl Selmer, George Kelly, Cletus Fisher, Mike Corgan
FRONT ROW:	Dick Beechner, Rudy Gaddini, Bob Devaney, Larry Kramer, Tom Osborne

RECORD: 10-1-0

- Undefeated in regular season
- Big Eight Champion
- Only loss to Alabama (28-39) in Orange Bowl cost the National Championship
- Average score 30.7 - 11.7 in 11 games
- All-Americans: Walt Barnes, Tony Jeter, Freeman White
- All-Big 8 Conference: Frank Solich, Tony Jeter, Freeman White, Mike Kennedy, Walt Barnes, Dennis Carlson, LaVerne Allers

STARS FROM DEVANEY'S EARLY YEARS

(1962 - 1966)

WALTER BARNES '65
- All-American Middle Guard
- Washington Redskins (66 - 71)

BOB BROWN '63
- All-American Guard
- All-Pro Oakland Raiders
- College and Pro Football Halls of Fame

TONY JETER '65
- All-American End
- Academic All-American
- Pittsburgh Steelers (66 - 68)

LARRY KRAMER '64
- All-American Tackle

WAYNE MEYLAN '66
- All-American Noseguard
- NFL 3 years (Vikings, Browns)

FREEMAN WHITE '65
- All-American End
- New York Giants (66 - 69)

BOB CHURCHICH '66
- All-Big 8 Quarterback

HARRY WILSON '65
- All-Big 8 Back
- Philadelphia Eagles (67 - 69)

AN ERA OF GREATNESS: COACH BOB DEVANEY'S FINAL FOUR SEASONS (1969 - 1972)

COLORFUL COMMENTS
BY AND ABOUT COACH BOB DEVANEY ("THE BOBFATHER")
(1962-1972) – HEAD COACH
(1967-1993) – ATHLETIC DIRECTOR

(1) *"I'd like to win just enough to keep the administration happy, but not warrant an NCAA investigation."*

(1962)

(2) *"800 million Chinese don't care about Nebraska football."*

(1967)

(3) *"I believe the size of my funeral will depend largely on the weather."*

(1995)

(4) *"In order to avoid confusion, I want the press to know that the pronunciation of my last name rhymes with "fanny".*

(1962)

(5) *"Phyllis and I have decided we can't leave Nebraska. She just bought new snow tires."*

(1969, on turning down an offer from Miami U.)

(6) *"I really feel bad about getting you guys into this mess today. I know it's a terrible day and this won't be much fun, but it kind of reminds me of the old back-alley fights we used to have when I was a kid in Michigan. There's nobody here to watch, but the toughest son-of-a-bitch is going to win."*

(1962) - a speech to the team before defeating Miami (34-31) on an icy field in the Gotham Bowl at Yankee Stadium.

(7) *"If Devaney ever loses two in a row, I'll have to declare a state-wide emergency."*

Jim Exon, Governor of Nebraska (1971)

(8) *"I know they (the fans and media) like me and respect me, but they loved Bob."*

Coach Tom Osborne, (1994)

(9) *"Bob could cuss you out in a heart beat and then joke with you the next moment. He could pull the best out of you, because you knew he cared about you."*

Johnny Rodgers, (2004)
N.U.s' 1st Heisman winner

(10) *"Winning isn't everything in Nebraska football, but we rate it right up there with oxygen."*

(1974)

(11) *"Bob Devaney came as close to duplicating (Notre Dame's Knute) Rockne as any coach I've known – his personality on and off the field and the way he carried the respect of his own players and that of his opponents.*

Ed Weir, N.U. All-American tackle (1923-24), as quoted in Bryant's "Tales from the Nebraska Sidelines" (2001) p. 49

(12) *"Good afternoon, officer. I want to commend you for your public service in stopping our car. I admit I was driving a little strangely, but my friend, Jim (Ross) here, and I are the new football coaches at Wyoming U., and one of our duties is to get out and meet the good folks in the local communities. We did that by dropping in at your local tavern on main street. We might have had 1 or 2 beers, but we were just trying to be sociable."*

(1957) The Wyoming State patrolman did not issue Devaney a ticket, and was later seen in his car laughing uncontrollably.

CHAPTER FIVE

THE TWO MIDDLE YEARS: (1967-1968)
SLIPPING TOWARD MEDIOCRITY

"I know the fans are with me,
win or tie."

Coach Bob Devaney (1968)
[after a 0-12 loss to Kansas State]

"You are either getting better
or getting worse –
It never stays the same."

Coach Bob Devaney (1968)

1967

Won 6, Lost 4, Tied 0

OPPONENT	AP RANK NU/OPP.	RESULT
Washington		**W 17-7**
Minnesota	7/	W 7-0
Kansas State	**7/**	**W 16-14**
Kansas	**8/**	**L 0-10**
Colorado	/4	L 16-21
Texas Christian		**W 29-0**
Iowa State		W 12-0
Oklahoma State		W 9-0
Missouri		**L 7-10**
Oklahoma	/5	L 14-21

NOTE:
Stadium capacity expanded to 64,170

FINAL RANKING:
None

1968

Won 6, Lost 4, Tied 0

OPPONENT	AP RANK NU/OPP.	RESULT
Wyoming	14/	W 13-10
Utah	14/	W 31-0
Minnesota	**9/17**	**W 17-14**
Kansas	9/6	L 13-23
Missouri	13/20t	L 14-16
Oklahoma State		**W 21-20**
Iowa State		**W 24-13**
Kansas State		L 0-12
Colorado		**W 22-6**
Oklahoma	/14	L 0-47

FINAL RANKING:
None

*Away games in bold.

The seasons of 1967 and 1968 were disappointing. NU finished each season with a 6-4 record and was not invited to a Bowl Game.

NU still had many good players and solid defenses, but overall the team's performance was slipping. It was gravitating toward mediocrity for these reasons:

(1)   NU was losing overall team speed. In the January, 1967 Sugar Bowl NU was soundly defeated (34 - 7) and outquicked by a fast Alabama Team. This trend continued for the next two years. NU had lost some of its speed on both sides of the ball and was particularly vulnerable to a sharp passing attack.. As stated by Coach Jim Ross: "We just quit recruiting for a while."

(2)   NU lacked a "big play" player on offense – a long strike threat on passes, runs, and kick returns.

(3)   NU's offensive production had fallen substantially. These two teams scored an average of only 14.1 points per game, in contrast to the 24.4 average of the 1962-1966 offenses. A scoring loss of over 10 points per game is significant. The Total Offensive yardage fell per game from 404 in 1965 to 279 in 1968, a decrease of almost 30%.

(4)   NU lacked a quarterback who could both run and pass, and this hurt the versatility of the offense. The offense overall was not well balanced between running and passing.

(5)   NU's offensive formation was out-dated. It still used an unbalanced line and a "full house" backfield [2 halfbacks and the full back behind the quarterback]. There was very little deception. (see p. 47)

(6)   The important "Turnover Margin" had shifted for the worst. NU was fumbling and getting intercepted more often than its opponents. [-18 in 1967 and -10 in 1968]. Turnovers killed drives and created field position and scoring opportunities for the opponents.

(7)   NU's opponents were getting better. The Big 8 Conference was emerging as the toughest conference in the country. It was no longer dominated by Oklahoma and Nebraska. Kansas won the Big 8 in 1968 and Missouri shared the title in 1969. Colorado was rated #3 in the nation in 1971.

NU's overall performance was slipping toward mediocrity. As remembered by Coach John Melton: "The players weren't playing very well, and we weren't doing a good job of coaching."

Changes were needed. Fortunately, Coach Devaney and the assistant coaches adjusted in both recruiting and in their formations, and this prepared NU for the "Era of Greatness" that would emerge during the next four seasons (1969 - 1972).

Dick Davis, All-Conference Fullback (1968)*

*"I won't know why
we lost the game until my barber
tells me on Monday."*

Knute Rockne (1923)

THE TWO MIDDLE YEARS

"Slipping Toward Mediocrity" (1967-1968)	1967	1968	2 Year Summary; Averages
(1) Won/Loss Record	6 - 4	6 - 4	12-8-0 .600 winning %
(2) National Ranking (Associated Press)	none	none	none
(3) Big 8 Conference	5th (3 - 4)	4th (3 - 4)	6 - 8 - 0 .444 winning %
(4) Bowl Game	none	none	none
(5) UNL Average Score	12.7	15.5	14.1
(6) Opponent's Average Score	8.3	12.8	11.0
(7) Average Point Differential	4.4	2.7	3.1

967, Oklahoma (14 - 21)*

AN ERA OF GREATNESS: COACH BOB DEVANEY'S FINAL FOUR SEASONS (1969 - 1972)

Green (N)

Halfback Mike Green scores (1968)

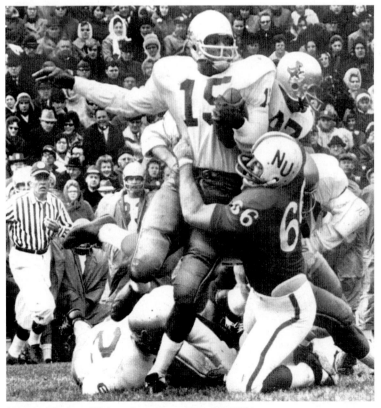

Wayne Meylan, All-American Nose Guard (1967)

Bob Liggett tackles Kansas State's Mac Herron (1968)

> *"Meylan played when he was hurt. He was a bear."*
>
> Coach Jim Ross (2006)

Coaches Devaney and Corgan viewing the loss to
Kansas State (1968)*

"We played like a
bunch of farmers."

Coach Bob Devaney
(after the K-State loss)

"I meant to say that
we played like a bunch of
farmers doing their normal
good job."

Coach Bob Devaney
(at a press conference 2 days
after the game)

Barry Alvarez and Adrian Fiala recovering a fumble (1967)*

AN ERA OF GREATNESS: COACH BOB DEVANEY'S FINAL FOUR SEASONS (1969 - 1972)

NU FOOTBALL IS FUN
(EVEN IN A 6-4 SEASON)

Fan support was loyal, but some natives were getting restless*

The Pause that Refreshes*

Go Big Red*

COMPARATIVE STATISTICS ON OFFENSE, DEFENSE AND TURNOVERS

		1967	1968
(1)	Total Offensive Average:	317	279
	(a) Rushing Average	162	150
	(b) Passing Average	155	129
(2)	Total Defense Against Opponents	158	260
	(a) Opponent Rush Yardage	68	137
	(b) Opponent Pass Yardage	90	123
(3)	Turnover Margin	- 18	- 10

All-American Joe Armstrong makes a tackle (1968)*

Joe Orduna highsteps for yardage (1968)*

Power running by Dick Davis and Ben Gregory (1967)*

AN ERA OF GREATNESS: COACH BOB DEVANEY'S FINAL FOUR SEASONS (1969 - 1972)

FRIENDLY MASCOTS
AND GOOD NATURED RIVALRIES (1967-1968)

Colorado Buffalo Fans*

The Kansas State Wildcat*

Big Red and the Missouri Tiger*

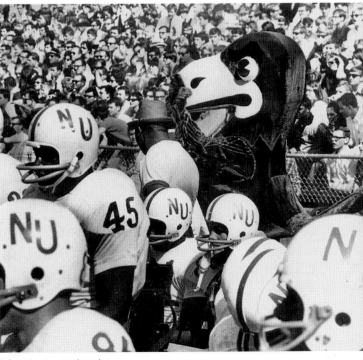

The Kansas Jayhawk*

CHAPTER SIX

THE 1969 SEASON: THE DAWN OF A NEW ERA AND MOMENTUM FOR THE FUTURE

"My favorite player in every game is named "Mo" – good old "Mo-mentum", the guy who changes jerseys several times during every game."

"Dandy" Don Meredith, (1972)
Dallas Cowboys All Pro QB in the 1960s and
Commentator on "Monday Night Football" in the 1970s.

1969

9-2-0
Big Eight Champion
Sun Bowl Champion

OPPONENT	AP RANK NU/OPP.	RESULT	
USC	/5	L	21-31
Texas A&M		W	14-0
Minnesota		**W**	**42-14**
Missouri	**20/7**	**L**	**7-17**
Kansas		W	21-17
Oklahoma State		W	13-3
Colorado	/18	W	20-7
Iowa State	20/	W	17-3
Kansas State	**17/**	**W**	**10-7**
Oklahoma	**16/**	**W**	**44-14**
SUN BOWL			
Georgia	14/	W	45-6
FINAL RANKING:			
	11th AP	(post-bowl),	
	12th UPI	(regular season)	

*Away games in bold

The 1969 Season started slowly, built momentum and ended with a "Bang" with lopsided victories over Oklahoma (44-14) and Georgia in the Sun Bowl (45-6). NU's record improved to 9 - 2, and NU would be ranked 11th in the final AP Poll.

N.U. had one of the toughest schedules in the nation, and had two losses in its first four games – 31 - 21 to Southern Cal (USC) and 17 - 7 at Missouri. But in both losses NU was competitive and the outcome was not decided until the 4th Quarter. Both losses were to high quality traditional powers. That year USC would play in the Rose Bowl and Missouri in the Orange Bowl.

Nebraska was clearly improving and was more competitive than the 1967-1968 teams. There were several reasons:

(1) The terrific 1968 Freshman class had an immediate positive impact with increased speed on both sides of the ball. NU's coaches had placed a priority on recruiting faster and quicker players. All-American safety Bill Kosch was a freshman in 1968 and he remembers: *"Recruits in `68-69 were smaller. . . We were lean and fast compared to the guys before us."*

(2) Under the guidance of the new Offensive Coordinator, Coach Tom Osborne, UNL changed from a "full house" backfield (2 halfbacks and fullback behind QB) to a more stream-lined "I Formation" with only the I-back and fullback directly behind the QB, and the "wingback" spread out right or left past the ends. This allowed for more deception and power running on Isolation plays up the middle as well as "inside-reverses" to the wingback. It also enabled more passing to the wingback. A wide receiver was also split out on the opposite side of the wingback. Thus, NU adopted the pro "spread" passing offense. (see p.47)

(3) NU had two very talented Sophomore Quarterbacks – Jerry Tagge and Van Brownson. Both could run and pass effectively. Both were mature leaders and talented field generals who sparked a dynamic offense by the end of the season. As a result, the offense became more "balanced" and the passing game was spread around to **all** receivers – wideouts, tight end, wingback, I-back and fullback. I-back Jeff Kinney would be the leading pass receiver in 1969.

(4) NU could rotate two young and talented I-backs – Junior Joe Orduna (Omaha) and sophomore Jeff Kinney (McCook). Orduna was fast and elusive. Kinney was powerful and reliable up the middle. Orduna became injured in preseason drills and was out for the season, and thus the entire burden was on Kinney who showed consistent improvement from game to game.

(5) Under Defensive Coordinator, Coach Monte Kiffin, the Defenses were faster and more aggressive in "attacking" the offense. Except for the opening game against USC (21-31), no opponent would score more than 17 points against NU. The other 10 opponents averaged only 8.8 points against the rugged NU defense.

(6) There was a dramatic improvement in the important "Turnover Margin" [from -18 in 1967 and -10 in 1968 to plus 6 in 1969]. NU was fumbling less and giving up fewer interceptions than its opponents.

UNL would go on to sweep its final 7 games, finishing 9 - 2, and concluding with a romp over Oklahoma and with a huge blowout win over Georgia in the Sun Bowl. The average score in the final 7 games was 28-8, a 3 touchdown differential. NU was "back" as a contender at the national level. Momentum had shifted. The genie was out of the bottle, and confidence was growing.

One vivid example of Coach Devaney's sense of humor and motivational ability was in his pre-game speech to the team before the Georgia game in the Sun Bowl (1969) as revealed by Don "Fox" Bryant in "Tales from the Nebraska Sidelines" (p. 121):

"Let's go out there and do a good job – but be careful running on the field, because half the state of Nebraska is out there in a spirit line waiting for you, and the other half is back home praying for you."

Left: Coach Bob Devaney

"Coach Devaney cared about each player on and off the field. This is very important."

Coach Monte Kiffin
(2006)

Right:
Coach Monte Kiffin:
"The Master of Disaster"
teaches dynamic
defensive techniques
(1969)

A.   Further Analysis of the Turnaround

Guy "The Fly" Ingles
Nebraska Football Hall of Fame

Omaha Investment advisor, Guy Ingles, starred on the 1968-1970 teams as a wide receiver and kick returner and is a member of the Nebraska Football Hall of Fame. Guy remembers the reasons for the "turnaround" in 1969.

"1967 and 1968, my freshman and sophomore years were the "6-4" years and 1969 the initial start of 33 consecutive "Nine Win" years through 2001. In other words, UNL went from the depths to the start of something special and unsurpassed in College Football for 35 years. From No Bowls to National Champions in less than 26 Months. (Thanksgiving 1968, and 47-0 vs. Oklahoma in Norman to the Orange Bowl on January 1, 1971 vs. LSU (17-12).

The reasons for the change were (a) a tremendous coaching staff; (b) 2 or 3 great recruiting classes, (c) a switch to the "I" formation and the "spread" passing offense. The Huskers were Off To The Races."

The reasons for the "turnaround" are also explained by Lincoln attorney Jim McFarland, an All-Conference tight end in 1969:

"When we talk about the transition that occurred between 1968 and 1969, and those 6-4 years in 1967 and 1968, our defense was always good. Our defense statistically was always near the top in all the defensive categories in the nation.

But our offense in 1967 and 1968 had really been stifled because a lot of teams were blitzing us and playing what Devaney called "pressure defenses." They would get 9 players up on the line of scrimmage and they would just come after us. And in 1967-1968, we really did not know how to adapt or attack and exploit that type of blitzing defense. We were still running the unbalanced line and full house backfield.

In 1969, the transition occurred and it made all the difference. Coach Devaney turned the offense completely over to Coach Osborne in 1969. We replaced the unbalanced line with a split end and then the pro formation. We went to the "I" formation and the spread formation. The coaches wanted a quarterback who could run. They couldn't just attack a defense with a pure passing quarterback and they wanted a more mobile quarterback. So they recruited Jerry Tagge and Van Brownson because they could run and were more like option style quarterbacks. They could drop back and pass, but they could also run the option and were more versatile. So, we changed that offense all around and we started out with a lot of sophomores who were very good. We had Tagge, Van Brownson, Jeff Kinney, and Larry Jacobson on defense.

We won two and lost two at the beginning of the year, and it looked like we would have another 6-4 season but then we beat Kansas, and got on a roll and won the last seven in a row. By the end of the year we were scoring 40 points a game.

There were two factors for the turnaround in 1969 (1) a lot of the sophomores really progressed from the beginning to the end of the year. (2) We all adapted to the new offensive scheme. We got better at it and the coaches got better at it. By the end of the year we were a tough team to stop offensively and our defense was as sound as ever. For example, we beat Texas A&M 14-0 and it was the defense that won the game. Kansas State was a very close game (10-7), and the defense won that for us too."

B.   The One Play that Changed the '69 Season

Most seasons have one game that is a critical turning point. In 1969 it was the Kansas game in Lincoln. And UNL was the beneficiary of an incorrect penalty call by the officials. NU was 2-2, and winning this KU game would add tremendous momentum for the future.

Here is what happened, as described by Jim McFarland:

"The most remarkable play I witnessed was the interference call that was made on my defender in the 1969 game against Kansas. It turned the game around. We were behind (14-17) in the 4th quarter with just a couple of minutes left. We had the ball around midfield and it was 4th and 14. We needed to make a first down and Jerry Tagge called what we called the "two minute pass". I was basically the primary receiver because Kansas was playing a zone prevent defense. I was supposed to run my pattern at about 12 yards. I took an extra two steps before I made my cut and I ran it to about 15 yards. By that time, Jerry was scrambling because the pocket had broken down. He was running around in the back

field and ran towards the east sideline. So I spun around and started heading downfield. And out of desperation, Jerry threw the ball in my direction, because the defensive back that was covering me was a smaller guy.

I realized that I was probably not going to catch it but I had a habit of diving for balls. I also knew that if we did not complete that pass, the only way we had of making a firstdown was to get a penalty. So, when I dove for the ball I intentionally dove into the defensive back that was running along side of me. I dove toward him and wrapped my leg around his leg, so he went down too. We both went down and the ball probably went 5 or 10 yards beyond. I probably could not have touched the ball because it was overthrown.

Nevertheless, it was right by our bench and Coach Monte Kiffin came running out onto the field pointing to the official that K.U.'s defensive back had knocked me down. Well, I had actually knocked him down but they threw a flag for pass interference on the defender. The official could not see who knocked who down. Then Emery Hicks, their middle guard, swore at the official and so they penalized Emery 15 yards for unsportsmanlike conduct. Then we got the ball around the 15 yard line and in 3 plays we scored a touchdown. We kicked the extra point and ended up winning 21-17 in the closing minute.

That play is significant because it started NU's streak of 32 consecutive games without a loss. We were on a roll and won our last 6 games by an average score of 25-6."

Celebrating the 1969 Sun Bowl Victory over Georgia (45-6), from Left to Right: Bob "Fig" Newton, Jeff Hughes, Jerry Murtaugh and Wally Winter

THE 1969 COACHES

ront row, L/R: Warren Powers, Mike Corgan, Bob Devaney, Cletus Fischer
nd row, L/R: Jim Ross, Monte Kiffin, John Melton
rd row, L/R: Carl Selmer, Bill Thornton, Tom Osborne

COMPARATIVE STATISTICS ON OFFENSE, DEFENSE AND TURNOVERS

		1967	1968	1969
(1)	**Total Offense Per Game**	317	279	372 (93 yard increase)
	(a) Rushing Average	162	150	172
	(b) Passing Average	155	129	200
(2)	**Total Defense Per Game Against Opponents**	158	260	253
	(a) Opponent Rush Yardage	68	137	130
	(b) Opponent Pass Yardage	90	123	123
(3)	**Turnover Margin**	- 18	- 10	+6 (+16 increase)

THE 1969 TEAM
BIG 8 & SUN BOWL CHAMPIONS

RECORD: 9-2-0

- Big Eight Champion
- Sun Bowl Champion
- Ranked 11th in the Nation

All Conference end Jim McFarland (1969)*

A COMPARISON OF 1969
WITH THE '67-'68 SEASONS

		(1967-1968) 2 year Summary Averages	Improvements in 1969
(1)	Won/Loss Record	12-8-0	9-2
(2)	National Ranking (Associated Press)	none	11th
(3)	Big 8 Conference	6-8 .444 winning %	6-1 Tie for 1st Place
(4)	Bowl Game	none	Sun Bowl 45-6 Over Georgia
(5)	UNL Average Score	14.1	28.2 (2 touchdown increase)
(6)	Opponent's Average Score	11.0	10.7 (about the same)
(7)	Average Point Differential	3.1	17.5 (2 touchdown increase)

1969

No.		Name	Pos.	Ht.	Wt.	Hometown
7		Adkins, John	DRE	6-3	192	Lynchburg, Va.
		Ahlmann, Harold	DMG	5-11	237	Norfolk
8		Anderson, Jim	DRCB	5-11	180	Green Bay, Wis.
3	**	Ashman, Carl	OLG	6-1	235	Burwell
6	*	Bomberger, Bill	OFB	6-0	187	Columbus
		Boyd, David	ORE	6-2	186	Wichita, Kan.
		Branch, James	WLB	5-9	187	Chicago, Ill.
2		Brownson, Van	OQB	6-2	176	Shenandoah, Ia.
2	*	Buda, Joe	OC	6-3	248	Omaha
		Carstens, James	OFB	5-11	214	Glen Ellyn, Ill.
3		Chandler, George	WLB	5-8	187	Park Forest, Ill.
		Coppa, Rich	OC	6-2	194	Steubenville, Ohio
		Davis, Harold	OLG	6-3	201	Gothenburg
1	*	Decker, John	LCB	5-10	178	Saginaw, Mich.
		DeOrio, Lonnie	DRT	5-11	223	Pittsburgh, Pa.
4		Didur, Dale	ORE	6-0	180	Long Beach, Calif.
1	*	Drakulich, Ron	DLT	6-2	219	Omaha
8		Dumler, Doug	OLT	6-3	216	Melrose Park, Ill.
1		Dvorsak, Tony	OQB	5-11	179	Burgettstown, Pa.
2	**	Fiala, Adrian	WLB	6-2	210	Omaha
8	**	Frost, Larry	ORHB	6-1	205	Malcolm
7	**	Geddes, Ken	DMG	6-3	212	Boys Town
		Graves, Lanny	OFB	5-11	203	Omaha
4	*	Green, Mike	OFB	6-0	205	Omaha
9		Grenfell, Bob	OLG	6-6	228	Philadelphia, Pa.
9	*	Gutzman, Dennis	DRE	6-2	211	Green Bay, Wis.
		Hacias, Greg	DS	6-0	175	Detroit, Mich.
3		Harvey, Phil	OLE	6-0	193	Kansas City, Kan.
8		Hauge, Bruce	SLB	6-0	204	Bloomington, Ill.
5		Hinckley, Ron	ORG	6-1	195	Wichita, Kan.
9		Hollstein, Gary	DS	5-11	175	Rushville
		Holmes, Bill	OLE	6-0	211	Birmingham, Mich.
9		Hopkins, John	ORT	6-3	203	Bellevue
5	*	Hornbacher, Bill	DRT	5-11	216	Rogers City, Mich.
6		Hughes, Jeff	OLHB	6-0	198	Burlington, Vt.
8		Hyland, John	DLE	6-1	185	Lincoln
8	*	Ingles, Guy	ORE	5-9	155	Omaha
5		Jacobson, Larry	DRT	6-6	240	Sioux Falls, S.D.
0		Jamail, Doug	OC	5-9	189	Bellaire, Tex.
2		Janssen, Bill	DLE	6-3	203	Grand Forks, N.D.
1	*	Jarmon, Sherwin	DRE	6-2	201	Detroit, Mich.
8		Jennings, Henry	Mon.	5-10	198	Kimball
		Jones, George	DS	6-0	185	Clairton, Pa.
5		Kinney, Jeff	ORHB	6-1	196	McCook
		Kinsel, John	OC	6-2	200	Council Bluffs, Ia.
9	**	Kobza, Dan	WLB	6-1	209	Shelby
		Kontos, Ken	SLB	6-1	189	Wahoo
4		Kosch, Bill	DRCB	6-0	170	Columbus
0	**	Larson, Al	Mon.	6-1	202	Sioux City, Ia.
1		Liddle, Kent	OC	6-0	215	Deerfield, Ill.
1	*	Liggett, Bob	DLT	6-2	250	Aliquippa, Pa.

1969

No.		Name	Pos.	Ht.	Wt.	Hometown
85		List, Jerry	OLE	6-0	193	Bay City, Mich.
16		McClelland, Tom	DS	6-0	179	Turtle Creek, Pa.
80	*	McFarland, Jim	OLE	6-4	223	North Platte
27		McFarland, Bob	DRCB	6-0	166	North Platte
70	*	McGhee, Donnie	ORT	6-1	260	Flint, Mich.
15		McGuire, Mike	Mon.	6-2	182	Bellevue
		McGowan, Tom	WLB	6-2	200	Superior
39		Mabin, Wes	DLCB	6-1	181	W. Bridgewater, Pa.
		Malone, Danny	DLT	6-1	238	Longview, Tex.
87		Mason, David	ORE	6-0	185	Green Bay, Wis.
63		Menser, Charles	ORG	5-10	230	Omaha
86		Miller, Jim	DLE	6-1	203	Oshkosh
		Minzak, Ed	ORG	5-10	211	Aliquippa, Pa.
47		Montgomery, Al	ORHB	6-0	194	St. Paul, Minn.
40		Morell, Pat	SLB	6-2	197	Wichita, Kan.
43		Morock, David	Mon.	5-9	184	Clairton, Pa.
42		Murtaugh, Jerry	SLB	6-2	201	Omaha
74		Newton, Bob	OLT	6-4	240	LaMirada, Calif.
		Newton, Clint	OLE	5-10	161	Philadelphia, Pa.
31	**	Orduna, Joe	OLHB	6-0	196	Omaha
17		Osberg, Chuck	OQB	6-0	180	Omaha
66		Pabis, Bob	DMG	5-9	196	Monessen, Pa.
10	**	Patrick, Frank	OLE	6-7	217	Derry, Pa.
72	**	Patterson, Glenn	OC	6-3	217	Worland, Wyo.
56	*	Periard, Ed	DMG	5-8	195	Saginaw, Mich.
54		Pitts, Johnny	DRE	6-0	194	Flint, Mich.
		Pogge, Bill	OFB	6-2	199	Omaha
25	**	Reeves, Randy	DS	6-2	195	Omaha
30	*	Rodgers, Paul	ORHB, K	5-11	187	Rock Rapids, Ia.
69		Schloof, Merle	DLT	6-4	230	Mahtomedi, Mich.
22	*	Schneiss, Dan	OFB	6-2	222	West Bend, Wis.
23		Smith, Jimmy	OLHB	5-8	177	Midland, Pa.
		Snyder, Bob	ORT	6-4	225	Concordia, Kan.
		Sobota, Joe	DRT	6-0	229	Schuyler
68		Stejskal, Greg	OLT	6-4	223	Omaha
36	**	Stephenson, Dana	DLCB	6-2	183	Lincoln
14		Tagge, Jerry	OQB	6-1	220	Green Bay, Wis.
		Tegels, John	WLB	6-0	195	Omaha
45		Terrio, Bob	OFB	6-2	200	Fullerton, Calif.
73	**	Topliff, Paul	ORT	6-2	205	Lincoln
19		Vactor, Frank	OLHB	5-8	178	Washington, Pa.
64		Volberding, Ron	ORG	6-1	202	Omaha
76	*	Walline, Dave	DRT	6-2	230	Ypsilanti, Mich.
61		Weber, Bruce	OLG	5-11	206	Omaha
		Wenner, Rick	DS	6-1	192	Detroit, Mich.
77	**	Williams, Gale	ORG	6-1	235	Meadow Grove
67		Winter, Wally	OLT	6-4	238	Eagle
		Witliff, Frank	ORHB	5-11	196	Port Huron, Mich.
90	**	Wynn, Mike	DLE	6-5	242	Evanston, Ill.
44		Yanda, Steve	SLB	5-10	214	Edina, Minn.

AN ERA OF GREATNESS: COACH BOB DEVANEY'S FINAL FOUR SEASONS (1969 - 1972)

Passing more often opens up the Running Game.
(Jeff Kinney finds the hole). *

Quarterbacks who can run and pass.
(Van Brownson scores). *

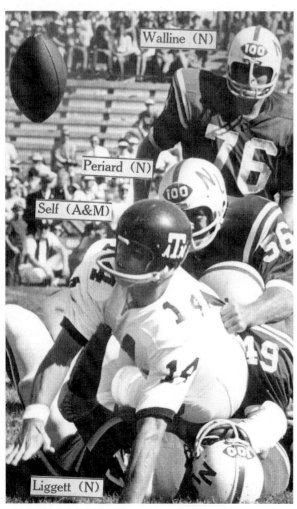

Great Defenses win Championships. *

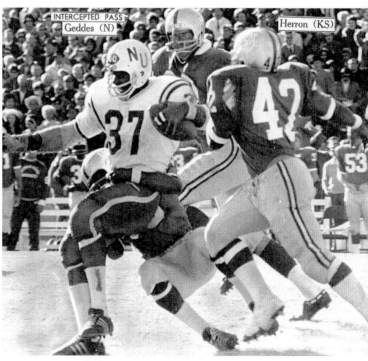

The Turnover Margin Improved.
(Ken Geddes intercepts a Kansas State pass). *

HAPPY DAYS ARE HERE AGAIN
(1969)

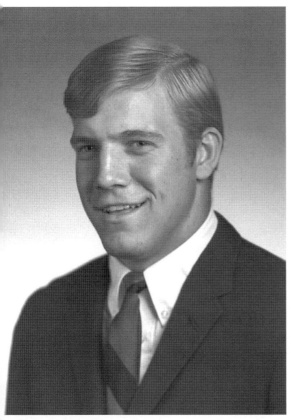

The Kicking Game Improved.
Paul Rogers kicked 4 field goals vs. Georgia and was named the Most Valuable Player in the 1969 Sun Bowl.

Rising Expectations. *

An early version of the West Coast Offense – passing to all receivers. Tight End Jim McFarland scores. *

Sherwin Jarmon and Dave Walline disrupt the passer. *

AN ERA OF GREATNESS: COACH BOB DEVANEY'S FINAL FOUR SEASONS (1969 - 1972)

OFFENSIVE FORMATIONS

A.   THE OFFENSIVE FORMATION IN 1967-1968:
     AN UNBALANCED LINE AND A FULL HOUSE BACKFIELD

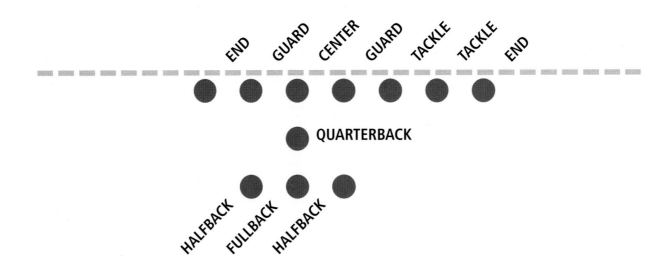

B.   THE KEY CHANGE IN 1969 TO THE "I" AND PRO SPREAD FORMATIONS
     CREATED MORE DECEPTION AND PASSING TO ALL RECEIVERS.

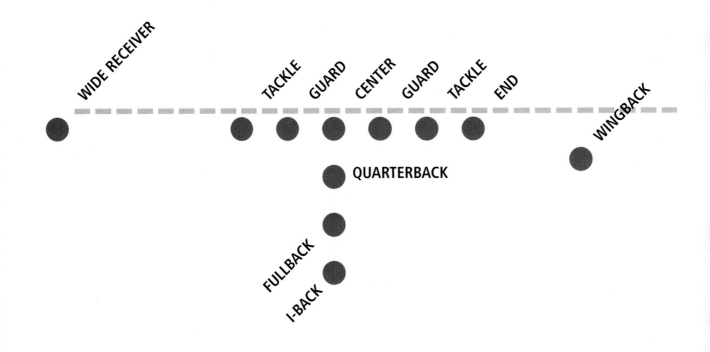

CHAPTER SEVEN

THE 1970 SEASON AND THE FIRST NATIONAL CHAMPIONSHIP

"Even the Pope wouldn't vote for Notre Dame as Number One"

Coach Bob Devaney (January 1, 1971)
[after NU's victory over LSU in the Orange Bowl;
The A.P. voted NU #1]

1970

11-0-1
National Champion
Big 8 Champion
Orange Bowl Champion

OPPONENT	AP RANK NU/OPP.	RESULT
Wake Forest	9/	W 36-12
USC	**9/3**	**T 21-21**
Army	8/	W 28-0
Minnesota	**6/**	**W 35-10**
Missouri	6/16	W 21-7
Kansas	**5/**	**W 41-20**
Oklahoma State	4/	W 65-31
Colorado	**4/**	**W 29-13**
Iowa State	**4/**	**W 54-29**
Kansas State	4/20	W 51-13
Oklahoma	3/	W 28-21
ORANGE BOWL		
Louisiana State	3/5	W 17-12
FINAL RANKING:		
	1st AP	(post-bowl),
	3rd UPI	(regular season)

*Away games in bold

W inning the final 7 games in 1969, sharing the Big 8 championship and winning the `69 Sun Bowl provided tremendous momentum going into the 1970 season. The terrific sophomore class of `69 had now become experienced Juniors, and the fast and elusive running back, Joe Orduna, returned to action.

The only question mark was the defense which returned only 3 starters – Jerry Murtaugh, Dave Walline, and Jim Anderson.

In retrospect there were only 3 close games (0-7 points) and all 3 were against perennial national powers (USC, Oklahoma and LSU).   The other 9 games were "Blowout wins" with an average margin of victory of 3 touchdowns.

1970 Wins and Ties:

A. 0-7 Point Margin
  1. 17-12 . . . LSU
  2. 28-21 . . . Oklahoma
  3. 21-21 . . . U.S.C.

B. 8-13 Point Margin
  • none

C. 14-38 Point Margin
  • 9 games with an average score of 41-19

A. The Southern Cal. Game (21 - 21)

On September 19th , the Huskers played the U.S.C. Trojans in the historic Coliseum in Los Angeles. And NU quickly served notice that it was a national contender.

Joe Orduna shocked the USC crowd by going 70 yards for NU's first touchdown in the 1st quarter. NU never trailed, and should have won the game. The Trojans tied the score (21-21) in the 4th quarter after NU failed on a 12 yard field goal attempt which would have iced the game.

There is an old saying in sports that "a tie is like kissing your sister." But in this case a tie was almost as good as a victory because it was on USC's home field, USC was ranked #3, and had a long tradition of success under legendary Coach John McKay (national championships in 1962, 1967, and 1972).

A LEGENDARY COACH
OF OPPONENT USC

JOHN McKAY
SOUTHERN CAL (U.S.C)
(1960 - 1975)

NU's tie (21 - 21) with USC in the Coliseum in Los Angeles (1970) preserved an undefeated season and Devaney's first National Championship.

■ 3 National Championships at Southern Cal (1962, 67, 72)

■ 9 Pacific Ten Conference Titles

■ 3 Undefeated Seasons

■ 5 Rose Bowl Victories

■ .749 Winning Percentage

■ College Coach of the Year in 1962 and 1972

■ College Football Hall of Fame

s later noted by Adrian Fiala, Omaha attorney and sports broadcaster, the tie with USC was "a springboard to success in future years." NU was #9 going into the game. The Huskers moved up to #8 and would win its next 23 games (10 in 1970 and 13 in 1971).

NU dominated its Big 8 Conference foes and elevated to No. 3 in the rankings with a late season blowout over Kansas State [51-13] The Wildcats had been ranked No. 20 before the game, but NU intercepted quarterback Lynn Dickey a school record 7 times.

The Oklahoma Sooners (28 - 21)

NU's second close game of the season was against Oklahoma in Lincoln. The Sooners were young but talented and a victory would have given Oklahoma a share of the Big 8 crown. NU trailed twice but came back to win the game (28-21) and the Big 8 championship.

No. 3 NU was headed for the Orange Bowl but would need some help to win the national title. Texas was ranked No. One and Ohio State Number Two. But Notre Dame upset Texas in the Cotton Bowl (24-11), and Stanford upset Ohio State in the Rose Bowl (27-17).

C.   The Louisiana State (LSU) Tigers in the Orange Bowl (17 - 12)

The door was open but NU had to defeat formidable LSU, ranked #5 and the Southeastern Conference Champion. NU started fast and led 10-0 in the first quarter, but LSU played well and took the lead (12-10) at the end of the 3rd quarter.

This set the stage for one of the most storied drives in NU history. NU was poised and confident and drove 67 yards for the winning touchdown on a quarterback sneak by Jerry Tagge.

The Associated Press voted NU No. One in its final poll. Two weeks later President Richard Nixon visited Lincoln to endorse the national title in a presentation at NU Coliseum to Coach Devaney and Captains Jerry Murtaugh and Dan Schneiss.

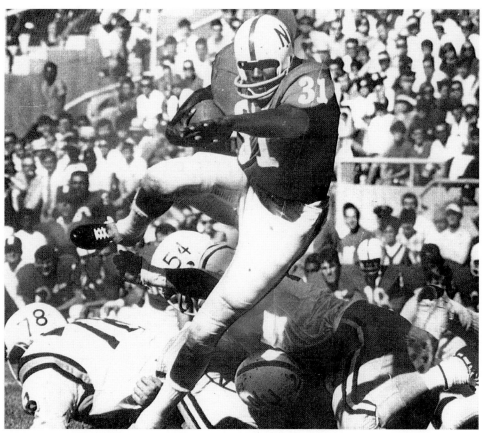

Graceful and powerful.
All Conference I-Back Joe Orduna scores again. *

THE 1970 TEAM
NATIONAL CHAMPIONS

"AN ERA OF GREATNESS"
A COMPARISON OF 1969 AND 1970

RECORD: 11-0-1

■ National Champion
■ Big Eight Champion
■ Orange Bowl Champion

*"When the one Great Scorer
comes to mark against your name,
He writes not that you won or lost,
but how you played the game."*

Grantland Rice (1922)
(renowned sportswriter for
the New York Post)

		1969	1970
(1)	**Won/Loss Record**	9-2	11-0-1
(2)	**National Ranking**	11th	1st
(3)	**Big 8 Conference**	6-1 Tie for 1st Place	7-0 1st Place
(4)	**Bowl Game**	Sun Bowl: 45-6 Over Georgia	Orange: 17-12 Over LSU
(5)	**UNL Average Score**	28.2	33.5
(6)	**Opponent's Average Score**	11.0	10.7
(7)	**Average Point Differential**	17.2	22.8

NEBRASKA FOOTBALL OFFICIAL ROSTER

1970

No.		Name	Pos.	Ht.	Wt.	Hometown
7		Adkins, John	DE	6-3	222	Lynchburg, Va.
9		Anderson, Frosty	SE	6-0	165	Scottsbluff, Nebr.
8	*	Anderson, Jim	RCB	6-0	180	Green Bay, Wis.
8		Austin, Al	OT	6-5	208	Lincoln, Nebr.
2		Beran, Mike	OG	6-0	228	Ord, Nebr.
7		Blahak, Joe	LCB	5-10	175	Columbus, Nebr.
6	*	Bomberger, Bill	FB	6-2	210	Columbus, Nebr.
1		Branch, James	LB	5-9	187	Chicago, Ill.
2	*	Brownson, Van	QB	6-2	181	Shenandoah, Ia.
6		Butts, Randy	LHB	6-2	200	Grand Island, Nebr.
7		Carstens, James	FB	6-0	220	Glen Ellyn, Ill.
3		Cox, Woody	SE	6-0	180	Grosse Point, Mich.
1	**	Decker, John	LCB	5-10	181	Saginaw, Mich.
		Deyke, Tom	DE	6-3	212	Columbus, Nebr.
4	*	Didur, Dale	SE	6-0	184	Long Beach, Calif.
2		Duffy, Joe	MG	6-2	205	Pittsburgh, Pa.
4		Dumler, Doug	OC	6-3	230	Melrose Park, Ill.
0		Dutton, John	DT	6-7	235	Rapid City, S.D.
9		Glover, Rich	DT	6-1	225	Jersey City, N.J.
8		Goeller, Dave	LHB	5-11	180	Pilger, Nebr.
9	*	Grenfell, Bob	OG	6-6	242	Philadelphia, Pa.
1		Harper, Willie	DE	6-3	205	Toledo, Ohio
2		Harvey, Phil	TE	6-2	210	Kansas City, Kan.
8		Hauge, Bruce	LB	6-2	220	Bloomington, Ill.
3		Henderson, Joe	OT	6-2	215	Red Cloud, Nebr.
9		Hollstein, Gary	S	6-0	173	Rushville, Nebr.
3		Hughes, Dennis	OG	6-1	206	Fremont, Nebr.
6	*	Hughes, Jeff	LHB	5-11	196	Burlington, Vt.
8		Hyland, John	DE	6-2	198	Lincoln, Nebr.
8	**	Ingles, Guy	SE	5-9	158	Omaha, Nebr.
5	*	Jacobson, Larry	DT	6-6	247	Sioux Falls, S.D.
0		Jamail, Doug	OC	5-11	204	Bellaire, Tex.
5	*	Janssen, Bill	OC	6-3	218	Grand Forks, N.D.
8		Jennings, Henry	Mon.	5-10	201	Kimball, Nebr.
1		Johnson, Carl	OT	6-4	245	Phoenix, Ariz.
4		Johnson, Doug	DE	6-4	210	Omaha, Nebr.
7		Johnson, Monte	DE	6-6	225	Bloomington, Minn.
5		Jones, Bob	QB	6-4	210	Oaklawn, Ill.
5	**	Kinney, Jeff	LHB	6-2	202	McCook, Nebr.
4		Kinsel, John	OC	6-2	225	Council Bluffs, Ia.
9	*	Kosch, Bill	DRCB	6-0	170	Columbus

1970

No.		Name	Pos.	Ht.	Wt.	Hometown
11		Linder, Max	QB	6-3	200	Plattsmouth, Nebr.
86		List, Jerry	TE	6-0	210	Bay City, Mich.
91		Longwell, Brent	P	6-4	205	Homer, Nebr.
5	*	Mason, David	Mon.	6-0	195	Green Bay, Wis.
16	*	McClelland, Tom	S	6-1	180	Turtle Creek, Pa.
10		McFarland, Bob	LCB	6-0	169	North Platte, Nebr.
70	**	McGhee, Donnie	OT	6-1	225	Flint, Michigan
40	*	Morell, Pat	LB	6-2	227	Kansas City, Mo.
43	**	Morock, Dave	Mon.	5-10	199	Clairton, Pa.
42	**	Murtaugh, Jerry	LB	6-3	212	Omaha
42		Newton, Clint	RCB	5-10	161	Philadelphia, Pa.
74	*	Newton, Bob	OT	6-4	248	LaMirada, Calif.
32		Norberg, Bill	RHB	6-0	191	Palo Alto, Calif.
34		O'Connell, John	S	6-2	187	Sidney, Nebr.
44		Olds, Bill	FB	6-1	210	Kansas City, Kan.
31	**	Orduna, Joe	LHB	6-0	196	Omaha, Nebr.
66		Pabis, Bob	MG	5-10	205	Monessen, Pa.
33		Peetz, Mike	Mon.	6-1	197	Sidney, Nebr.
56	**	Periard, Ed	MG	5-9	201	Birch Run, Michigan
80		Pitts, Johnny	DE	6-1	209	Flint, Mich.
17		Pogge, Bill	DE	6-2	205	Omaha, Nebr.
41		Powell, Ralph	FB	6-2	212	Detroit, Michigan
68		Robison, Tom	DT	6-3	235	Detroit, Michigan
20		Rodgers, Johnny	RHB	5-10	171	Omaha, Nebr.
30	**	Rogers, Paul	RCB-K	6-0	192	Rock Rapids, Ia.
77		Rupert, Dick	OT	6-2	216	Los Angeles, Calif.
69		Schloof, Merle	DT	6-4	226	Mahtomedi, Mich.
23		Schmit, Bob	RHB	6-1	187	Boys Town
22	**	Schneiss, Dan	FB	6-2	222	West Bend, Wis.
87		Schultz, Kelly	TE	6-4	212	Palo Alto, Calif.
49		Strong, Jon	LB	6-2	204	Fremont, Nebr.
14	*	Tagge, Jerry	QB	6-2	215	Green Bay, Wis.
45		Terrio, Bob	LB	6-2	208	Fullerton, Calif.
19	*	Vactor, Frank	LHB	5-9	178	Washington, Pa.
76	**	Walline, Dave	DT	6-2	238	Ypsilanti, Mich.
61		Weber, Bruce	OG	6-0	221	Omaha, Nebr.
72		White, Daryl	OT	6-4	236	East Orange, N.J.
67	**	Winter, Wally	OT	6-4	248	Eagle, Nebr.
86		Wolfe, Bob	TE	6-5	232	Omaha, Nebr.
65		Wortman, Keith	OG	6-3	237	Whittier, Calif.
39		Yanda, Steve	LB	5-11	196	Edina, Minn

AN ERA OF GREATNESS: COACH BOB DEVANEY'S FINAL FOUR SEASONS (1969 - 1972)

HAPPY DAYS CONTINUE IN 1970

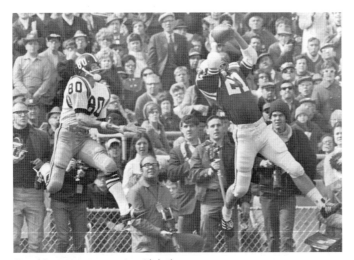

Breaking up passes – Joe Blahak

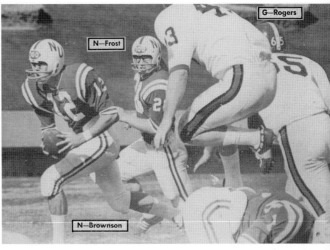

Running the option – Van Brownson

Catching long passes – Larry Frost*

LSU QB Bert Jones gets a Big Red Squeeze in the Orange Bowl.

Coach Corgan teaching the running game.

Team camaraderie –
Dave Walline, Bill Kosch and John Decker

Winning the Big 8 Championship over Oklahoma (28 - 21)

HAPPY DAYS IN 1970
GOING "UP AND OVER" SCORES TOUCHDOWNS

I-Back Joe Orduna hurdles for a gain.*

Schneiss (N)

Fountain (M)

Schnietz (M)

Wingback Johnny Rodgers.*

Fullback Dan Schneiss.*

I-Back Jeff Kinney.*

HAPPY DAYS IN 1970
GREAT DEFENSES WIN CHAMPIONSHIPS

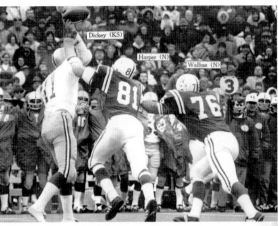

An interception against Kansas State.*

Jerry Murtaugh tackles KU's John Riggins.*

"The Long and Short of it" – Larry Jacobson & Eddie Periard harass Colorado.*

Joe Blahak makes an interception.*

"Little Eddie" Periard makes a big impact against Wake Forest.*

ORANGE BOWL BOUND
(TO FACE LSU)

*December 1970 – From bottom to top:
Willie Harper, John Pitts, Doug Johnson,
Ralph Powell, Johnny Rodgers and
Ken Kontos.*

*Miami, Orange Bowl, 1970 at the
Ike & Tina Turner Show
Right to left: Bruce Weber, Jeff Hughes,
Doug Dumler, Doug Jamail,
Johnny Rodgers, Frank Vactor,
Jim Carstens, Carl Johnson, Bob Jones
and Keith Wortman*

VICTORY IN THE ORANGE BOWL
(17 -12 OVER LSU)

President Richard Nixon awards the Championship to Coach Devaney and Captains Dan Schneiss and Jerry Murtaugh.

Quarterback Jerry Tagge's T.D. wins the National Title.

The celebrating begins.

AN ERA OF GREATNESS: COACH BOB DEVANEY'S FINAL FOUR SEASONS (1969 - 1972)

MEDIA SATURATION
AND "THE VOICE" OF NU FOOTBALL
AS PART OF THE TRADITION

"Holy Moley! Man, woman and child!
Johnny "The Jet" Rodgers just shook 'em loose
from their shoes. He just put 'em in the aisles."

Lyell Bremser (1971)
Legendary KFAB Radio Announcer and "the Voice" of NU football for 44 years from the late 1930s into the 80s; Quote made after Rodgers T.D. on a punt return in the 1971 "Game of The Century" against Oklahoma (NU 35 - O.U. 31).

From July to January, the various newspapers, radio and television sports news and programs are dominated by Big Red information and commentary. You simply "cannot get away from it", and it becomes "the only game in town" because Nebraska has no professional football team and no other Division 1-A college football team.

For 44 years (1939 through 1983) on KFAB Radio Lyell Bremser was, "The Voice" of Nebraska Football. Bremser dominated the airwaves as "Mr. Football" and some of his eloquent descriptions became part of the Husker Tradition. He could take any play and enhance it with his color and flair. For example:

■ *"And Tagge, the Master of Deception, just mesmerized the Okies with a myriad of moves."*

■ *"And Dave the Dealer (QB David Humm from Las Vegas) just riddled the Tiger with his darts."*

Lyell spread optimism and happiness and will forever be a significant part of Husker Tradition.

Left to right: Lyell Bremser, Dave Blackwell and Jack Payne (1970 – KFAB). NU 31 - Wake Forest 7.

"The 1971 Nebraska Team is
the best college team I have seen."

Coach Bear Bryant (1972)
(after Alabama's loss to N.U. in the Orange Bowl (38-7))

"Faster than a speeding bullet!
More powerful than a locomotive.
Able to leap tall buildings in a single bound."

Introduction to the Superman Radio Serial

1971

13-0-0
National Champion
Big 8 Champion
Orange Bowl Champion

OPPONENT	AP RANK NU/OPP.	RESULT
Oregon	2/	W 34-7
Minnesota	1/	W 35-7
Texas A&M	1/	W 34-7
Utah State	1/	W 42-6
Missouri	**1/**	**W 36-0**
Kansas	1/	W 55-0
Oklahoma State	**1/**	**W 41-13**
Colorado	1/9	W 31-7
Iowa State	1/	W 37-0
Kansas State	**1/**	**W 44-17**
Oklahoma	**1/2**	**W 35-31**
Hawaii	**1/**	**W 45-3**

ORANGE BOWL

Alabama	1/2	W 38-6

FINAL RANKING:

1st AP & UPI

*Away games in bold

AN ERA OF GREATNESS: COACH BOB DEVANEY'S FINAL FOUR SEASONS (1969 - 1972)

The Big Red Machine continued to roll in 1971. Confidence was abundant in players, coaches and fans. With the exception of the Oklahoma game (35-31) in Norman, NU dominated its opponents to a degree rarely seen in any team sport.

The average score in the other 12 "Blowout" wins was 40.2 - 4.7, a 5 touchdown differential. The closest any other opponent came was 24 points against Colorado (31-7) and Colorado would finish 3rd in the nation that year.

An age-old maxim in football states that "Great Defenses win Championships," and the NU defense was tremendous. In all 13 games the opponents scored an average of only 8 points. Excluding the OU game, the other 12 opponents averaged only 4.7 points. The NU defense ranked in the top five nationally in every defensive category. Anchored by All-Americans Rich Glover (nose guard), Larry Jacobson (tackle) and Willie Harper (end), the 1971 NU defense allowed the lowest average yards per rush (2.06) over a season. This is still an NCAA record.

Nebraska was also well balanced on offense (averaging 258 yards running and 179 yards passing) and the passing was diversified to all receivers - I-back, wingback, fullback, tight end and wide receiver.

A.   The Oklahoma Game
of the Century (35 - 31)

Oklahoma had the most prolific offense in the country. OU had perfected the "wishbone" offense where the fullback lined up tightly behind the quarterback and in front of the 2 halfbacks. OU's wishbone featured the option running of quarterback Jack Mildren, the outside running of Greg Pruitt, and the power running of fullback Leon Crosswhite. As stated by All-American Pruitt, "the wishbone on paper looked easy to stop, but Oklahoma's speed made it difficult to defend."

Thus, on Thanksgiving Day, 1971, the NU-OU game in Norman was for "all the marbles." The nation's best offense vs. the best defense. The media described the shootout as "The Game of the Century." On television it would be the most heavily watched college game of all time up to that point.

The game lived up to its billing. Both teams played exceptionally well, and there was only one penalty in the entire game. NU led twice (14-3 and 28-17), but OU came

back twice to lead (17-14 at half-time and 31-28 in the 4th quarter). Oklahoma's star quarterback, Jack Mildren was outstanding in passing for 2 TDs and running for 2 TDs. NU's defensive plan was to stop Greg Pruitt's running, and Mildren surprised with his pin point passes to the speedy John Harrison.

One point should be emphasized. Oklahoma had one of the most dynamic offenses in college history. OU had greatness and either team could have won. The OU shootout was the only time during the entire season that NU had trailed.

Two events will forever be etched into the minds of NU fans: (a) Johnny Rodgers dramatic twisting 72 yard punt return for a TD in the first quarter; (b) the final NU drive in the 4th quarter to go ahead and win (35-31). On a crucial 3rd down and 8 yards to go, Tagge passed 9 yards to Johnny Rodgers for the 1st down. The team was confident. Oklahoma's defense was becoming tired, and Jeff Kinney ran relentlessly up the middle to score the winning TD with four minutes left.

Oklahoma went on to demolish Auburn in the Sugar Bowl. NU would go on to overwhelm Alabama in the Orange Bowl (38-6). Alabama's legendary coach, Bear Bryant, described the 1971 Nebraska team as "the best college team I have seen."

In retrospect, two additional and often overlooked factors added to the greatness of the season:

(1)   NU's defense caused a school record "turnover" margin of plus 26 (20 fumbles and 27 pass interceptions).

(2)   Superior field position. As stated in the Interviews by Jerry Tagge and Coach Tom Osborne, because of defense and the kicking team NU usually started at its own 40 yard line or better.

The success of the 1971 season is succinctly summarized by Coach John Melton:

"In 1971, we never showed anybody any mercy. We could beat you running, passing, defense, punt returns. They never had a chance to rest against us. I don't think we had any weaknesses."

3. The Burning Question That Can Never Be Answered With Certainty

Was the 1971 NU team the best individual college team of all-time?

The best answers are "perhaps" or "probably" or "arguably." It can never be decided for certain, but it is fun to ponder and debate.

(1) In 1972, Alabama Coach Paul "Bear" Bryant, a legend and an expert, said that the '71 NU team was the best he had seen.

(2) The Jeff Sagarin Computer Ratings (2002) stated that the Nebraska Teams of 1971 and 1995 were the two best teams of all-time [with an edge to the '95 team]. The Sagarin Ratings (2002) ranks the best college teams since 1956. It also ranked Oklahoma '71 in 4th place and Nebraska 1972 in 10th place:

1.	**Nebraska**	**1995**
2.	**Nebraska**	**1971**
3.	Mississippi	1959
4.	Oklahoma	1971
5.	Ohio State	1973
6.	Washington	1991
7.	Oklahoma	1973
8.	Oklahoma	1974
9.	U.S.C.	1972
10.	**Nebraska**	**1972**

(3) The question can also be analyzed in the context of comparing the four best seasons and the best eras in Husker History. (see pp 71 - 72)

STATISTICAL COMPARISONS OF THE 2 NATIONAL CHAMPIONS

	1971 NU	1995 NU
1. Record	13-0-0	12-0-0
2. National Ranking	1st	1st
3. Average Points Scored	36.6	53.1
4. Average Points by Opponent	8.6	14.5
5. Point Differential	28	38.6
6. Rushing Yardage Average	258	399.8 [NCAA Record of 7 yards per rush]
7. Passing Yardage	179	156.5
8. Total Yardage	437	556.3
9. Opponent Rushing Yardage	85.9	78.4
10. Opponent Passing Yardage	117	215.7
11. Opponent Total Yardage	202.9	294.1
12. Turnover Margin	+26	+13
13. Closest Game	4 points (OU, 35-31)	14 points (Washington, 35-21)
14. Bowl Game	38-6 (#2 Alabama)	62-24 (#2 Florida)

"We hear you knocking, but you can't come in."

A famous song from the 1950s

JOHNNY RODGERS PUNT RETURN IN THE 1971 GAME OF THE CENTURY NEBRASKA VS. OKLAHOMA

Johnny Rodgers 72 yard punt return.

(3)   Tom Shatel, the Omaha World-Herald's astute analyst and sportswriter, addressed the subject in an analytical article on January 1, 2006 comparing the 2005 USC Trojans and the 1971 and 1995 Huskers. It should be noted that Shatel's article was written three days before USC would lose to Texas in the Rose Bowl.

"There's no such thing as a greatest team ever.

There's only the debate. The conversation.

The idea of comparing the athleticism and the speed of the game from era to era is ludicrous. Even stats don't translate over time.

Each statistic was made in a different time, against different competition. Was it easier to score on 1944 Fordham than 2005 Oregon? Who knows?

Those who scoff at the greatest ever tag for 2005 USC point to a less-than-stellar defense. The Trojan offense will win all the Oscars. The defense has been the stage hand, allowing an average of 344.7 yards and 21.3 points a game – and 28 points or more three times.

The '95 Huskers, widely lauded as the most complete team of our generation, allowed 294.1 yards and 13.6 points per game and allowed more than three touch-downs in a game once.

Herbstreit says the '95 Huskers couldn't pass and defenses today are too fleet to get hammered by a one-dimensional running game. Ingles says teams today face too many spread options and "aren't used to getting hit in the mouth like they would by Nebraska."

Tommie Frazier and Co. [1995] actually averaged 156.5 yards in the air and used it when they needed it.

Of course, both would lose to the 1971 Huskers.

Forget this "best team" debate. There's no such thing. What's more plausible is a team with the "greatest season" or "greatest accomplishment."

Let's measure the 1971 and 1995 Huskers and 2005 Trojans.

Start with the pressure of repeating. NU in 1971 and 1995 was going for back-to-back titles. The 2005 Trojans have the weight of a third on their shoulders. Advantage, USC.

Now, what about sheer dominance? Nebraska, in 1995, never got pushed. The Huskers never needed a last-minute touchdown or drive to save them. But the Big Eight 10 years ago wasn't so big.

OK, so what about schedule? Advantage, 1971 Huskers. The Big Eight in 1971 was the best league in the nation. The top three teams in the final poll were NU, Oklahoma and Colorado. NU won the "Game of the Century" on No. 2 OU's home field, then beat Bear Bryant's No. 2 Alabama team by 32 points in the Orange Bowl.

Give me the 1971 Huskers as having the "greatest season" in history."

A LEGENDARY COACH
WITH A TRIBUTE TO BIG RED

PAUL "BEAR" BRYANT
UNIVERSITY OF ALABAMA
(1959 - 1983)

*"The 1971 Nebraska Team
is the best college team I have seen."*

- 5 National Championships at Alabama (1961, 64, 65, 78, 79)
- College Football Hall of Fame
- In the 1972 Orange Bowl, Devaney's defeat of Alabama (38 - 6) won N.U.'s 2nd consecutive National Championship

COMPARATIVE STATISTICS ON OFFENSE, DEFENSE AND TURNOVERS

		1969	1970	1971
(1)	Total Offensive	372 (+93 yards)	421	437
	(a) Rushing Average	172 (46%)	232 (55%)	258 (59%)
	(b) Passing Average	200 (54%)	189 (45%)	179 (41%)
(2)	Total Defense Against Opponents	253	271	203*
	(a) Opponent Rush Yardage	130	148	86*
	(b) Opponent Pass Yardage	123	123	117*
(3)	Turnover Margin	+6	+17	+26

(*Led conference)

*"We were like brothers.
We fed off each other.
What made us a great team was
our unity on and off the field."*

*John Pitts (2006);
Monster Back '71*

THE 1971 TEAM
NATIONAL CHAMPIONS

RECORD: 13-0-0

■ National Champion
■ Big Eight Champion
■ Orange Bowl Champion

"I would like to relive the whole darn dream. Our players were so close. It was a team thing. It was a brotherhood."

Bob Terrio (2006); All Conference Linebacker (1971)

A COMPARISON OF THE 1969, 1970 AND 1971 SEASONS

		1969	1970	1971
(1)	**Won/Loss Record**	9-2	11-0-1	13-0
(2)	**National Ranking** (Associated Press)	11th	1st	1st
(3)	**Big 8 Conference**	6-1 Tie for 1st Place	7-0 1st Place	7-0 1st Place
(4)	**Bowl Game**	Sun Bowl: 45-6 Over Georgia	Orange: 17-12 LSU	Orange: 36-6 Alabama
(5)	**UNL Average Score**	28.2	33.5	38.2
(6)	**Opponent's Average Score**	10.7	14.9	8.0
(7)	**Point Differential**	17.5	18.6	30.2

NEBRASKA FOOTBALL
OFFICIAL ROSTER

1971

No.		Name	Pos.	Ht.	Wt.	Hometown
7		Adkins, John	DLE	6-3	221	Lynchburg, Va.
9		Anderson, Frosty	SE	6-1	176	Scottsbluff, Nebr.
7		Anderson, Dan	ORG	6-1	225	Fremont, Nebr.
8	**	Anderson, Jim	RCB	6-0	180	Green Bay, Wis.
8		Austin, Al	ORT	6-5	222	Lincoln, Nebr.
1		Bell, John	MG	6-0	203	Anaheim, Calif.
2	*	Beran, Mike	ORG	6-0	232	Ord, Nebr.
7	*	Blahak, Joe	LCB	5-10	184	Columbus, Nebr.
9		Borg, Randy	RCB	6-0	189	Alliance, Nebr.
1	*	Branch, James	SLB	5-9	203	Chicago, Ill.
2	**	Brownson, Van	QB	6-3	185	Shenandoah, Ia.
6		Butts, Randy	LHB	6-2	197	Grand Island, Nebr.
7	*	Carstens, James	FB	6-0	218	Glen Ellyn, Ill.
		Coleman, Ron	QB	6-3	195	Ulysses, Nebr.
2	*	Cox, Woody	SE	5-9	167	Grosse Point, Minn.
0		Crenshaw, Marvin	ORT	6-5	223	Toledo, Ohio
6		Damkroger, Maury	FB	6-2	215	Lincoln. Nebr.
4		Deyke, Tom	DRT	6-3	218	Columbus, Nebr.
4	*	Didur, Dale	SE	6-0	184	Long Beach, Calif.
2		Dixon, Gary	LHB	5-10	201	Oxnard, Calif.
3		Doak, Mark	OLT	6-4	236	Whittier, Calif.
2		Duffy, Joe	OLG	6-2	217	Pittsburgh, Pa.
4	*	Dumler, Doug	OC	6-3	237	Melrose Park, Ill.
0		Dutton, John	DRT	6-7	241	Rapid City, S.D.
8		Fuller, Bruce	S	6-0	181	Kanas City, Mo.
9		Garson, Glen	RHB	6-0	184	Fullerton, Calif.
9	*	Glover, Rich	MG	6-1	234	Jersey City, N.J.
8		Goeller, Dave	LHB	5-11	188	Pilger, Nebr.
7		Gulbord, Greg	DLE	6-4	197	Dearborn Hts., Mich.
1	*	Harper, Willie	DRE	6-3	207	Toledo, Ohio
2	*	Harvey, Phil	TE	6-1	208	Kansas City, Kan.
8	*	Hauge, Bruce	SLB	6-2	216	Bloomington, Minn.
2		Hegener, Stan	OLT	6-4	231	Lincoln, Minn.
3		Henderson, Joe	ORG	6-2	225	Red Cloud, Nebr.
6		Henrichs, Dennis	OLG	6-2	210	Beatrice, Nebr.
8		Hill, Jeff	SE	6-2	190	LeGrange, Ill.
9	*	Hollstein, Gary	LCB	6-0	175	Rushville, Nebr.
6	*	Hughes, Jeff	RHB	5-11	196	Burlington, Vt.
0		Humm, David	QB	6-2	186	Las Vegas, Nev.
8	*	Hyland, John	DLE	6-2	202	Lincoln, Nebr.
5	**	Jacobson, Larry	DLT	6-6	250	Sioux Falls, S.D.
0	*	Jamail, Doug	OC	5-11	205	Bellaire, Tex.
5		Janssen, Bill	DRT	6-3	228	Grand Forks, N.D.
1	*	Johnson, Carl	ORT	6-4	252	Phoenix, Ariz.
4	*	Johnson, Doug	DRE	6-5	218	Omaha, Nebr.

1971

No.		Name	Pos.	Ht.	Wt.	Hometown
37		Johnson, Monte	MG	6-6	232	Bloomington, Minn.
35	**	Kinney, Jeff	LHB	6-2	210	McCook, Nebr.
53		Kinsel, John	OC	6-2	210	Council Bluffs, Ia.
24	**	Kosch, Bill	S	6-0	176	Columbus, Nebr.
80		Lackovic, Tim	SE	6-1	186	Omaha, Nebr.
88		Linder, Max	SE	6-3	200	Plattsmouth, Nebr.
85	*	List, Jerry	TE	6-1	218	Bay City, Mich.
86		Longwell, Brent	TE	6-4	222	Homer, Nebr.
73		Lynch, Dab	DLT	6-5	250	Yankton, S.D.
11		Manstedt, Steve	DLE	6-2	210	Wahoo, Nebr.
25	*	Mason, David	Mon.	6-0	199	Green Bay, Wis.
16	**	McClelland, Tom	S	6-1	193	Turtle Creek, Pa.
69		McKinley, Kim	DRT	6-3	233	Greeley, Colo.
30		Moran, Jeff	LHB	6-1	191	Huron, S.D.
40	**	Morell, Pat	WLB	6-2	215	Wichita, Kan.
99		Nelson, Chris	TE	6-4	210	Albion, Nebr.
34		O'Connell, John	S	6-2	192	Sidney, Nebr.
38		O'Holleran, Mike	RHB	6-1	197	Sidney, Nebr.
44		Olds, Bill	FB	6-1	210	Kansas City, Kan.
66	*	Pabis, Bob	MG	5-10	205	Monessen, Pa.
No.		Name	Pos.	Ht.	Wt.	Hometown
33		Peetz, Mike	Mon.	6-1	200	Sidney, Nebr.
56	*	Pitts, Johnny	Mon.	6-1	196	Flint, Mich.
41		Powell, Ralph	FB	6-2	218	Detroit, Michigan
74		Righetti, Phil	OLT	6-2	235	Phoenix, Ariz.
68		Robison, Tom	DLT	6-3	236	Detroit, Michigan
20	*	Rodgers, Johnny	RHB	5-10	171	Omaha, Nebr.
13		Runty, Steve	QB	5-11	186	Ogallala, Nebr.
77	*	Rupert, Dick	OLG	6-2	221	Los Angeles, Calif.
43		Sanger, Rich	WLB	6-0	214	Ovid, Colo.
23		Schmit, Bob	RHB	6-1	192	Boys Town, Nebr.
42		Sloey, Bill	SLB	6-1	224	Hawthorne, Calif.
15		Starkebaum, John	Mon.	6-2	198	Haxtun, Colo.
49		Strong, Jon	WLB	6-3	211	Fremont, Nebr.
14	**	Tagge, Jerry	QB	6-2	215	Green Bay, Wis.
45	*	Terrio, Bob	WLB	6-2	209	Fullerton, Calif.
17		Thornton, Robert	RCB	6-0	187	Lomita, Calif.
61	*	Weber, Bruce	OLG	6-0	223	Arlington Hts., Ill.
21		Westbrook, Don	RHB	5-11	185	Cheyenne, Wyo.
72		White, Daryl	OLT	6-4	238	East Orange, N.J.
83		Wieser, Steve	DRE	6-0	196	Columbus, Nebr.
76		Wolfe, Bob	OLT	6-5	242	Omaha, Nebr.
65	*	Wortman, Keith	ORG	6-3	238	Whittier, Calif.
59		Zanrosso, Dennis	OC	6-2	223	Arleta, Calif.

AN ERA OF GREATNESS: COACH BOB DEVANEY'S FINAL FOUR SEASONS (1969 - 1972)

BALANCED OFFENSES WIN CHAMPIONSHIPS
58% RUSHING AND 42% PASSING

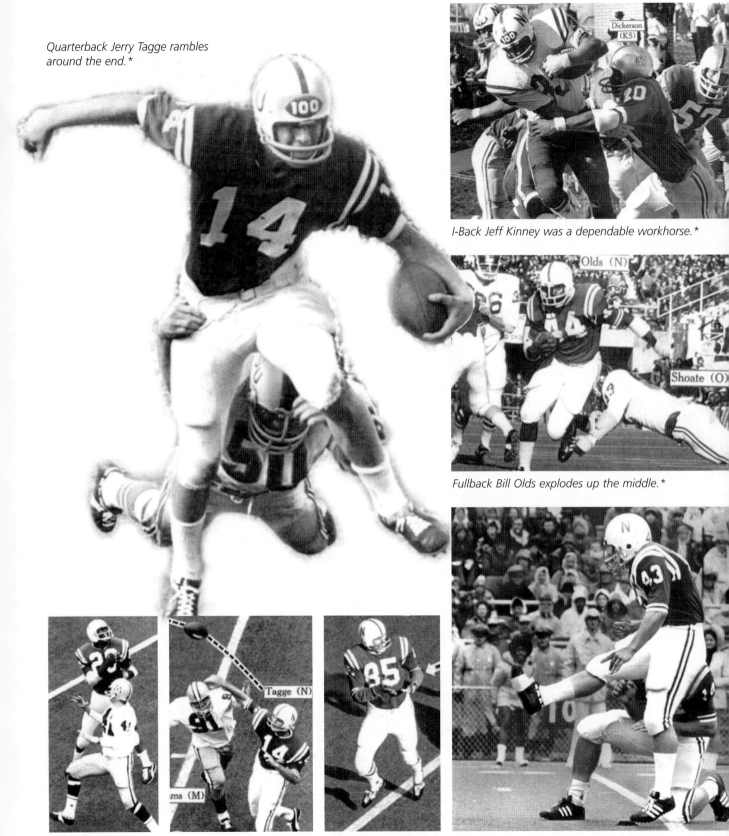

Quarterback Jerry Tagge rambles around the end.*

I-Back Jeff Kinney was a dependable workhorse.*

Fullback Bill Olds explodes up the middle.*

Tagge to Rodgers was a reliable combination.*

Tight End Jerry List.*

Kicker Rich Sanger set a record for points scored.*

GREAT DEFENSE WINS CHAMPIONSHIPS

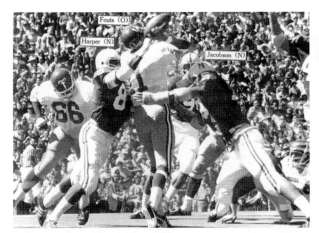

Oregon QB Dan Fouts is welcomed to Lincoln.*

A fumble recovery by All-Conference defender Bob Terrio.*

Meet Mr. Blahak.*

A Big Red Sandwich.
Bill Janssen and John Hyland.*

AN ERA OF GREATNESS: COACH BOB DEVANEY'S FINAL FOUR SEASONS (1969 - 1972)

QB JERRY TAGGE WAS CONSISTENT
IN RUSHING AND PASSING

Quarterback Jerry Tagge looking for a block from Dan Schneiss.

Thousands of fans at the Lincoln Airport await the team's return.

WINNING THE '72 ORANGE BOWL
AND THE NATIONAL CHAMPIONSHIP

The final scoreboard says it all (38 - 6).*

Fans agree (38 - 6).*

Jeff Kinney rips up the middle.*

Joe Blahak intercepts.*

Captains Jim Anderson and Jerry Tagge with the National Championship trophy.*

Mike Beran & Jim Branch with the Orange Bowl trophy.*

AN ERA OF GREATNESS: COACH BOB DEVANEY'S FINAL FOUR SEASONS (1969 - 1972)

THE 4 GREATEST ERAS
IN HUSKER HISTORY

*"The final proof of greatness
lies in being able to endure contumely
without resentment."*

Elbert Hubbard (1900)
"Get Out Or Get In Line."

	1900-1903 4 Years	1911-1915 5 Years	1969-1972 4 years	1993-1997 5 years
1. Record	31-3-1	35-2-3	42-4-2	60-3
2. Winning %	.900	.913	.895	.945
3. Coach	"Bummy" Booth (.845 career winning % 2nd in NU history)	"Jumbo" Stiehm (.913 career winning % 1st in NU history)	Bob Devaney (.829 career winning % 4th in NU history)	Tom Osborne (.836 career winning % 3rd in NU history)
4. Average Points Scored	23.4	27.0	35.4	42.8
5. Opponents Average Score	2.4	4.0	10.5	14.6
6. Avg. Point Differential	21.0	23.0	24.9	28.2
7. Consecutive Undefeated Games	24 (1901-1904)	34 (1912-1916)	32 (1969-1972)	26 (1994-1996)
8. Shutouts by Defense	37 in 55 games	21 in 40 games	9 in 48 games	6 in 63 games
9. Conference Championships	Inapplicable (played as Independent)	5 Consecutive Missouri Valley	4 Consecutive Big 8	4 out of 5; Big 8; Big 12
10. National Championships	Strong Claim in 1902-03	Strong Claim in 1913-14-15	2 1970,1971	3 1994,1995,1997
11. Bowl Championship	N/A	N/A	4 Straight	4 out of 5
12. Undefeated Seasons	2 (1902-1903)	3 (1913, 1914, 1915)	2 (1970-1971)	3 (1994, 1995, 1997)
13. Comments	Forward pass not used until 1913	Team averaged 160 lbs per man Billingsley Computer Ratings ranks NU #1 in 1915	Led the Nation in total wins and winning % over the 4 year period	*Only 1 of 2 schools to win 3 National Titles in 4 years (Notre Dame, `46,`48,`49)

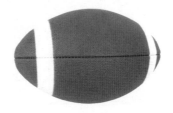

THE 4 GREATEST SEASONS
IN HUSKER HISTORY

	1902	1915	1971	1995
1. Record	9-0-0	8-0-0	13-0-0	12-0-0
2. Coach	"Bummy" Booth	"Jumbo" Stiehm	Bob Devaney	Tom Osborne
3. Average Points Scored	17.7	35.2	39.1	52.4
4. Opponents Average Score	0	4.9	8.2	13.6
5. Point Differential	17.7	30.3	30.9	38.8
6. Closest Game	6 (6-0 Minnesota)	1 (20-19, Notre Dame)	4 (35-31, Oklahoma)	14 (35-21, Washington)
7. Shutouts by Defense	NA	None (Turned down Rose Bowl)	Orange (38-6, Alabama)	Fiesta (62-28, Florida)
8. Conference Championships	NA (Independent)	Missouri Valley (5-0)	Big 8 (7-0)	Big 8 (7-0)
9. National Championships	Strong Claim	Strong Claim	1st A.P.	1st A.P. & U.P.
10. Offense Total: (a) Rushing (b) Passing*			437.6 258.3 179.3	556.3 399.8 156.5
11. Turnover Margin			+26	+13
12. Comments	Minnesota's only loss	Notre Dame's only loss	Oklahoma's only loss	Florida's only loss

(* Passing started in 1913)

ESPN'S 10 GREATEST TEAMS

In 2006 the influential ESPN produced its opinion of the 10 Best College Football teams of all time:

1. NEBRASKA (1971)
2. USC (1972)
3. NEBRASKA (1995)
4. Army (1945)
5. Miami (2001)
6. Michigan (1947)
7. Notre Dame (1947)
8. Oklahoma (1956)
9. Oklahoma (1974)
10. Alabama (1971)

ESPN's specific analysis of the `71 and `95 Husker teams is as follows:

1. NEBRASKA (1971)

Many consider the 1971 version of the Cornhuskers the best college football team ever, and we can't find any reason to disagree. The team averaged more than 39 points a game on offense, and surrendered only 8.2 points a game. Led by kick and punt returner par excellence Johnny Rodgers (who won the 1972 Heisman), the top-ranked Cornhuskers defeated No. 2 Oklahoma 35-31 on Thanksgiving Day, in what some have called the "Game of the Century." They rounded out their 13-0 season with a 38-6 drubbing of Alabama in the Orange Bowl.

3. NEBRASKA (1995)

Combine a great offense – 50-plus points per game – with a great defense. Add a tough schedule, including four Top 10 teams, which the Cornhuskers trounced by no fewer than 23 points. Stir in Ahman Green and Lawrence Phillips for an incredible running attack. Presto. You've got a second straight National Championship, topped by a 62-24 humiliation of second-ranked Florida in the Fiesta Bowl, and one of the best teams ever.

AN ERA OF GREATNESS: COACH BOB DEVANEY'S FINAL FOUR SEASONS (1969 - 1972)

*"It's not easy to win a National Championship,
and it shouldn't be easy."*

Oklahoma Coach Barry Switzer (1986)
(after winning his 3rd title in the Orange Bowl vs. Penn State)

*"If "ifs" and "buts" were candy and nuts,
what a wonderful world it would be."*

"Dandy" Don Meredith (1973),
Dallas Cowboys All-Pro quarterback and
Commentator on "Monday Night Football"

1972

9-2-1
Big Eight Champion
Orange Bowl Champion

OPPONENT	AP RANK NU/OPP.	RESULT	
UCLA	**1/**	L	**17-20**
Texas A&M	10/	W	37-7
Army	**9/**	**W**	**77-7**
Minnesota	7/	W	49-0
Missouri	6/	W	62-0
Kansas	**5/**	**W**	**56-0**
Oklahoma State	3/	W	34-0
Colorado	**3/15**	**W**	**33-10**
Iowa State	3/17	T	23-23
Kansas State	5/	W	59-7
Oklahoma	5/4	L	14-17
ORANGE BOWL			
Notre Dame	9/12	W	40-6

FINAL RANKING:

4th AP	(post-bowl),	
9th UPI	(regular season)	

*Away games in bold

It was "Close But No Cigar."

This is "the one that got away." UNL had tremendous returning talent, the same successful coaches, and a chance to be the only team in college history to win 3 consecutive National Championships.

It could have happened, but the fact that it didn't should not obscure the greatness of the 1972 NU team. NU would finish 4th in the Final A.P. Poll, and the `72 team was ranked the 10th best team of all-time by the Sagarin Computer Ratings. Rich Glover won both the Lombardi and Outland Trophies, and Johnny Rodgers was awarded the Heisman Trophy.

Two curious facts emerge in analyzing the `72 season. First, there were only 3 close games, and NU didn't win any of them (one tie and two losses, each by 3 points). The second unusual fact is that all 9 victories were monumental "Blowouts" by colossal point differences. The average score was a lopsided 52-4, an amazing differential of 7 touchdowns.

A.   Losses & Ties (3):

- 3 points   . . .   UCLA   (17-20)
- 3 points   . . .   Oklahoma   (14-17)
- 0 points   . . .   Iowa State (23-23)

B.   Margins of Victory in "Blowout" wins (9):

(1)   **23-34 points (4):**

- 23 . . . Colorado
- 30 . . . Texas A&M
- 34 . . . Notre Dame
- 34 . . . Oklahoma State

(2)   **49-62 points (5):**

- 49 . . . Minnesota
- 52 . . . Kansas State
- 56 . . . Kansas
- 60 . . . Army
- 62 . . . Missouri

There were several reasons that cumulatively denied the 3-peat.

1) Obviously, every opponent was "up" and "gunning" to upset the 2-time defending National Champion. They would give NU their "best shot."

2) The "turn-over" margin made a huge swing for the worse. From +26 in 1971 to -4 in 1972. That equals 2.5 turnovers per game.

3) Lack of an experienced quarterback. For 3 years NU had benefited from the "dynamic duo" of Jerry Tagge and Van Brownson. As Coach Osborne later said: "experience at QB can cost a couple of games." Sophomore quarterback David Humm would later become All-Conference and All-American and play for the Oakland Raiders. But it took a while for Humm to mature. As remembered by All-Conference safety, Joe Blahak: "In 1969-1971 quarterback Jerry Tagge held everything together. This became clear in 1972 when NU lacked a QB with experience."

4) A decline in the running game. Humm was a great passer but not a runner. Also, NU did not have an I-back with the skills or experience to replace All-American Jeff Kinney.

5) Of possible importance was having a "two" head coaches system. Devaney announced before the `72 season that he would be retiring, and Tom Osborne became "Assistant Head Coach." This was probably a mistake. It disrupted old patterns of responsibility and created some confusion among the players and coaching staff.

6) One obscure fact that may have had an impact was that the NU coaching staff in the summer coached the college All-Stars in the annual Kickoff game against the defending NFL champion. Coach Monte Kiffin recalls that the All-Star commitment gave NU's coaches less time to prepare for the opening game against UCLA (17-20).

7) Finally, some overconfidence may have crept in. As remembered by Assistant Coach Jim Walden:

"Our biggest challenge was not being over-confident. There were two football games where I thought we just kind of got caught looking. (a) UCLA game in 1972 was the opening game of the season, and they weren't a great team (b) the other one was Iowa State. We had ourselves in the position to be Number One, and we go to Iowa State in 1972 and tie the game (23-23). We were not ready and did not play with the intensity that we were known for. And those teams played well at that time."

In summary, NU's Defense was still "rock solid," but the offense was not as consistent as in 1971. As stated by All-American Defensive end, Willie Harper:

"Our problem in 1972 was that offensively we found ourselves in situations and holes too deep, and the defense could not pull us out."

From the 5th game of 1969 through the end of the 1972 season, NU lost only 2 games. Over 3 (`70 - `72) seasons, the record was a remarkable 33 - 2 - 2 (.918 winning percentage). Each of the two losses in `72 were by only 3 points, and they deserve further analysis.

A.   The UCLA Bruins (17-20)

This was the season opener in the Los Angeles Coliseum. Mark Harmon, later a movie and TV star, was UCLA's quarterback.

This was NU's first loss in 33 games, and the two basic reasons for the loss were (1) inconsistency on offense. NU out gained UCLA in total yardage by 320 to 284. NU had 148 yards passing and 174 rushing, but this was far below NU's 1972 average of 442 yards per game. (2) Turnovers were a key factor. NU had 4 fumbles and 2 interceptions. In essence, NU "beat itself."

The game was tied 10-10 at Half-time and 17-17 in the 4th quarter. And NU had two chances to win when drives bogged down. UCLA's Herrera kicked the winning field goal with only 22 seconds left.

B.   The Oklahoma Sooners (14-17)

This was the last regular season game in Lincoln, and NU still had an outside chance for the national title. NU was undefeated in 26 consecutive Big 8 games (1969 - 1972).

NU led 7-0 at Halftime and 14-0 in the 3rd quarter. But OU refused to buckle. (1) Key plays were short passes to wide receivers Al Chandler and Tinker Owens. (2) led by the Selmon brothers, OU's great defense shut down NU the last 20 minutes. (3) And, again, an NU turnover was crucial. With 10 minutes left, quarterback David Humm fumbled. OU drove to the NU 27 and Rick Fulcher kicked the winning field goal. It was NU's first conference loss at home since 1968.

In retrospect, Oklahoma clearly deserved the win. OU outgained NU in total offense by 327 to 181. Nebraska completed only 10 of 33 passes for 104 net yards. OU's defense dominated the second half, and NU's pass defense was unusually porous in giving up 186 yards on 10 passes, an average of 18.6 yards per pass.

Nebraska finished the season 8 - 2 - 1. NU would get a chance to redeem itself in the Orange Bowl against Notre Dame.

C.   The Orange Bowl vs. Notre Dame (40-6)

The Huskers routed Notre Dame (40-6), and NU became the first team to win 3 straight Orange Bowls. In a surprise move, the coaches moved Johnny Rodgers from wingback to I-back. Rodgers scored five touchdowns - 3 by running one by passing (to Frosty Anderson), and one by receiving a pass from QB Dave Humm.

Notre Dame's coach, Ara Parseghian, described the game as "the worst loss" of his career. The statistics were lopsided with NU out gaining N.D. 560 yards to 207 yards. NU had 300 yards rushing and 260 passing.

NU was ranked 4th in the final A.P. Poll. Coach Devaney's 3 year record was 33 - 2 -2 (.918 winning percentage). Devaney retired as the winningest active coach in college football. It was the end of an illustrious Era of Greatness

A 3-YEAR RECORD OF 33- 2- 2
(1970 – 1972) (.918 WINNING PERCENTAGE)

andy Borg take it to The House.*

Manstedt and Borg seal off the end.*

AN ERA OF GREATNESS: COACH BOB DEVANEY'S FINAL FOUR SEASONS (1969 - 1972)

THE 1972 TEAM
BIG 8 AND ORANGE BOWL CHAMPIONS

RECORD: 9-2-1

- Big Eight Champion
- Orange Bowl Champion
- Ranked 4th in the Nation (A.P.)

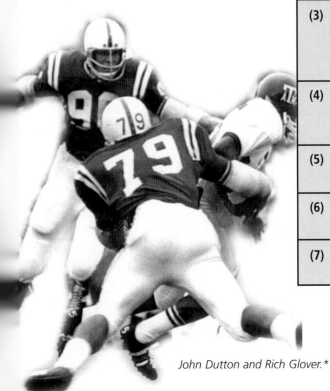

John Dutton and Rich Glover. *

A COMPARISON OF THE 1969, 1970, 1971 AND 1972 SEASONS

		1969	1970	1971	1972
(1)	Won/Loss Record	9-2	11-0-1	13-0	9-2-1
(2)	National Ranking (Associated Press)	11th	1st	1st	4th
(3)	Big 8 Conference	6-1 Tie for 1st Place	7-0 1st Place	7-0 1st Place	5-1-1 1st Place
(4)	Bowl Game	Sun: 45-6 Georgia	Orange: 17-12 LSU	Orange: 36-6 Alabama	Orange: 40-6 Notre Dame
(5)	UNL Average Score	28.2	33.5	38.2	40.9
(6)	Opponent's Average Score	10.7	14.9	8.0	8.1
(7)	Point Differential	17.5	18.6	30.2	32.8

NEBRASKA FOOTBALL
OFFICIAL ROSTER

1972

No.		Name	Pos.	Ht.	Wt.	Hometown
		Alward, Tom	OLG	6-4	215	Flint, Mich.
		Anderson, Bill	MG	6-2	214	Toledo, Ohio
		Anderson, Dan	ORG	6-1	214	Fremont, Neb.
	*	Anderson, Frosty	SE	6-1	176	Scottsbluff, Neb.
	*	Austin, Al	ORT	6-5	222	Lincoln, Neb.
		Bahe, Ritch	WB	5-11	182	Fremont, Neb.
		Bell, John	MG	6-0	203	Anaheim, Calif.
	**	Beran, Mike	ORG	5-11	225	Ord, Neb.
	**	Blahak, Joe	LCB	5-9	179	Columbus, Neb.
	*	Borg, Randy	RCB	6-0	189	Alliance, Neb.
	**	Branch, James	SLB	5-9	203	Chicago, Ill.
	**	Adkins, John	DLE	6-3	221	Lynchburg, Va.
		Butts, Randy	IB	6-2	197	Grand Island, Neb.
	**	Carstens, James	FB	5-11	222	Glen Ellyn, Ill.
		Coleman, Ron	TE	6-3	195	Ulysses, Neb.
		Costanzo, Rich	ORT	6-5	240	Jersey City, N.J.
		Crenshaw, Marvin	ORT	6-5	223	Toledo, Ohio
	*	Damkroger, Maury	FB	6-2	215	Lincoln. Neb.
		Davis, Tony	IB	5-11	205	Tecumseh, Neb.
		DeNell, Jake	RCB	6-2	180	Fond du Lac, Wis.
	*	Dixon, Gary	IB	5-8	188	Oxnard, Calif.
		Doak, Mark	OLT	6-4	220	Whittier, Calif.
		Drinkwalter, Bob	ORG	6-3	220	Billings, Mont.
		Duda, Rich	C	6-3	215	Westchester, Ill.
	**	Dumler, Doug	C	6-3	230	Melrose Park, Ill.
	*	Dutton, John	DRT	6-7	248	Rapid City, S.D.
		Fischer, Pat	LCB	5-9	160	Lincoln, Neb.
		Fuller, Bruce	LCB	6-0	180	Kansas City, Mo.
	*	Garson, Glen	WB	6-0	184	Fullerton, Calif.
	**	Glover, Rich	MG	6-1	233	Jersey City, N.J.
		Goeller, Dave	IB	5-11	188	Pilger, Nebr.
	**	Harper, Willie	DRE	6-2	208	Toledo, Ohio
		Hegener, Stan	ORG	6-4	231	Lincoln, Minn.
		Henrichs, Dennis	OLT	6-2	210	Beatrice, Nebr.
		Heydorf, Mark	S	6-2	185	La Crescenta, Calif.
		Hill, Jeff	SE	6-2	190	LeGrange, Ill.
		Humm, David	QB	6-2	186	Las Vegas, Nev.
		Humm, Tom	WB	5-10	170	Las Vegas, Nev,
	**	Hyland, John	DLE	6-2	193	Lincoln, Nebr.
	**	Janssen, Bill	DLT	6-3	230	Grand Forks, N.D.
		Jenkins, Brad	SE	6-2	190	Kimball, Neb.
		Johnson, Ardell	RCB	6-0	170	Chillicothe, Mo.
	**	Johnson, Monte	DLT	6-6	239	Bloomington, Minn.
		Jones, Chuck	LCB	6-0	170	Beatrice, Neb.
		Kinsel, John	C	6-2	220	Council Bluffs, Iowa
		Knudsen, Tom	MG	6-2	215	Lakewood, Calif.
		Kyros, George	S	5-9	155	Grand Island, Neb.
		Lackovic, Tim	SE	6-1	190	Omaha, Nebr.
		Leonardi, Chad	OLG	6-1	205	Canonsburg, Pa.

1972

No.		Name	Pos.	Ht.	Wt.	Hometown
85	**	List, Jerry	TE	6-1	218	Bay City, Mich.
4		Loewenstein, Ron	Mon.	6-0	185	Grand Island, Neb.
86	*	Longwell, Brent	TE	6-4	222	Homer, Nebr.
11		Luck, Terry	QB	6-3	208	Fayetteville, N.C.
96		Lynch, Dab	DLT	6-5	250	Yankton, S.D.
82	*	Manstedt, Steve	DLE	6-2	210	Wahoo, Neb.
25	**	Mason, Dave	Mon.	6-0	199	Green Bay, Wis.
31		Mazon, Frank	RCB	5-10	165	Anaheim, Calif.
93		McGuire, Tim	OLG	6-1	230	Omaha, Neb.
65		McKinley, Kim	DLT	6-3	233	Greeley, Colo.
98		Meyer, Bob	DRE	6-3	200	Hooper, Neb.
69		Mills, George	DRT	6-5	210	Omaha, Neb.
30		Moran, Jeff	WB	6-1	191	Huron, S.D.
88		Mushinskie, Larry	TE	6-2	210	Temple City, Calif.
57		Nelson, Bob	SLB	6-5	230	Stillwater, Minn.
94		Norrie, Rod	DRT	6-4	240	Geneva, Neb.
34		O'Connell, John	S	6-2	192	Sidney, Neb.
95		Offner, Mike	DLE	6-2	190	Red Cloud, Neb.
38		O'Holleran, Mike	FB	6-1	197	Sidney, Neb.
44	**	Olds, Bill	FB	6-1	224	Kansas City, Kan.
99		Osborne, Mike	DRT	6-5	240	Long Beach, Calif.
68		Pate, Tom	DRE	6-3	190	Omaha, Neb.
7		Peterson, Matt	SE	6-3	195	Cedar Rapids, Iowa
56	**	Pitts, Johnny	WLB	5-9	196	Flint, Mich.
10		Potter, Dana	QB	5-11	180	Des Moines, Iowa
41		Powell, Ralph	FB	6-2	212	Detroit, Michigan
91		Redding, Dave	DRE	6-1	190	North Platte, Neb.
84		Revelle, Bob	SE	6-2	195	Sierra Madre, Calif.
74		Righetti, Phil	OLT	6-3	233	Phoenix, Ariz.
20	**	Rodgers, Johnny	WB	5-9	173	Omaha, Neb.
40		Rodgers, Terry	Mon.	5-11	180	Columbus, Neb.
13		Runty, Steve	QB	5-11	186	Ogallala, Neb.
15		Rutan, Bob	QB	6-1	200	Blue Springs, Neb.
45		Ruud, Tom	WLB	6-3	212	Bloomington, Minn.
43	*	Sanger, Rich	K-SLB	6-0	214	Ovid, Colo.
23		Schmit, Bob	SLB	6-1	187	Boys Town, Neb.
16		Seeton, Jim	S	6-2	188	Lakewood, Colo.
42	*	Sloey, Bill	SLB	5-11	225	Hawthorne, Calif.
48		Starkebaum, John	Mon.	6-2	198	Haxtun, Colo.
3		Stinner, John	WLB	6-0	195	Pittsburgh, Pa.
49		Strong, Jon	WLB	6-3	211	Fremont, Neb.
17		Thornton, Robert	S	6-0	197	Lomita, Calif.
21		Westbrook, Don	IB	5-11	185	Cheyenne, Wyo.
72	*	White, Daryl	OLT	6-0	196	East Orange, N.J.
83		Wieser, Steve	DLE	6-0	196	Columbus, Neb.
76	*	Wolfe, Bob	OLG	6-5	242	Omaha, Neb.
52		Young, Vic	C	6-3	220	Louisville, Miss.
59		Zanrosso, Dennis	C	6-2	223	Arleta, Calif.

A STRONG DEFENSE
4 STRAIGHT SHUTOUTS AND ONLY 8.1 POINTS PER GAME

*Applying pressure on defense.**

COMPARATIVE STATISTICS ON OFFENSE, DEFENSE AND TURNOVERS

		1969	1970	1971	1972
(1)	Total Offensive Average	372	421	438	442
	(a) Rushing Average	172 (46%)	232 (55%)	258 (59%)	221 (50%)
	(b) Passing Average	200 (54%)	189 (45%)	179 (41%)	221 (50%)
(2)	Total Defense Against Opponents	253	271	203*	217
	(a) Opponent Rush Yardage	130	148	86*	108
	(b) Opponent Pass Yardage	123	123	117*	109
(3)	Turnover Margin	+6	+17	+26	-4 (30 Turnover Decrease)

(*Led conference

A POTENT OFFENSE
9 "BLOWOUT" WINS WITH A 52-4 AVERAGE SCORE

avid Humm throws a
uchdown pass to Frosty
nderson. *

Q.B. David Humm became the most
prolific passer in Husker history. *

Johnny Rodgers
catches a pass against Missouri. *

AN ERA OF GREATNESS: COACH BOB DEVANEY'S FINAL FOUR SEASONS (1969 - 1972)

CHAPTER TEN
THE REASONS UNDERLYING
THE SUCCESS

"All for one, and
one for all"

Alexander Dumas (1844)
"The 3 Musketeers"

(1) **A Head Coach who had Extraordinary Skills in Organization, Delegation, Strategy, and Motivation**

Bob Devaney was the rare infectious personality who combined all the qualities needed in a successful head coach:

(a) a tremendous recruiter (with both parents and players);

(b) an astute teacher of fundamentals;

(c) a masterful strategist on the field during games;

(d) a generosity that inspired loyalty in his Assistant Coaches;

(e) an infectious sense of humor and ability to make others feel comfortable and happy;

(f) a wonderful gift at public relations with the fans and the media; but also a controlled temper that could be unleashed to gain attention or to motivate;

(g) confidence in himself and an ability to instill confidence in his players.

(h) a leader and one of his least remembered and greatest qualities was his organizational skills and lack of ego in taking credit – he selected excellent Assistant Coaches and let them do their jobs.

(9) a fierce competitor with a "heart" and burning desire to win. The greatest professional foot ball coach of all time, Vince Lombardi, once observed that the difference between men:

"is in the energy, in the strong will, in the settled purpose and in the invincible determination."

Maraniss, <u>When Pride Still Mattered</u>
1999) p. 47.

Devaney's vision, strength of character and his will to prevail transformed him, his players, the people of the state of Nebraska and ultimately the entire collegiate world of football.

Bob Devaney unquestionably belongs in the All-Time Pantheon of the Greatest College Coaches who possessed all of the necessary attributes for success and which allowed them to stand apart from the coaching multitudes, e.g. Notre Dame's Knute Rockne, Minnesota's Bernie Beerman, Pittsburgh's Jock Sutherland, Army's "Red" Blaik, Oklahoma's Bud Wilkinson, Alabama's "Bear" Bryant and Southern Cal's John McKay.

Guy Ingles (UNL `72) starred as a pass receiver and kick returner on Devaney's first National Championship team in 1970. Guy summarizes the complex personality of Coach Bob Devaney:

"Bob Devaney was a great football coach and a better man. The perfect optimist to give a strong re-birth to a dead football program. People genuinely loved him, even opponents and players who disagreed with him over their fortunes.

Johnny Rodgers (UNL `73) was twice All-American at wingback and NU's first Heisman Trophy winner. Johnny remembers:

"Bob was the best motivator of people I have seen. Bob was a leader and he taught leadership skills and the faith that leadership needs.

ob Brown (UNL `63) is the second Husker to be ashrined in both the College and Pro Hall of Fames (Guy hamberlin `15 was the first). In his acceptance speech /8/04) Brown stated on national television, "Bob Devaney as the best teacher of college football, **EVER!**"

2) Talented Assistant Coaches with Great Chemistry and Teaching Ability

evaney knew that continuity was key. His assistant oaches liked each other, and Devaney "let them coach". hey had the freedom to teach and to inspire their players.

s told by Coach Jim Ross, Devaney wanted initial debate d discussion among all the coaches and then would ach a consensus. In practice and games there was "no ckering." They were all on the same page.

here was a respect from the players for their coaches and a nse of trust that NU would be prepared better than its ponents.

3) Recruiting High Quality Athletes with Speed

"Jimmy and Joes are more important Than "Xs" and "Os""

here is no substitute. Championship teams must have the ayers to run the plays. NU's coaches admittedly did not cruit well in 1966 and 1967. But they adjusted and had xcellent recruiting classes in `68 and `69. They also were telligent in going to California to recruit "JUCO" players unior College) who brought maturity and experience.

4) Great Defenses Win Championships and they are Built on Overall Team Speed Pursuing to the Ball

his fundamental principle has been espoused by Knute ockne, Vince Lombardi, Bear Bryant, Bob Devaney and umerous other legendary winning coaches.

reat defenses cause turnovers and can score points. They rovide good field position through turnovers or forcing unts. They can emotionally inspire the team in all areas, s well demoralizing the opponent. Then can "hold" the am in the game until the offense gets moving. Great efense are key because the opponent cannot win if it annot score.

(5) Balanced Offenses Win Championships

Coach Devaney and Coach Osborne were "ahead of their time" in 1969 when they installed an early version of the "West Coast Offense." They discarded an outdated power running game (full house backfield) and went to the modern "I" formation with the wingback and wide receiver split out wide. This provided more versatility and deception.

This also allowed passing to all eligible receivers – fullback, I-back, wingback, tight end and wide receiver. This versatility in passing in turn "opened up" holes for the running game. Indeed, in 1969 I-back Jeff Kinney was the leading receiver on the team, and the offenses on all 4 championship teams averaged passing on 40-50% of the plays.

In essence, successful teams over an era, or period of years, need both an effective passing and running game. Devaney and Osborne adjusted and perfected both.

(6) The Respect, Admiration and Camaraderie Among the Players – A Sense of Humor is Helpful

It was highly unusual and beneficial. Like a brotherhood, it made players want to go "the extra mile." As Coach Kiffin stressed, "do it for your teammates." The enthusiasm was contagious, and it made practice fun and enhanced teamwork.

(7) Practice Smarter, not Longer

The greatest golfer of the 1940s and 1950s was Ben Hogan who perfected his swing through hours upon hours of repetition. Hogan once quipped, "The more I practice, the luckier I get." But practices can be counterproductive if they are not well planned. For example, Coach Devaney's predecessor, Bill Jennings (1957-1961) was often criticized for holding 3 hour practices which tired the players and hurt their energy levels and performance in the games.

Devaney was smart in limiting practices to 90 minutes. There would also be a "break" for water or juice, so practices were intense but tolerable.

Coach Osborne also describes how people were always moving and not standing around because the "walk-on" program created enough players to have multiple offenses and defenses operating against each other at all times. This produced efficiency and productivity.

(8)   Luck and Avoiding Injuries

As Trainer George Sullivan observed, things were going so well in 1970-'71 that there were almost no injuries.

Devaney also limited contact in the practices, and this helped to minimize injuries.

(9)   The Ability and Willingness to Change and Adjust

As explained by Coach Tom Osborne in his Foreword, the changes before the 1969 season were highly productive:

(a)   NU was one of the first colleges to use an "audible" system where the quarterback could verbally create a new play at the line of scrimmage.

(b)   Under the expert supervision of Boyd Epley, NU developed one of the first weight lifting and conditioning programs. It became a model for the nation and other colleges. Coaches visited NU to learn the most modern techniques.

(c)   Changed the offense to a modern "I" and "pro spread" formation, which enabled more deception on reverses and counter plays, as well as a more diversified passing attack to all eligible receivers.

(d)   Recruiting Junior College players who added immediate maturity and experience.

(10)   Excellent Field Position

The defenses and kick return teams were so effective that NU in 1969-1972 almost always had great field position. All-American QB Jerry Tagge estimates that in his 3 years ('69-'71) the average starting position for the offense was at NU's 40 yard line.

(11)   A Favorable Turnover Margin

As seen in earlier statistics, NU's all important "turnover margin" improved each year in 1969, 1970, and 1971. In 1971 set a school record of plus 26. NU's defenses were recovering fumbles and getting interceptions much more often than its opponents.

Then, in 1972 for some unknown reason, the turnover margin reversed to minus 4, a 3 turnover per game reversal which undoubtedly contributed to the failure to win a 3rd consecutive National Championship.

(12)   The Best Fans in America

Don "Fox" Bryant is UNL Assistant Athletic Director and Sports Information Director Emeritus (1963-present). Don observes (2006):

> *"The UNL fans have been tremendous and they are a key part of the success."*

Legendary television commentator Keith Jackson agrees in stating frequently on national television:

> *"Without question, Nebraska has the best fans in the country."*

And ESPN analyst Lee Corso concurred (2003):

> *"Of all the fans in America, Nebraska's are the most in-tune with college football, and they have the most respect for the way a college football game should be played."*

Dozens of interviews in this book confirm the emotional and psychological lift that the NU fans provided (and still provide) for the players.

In 1978 the fabled "Voice of Nebraska," KFAB radio announcer Lyell Bremser exclaimed at the end of an NU-OU game:

> *"It is impossible to describe in words **what NU football means to the people of Nebraska. It unites our people,** both east and west, and north and south of the Platte."*

(13)   Playing in the Toughest Conference in America is the Best Preparation for National Greatness

In the late 1960s the Big Eight Conference had clearly emerged as the best in the nation. Playing in a tough conference is the best preparation for attaining national greatness.

Before Nebraska's four year Era of Greatness (1969-1972) it should be remembered that NU's coaches experienced a "wake up call" in the 1967-1968 seasons in losing games to high quality Big 8 opponents: 2 straight to Oklahoma, Missouri and Kansas, and one loss to Colorado and Kansas State. The high level of play within the conference was a challenge and elevated the level of play for all of its teams.

In 1996 the Big 8 merged with 4 teams from the old Southwest Conference (Texas, Texas A&M, Baylor and Texas Tech). The new conference is called the Big Twelve.

Since 1969 the Big 8 Conference and its continuation into the Big 12 Conference in 1996, overall continued to be the toughest conference in America when measured by comparative National Championships won by its members over the past 37 years (1969-2005)

- 13 National Titles   (36%)
- 5 Runner Up   (13%)
- 14 Third Place   (38%)

The following chart reveals the preeminence of NU's Conferences in terms of national titles and strong competition for the title.

"The closeness of the players and coaches is a strong memory for me. There was a powerful loyalty and camaraderie among all of those involved."

Tom Osborne (2006);

Conference	National Championships (College/Year) (Since 1969)
(1) Big Twelve	13 ... 5 Nebraska (70, 71, 94, 95, 97); 4 Oklahoma (74, 75, 85, 2000); 3 Texas (69, 70, 2005); 1 Colorado (90)
(2) Big Ten	2 ... 1 Michigan (97); 1 Ohio State (2002)
(3) Southeast	7 ... 3 Alabama (78, 79, 92) 1 Georgia (80) 1 Florida (96) 1 Tennessee (98) 1 LSU (2003)
(4) Atlantic Coast	2 ... 1 Clemson (81) 1 Florida State (99)
(5) Pacific Ten	5 ... 4 Southern Cal. (USC) (72,73,2003, 2004) 1 Washington (91)
(6) Big East	1 ... 1 Miami (2001) (joined in Mid-90s)
(7) Independents	12 ... 1 Florida State (93) 1 Pittsburgh (76) 2 Penn State (82, 86) 4 Miami (83, 87, 89, 91) 1 Brigham Young (84) 3 Notre Dame (73, 77, 88)
2nd Nationally:	6... Big Twelve: 2 Nebraska (83, 99) 3 Oklahoma (71, 72) 1 Texas (81)
3rd Nationally:	13... Big Twelve: 2 Colorado (71, 94) 1 Texas (72) 3 Nebraska (82, 84, 93) 7 Oklahoma (73, 78, 79, 80, 86, 87, 2003)

*"Bob Devaney brought Greatness
to Nebraska Football, and
Tom Osborne maintained it."*

*Barry Switzer (2006),
Oklahoma Head Coach (1973-1990);
3 National Championships, College Football Hall of Fame*

After the 1973 Orange Bowl, Coach Devaney was carried out of history into legend. His 11 years left an indelibile stamp on his players, the University, the people of Nebraska and the entire world of College Football. He retired to become full-time NU Athletic Director, and Tom Osborne became Head Coach for the next 25 years (1973-1997).

Osborne kept the momentum going forward. He won 13 Conference Championships, 3 National Titles and would finish as the 5th winningest coach in NCAA history (.836 winning percentage). Both Devaney and Osborne "went out on top" in winning their National Championships and having their best seasons at the end of their careers. Both are enshrined in the College Football Hall of Fame.

Devaney established a solid foundation for success. Osborne maintained the tradition, and NU led the nation by a wide margin over the combined 36 year period (1962-1997):

36 SEASONS
THAT LED THE NATION BY A WIDE MARGIN

A. THE BASIC STATISTICS UNDER 36 YEARS OF COACHES BOB DEVANEY (1962-1972) AND TOM OSBORNE (1973-1997):

(1)	Wins/Losses/Ties:	356 – 69 – 5	
(2)	Winning Percentage:	.832	(NU led the nation by a wide margin over this 36 year period.)
(3)	Conference Championships: (Big 8 and Big 12)	21	(58.4%)
(4)	National Championships:	5	(70, 71, 94, 95, 97)
(5)	Average Points Scored:	33	
(6)	Average Points Allowed By Defense:	12.5	
(7)	Average Point Differential:	20.5	
(8)	Bowl Victories:	18	
(9)	Bowl Losses:	16	
(10)	1st round NFL Draft Selections:	26	
(11)	Consecutive Winning Seasons:	36	(1962-97)
(12)	Nine-Win Seasons:	34	(1969 - 1997)
(13)	Husker Student/Athletes Named Academic All-Americans:	44	
(14)	NCAA record of consecutive sellouts:	255	(ongoing)
(15)	All-American players coached:	64	

COACH TOM OSBORNE
NU Head Coach
(1973 - 1997)

- 5th Winningest Coach of All-time (.836)
- 3 National Championships (1994, 95, 97)
- 13 Conference Championships
- College Football Hall of Fame

AN ERA OF GREATNESS: COACH BOB DEVANEY'S FINAL FOUR SEASONS (1969 - 1972)

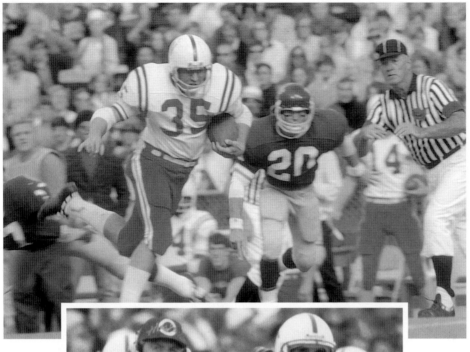

**Coach Tom Osborne and
Quarterback Brooke Berringer** *(1994)
Osborne's 1st National Championship Season*

*For an excellent analysis of the Osborne years
(1973-1997) see Mike Babcock's book, "Heart
of a Husker: Tom Osborne's Nebraska Legacy"
(2006).*

CHAPTER TWELVE

MEMORIES AND THOUGHTS OF THE COACHES, TRAINERS AND MEDIA 35 YEARS LATER

"They call it coaching,
but it is teaching.
You do not just tell them it is so,
but you show them
the reasons why it is so,
and you repeat and repeat
until they are convinced,
until they know."

Vince Lombardi (1967)
(Maraniss, "When Pride Still Mattered")
(1999) p. 213

"A teacher affects eternity;
he can never tell where
his influence stops."

Henry Brooks Adams (1907)
"The Education of Henry Adams" (ch.20)

COACH MONTE KIFFIN
DEFENSIVE COORDINATOR
**Graduated from N.U. in 1963. Played `59-`63;
Position: Offensive/Defensive Tackle**

HUSKER REFLECTIONS

1. When we played Oklahoma in 1971 in Norman in the "shoot out" game, in the first half OU was going up and down the field like a track meet. Devaney was the kind of head coach that let the assistant coaches do the coaching. But he said "Monte, get the defense together on the sidelines." So, I got them over on the sideline and he says "Glover is tackling the dive, the quarterback, and the pitch. What the hell are the rest of you guys doing?" That was the first half. He was hot but then the guys all just rallied. Glover killed OU's center (Brahaney) that day.

   On TV they show the NU-OU classic shoot out of 1971 every year, and the players get excited because they know I am from Nebraska. They always give me a bad time and they say "Oh, we have to hear about the Nebraska game again". I have a lot of fun with that stuff. Anyway, we get to watch Johnny's punt return once a year.

2. The coaches in the back room of our offices at UNL had what they now call a "cigar bar". Jim Ross, John Melton, and all the coaches smoked cigars and they would play pitch. I was a young grad assistant and other grad assistants were Warren Powers, Barry Alvarez, and Jimmy Walden. Our goal was to sit at that pitch table. There was only room for 5 guys and they played pitch every noon. If you ever got to play in a game you knew you were accepted. It took a couple years to get one. Coach Selmer and Coach Corgan played. Coach Jim Ross always started the pitch game, and he loved to play. Devaney, Ross, and Corgan had been together since Michigan and then at Wyoming. Then they hired Selmer and Melton in Wyoming and they all came to N.U. in 1962.

3. Regarding Coach Osborne, I remember when Tom first started Nebraska's first football camp at Lake Mary Jane Ranch in Central City, Nebraska. There were about 25 kids there from nearby Central City. These football camps nowadays have become a big deal with thousands of kids. Anyway, Warren Powers and I worked at the

camp and stayed in some old beat up cabin and Tom ran the camp. We were all assistants at that time.

4. In the mid-1960s Tom and I used to hit that old racquetball court in the old field house. Back in those days we played handball. Tom and I were both grad assistants. We would play two out of three, and we would come out of there dripping wet. We were real competitive. Like offense and defense.

5. Nebraska fans are the best. When the bus is pulling up to the stadium with all those fans out there and all that red, it was just an unbelievable feeling. It has not changed. I still hear stories every time I talk to someone who was at a Nebraska game, and they were from another school (players or parents or whatever). They always say what great fans Nebraska has. If you played hard and even though you would not win, Nebraska fans always gave you a good hand when you walked off the field.

6. The most remarkable offensive play I witnessed was Johnny Rodgers' punt return in 1971 against Oklahoma. Also when I was playing against Kansas (1963) and Gale Sayers went 99 yards against us. I said to myself "why is he playing for Kansas and not Nebraska?"

7. My first year as a varsity coach was 1969, and I recall us beating Georgia in the Sun Bowl in El Paso (45-6). I was just a young coach (29 years old). Mike Wynn, Sherwin Jarmon, Bob Liggett, Ken Geddes. I remember those guys coming up to me after the game. I was just a young coach and they said "Coach, thanks a lot, your first year as a coach you really meant a lot to us." That is something I will never forget. That meant a lot to me because I was a young pup and had just moved up from the freshman job. That is a sentimental story.

   I owe so much to the players from Nebraska. You are only as good as your players. What Mike Wynn meant to me at UNL was the same as what Warren Sapp or Simeon Rice have meant to me at Tampa. It is all the same. You have to relate to your players, and you have to get your players to work hard and respect each other

8. Football never changes. Players are not one bit different. Johnny Rodgers or Cadillac Williams are the same. Players don't change but they make more money now. Our saying in Tampa is "We play hard, we play fast, and we play together". And that is the way Nebraska played. I coached the same way back then and I don't coach any different now. I am 66 going on 46. Some people are 66 going on 86. It's how you act.

9. Coach Devaney was like my second dad. My father was a high school coach in Lexington, Nebraska. I always have believed that you need to give players a second chance. Devaney suspended me from the Gotham Bowl in 1962 when I was a Junior in college and I never got to play in the Gotham Bowl. That was for the milk truck deal. I got suspended, but he gave me a chance to come back that next spring. I ended up starting my senior year (1963). Then he hired me as a coach in 1967. It just goes to show that the guy that kicks you off the team can give you a chance to come back. I believe in the same thing. I would not be where I am today if it was not for Coach Devaney giving me that second chance. Bob meant a lot to my career.

10. I would like to go back and relive the "flea flicker" pass by Oklahoma that beat us in 1976 (21-17). It was the last game I coached at NU. It was a 3rd and 19 with about one minute left in the game. They usually ran the wishbone and the option but they threw a short pass in the flat, and the receiver lateraled the ball to Elvis Peacock who ran 60 yards. They went to the end zone and won. It was the fifth year in a row that they beat us. We had them beat. They threw the "flea flicker" and we should have been defending the pass better. If I ever had a call to make over again that would be it.

11. I don't know if I would change a whole lot because my career at UNL went well. I was fortunate.

12. All of our assistant coaches were great coaches. Devaney brought great assistants from Wyoming and he hired Clete Fischer from Nebraska. That was a big high because Clete was a former Nebraska player and an excellent coach.

13. Regarding outstanding players, I have to start with Rich Glover. He did not talk, but he led by example. He missed one practice in all the years I was there. It was before a bowl game and he was so beat up that we made him take a day off from practice. He was as tough as they ever came. He could have lined up against Alabama and they could wear pads and he could wear sweats. It did not matter to him. He was going to stop Johnny Musso no matter what.

14. Our goal in 1969 was just to win. Devaney had just finished back to back 6-4 seasons. I just wanted to win so I could keep coaching. And I also wanted to win so badly for Coach Devaney. I wanted to win for Nebraska because I love Nebraska.

15. The most important reasons for the wins were that (1) Devaney brought unity to the team; (2) And we had some great recruiters who got some good football players.

16. We had that 32 game winning streak (1969-1971) and UCLA finally beat us in 1972 in Los Angeles (14-17). We spent three weeks before that game coaching the College All Star team in Chicago, and I still think to this day that might have hurt us. We did not spend enough time preparing for UCLA.

17. It meant a lot to be considered the best in 1970 and 1971. I will never forget that. I have my Championship ring. It was unbelievable.

18. To motivate the players before the game, we did not do much the day of the game. It was mostly the night before the game. We would get pretty fired up. We always talked about playing hard and together.

19. I got the players to play hard because I would get fired up myself. I would just kind of wing it. I was very emotional. I think all coaches are different and that is why I respect Coach Osborne a lot. You have to coach within your own personality, and Coach Osborne was more low key. I worked for Coach Tony Dunge with the Buccaneers. He is low key and he reminded me of Tom. I am sort of the other way. And sometimes that is a good mesh. I still am very emotional. You can win a lot of different ways.

20. One of the biggest challenges happens when the expectations become so high. We had to learn how to coach under pressure. In 1972 I had to learn how to handle that pressure and not let it get to the players. The expectation level was just so high and it ran rampant.

21. Coach Devaney was very good at handling the high expectations. He never got a big head. He kept the players on an even keel. Bob did not care who you were. You could have a lot of money or be a blue collar guy off the street and he would treat everyone the same. He treated the staff that way as well.

22. I would not let a player quit.

23. The game that was biggest challenge for the team without a doubt was the Oklahoma shoot out in 1971. We went down and scored at the end of the game to lead 35-31. And we had not stopped them a whole lot during the game. They got the ball again, and Oh, my gosh we need to stop them. Jacobson and Glover got a couple of good rushes and Blahak covered the corner good. That last stop was the biggest one that I have ever been in.

24. My biggest disappointment was losing that opener against UCLA in 1972. My son (Lane Kiffin) just experienced that because he is the Offensive Coordinator at Southern Cal. We had a 32 game undefeated streak, and they had a 37 streak, but they lost to Texas in the Rose Bowl last January, 2006.

25. The most important aspect that made the team work so well together was attitude, Bob Devaney's attitude. He would get the players to play for him because his communication rapport with the players was so sincere. Some coaches are phony, and players can see through that. Devaney cared about each player off the field and not just on the field. I learned that from him and that is very important.

26. The most talented players were (a) Johnny Rodgers on offense. He was unbelievable. Johnny was the Reggie Bush of the 1970s (b) on defense those 3 years it was Richie Glover.

27. The most inspirational player was Joe Blahak. He would get me fired up because he just loved football. He would come up with some of the goofiest stuff. I still laugh at him. He would get all fired up.

28. I would always talk about commitment to your teammate. If the guy next to you is working hard, you better be working hard. I told them not to be playing for Monte Kiffin or Bob Devaney, but to play for your teammates. That is what it is all about. We watched tape all together on Sundays, and we also do that on Mondays with Tampa. We watched the whole defensive tape together and the red dot would go on you if you loafed. If you make a great play, the red dot goes on you too. You have to be accountable to your peers. I do believe in peer pressure in the right sense. It did not matter if you were second or third string because when you went out on that field you needed to play like a starter.

29. To be Number One takes commitment from staff and players. Total commitment. You all have to be drinking the same Kool-Aid. All the success we had goes back to the players.

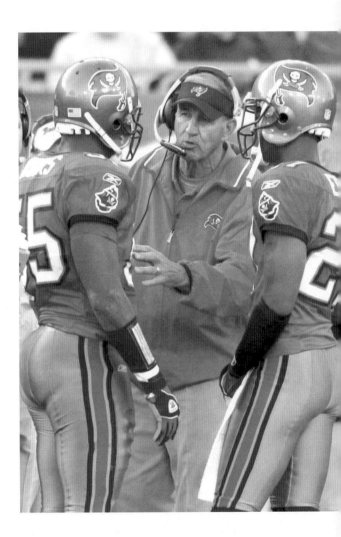

"Coach Kiffin had the uncanny ability to get us to believe in ourselves and in each other."

Willie Harper (2006)
All-American Defensive End
('70 - '71)

*"I got the players
to play hard
because I would
get fired up myself.
I love Nebraska."*

Monte Kiffin (2006)

**Defensive Coordinator
Tampa Bay Buccaneers
    Super Bowl Champions 2002**

Coached 11 years at UNL

(1967-1977)

University of Arkansas with Lou Holtz;

**North Carolina State
    (head coach for 3 years);**

**Pro football
    Green Bay 1983; Buffalo Bills 1984-85;
    Vikings 86-89; Jets 90; Vikings 91-94;
    Saints 95; Tampa 1996- current, ten
    years.**

AN ERA OF GREATNESS: COACH BOB DEVANEY'S FINAL FOUR SEASONS (1969 - 1972)

COACH JOHN MELTON

COACHED: 1962 – 1988

HUSKER REFLECTIONS

1. Regarding Coach Devaney, every time we played a team we would be sitting there and we would watch film and the assistant coaches would be tighter than the dickens. And Bob would always say "God, if we can't beat this club, we ought to quit coaching". He never figured that anyone should beat us. Bob did not take defeats gracefully. But he never did blame any one guy or one thing. He would just get ready for the next one.

2. Devaney was a great recruiter. The thing that used to get me was when Bob and I would go to a home on a recruiting trip. They would always have cookies or something like that and he would say to the mother "Would you mind taking a minute and writing down the recipe for these cookies. They are the best cookies I have ever tasted". I used to think "God damn liar". I bet I heard him say that at least 5 or 6 times. The mothers would giggle. Bob always said "If you get the mothers on your side, you will get the kid".

3. Coach Mike Corgan loved his wine. He would make it in the morning, and drink it the afternoon. The "aging period" for his wine was about 2 hours.

4. Coach Cletus Fischer used to love betting on the horses. He would bet on any grey horse in a race. His "daily double" was always 1 & 4 and 4 & 1.

5. Coach Osborne was always a saint. He never had any highs or lows. When he was really mad, he would say "dang gummit".

6. Coach Jim Ross used to beat Bob (Devaney) in golf all the time. He was a great golfer. He liked to keep it close. If Bob shot an 80, he would shot a 79. Jim was the only guy who could control Bob a little bit because they went way back. When they graduated from college, they both applied for this head coaching job in high school football and Jim got it. Jim was the head basketball coach and assistant football coach and Bob was the head football coach and assistant basketball coach in Alpena high school (in Michigan).

7. Overall my favorite memory was winning the National Championship.

8. The thing that I really liked about Nebraska fans was that they traveled a lot. Like they often say, Nebraska really never played a "road game". They are great fans and they like to win just like any other fans.

9. I never did like Coach Eddie Crowder from Colorado. He looked just like Colonel Clink on TV. And that is what I used to call him. And he really used to cuss me out. He and I got into some really good recruiting battles. In those days fans were able to drink in the stands and I remember "how wonderful their fans used to be". They would throw snowballs at us.

10. UNL treated the coaches well. They took good care of us. The people in Nebraska still love the Cornhuskers and they always will. We are fortunate that UNL is the only school in the state that plays big-time football.

11. The most remarkable offensive play I ever witnessed was Johnny Rodgers' punt return against Oklahoma (1971) in the "Game of the Century". He deserved that touchdown. And there has never been a better one. Johnny is the best all around football player I ever saw at NU.

12. Defensive – When Jerry Murtaugh intercepted the pass against Kansas State (1970) and ran it for a touchdown off of quarterback Lynn Dickie. What a great line-backer that guy was. That guy Ruud just broke his record (tackles) but it took him four years to do it and Murtaugh made the record in 3 years. Could you imagine the records Murtaugh or Rodgers would have had if they were able to play all 4 years. They would never be broken.

13. I remember that Johnny Rodgers used to miss some Monday practices, always claiming that he was "hurt a little bit". Everyone else would have to come and practice but his big daddy, Bob, would always step in and say "that's okay Johnny, you don't have to practice today".

4. Coaching football taught me patience. Things like waiting in airports and waiting for parents and schools to see the kid on recruiting trips. You learned patience.

5. This rule they have now about signing kids in February, we did not have a signing date. We would recruit all summer. We didn't sign Dave Humm till May 12th. So we would be coaching spring ball and still be recruiting. That made a long year.

6. The players were all good leaders but there wasn't anyone who was an outspoken leader. Each guy did his job. Jerry Tagge and Jeff Kinney were not outspoken. Rich Glover never said a word. He has not been blocked yet. God, he was good. He had a quiet confidence.

7. Our goal was to win a National Championship when we came to NU in 1962. I reached my goals. In my opinion the Game of the Century in 1971 vs. Oklahoma is still the best football game ever played.

8. One game I enjoyed was when we put it on Notre Dame in the `73 Orange Bowl (40-6). Rodgers played I-back that game. We did not put Johnny there too much for fear that he would get hurt. Bob did not want "his baby" to get hurt. Had to protect "his baby."

9. Our team goals were to win one game at a time.

10. The 3 most important qualities for the wins were (a) Toughness; (b) Pride. The guys figured no one could beat them, (c) Good football players who played hard.

11. We were confident NU would win the National Championship in 1971. More confident as time went by and we saw other teams. The Big Eight was a tough league. In 1971, NU was #1, Oklahoma #2, Colorado #3. There was never a better football team in the country than the `71 team. They talk about the Southern Cal teams in 2003-2004, but I don't know if they could take the pounding we used to do in the Big 8. We knocked the hell out of each other.

12. The biggest challenge was playing Oklahoma in 1971 to show who was the boss for a long time. We had to play at Oklahoma, Colorado and Missouri and they were all good. In those days in the Big 8 winning on the road was the biggest challenge. The players overcame the challenge. The guys went out and took it to them. The guys were tough. We never showed anybody any mercy. In 1970-1971, we could beat you running, passing,

defense, punt returns. They never had a chance to rest against us. I don't think that we had any weaknesses.

23. I never thought about quitting. I enjoyed coaching but the traveling got old sometimes. We recruited all over the United States. We did not have specific areas at the time. That came later.

24. I didn't like trick plays. We were so damn aggressive that sometimes trick plays hurt us.

25. My biggest disappointment was the whole 1967 year. We were not doing a good job of coaching, and the players were not doing a good job of playing. We did not do a very good job at recruiting, but after that we worked hard and recruiting improved. If I could go back and change one thing we would have worked a little harder in 1967. They had a petition to fire us. We were so bad, I was going to sign the petition myself.

26. Bob Devaney's salary in 1962 was $17,000. That was the best investment the State of Nebraska ever made. They got Bob for $17,000. And the Assistant coaches started out at about 7 to 9 thousand. After we starting winning we got little raises (ha-ha). NU took very good care of us.

27. Devaney announcing his retirement before the `72 season did not affect the coaching staff. Bob never interfered. He let his assistant coaches coach.

28. The most important aspect that made the team work so well together was chemistry. We liked the kids, and they liked us. They played for us, and we coached for them. They were a damn good bunch of kids.

29. I remember Coach Corgan saying during the drills when someone fumbled: "Get her out of here before she hurts herself". Bob did not like that very much. He was a tough one. I remember Coach Monte Kiffin and the incident with the milk truck (1962). He was a nervous wreck. Very intense.

30. The most talented player I ever saw was Johnny Rodgers. But Oklahoma State's Barry Sanders was almost as good as Rodgers. [Editors' Note: Sanders won the Heisman Trophy and became All-Pro with the Detroit Lions].

31. The most inspirational players were the guys who were "walk-ons" and became regular players. Walk-ons really saved us. You got them for nothing, and they worked hard.

32. Just take a look at the toughness of the schedule that NU played in 1969 - 1971. Now, they play some teams that I have never heard of. We played some damn good football teams in `69 - `71.

33. The most outrageous player was linebacker Jerry Murtaugh. He was always good for 15 yards in a game – in penalties, that is. Always one a game. But Murtaugh was a leader. He was a well conditioned athlete.

34. The hardest worker in practice was Johnny Rodgers. But no one on the team really loafed. If they did, they would not be on the team.

35. The player who surprised me the most was Johnny Pitts. He worked himself into a good football player. I think a lot of him.

36. Coaching Nebraska football helped me in the after football life. I met a lot of people. I worked on the Board of Directors for Madonna, and for the chairman of the foundation for Madonna.

37. I feel appreciated by the University for the time I put in. I have not been to a football practice since I stopped coaching, but I go to all the games.

38. Richie Glover in `71 - `72 just sticks out in my mind. You could not block him. He was strong. They would double-team him but he was always around the ball. When the quarterback would go back to pass, he would have one eye on Glover and the other on the receiver. He was one of the best defensive players I have ever seen.

39. I will match the `71 NU football team with anyone in the country. It was harder back then to get into a Bowl game because there were not as many as there are today. Today you can win only 6 games and get into a Bowl. In our day if you won 6 games in Nebraska you got fired.

*John Dutton and Richie Glover (1972)**

"Coach Melton was like a father figure to me. He always calmed me down when I would get angry."

Jerry Murtaugh (2006);
All American Linebacker (1970)

COACH TOM OSBORNE

UPDATE

Married to Nancy for 43 years, 3 children, 4 grandchildren
Currently: Member of U.S. Congress (6 years) from Nebraska

HUSKER REFLECTIONS

1. I started coaching at NU in the Spring, 1962. Bob Devaney had accepted the head coaching job while still working at Wyoming. I was an assistant for the next 11 years. Then, Head Coach from 1972 to 1997. Last game in January 1998.

2. Bob's happiest time was after we beat Alabama in the 1972 Orange Bowl (38-6) because Bob had a tough time with Bear Bryant in the bowl games. That game brought everything full circle, undefeated seasons, national champions, and defeating Bear Bryant. I remember Bob after the game as being very excited. The Press had voted Bear Coach of The Year. I remember Duffy Daugherty going over to Bear after the Bowl game and asking if he would let Coach Devaney be co-coach of the year. Bear's answer was "no, I won the vote but he (Bob) is the Coach of The Year."

3. Monte Kiffin was a player when I first came to NU in 1962-63 and he was a good defensive lineman. He ended up being a grad assistant coach, and he really had a strong passion for coaching. He was totally devoted to it. I always admired the amount of energy and attention he put into coaching.

4. Coach Cletus Fischer was totally devoted to Nebraska. If it was from Nebraska it was all good and if it was not from Nebraska then it was not very good. He really spent a lot of time working with Devaney early trying to sell the state to Bob. He took him around and introduced Bob to people. Clete was a Nebraskan first and foremost. He understood the kicking game very well. He believed in recruiting Nebraska players. He had a strong desire to make sure that we did not lose anyone in the state. I also bought into that theory. You can recruit all over the country, but you did not want to lose a good player from your state. He recruited Nebraska most of his life. Clete was a salesman for Nebraska.

5. Coach Mike Corgan's trademark was toughness. He wanted backs who blocked and ran hard. I remember he had his backs-on-ends drill and one of the backs would get about a 6 or 7 yard run against the defensive ends. Of course he always wanted them to hit them with their foreheads. So, he took a lot of pride in that. His backs were tough, good blockers, and runners. He always said tough backs don't fumble. He was a very sound fundamental football coach.

6. Coach Carl Selmer was an intellectual guy. He had a good understanding of blocking schemes and a good grasp of the different ways to attack a defense. He did a good job of coaching the offensive line. He was a high school coach in Wyoming. John Melton was a Wyoming high school coach as well.

7. Coach Bill "Thunder" Thornton was a good coach and player. He was the starting NU fullback in 1962, which was Bob's first year and then he played pro football for the St. Louis Cardinals.

8. Coach Jim Walden played for Bob at Wyoming as a quarterback. He came to Nebraska as a grad assistant and then became a full time coach. He left with Coach Carl Selmer when I took over. Carl ended up at Miami. Jimmy went to Washington State and then Iowa State.

9. Coach Warren Powers played at NU (1960-1962). At that time players played both ways, and he played with the Oakland Raiders for a couple of years. Then he came back as a grad assistant. Eventually he became a full time coach, and got the job at Washington State. Went to Missouri after that. He did a good job.

10. One humorous story about Bob Devaney: One time he got arrested in South Dakota and he had been going 100 mph. He told the cop that he had just gotten off the interstate and had not had time to adjust.

11. The Nebraska fans are tremendous. I remember one game at Kansas and well over half of the fans were from Nebraska. You could tell because of all the red.

We did not have much of a disadvantage on road games like other teams did.

12. The NU players in general had a strong work ethic. The pro scouts would always tell me when they came through that Nebraska players worked awfully hard.

13. The Oklahoma game had a special intensity and rivalry. Over a period of 30 years there were about 29 of the games where the conference champion came out of that game. About 7 or 8 national champions came out of that game as well. Colorado would always claim in my later years that they were our rival, but a true rivalry grows over a period of time and quality of play. The NU and OU rivalry exemplified that because we had so many great teams and the champion of the conference almost always came out of that game.

Playing at Colorado was always tough because the fans were right on top of you. Missouri at times was a tough place to play because they were really intense. And of course the most difficult was playing Miami in the Orange Bowl on their home field because it was a night game, and they were pretty intense. You also had humidity and heat.

14. I spent 36 years coaching at NU and that is a lot of memories. Generally, the character of the players and people was outstanding. Over time the fans always showed a good deal of respect to our opponents. They were very knowledgeable and were respectful of a good performance by our opponents.

15. The most remarkable offensive plays I witnessed were in the kicking game with some of the punt returns that Johnny Rodgers had against Colorado. He had 2 or 3 great returns. And everybody chooses the Oklahoma punt return in 1971 but it seemed like in the Colorado game he had 2 or 3 long returns that were outstanding. From scrimmage it would be that run against Florida State in 1986 when Roger Craig broke a bunch of tackles. The Tommy Frasier run against Florida in the Fiesta Bowl (1996) when he broke a bunch of tackles was outstanding. The 3rd down and 8 pass against Oklahoma in 1971 that Johnny Rodgers caught was a key play to keep the drive alive.

16. Coaching requires self-discipline and long hours. I learned a lot from the players because we recruited all over the country from wealthy suburbs and from inner cities. I learned that all people fundamentally are pretty much the same in terms of what is important to them. Over the years we developed a good atmosphere where players felt that they mattered and that the people cared about them beyond what they could do on the football field. That environment was important.

17. I could go back and relive the last couple of touchdown drives against Miami in the 1995 Orange Bowl. We were down 17-10 and came back and won the National Championship (24-17).

18. We came very close to a couple of National Championships in 1982 and 1983. I would like to go back and get the two point play against Miami at the end of the 1984 Orange Bowl (30-31).

19. The thing that was remarkable about 1969 was that in 1968 we lost to OU (47-0) down at Norman, and the next year we reversed it and we beat them (44-14) at Norman. With a lot of the same players it was quite a turnaround. The lowest point of Nebraska football when I was there was the 1968 game at OU where we were just totally dominated (47-0). Of course that year we also lost to Kansas State at home (0-12) and our record was 6-4.

I remember people circulating a petition to fire Devaney after that year. As a young assistant that was an eye opener to me because a coach who had won as many games as Bob had and turned that program around in a period of 2 years was suddenly unpopular. 1969 season was a big year. I remember we went to Kansas State and won 10-7. That was a nerve racking game, and on the way back Bob called me to the front of the bus and said that he was getting ready to retire, and he wanted me to take over. But things got better and he ended up coaching another 3 years.

20. In 1969, Jerry Tagge, Van Brownson, and Jeff Kinney were all sophomores. They made a big difference on our football team. After the 1968 season Bob told me that we ought to go after some Junior College (JC) guys. I recruited Bob Newton out of California and he was an All-American and a leader. In 1969 there was a sense of optimism that we could win. I felt that slipping in the two previous years when we did not have as much confidence. There are other players like Jerry List and Joe Blahak and Bill Kosch. Those guys played well in 1971. In 1968 we had a really good freshman team and a bunch of good recruits.

1. In the early 1990s I decided to give the players more ownership, and let the players set the goals. I was going to give them ownership, and if they want to set certain goals they are going to have to help produce them. It did build a more unified and goal oriented team. In the 90s we had tremendous focus.

   Some of that also happened during 1970-71. I think 1970 just kind of happened. We played that game at USC and used that trick play and ended up 21-21. That was a real springboard. We were a very good team that year but probably not overwhelming. We kind of backed into that National Championship because we were rated 3rd and the teams in front of us (Texas and Ohio State) got beat and we beat LSU to become National Champions. In 1971, we were just a dominating team and that was gratifying. We had a great football team from start to finish. A lot of players had pride and confidence. That was a very complete team because we had a good offense and defense and kicking game.

2. In 1972, NU had a chance to win a 3rd straight national championship, but there was one problem. Whenever you have a new quarterback you are going to lose a couple of games because of inexperience. David Humm played well, but having experience at quarterback is critical. Overall, we still had a great team. We got tied over at Iowa State (23-23) and that was a game that was tough to take. We did not play well against UCLA and we lost (17-20).

3. Better recruiting was a most important reason for the wins in 1969-1971. We really had some great athletes and the 1968 recruiting class was outstanding. With guys like Tagge, Brownson, Kinney, Olds, Mason, Jimmy Anderson, Dumler, Blahak, Kosch, and a lot of really good players. The talent level went up. We learned in losing those two games to Alabama (1966-1967). Alabama was using some small linemen. Their linemen were 5'11" to 6 ft and 190 - 205 lbs. and mostly high school fullbacks that were quick and got low and scramble blocked you. We decided that was the way to go and so we started recruiting small quick lineman. We were just getting pushed around in the Big 8 in 1967-68.

4. There were three big changes that turned things around in 1969. (1) Bob asked me to redesign the offense and started going away from the old unbalanced line and "full house" backfield. I looked at OU and went to the "I" formation; (2) we started recruiting junior college players and ended up with guys like Bob Newton, Carl Johnson, Keith Workman, Dick Rupert. So in 1970 and 1971 four or five of the starters were JC players; (3) we started an off-season weight program. Clete Fischer had commented on the fact that Alabama was using an off-season weight program. We had never done that. We installed some stations and drills and started a weight program.

Boyd Epley came to me and Bob and talked and Bob was not real excited because he was from the old school where weight lifting made you muscle bound. But after those two 6-4 seasons Bob was willing to look at almost any new idea so he went ahead with it. We were one of a few teams that did that. We developed some linemen that were not little quick guys but fairly quick guys that were big and strong. Those things were really the spring board. And of course Johnny Rodgers came in 1969.

25. I don't think anyone really imagined that we would just dominate like we did and win the National Championship in the 1971 season. But after the 1970 season people thought we could win another National Championship.

26. We had good players and a sound program and system. I had a good relationship with the players for the most part. That has become more important to me over time than the wins and losses and the rings. Relationships are the most important thing.

27. Just knowing that you could get fired was a motivation. At Nebraska I always felt I was one year away from getting fired. I saw that so clearly with Bob when he turned that program around and won all those games, but after two 6-4 seasons there were people that wanted to get rid of Bob. I was at that time 32 years old with a wife and 3 little kids. Bob told people "if one guy goes we all go. We are a package deal and I am not having sacrificial lambs." That meant a lot to me and that is one reason I was very loyal to Bob because he demonstrated that loyalty to the coaches.

28. The biggest challenge when Bob first got to NU was mainly turning attitudes around. I don't think the players thought they could win. When NU went up to Michigan in 1962 and beat them (25-13), that was a big deal. People in Nebraska could not believe we won 9 games in 1962.

29. Temporary insanity made me run for Congress in 2000. I wanted to make a difference.

30. My biggest disappointments were (a) 1991 and (b) losing to OU my first few years (1973-1977). People

sometimes looked at it as a one game season. What other places would consider a good season, people at NU would sometimes consider it a bad year if you only won 9 or 10 games and did not beat the right people.

31. The most important factor that made the team work so well together was the ability to change and adjust. After those two 6-4 seasons Bob was ready to change and the changes we made were good.

32. Our teams had chemistry and worked well together. Success breeds success. When you are winning it is easy to keep things together but when it starts unraveling is when finger pointing starts to occur. Those were good years in 1968-1972. Leadership was good.

33. I remember going to El Paso and playing Georgia in 1969 in the Sun Bowl. Georgia did not want to be there, because they had been in better Bowls. It was the first Bowl game our players had been to in three years, and they were excited about going. Bowl games are a little different from regular season games, and your team had better want to play. So that was a big win (45-6). You could tell that Georgia was not excited about being in that game.

34. My biggest fear was players getting hurt. Somebody doing something crazy. Every weekend you never knew what was going to happen.

35. We emphasized fundamentals. If you don't know the basics you can't hold everything together. We always tried to structure group work so that we had good work on fundamentals and technique. One thing that could always get away was tackling. As the season goes along we did not want to hurt anyone so we did not do some of the fundamentals. I don't think you can ever let that slip.

In my later years of coaching one thing that we began to notice was that the "scout team" as the season went along would become more passive and just go though the motions. As a result your top units were not getting very good pictures. So we would spend about a 10-15 minutes on Tuesday and Wednesdays where we would put in the first team offense and first team defense against each other. I thought that really helped.

36. In terms of talent, Johnny Rodgers was the most talented player we had. He could do the most things in terms of punt returns, pass receptions, and running from scrimmage. Johnny could beat people in more different ways and on game day he was always a com-

petitor. In terms of day in and day out practice, Jerry Tagge was a good solid leader during that period.

37. Overall, the "walk-ons" made a tremendous difference at NU. They tended to set the tone in terms of work ethic and self sacrifice. The scholarship guys were a little bit more talented and were recruited but it was not long before they realized that if they did not work hard that a walk-on would take there place. Walk-ons almost by definition were overachievers.

The other thing the walk-ons did was give us repetition. The way most teams practice is that they will have one offensive station and one defensive station and as a result, you have a lot of guys on the second team just standing around. In most of our practices all of the players were going all the time. We had 2 offensive and 2 defensive stations and without the walk-ons there would not have been enough players to do that.

38. The most outrageous player was Langston Coleman who was a walk-on from Washington D.C.

39. Terry Luck played hurt the most but he had great potential. He had a knee injury, but came back and played. I always admired his willingness to rehab.

40. Everyone worked hard in practice. Jimmy Pillen always put forth a great effort. A couple of times they had to pack him in ice after 2 a days.

41. Who surprised me the most was Ernie Sigler. He was not that big or that fast but he had a good attitude and was a diligent player. Gary Dixon again was not the biggest or fastest but hung in there and started for us.

42. The good thing about Nebraska was that you knew the fans cared and paid attention. You get something written everyday about football year round. It is hard to get away from it, but it is better to have scrutiny and have people care.

43. To be Number One you need three factors: (1) talent; (2) chemistry and having a fair number of people willing to sacrifice for the common good; (3) a coaching staff that knows what they are doing. What benefited us was continuity in our coaching staff.

44. I feel appreciated by the University for the time I put in. Most people have been very generous with their appreciation. I had a good experience.

COACH JIM ROSS

COACHED 1962 – 1977
Married to Maurine for over 50 years.
3 daughters (Sharon, Margaret, Kathy) and a lot of grandchildren.
Lives in Lincoln, Nebraska.

HUSKER REFLECTIONS

1. The problems in 1967-68 happened because we just quit recruiting enough good athletes. We weren't recruiting very well for 2 years. And some of the teams in the Big 8 were playing a little better back then. It just came down to manpower. Then is when the freshman classes of `68-69 came in and it solved the manpower situation quickly.

2. Oklahoma was always the toughest for us when we first started in 1962. Missouri was also very good at that time. We tangled up with Kansas State when they had that real good quarterback, Lynn Dickey, and they beat us a couple years in 1967-68. We were out manned a little bit. And probably out coached a bit too. Then in 1968 we made the big change and I took over the freshman. George Kelly left to go to Notre Dame and Monte Kiffin took his place. Monte had been coaching the freshman, and then I decided I was getting to the age where I should retire. Bob asked me to do more of the Athletic Director stuff and so I took the freshman and Warren Powers took the Varsity as defensive backfield coach. In 1962-1967 I was the defensive backfield coach.

3. My memories of Bob Devaney have all been told. Bob and I coached together in Alpena, Michigan high school. He was the football coach and I was the basketball coach. And I was his assistant in football and he was my assistant in basketball. We always got along just great. Bob had great teams. Bob's first two years in high school coaching he was undefeated. So, we were real lucky there and when we went to Wyoming we were real lucky. We had good kids there, and we had great kids here in Nebraska. Bob loved football and that is what he lived for. He was a great coach to play for.

4. Our coaching staff got along great at Nebraska because we had the same coaches that we had at Wyoming. There was a period there for about 20 years that we had the same bunch of coaches. We got to know each other pretty well.

5. I was the defensive backfield coach and Coach Devaney let me do what I wanted. He was always there if you needed help. Bob was not only a good offensive coach but also a good defensive coach. He knew football, and if you needed help you could go to him and he was always willing to help you. He let you run the kids out on the field and the kids felt you were coaching them. He just got along with everybody.

6. The Nebraska fans were great. Of course most fans are with you when you are winning but not so much when you are losing. But our Nebraska fans have been wonderful. NU is a tough place to coach football but it is a great place to coach football if you can win.

7. The most remarkable offensive play I witnessed was Johnny Rodgers' punt return down at Oklahoma in 1971. No question about that. When he ran that punt back to start the ball game. On defense it was Wayne Meylan. Every week he would block punts and make tackles in the back field. Wayne was the most spectacular player we had defensively.

8. I learned to do the best you can all the time. And you better get along with all the other coaches. That is one thing Bob would not stand for. There was never any bickering in the coaching staff. He let you have your say, and then he would say it is going to be this way and with no bickering. That is the most important thing.

9. The best leaders were Willie Harper, Rich Glover, Johnny Rodgers, Joe Blahak and Jim Anderson.

10. We all wanted to win. It was hard to leave Wyoming to come to NU in 1962 because NU was not doing real well then, and we had five great years at Wyoming. We won the Big Sky Conference Championship four years in a row. It was tougher to recruit in Wyoming. There were only 27 Wyoming high schools that played 11 man football.

11. The three most important reasons for the wins were (a) We had good material. We had good kids; (b) Bob was a good organizer. He always had you ready to play. (c) Winning is just like losing. It is a habit. You can get into a habit of either winning or losing.

12. How confident were you that NU would win the National Championship? We did not talk much about that for a while. But that was always in the back of Bob's mind. The second year we were here (1963) we had Bob Brown and Thunder Thornton and all that bunch and they were excellent football players. Then we got a great 1968 freshman class in 1968. If you win a few conference championships, you start thinking you can go one step further and get the National Championship. That was always our final goal.

13. What does it mean to be considered the best? I was thrilled to be with the group. I had never coached college football until I went to Wyoming with Bob. So it was a new experience for me. The first coaching team we had at Wyoming in 1957 had four high school coaches (myself, Corgan, Melton, Selmer). We had never coached in college. Bob knew us and knew what we could do. He wanted his own crew and not someone else's.

14. The biggest challenge for Bob putting together winning teams all boils down to the players. When we had the kids, we did pretty well. And I am talking about `63-`64 and `70-`72. But if you don't have the kids, I don't care how hard you work. You are not going to get it down. We let our recruiting slack off a couple years (1966-1967) and we had to catch up again.

15. It was important for Bob to beat Bear Bryant in the Orange Bowl in 1973. Bear talked Bob into a couple ball games we probably should not have gone to (Bowl games in 1966-1967) because he just had better kids. In 1967 in the Sugar Bowl in Louisiana Bear had all those kids that played pro ball later.

16. That day in Miami (1973), we played Alabama in the Orange Bowl Game and won 38-7. That erased a lot of things. Bear was not too anxious to play us after that. Nobody thought we could beat Bear as badly as we did that day.

17. The most important aspect that made the team work so well together was having the coaches who can run the show. Bob could run the show, and then he had a bunch of assistant coaches that he had put together 15-20 years. They knew what the other coaches were thinking and that helped. And we had a bunch of players that wanted to win. That Dutton bunch that JR was with contributed so much to that.

18. The most talented player I ever coached at NU was probably Dana Stevenson. He was a hell of an athlete and a good kid.

19. The most inspirational was Bob Devaney. Johnny Rodgers did a good job too. He used to get on those kids a bit.

20. Wayne Meylan played hurt the most. He was just a bear.

21. It all boils down to recruiting. You have to recruit good kids to come to Lincoln. We were lucky that we inherited a bunch of great kids in 1962. When we came Bob Brown and Thunder Thornton were there. And we recruited pretty good that first year. So for about 5-6 years we just had a bunch of excellent players coming. We just fell off in 1966-1967 and started over again in 1968. The class of 1968 got us going again. It helps a lot if you are winning, kids want to come.

22. I feel appreciated by the University for the time I put in. I love Nebraska. They were great to me, and I wish NU a lot of success.

Coached the great freshman team in 1969.
(Johnny Rodgers, Willie Harper, Rich Glover and others).

"Jim Ross was really a stabilizing force for Bob. Devaney always bounced ideas off of Jim."

Tom Ash (2006);
World Herald Sports Reporter (1970-1981)

COACH CARL SELMER

COACHED OFFENSIVE LINE 1962 – 1972
Later coached at Miami, North Texas State, Kansas State, BC Lions, Notre Dame and Northwestern
Lives in Bellevue, Nebraska

HUSKER REFLECTIONS

1. My best memories were the Oklahoma game in 1971, and 1972 against Notre Dame game in the Orange Bowl. There were so many great games and experiences.

2. Coach Bob Devaney was a great person and a great coach. Humorous and quick witted and fun to be around. I always joked with him that when the games were easy is when he would try and do a lot of coaching. But when the games were tough, he let us coach. We had a great system and we were together for a long time.

3. Coach Cletus Fischer and I were horse racing buddies. Fischer was Mr. Nebraska. He lived and breathed Nebraska.

4. Clete and I used to joke about the horse races a lot. He was a good handicapper. Clete never did drink and every time you would go to his house he would always offer you a beer, but we knew that he didn't have any. He was always teasing about that.

5. I got to work with one of the coaches from Alabama (Mel Moore) who is now their Athletic Director. He once told me that their biggest mistake in the 1972 Orange Bowl was kicking the ball to Johnny Rodgers.

6. The Nebraska fans are wonderful people. They always stuck with us.

7. The most remarkable offensive play I witnessed was in the `71 Oklahoma game. The 3rd down catch J.R. made from Tagge in the 4th quarter against Oklahoma and he was almost on the ground. That was the key play. Also, the final touchdown when Jeff Kinney put us ahead and we won (35-31).

8. It was a pleasure coaching at NU. We were treated well. I found coaching at other places a little harder where you do not win as often. After NU, I coached at Miami, North Texas State, Kansas State, one year in Canada at BC Lions, then to Notre Dame, and finished up at Northwestern.

9. At NU in the early 60s we were not expected to win, but we did win. That experience helped me as a coach. I was a high school coach for nine years and I had a lot of fun. Sometimes I think if I would have stayed as a high school coach that would have been just as gratifying.

10. I had a chance to go to Iowa when I was with the BC Lions. If I could do it over, I would have taken that job with Hayden Fry at Iowa because they had a lot of excellent coaches whom I worked with at North Texas.

11. We all had different ways of approaching things. Coach Mike Corgan always let you know exactly where you stood and that is very important. Coach Fischer was a great guy to keep you going and kept you laughing. Coach Kiffin developed into a solid coach at NU and went on to be considered one of the best in the country in the professional football.

12. I remember the first thing they told us in 1962 when we played Colorado at Boulder. They kept harping that the 1961 NU team did not even make one 1st down. We were anxious to do well. The 1962 players surprisingly were fantastic. We won the Gotham Bowl in Yankee Stadium against Miami (36-34).

13. The most important reasons for the wins were that we had a lot of bodies at practice, and everyone got along. Excellent teamwork and cooperation made for a good team.

14. It is exciting to be considered the best team in `71. Willie Harper, Johnny Rodgers and Rich Glover were such great players. Larry Jacobson, Bill Janssen, Bill Olds. Excellent players make great coaches.

15. We motivated ourselves before games by spending a great deal of time on Friday night preparing substitutions and things like that. We were probably nervous.

16. We always had to replace lineman which was a big challenge. And you had to anticipate the different defenses that we were up against. To prepare the drills, the offensive station and the passing station had to anticipate each play. This was before computers.

17. Oklahoma was the biggest challenge for the team. And Missouri had some very fine teams. The `69-`70 Southern California teams had some awesome players, and it was hard to believe that some of our guys were small compared to theirs.

18. My biggest disappointment was the loss in `68 to Kansas State. We played a miserable game and got beat (12-0). Also, the 1966 loss in the Orange Bowl to Alabama (28-39). We had a chance to be National Champs. We made a lot of teams Number One. The losses were always disappointments, and the wins were thrilling.

19. Coach Devaney's announced retirement before the `72 season put us in a difficult situation. It was like having 2 head coaches. Who do you pay attention to? One guy is leaving and one (Coach Osborne) is taking over. I think we lost a little something. I wished that Coach Devaney would have waited until after the season to announce his retirement.

20. You can't really put your finger on the most important aspect that made the team work so well together. I think that Bob just worked well with the players and got a lot out of them, and he also did that with his coaches.

21. We had wonderful team chemistry and we enjoyed going to work. We wanted to succeed and did.

22. Johnny Rodgers had the biggest impact, and Jeff Kinney and Bob Newton were also big impact players.

23. Richie Glover was the most inspirational player because he did so many things. He was quiet but could inspire you by his tremendous effort. The center from Oklahoma (Brahaney) was supposed to be All-World, but Glover ate him up. The unsung heroes were Willie Harper, Atkins, Jimmy Anderson, Jerry List.

24. The hardest workers in practice were the lineman – The way Clete and I ran it. They all had to do it the same way or they were moved out. They all were good. Never had any complaints.

25. Dick Rupert surprised me the most because he was undersized. But he was excellent for what you asked him to do.

26. The fans were always behind us. I hated the fans from Colorado. They helped our team because it gave us something to play for.

27. Coaching at Nebraska helped me in the after football life. Everyone still calls me "Coach". I coached football for 45 years.

28. I don't know if I feel appreciated by the University for the time I put in. I have not been down there in a long time. I am sure that they appreciate what we did. The era under Devaney got everything going. The players in `69-`72 made it easier because it is easier to keep it going instead of getting it started. It was fun.

29. I have nothing but fond memories of Bob Devaney. I coached with him in Wyoming as well. He was a success wherever he went. He was clever. I am sure the players enjoyed playing for him. If things were tense, he would crack a joke and that made everyone feel good.

*"Carl Selmer was a
very good offensive line coach.
He was a very bright guy.
He was an
aeronautical engineer."*

Don "Fox" Bryant (2006);
NU Assistant Athletic Director Emeritus

GEORGE SULLIVAN

NU TRAINER (1953-1997)

Lives in Lincoln, Nebraska

HUSKER REFLECTIONS

1. In 1947, I played a couple of games at NU, but due to an injury the trainer asked if I would like to become a trainer. In 1949 - 1951 I went to Iowa University for Physical Therapy school. Then UNL wanted me to come back and become the physical therapist for the student health center and head football trainer under Potsy Clark, the athletic director. I started in 1953 and in about `72 moved to the athletic department to do all sports until 1997 when I retired.

2. When Devaney came in 1962 we all worked together like a family. 1970 and 1971 were just so much fun. It seemed like I did not have much work to do because no one got hurt.

3. In 1968, we put in a full program of spring conditioning. Before that we did not really have a program in place for conditioning. Clete Fischer and myself designed the whole program.

4. Coach Cletus Fischer had the punting team. During punting drills he used to race everyone back down the field. He had that bum knee from a car accident and then he pulled a hamstring. He was cheating because he started before everyone else. He was a good teacher.

5. Coach Corgan would always be chewing on somebody, especially Damkroger and a few of those fullbacks, because he thought he could make them tougher. Once he was trying to sneak a smoke with Devaney far down the field, and he started his pocket on fire. Smoke was rolling down. Even though he was gruff and rough, I think all his players liked him. Mike had a few drills that were a little questionable.

6. Against Missouri one of their coaches came across our sideline to see if we were cheating. Coach Devaney made him go back and was hollering at the officials. And while Devaney is chewing out the officials, the Missouri coach came back up and was smoking a cigar and he did not get off that field without that

cigar going in his mouth. Devaney jammed the cigar in his face.

7. Devaney was so good to work for. He would stick up for any of his coaches. If you had a disagreement with another coach, he would usually bring them right in and solve it real quick. During the process of solving the problem he would look madder than the dickens but two hours later you would not even know anything had happened. All family again.

8. Devaney had a lot of trust in Tom Osborne. He thought he was a top notch young coach.

9. The most remarkable offensive plays I witnessed were by Johnny Rodgers. The whole nation recognized that. The play I remember the most was down at Oklahoma State involving defensive nose guard Richie Glover. Johnny Rodgers took in the punt and I looked over, and an Oklahoma State player is coming right at me because I was fixing a chin strap. The next minute there is a big pileup and Richie saw that he was going to get me and Richie just threw himself at him and peeled two of them off me and J.R. went down and scored. I would have probably got my neck broken on that wall if Richie had not stepped in.

10. Bob Devaney and to a large extent Tom Osborne would let me make the decision on whether or not an injured player should play. I had a very good relationship with Bob, and he also let me help on dress code. I always made them remove their hats in the dining hall. During pictures some wanted to wear curls down to their shoulders, and I would not let them take a picture with hair like that.

11. I had great relationships with all the people at NU. When I first came back from Iowa after physical therapy school, they offered a good salary and were always honest with me.

12. I would not change anything. I think today the attorneys have changed everything so much that the guys who are trainers are almost scared to death to

touch an injured person. It's a different situation with all the lawsuits, not so much in Nebraska but across the country.

13. The best leaders were:
    a) Johnny Rodgers because everyone looked up to him.
    b) John Pitts, who did not shout but led by example.
    c) Richie Glover was kind to all his fellow players. He would not chew out anyone if it was the last thing in the world. He was a great, great, great person. He worked hard and was kind of quiet.

14. The three most important reasons for the wins were:
    a) I never saw any harshness between anybody;
    b) good students, everyone was very coachable;
    c) there was a strong togetherness and players just had a great relationship amongst themselves.

15. I had been through so much losing in the 1950s. I never even dreamt about winning the National Championship. In the 1960s we were starting to get exposure. For example, we would not have recruited Bob Terrio if we had not gone to a bowl game and gotten exposure.

16. There are many stories about Monte Kiffin's antics. The big one is in 1962 when Devaney left him home when we went to the Gotham Bowl. Monte was up a little late at night at a place called Millie's and a Meadow Gold milk truck was there and was running. So, Monte drove it up to the dorm. Monte could do anything in the way of sports. Good all around athlete. So good in fact that Bud Wilkinson himself flew into Lexington to recruit him.

17. Coach Carl Selmer was also an engineer. He could quickly calculate in his own mind somebody's speed and whether or not his linemen had the agility. He was a tremendous coach in that regard.

18. Devaney motivated players before the game. Many players motivated themselves by looking in little mirrors and talking to themselves. They all were very good film watchers.

19. Devaney and the assistant coaches were very close. The only time Bob thought about quitting was to coach a pro team. But Devaney asked his staff and none of them really wanted to move to a big city and they were raising families. And Bob believed in his staff so much he went with their decision. The whole staff passed up pro opportunities to stay and coach with Bob.

20. The biggest challenge to team chemistry was drugs and especially steroids even back then. I remember one kid from California wrote Winstrow as a medication and this was a steroid which his mother got for him. It was not illegal back then.

21. In 1960, we went down and won the game in Oklahoma (21-14). The year before Oklahoma went to Notre Dame and the big bettors had put something in their food which gave the players diarrhea when they went out on the field. Paul Schneider and I were scared that would happen to us so we brought all our own steaks and walked them to the kitchen and watched them being cooked. There was a lot of gambling going on in collegiate sports in the late 1950s.

22. The most inspirational player was Johnny Rodgers – especially his junior year in 1971. He was fantastic.

Sullivan bandages Van Brownson. *

COACH JIM WALDEN
COACHED OUTSIDE LINEBACKERS 1967-1972

Later coached at Miami and became head coach at Washington State
Radio broadcaster and analyst for Washington State - Lives in Harrison, Idaho

HUSKER REFLECTIONS

1. I think back about Mike Wynn, Bob Liggett and Ken Geddes. They were such good characters and athletes, and who could forget Jerry Murtaugh, Dana Stevenson, Bill Janssen, Al Larson, and our own Adrian Fiala. There were just so many great guys. I loved being there. I think we surprised ourselves. I was at NU in 1967-1968 and those two 6-4 seasons. And there was a lot of nervousness when the 1969 season came. The players just did a great job in 1969. Beating Oklahoma and Georgia back to back really set the tempo for the next 3 years and the greatness during that time.

2. In 1968 there were petitions to have the coaches fired. That was always the funny thing to me. I figured out that Nebraskans had 16 consecutive losing seasons prior to Coach Devaney coming in 1962 and then in 1967 he had his first bad year after he won 4 straight championships. And all of a sudden he goes 6-4 two years in a row and that is not good enough for Nebraska. And I thought "give me a break, man." Sometimes I just wanted to say to those Nebraskans "don't get too far into it now. It was not that many years ago that a winning season was a good year"

   But Coach Devaney bounced back and so did all the players. The 1969 season was a trampoline that set forth the action. It took the pressure off of everybody and let the coaches relax a little bit. The players were just excited and things happened because we got quarterbacks like Tagge and Brownson and runners like Joe Orduna and Jeff Kinney. And all of a sudden Johnny Rodgers shows up and that was not bad either.

3. We won the National Championship in the Orange Bowl in 1971 over LSU (17-12) Notre Dame beat Texas and that put us Number One. Our players and our coaches were so busy trying to win the Big 8 Conference that it never occurred to us that we were going to be a National Championship team. We just kept taking care of business, and the first thing you know we were undefeated. I remember talking with Monte Kiffin and Warren Powers. We were saying "God, we are National Champions and what do we do now." We did not know how to act.

4. We were a quality football team in 1970, but we got Coach Devaney a little upset. The 1969 team went 9-2 and then in 1970 we opened with a real good thumping of Wake Forest. Then we played USC in Los Angeles and it was difficult to beat them on their home field. We tied the game 21-21 and USC was a tremendous football team. Down deep all of our coaches thought we did a pretty good job. Coach Devaney had been out on the field a little longer than normal, and he came in the dressing room and none of us were really deflated but we were not happy that we tied. To go there and tie USC with the national prominence that they carried we thought was pretty good.

   Who didn't think it was very good was Coach Devaney. I never had my butt chewed so hard in my life. He jumped all over us saying "We are too proud to be tieing teams, and we have to have a stronger attitude about ourselves." He personally felt that we should have won that game, and he thought it was bad coaching and not bad playing. I can tell you when he came by my office I was working hard because I did not want to get fired.

5. My best memory of Coach Devaney was watching him walk around the first year I was there as a freshman coach. Once our freshman season got over we would go over and hang out with the varsity guys. The thing that always impressed me (having played for him and having coached for him) was his ability to communicate with the players while they were playing. He could move over to a group and he had a phenomenal memory for names. If someone told him Tommy Pate's mother wasn't doing well or Steve Manstedt's father was in the hospital, he had an unbelievable ability to go around a football field and say something to each person in some way that would

make you so proud, because he knew who you were. I was always amazed by that. He knew when to pick you up or when to jump on you a little bit.

6. He gave the assistant coaches the freedom to coach. He made you feel so good about going to work. We liked each other. He liked to go down to the Legion Club and take the staff out there after a game and relax. When Bob Devaney was the Athletic Director and he threw a staff party, it was not optional whether you came or not. It was required. He also had a great ability to make us all feel confident and to let you coach the way you thought it should be done. He gave you that freedom and I always respected that.

7. During the week before the OU game in 1971, the Sugar Bowl came out early and said they were going to take a chance. They said that OU was probably going to win the game and they were going to issue their bid to OU for the Sugar Bowl. And Bob never said a word to any of us. After the game, we are walking up the ramp to the dressing room and there is a representative of the Sugar Bowl right in front of our locker room. And Warren and I are 3 steps behind Coach Devaney, and the guy from the Sugar Bowl reaches out to shake his hand and Coach Devaney proceeded to take him apart verbally. He said "you said OU could beat us and things like that." He said things to that guy that he never said to me as a player. And Warren Powers and I are standing just there looking at each other.

    Coach Devaney was just that intense. Nobody truly understood how intense he was about protecting Nebraska and believing in NU. It just infuriated him that this guy would pick them over us and that was an insult as far as he was concerned. But they came back two years later and invited NU to the Sugar Bowl so it did not have any lasting effect.

8. I played for Bob when he was at Wyoming. I was his quarterback in his second and third years (1958-1959). We had a great relationship. I loved the NU staff and loved Mike Corgan, Selmer, Ross, and Melton. They were like fathers to me. When coach Devaney gave me the opportunity to coach, it was a dream come true.

9. The greatest single individual effort that I have ever seen by a defensive player was Rich Glover's performance against Oklahoma in 1971. Here is a middle guard that got 22 tackles playing nose guard against the wishbone. When you evaluate the blocking schemes of the wishbone, to see one middle guard do that was in my opinion maybe the greatest individual accomplishment in a college game that I have ever seen. Rich was on my staff at Washington State. I have a copy on film and sometimes I will get it out and watch it and I still marvel at how well he played that day. Rich Glover and Daryl White were the dynamic duo.

10. In 1969 I thought Coach Tom Osborne would do well coming from receiver coach to offensive coordinator. If you watch Tom's preparation habits, and if you could describe Tom Osborne in one word you would say "organized." Tom had a plan and knew how to work with it.

11. Coaching at NU catapulted everything I was trying to do. It gave me such a grounded feeling watching these guys work. The one thing I learned from Coach Devaney was not to mistreat assistants and to understand that they had families and needs. That breeds success. The one thing that makes the great winners keep winning is because the Head Coaches respect their Assistants to a point where they are not a dictator. They are just your boss. That is what I learned from him. You take all that you learn from watching assistants and the way Coach Devaney handled young people, and that is what he taught.

12. Regarding leadership, Mike Wynn was a dominating guy. He and Bob Liggett were such strong personalities. Over the long haul Jerry Tagge was a good leader and he went the extra mile. Jerry List was one of those quiet guys that did not say much, but everybody had great respect for him because he was a grossly undersized tight end playing at a high level. Rich Glover did not say much, but he was a dynamic football player. Johnny Rodgers played when he was hurting. And that is called leadership. It is not necessarily how much you are cheering in the dressing room. You are a leader by what you do.

13. One of the most important reasons for the wins was that the blackshirt defense just came out of nowhere. Coach Monte Kiffin changed the system. Warren Powers was a tremendous secondary coach and John Melton filled in where he could. The way the blackshirts played on defense seemed to inspire our offense. We believed in ourselves and it seemed to me that the players were having a lot of fun.

4. The mystique of the "blackshirt" came about accidentally. We would all be in white so you had to get differentiated. The first team got the blackshirts, second team got the gold, and third team got the green shirts. If you had a blackshirt you knew you were going to start. We were religious about not having more than 11 guys on the first. And believe me, the players wanted those blackshirts.

5. One funny story about Coach Monte Kiffin: During 2-a-days Monte would do up-downs with his kids. Well, he got this wild hair one time and each day we would try to add 3 or 4 up-downs. So by the time 2-a-days were over we would be up in the 50 and 60s. So one day he and I worked out together. When it came time to do up-downs Monte told the players that we would do them with them on the last day. Well, it was 70 up-downs, and I did that 70 times and for the next three days I could not even move my arms. I told him if he ever did that again I would kill him. My upper body was so sore that I literally could not use my hand to write.

6. In 1967-1969, the team that used to give us fits was Missouri. We had a mind set and a terrible time playing Missouri. I don't know why it was. They were a team that always frightened our guys more than you would expect.

7. It was just such a tribute to the players to be considered the best in 1970-1971. It was just so fun for me. Monte and Warren and I were so young. I learned later to appreciate it and the opportunity to be with a group of guys that were so good and worked so hard. We had a coaching staff that you just loved spending time with. It is mind boggling.

    I know that I am prejudiced, but nothing is ever going to beat the (1971) Nebraska and Oklahoma game because it was on Thanksgiving Day. It took us ten days to play after the regular season was over so there was all that build up and all that promoting, marketing and intensity. And then it was such a wonderful game. There will never be a greater build up of two 10-0 teams rolling head to head. You knew it was going to be a hell of a collision when we played, and it was.

8. Before the game Coach Devaney used to give one of his speeches that nobody listened to because it was right before we would get on the bus. By that time we were all so nervous nobody heard it. Most of the motivation came during the week. Our approach was letting the players know how important the game was.

19. Our biggest challenge was not being over-confident. There were two football games where I thought we just kind of got caught looking: (a) The UCLA game in 1972 was the opening game of the season, and they weren't a great team; (b) the other one was Iowa State in 1972. We had ourselves in position to be Number One, and we go to Iowa State and tie the game (23-23). We were not ready and did not play with the intensity that we were known for. And those two opponents played well at that time.

20. One of the most important reasons that made the team work so well together was that all our players knew that their coaching staff liked each other. There was that feeling of comfort. You knew that we were all in it together, and players pick up on that. The players believed in us. The players liked us and they had a great feeling that this was going work.

21. Nebraskans are the most intelligent football fans I have ever been around, and I have been in this business 35 years. The thing I loved about Nebraskans was they came early and they still do. When you go out on the football field to warm up, they are already there. They believed that they needed to be in the stands and they wanted to watch the punters and kickers and the pass receivers. That was such an uplifting thing. They are respectful and eager fans. They love their football and they want football to be big in the state. I love that.

22. Coaching for Nebraska helped me in the after football life. Once you get four conference championships and two national championships notches on your belt, your resume reads pretty good. NU helped in everything that I did after that in terms of coaching.

23. I am retired in Harrison, Idaho on Lake Courdelene. I have done radio broadcasts on WHO with my partner, Jim, on Sundays for ten years. I am the Adrian Fiala of Washington State. Now I just take care of my grandkids and that is a lot of fun.

24. I just want to tell the folks at Nebraska how much I miss them and how much I loved them when I was there. It was a pleasure and privilege for me to coach and live in Nebraska, and it has always been the highlight of my professional life.

HUSKER REFLECTIONS

1. The greatest time in college football history was the Big 8 in 1971, when NU finished 1, Oklahoma 2, and Colorado 3. It certainly does not get any better than that for a conference.

2. I started doing Big 8 sports reporting in 1970. Bob Devaney was unique in dealing with the press. My favorite memories of those days are the relationships. You could afford to be friends. Now, the press and the coaches and the players are kind of enemies, but back then we had a different relationship with Bob. He was always so honest and everybody knew where he stood. You could also taste the wrath of Bob. He let you know if he did not like something.

3. I had a project with the World Herald to compile an All Sports race for the conference. And Nebraska was always in the top in football but in some of the other sports like tennis and golf and wrestling they were really dragging anchor. Devaney did not think that the poll was valid. Bob said "Football paid the bills and that is where we are going to put our resources." And football and tennis counted the same in weight. He had a good point.

4. Devaney described his good natured relationship dealing with the press: "Never get into a pissing contest with a skunk." and "Never argue with a guy that buys ink by the barrel and paper by the roll." He was always available to the press and very charming. What was unique about Bob was he would carve you up and then say "let's go to the Legion Club and have a drink." He was a delightful character.

5. I had a great affection for Jim Ross. Jim was really a stabilizing force for Bob because Bob could be pretty volatile. Devaney always bounced ideas off of Jim.

6. Things have changed. Back then the sportswriters were part of the program. I had my own locker at the field house. I would be in the steam room with the coaches and working out with them. Or drinking with them.

During the summer I would be fishing with Tom, Milt Tenopir or Charlie McBride. These were my best friends back then. They don't do that now. The press is the enemy. And they don't have the same type of openness.

7. I was very close with Oklahoma's Coach Barry Switzer and still am. And Gaylen Hall and Larry Lacewell. Barry is a unique guy. He came up hard. He was a real player's coach. And his players and coaches would swear by him. Bob Devaney and Barry had a great relationship because they spent a lot of time in the bars together at conventions. They had a special and unique relationship. They used to play a lot of practical jokes on each other. Out in Kearney they had a dinner for the booster club and Bob was the speaker. Barry showed up and came in with a chef's hat and surprised Bob with a birthday cake. At first, Bob did not recognize Barry and then Bob recognized him and said "I did not recognize you without a bottle of Jack Daniels in your hand."

8. They don't have press parties anymore. Back in those days the night before a game the coaches would get together and have a press party at the Legion Club. In Oklahoma it was at Fuzzy's supper club in Oklahoma City. The coaches and sportswriters would come and there was such a fraternity in the conference. It was built on mutual respect and everybody enjoyed each other's company. It was not the dog eat dog stuff that you see now.

9. Sports should be fun. I was lucky because I came during a time when sports were still fun. We kept it in a proper perspective. But along about the late 60s early 70s, we went through a culture shift in the whole country during the Vietnam era. It seemed like the country became more cynical and more negative. The press started attacking everything and sports was not immune. I retired from that business in 1981 because the press had become more adversarial and more aggressive. You couldn't be friends with the coaches and players like we had.

10. Coach Tom Osborne initially had a hard time in bowl games and beating Oklahoma. Even though he won 90% of his games, Oklahoma basically was recruiting better athletes. That changed when Tom started recruiting speed and better athletes.

11. The most remarkable offensive play I witnessed was Johnny Rodgers' pass to Frosty Anderson against Notre Dame in 1972. We got to see Johnny throw so seldom.

12. The best defensive plays I saw were Richie Glover in the Oklahoma game in 1971.

13. The best leaders were Jerry Tagge and Johnny Rodgers. Tagge took charge and had the winning attitude as all the players did. Guys that led by example were Jimmy Anderson, Kosch, Blahak. Those guys were solid. Bob Terrio, Dutton, Branch, Pitts. It is almost the whole roster. There were no weaknesses. Everybody stepped up and it was a unique bunch. Even Jerry Murtaugh led by example by being nasty. Monte Johnson and Dick Rupert were some great athletes. Jeff Kinney was persistent and you wanted the ball in his hands.

14. There was only one goal and that was the National Championship. It started in 1969 in the Sun Bowl with a blowout against Georgia and Paul Rodgers kicked four field goals. That was really the start of greatness. From that moment you knew that Nebraska had a very special bunch of players.

15. The 3 most important reasons for the wins were (1) Great athletes. (2) Belief. That group had great faith; (3) A special coaching staff. Everybody loved each other and the coaches worked their butts off. They were like Bob and had a work hard/play hard mentality. Bob was a players coach. These guys were as competitive as could be and they really enjoyed life. After the games Bob would always have all the staff and their wives out to the Legion Club. It kept everybody loose and that was his style.

16. The 10 years that I covered the Huskers was a very special time. It was special to break in with a National Championship group. The last game of the 1971 season was the first game I saw the Huskers play. How do you get any better than that in the Alabama game (38-6).

17. This is a perfect example of how good Bob was. In 1971 I was a rookie and I had never covered this team. I walked out on the practice field the first day that I got in Miami and I was kind of intimidated. Don Bryant came over and welcomed me, and I said "I would like to talk to Coach Devaney." The next thing I know here comes Devaney and said "what can I do for you?" That blew me away that he would take the time to visit with me during practice for the National Championship game. He just dropped what he was doing and talked to me for as long as I wanted to talk to him. Tremendously impressive for a young sportswriter.

18. Are Nebraska's best years in the past or yet to come? They won't get any better. How do you better perfection? They did that twice. The 1971 season is still the best football team and season that college football has ever had. Nebraska was the king of the hill. The best football in history. The only thing you can do is to come close to it. 1995 was also pretty doggone good.

19. Nebraska fans in general have always been so well behaved. Nebraska fans treat the other teams like guests.

"How do you better perfection? 1971 is still the best football team and season in college history."

"Everyone stepped up and it was a unified bunch. There were no weaknesses."

DON BRYANT *(aka "Fox")*

UNL SPORTS INFORMATION DIRECTOR (1963-1994) AND
ASSISTANT ATHLETIC DIRECTOR, EMERITUS (1994-PRESENT)

HUSKER REFLECTIONS

1. The 1969 season was the trigger for considerable change. We went 6-4 two years in a row in 1967-1968, and we had relied on the unbalanced line and full house backfield. We were big but overall speed was lacking. Some of the schools that were beating us had more team speed. Bob and the coaches changed the offense and went to more wide open passing and the I-back offense. That made the big difference between '68 and '69. They decided to go for more speed but with big, strong and fast players. We opened things up and had that good year in 1969 and beat OU.

2. I always credited Tom (Osborne) as the guy who changed the offense in 1969. Plus they began to recruit faster and quicker players. And they went out and recruited some excellent Junior College players.

3. The relationship that Bear Bryant and Coach Devaney had was a unique deal. They became friends. Bob always joked about how we played them in 1965 in the Orange Bowl and they really beat us with some trick plays. We were undefeated going into that Orange Bowl, and then Bear beats us with a tackle eligible and onside kicks and all of that. Bobby Churchich had a great game against them and he threw a record of 3 TD passes in the Orange Bowl.

4. Bear called Bob and said our fans had such a good time with yours and let's get together at the Sugar Bowl. They did and Bear beat us pretty bad (34-6). And Bob said "that was the end of that. I am not going to let him fool me again." When we played them in 1972 Bob was ready for Bear (38-6).

6. I loved Devaney's psychology at the Gotham Bowl in 1963 at Yankee Stadium against Miami (36-34). He had his locker-room talk just before we went out on the field. And it was about 14 above zero and everybody had to put on tennis shoes because the field was frozen solid. Bob said: "Fellas, I am really sorry about getting you into this crummy deal. This isn't much fun but it reminds me of my old back alley days when I was a kid

in Michigan and we had those back alley fights. There was no one there to watch but the toughest son of a bitch won." And the players were laughing. He was great with locker-room talks.

7. At the Sun Bowl in 1969 we beat Vince Dooley and Georgia (44-16). A lot of Nebraska fans before the game went down on the field and formed a spirit line to welcome the team from the locker-room onto the field. They were hooping and hollering and Bob's last words to the squad as they started out the door was "Wait a minute fellas, be real careful going out the door. I don't want anybody to get hurt. Half the state of Nebraska is out there waiting for you, and the other half is home praying for you."

8. One of the unique things that made Bob a great success at NU was that many of the Assistant Coaches knew each other. He had a staff that coached together in high school and at Wyoming. All of those guys had been successful – Jim Ross, Mike Corgan, John Melton. And Jim and Bob played Mike Corgan nine games in Michigan competitively so they were friends. And Bob got those guys to go to Wyoming and they picked up Selmer and Melton out there. He had George Kelly from Nebraska and Cletus Fischer and all those guys had been successful high school coaches and/or college coaches and knew how to teach.

    They were a hell of a bunch of teachers. And they knew how to build guys. Everybody just melded in. And Bob would walk out of meetings in the morning and say "you guys know what to do." He let them coach. The coaches coached and it was the same with Sports Information. He told me that as long as I was not screwing up you know what to do and do it. Bob knew what was going on. He would review the defensive plans and they would all decide what to do on Sunday night and the assistants took it from there.

9. In his first year in 1962 what really helped was that Bob made practice fun for the guys. In those days a lo of coaches scrimmaged all week long and the players would be weak legged on Saturday. Devaney did not

have contact during the week. They did not battle everyday in the trenches. They worked on execution. Bob also wanted the guys to have a good time when they went to the Bowl games. It was a reward for a successful season. Bob enjoyed life and wanted the kids to have fun too.

10. Coach Cletus Fischer was tough. He went both ways with the New York Giants when he left NU. We were in school together and double dated in the 1940s. He was really a fine player and a good coach. He was a fireball. You could hear his laughter a block away. He took real pride in the special teams and did a great job.

11. Coach Mike Corgan was a tough sucker. He played at Notre Dame as a fullback before the war. And he went into the Navy and was a gunner officer on those Liberty ships taking supplies up to Russia. One time when we went out to play Colorado and Devaney says we have to do something to loosen the kids up. It was Thursday night and Bob said lets do something funny, let's pull something on Mike Corgan. So I got this old helmet just two pieces of leather going in different ways from 1900 and got it from a trophy case and I walked out on the field with it in a paper sack. Bob called the team together and "Coach Bryant has to tell you something really important" and I said "fellas, I got some information here. Notre Dame was cleaning out their old equipment room back when Mike Corgan was a star fullback for Notre Dame and they sent his helmet to me. In case we would like to have his old helmet as a souvenir." And I pulled it out and put it on my head and Mike hollered "Why you little fat son of a bitch." And the guys were hooping and hollering and laughing.

12. Bob knew when to loosen them up or pull something funny. We had a guy playing guard in 1964 named John Dervin. We played Iowa State and we won. But an Iowa State player made defensive player of the week. That Monday before practice we are down in the lockerroom in the coach's office and he had me go down to Western Union and get a form and I typed a message that he dictated. The message said: "please thank John Dervin for helping make me the Big 8 Defensive Player of the Week, best wishes, signed Jon VanSicklin, Iowa State University." Well Dervin was walking by the door Bob called him in and said I got a telegram here I have to read. And he read it and Dervin said "That son of a bitch." And he got all fired up. Bob was always pulling something funny.

13. The most remarkable offensive play I witnessed was JR's punt return against Oklahoma in 1971. That was just spectacular. Johnny Rodgers was the best and most exciting football player that I ever saw. He was the only guy that when he got ready to the touch the ball everybody got ready to stand up. He just had that dynamic appeal.

14. On defense, Rich Glover was a hell of middle guard. He was quick. He wasn't very big but he had some great plays. He had a hell of a play in that OU game at the end when they got the ball and there were just seconds left. They are coming down the field and he and Jake each got a sack.

15. Each coach had a different role. Jim Ross was a father figure and he was a brilliant coach and a very wise man. Carl Selmer was a very good offensive line coach and very bright guy. He was an aeronautical engineer. John Melton was the mouthy clown and had the needles out all the time. And Mike Corgan was just so damn funny with those kids.

16. A good leader who did not get a lot of credit was Jim Anderson. He was a co-captain in 1971. He was an unsung hero and really a leader by performance. He was not flashy and he did not get a lot of ink but he was a heck of a leader and so was Tagge. That 1971 team was something. More than anything they thought they were going to win. They always played like hell on Saturday.

17. The 3 most important reasons for the wins were (a) preparation (b) confidence and execution (c) and good luck.

18. 1971 is the best team that I have seen. I knew the players and worked with them and loved them. There was a closeness on that staff and just a phenomenal performance all the way.

"The NU fans have been tremendous and they are a key part of the success."

19. The biggest challenge in 1969 was shaking off the Missouri loss (7-17). And then bouncing back and going all the way and not losing again for 32 games. Kansas that year was a key game (21-17). They called pass interference on Kansas. Their captain cussed out the ref and was penalized and we pulled it out.

20. One time Devaney thought about leaving NU. He considered taking a pro offer in 1969. And we were all going to go. And the coaches talked him out of that.

21. My biggest disappointment was the Oklahoma game in 1976 when they beat us on the fleaflicker pass. We thought he had the game, and they won it in the last minute. That was a crusher. It hurt.

22. The most important reasons that made the team work so well together were coaches, player's talent and attitude. The coaches did a tremendous job of teaching and motivation. They cared about the players and tried to make it fun and provide them with as much leadership as they possibly could. We recruited some very fine people, and they bonded together. To have the success that we had in 1969-1972 you had to be a close bunch of guys. To come back from 1967-68 and put together what they did in four years was a heck of an accomplishment.

23. The fans gave great support to the efforts in the games. They followed you on the road. We would have lots of people in those stadiums on road games.

24. My greatest memory of the fans was that first National Championship against LSU in the `71 Orange Bowl. As we went off the field the fans were hollering and half of them were crying. We were all pretty juiced that night. That was a big win. It was very emotional for me and a lot of people. Also, arriving at the airport and there would be 5,000 people to greet you. The fans have been tremendous and they are a key part of the success.

25. On defense Coach Monte Kiffin was a great teacher, leader and motivator. He got the players juiced at practice.

"They were a hell of a bunch of teachers. And they knew how to build guys. Everybody just melded in. And Bob would walk out of meetings in the morning and say "you guys know what to do." He let them coach."

ALAN MACKIEWICZ

**WORKED ON KFAB RADIO BROADCAST TEAM
WITH LYELL BREMSER (1974-1983)**

Married, two children. Attorney at Law in Omaha.

HUSKER REFLECTIONS

1. Lyell was really in charge of the entire broadcast crew. He called the shots. His philosophy was that the play-by-play announcer needed to control the broadcast. He did not want people breaking in with commercials so we would often dump out of a commercial to go back to the play by play, if the team came out of the huddle early or if there was something unusual that needed to be reported.

2. KFAB was originally in Lincoln. And Lyell started doing play by play for KFAB in 1938. He broadcasted for 44 years. He was going to school at the University in Lincoln and working part time at KFAB. How he ended up getting on the broadcast crew was the fellow that had been doing the play by play was in poor health and they wanted to hire someone to help him out. They polled the employees and Lyell was the only one who was interested in doing it. He became the assistant to the play by play guy. Then the play by play guy died of a heart attack before the season started. So, Lyell without any prior experience was thrown into the job just cold. He started in 1938 and continued until 1983.

3. In the early 1970s when I first started working with the radio broadcast crew there were four stations that were doing origination broadcasts of the NU football games. Lyell was well regarded as the guy that most fans listened to simply because he was the sportscaster's name that was mentioned most often when people would write into the paper.

4. After Lyell retired after the 1983 season, I continued to work on the broadcast crew until 1996. Before the game we would have one spotting board set up for the opponent and a second spotting board set up for Nebraska. We would use a piece of plywood that was about 18 inches by 24 inches. We would have a piece of poster board that would have preprinted on it a 5/2 defensive formation on the back and one with the I-formation on the front.

And we would have little boxes where we could list the players across the offensive line and behind the offensive line e.g. the QB, fullback and I-back and wingback. We could list them 3 and 4 deep. By dividing the boxes we could add another depth to what we had on the board. And then we would use pushpins for the skill players who were in so Lyell could look down at the board and tell who was in the game at the skill positions at any one time. I would spot the opponents and what spotting involved was following the ball and indicating who was throwing a block or who was carrying or catching the ball, recovering a fumble, making a tackle, etc. Lyell and I used a simple set of hand signals so I could communicate with him without talking to him.

5. Did Lyell ever want to do TV? At the time Lyell came up in the 1930s he was the winner of the Iowa talent contest the same year that Donna Reed won it. But Lyell was not that photogenic. We always kid around when I get together with Pavelka and Saddlemeyer that Lyell had a good radio face.

6. Lyell's nickname of "Mr. Football" probably evolved from the fact everybody would listen to him doing the NU games on Saturdays. One time the World-Herald did an analysis of the four radio stations that were announcing the game. And they did a light polling of people to find out which of the broadcasters was being listened to. It was for an Oklahoma State game that was played in Lincoln. It turned out in the World Herald analysis that Don Gill was the most accurate compared to the NCAA official play by play, but that Lyell had about 80% of all people in the State listening to KFAB. The big advantage was KFAB was the only 50,000 watt stations in the state that carried football. KFAB reached most of the people in the state.

7. Coach John Melton would always hook up with us before a game because he would always have a couple of jokes.

8. The first Kick-off Classic in New Jersey in 1984 we ended up playing Penn State. Everybody thought they would bring in Penn State to fill up the stadium, but it turned out that there were just as many Nebraska fans there. Nebraska fans love to travel.

(9) Dave Blackwell and Jack Payne fit in beautifully with Lyell. Payne had been the play by play guy on WOW then KFAB hired Payne from WOW. Dave Blackwell was a laugh a minute. He was one of the best natural wits I ever met. He would always break up Lyell. Lyell liked him a lot. Lyell liked Jack a lot too. But Jack was kind of all business, even though he really liked to have some fun. It was really a good crew.

"Mr. Football" Lyell Bremser, 1970.

Alan Mackiewicz, Lyell Bremser and grandson James.

JACK PAYNE

NEBRASKA BROADCASTERS HALL OF FAME
Part of KFAB radio team with Lyell Bremser and Dave Blackwell (1970-1983)
WOW TV and Radio through 1967. Lives in Omaha, Nebraska.

HUSKER REFLECTIONS

1. I was with the Omaha Mustangs in 1968-1969 and I was the general manager. I went to KFAB radio in 1970. I was with WOW radio and TV through 1967. So I was in on one of those two 6-4 years that NU experienced (1968).

2. When Bob came to Nebraska in 1962 he realized and was fully convinced that we were determined in Nebraska and he had the State behind him. He did not walk into a cupboard that was empty. There were some darn good football players here when he came in 1962. Coach Bill Jennings and his staff were simply not able to put things together and click. Bob came in with a good staff from Wyoming. He kept Clete Fischer and George Kelly and also in 1962 an inspiring young graduate assistant came by the name of Tom Osborne.

3. Bob had some people that could recruit. He and his staff went around and gained the respect and rapport that was necessary. Bob always liked to say "re-cruiting." They had that great rapport and built it back all over the state. He would take the same line of stories with him. He was humorous, and everyone would roll in the aisle. That little Irish man had a way of doing it. He had a special way of communicating with the people and the players.

4. When Devaney came in 1962 and took us to the Gotham Bowl, that was NU's third Bowl in history and we got a win over Miami (36-34). And that set the stage for enthusiasm and they rolled through four consecutive Conference Championships (1963-1966) and started going back to the Bowls.

5. When NU rolled into 1967-68, when John Melton would speak he used to say "we were so bad that they were circulating a petition to fire us. If I would have been up there I would have signed it." We were not just recruiting in 1967-68 and the quality of our talent fell off quite a bit.

During that period of time teams like K-State and Kansas were coming up. We were sliding, but K-State and KU were getting better talent than we had. And Kansas put back-to-back wins on us in `67-68. KU shut us out 10-0 down there. Pepper Rodgers came along and he was the kind of Coach, like Devaney, who could put things together. Kansas State then beat us in Lincoln in 1968 (0-12) in a homecoming game. And that was a real omen. Vince Gibson was coaching at K-State and he said "we gonna win." So K-State and KU were coming up, and our supply of talent overall was falling off.

6. Something had to be done. Devaney and his coaches stepped up their recruiting and changed their philosophy. They said "we not only have to get strong kids but we have to improve our speed." Tom was in charge of the wingbacks in 1967. Then in 1969 he was instrumental in introducing the I-formation with the balanced line. That opened up the offense, and it changed the philosophy of unbalanced line strong side up the middle tackle football. It gave diversity and widened the scope of attack. And that began to attract different people.

The style of football that we started to play in 1969 was the earmark of greatness of Bob Devaney's coaching. He took the people that were around him (the assistant coaches) and they analyzed the situation. To play the formation we wanted to play they had to get the talent and speed. And then they started to win and in the last part of 1969 went to the Sun Bowl and ripped Georgia down there. That started a long streak of 9 win seasons.

7. Bob could communicate with a player. He could look at you and tell you something and make you believe it. He also had a way of handling the media and the administration and the fans. He had everything going for him. After two bad seasons, they definitely felt that they had to get with the times and modernize.

8. One of my favorite memories is Devaney's moment of greatness in the 1973 Orange Bowl against Notre Dame

AN ERA OF GREATNESS: COACH BOB DEVANEY'S FINAL FOUR SEASONS (1969 - 1972)

(40-6). When he shifted an aspiring and hopeful little kid (JR) from Omaha from wingback to I-back. And Johnny ran for 3 touchdowns threw for another and caught another. This young man named Johnny Rodgers was adept in running the football.

9. I first worked with Bob when he came to Lincoln in 1962. WOW radio and TV signed him to a contract agreement. He would drive up here on Monday morning and we would sit down in the radio studio at 6:30 and for about 25 minutes we would record a series of 5-five minute programs to run on Monday, Tuesday, Wednesday, Thursday, Friday. Then at 7 o'clock we would go in and tape the television show that ran on Monday night from 7-8 o'clock. Jim Ross would edit the film for him. Bob was known for being a "heavy foot on the gas pedal." And he would be ready at 6:30 a.m. and I would say "What time did you leave Lincoln?" He would say "Well, I think I left about 15 minutes of 6 o'clock." I said "Wow, you must of really flown up here" and he said "Yeah, I had to stay low to avoid the signals."

10. Regarding legendary announcer Lyell Bremser: "Man, Women and Child," what excitement there was sitting there with Lyell and Dave Blackwell during the 1971 OU football game in Norman. Lyell was a lot of fun but when you were on the air, it was strictly business.

11. One time we went to Oklahoma State and usually we would hire kids to spot for us. And the Sports Information Director furnished us a spotter and Lyell would give the kid $20. But this particular time he took his son-in-law with us to be the spotter, Al Mackiewicz. So we go up to booth and this kid came in and introduced himself and Lyell told him "I am sorry, we have our own man here, but I want to thank you for coming up." And he gave him a twenty dollar bill. And this kid asked "Do you mind if I stay in your booth. I am trying to get into journalism and see how you people do these things." And Lyell told him it was fine.

12. We called Lyell "Mr. Football". We would kid him about that and he built it on the air. The charisma in his voice was just magnetism. And listeners following the ballgame never knew when Nebraska wasn't in the game because he never put the team out of the game. Lyell was a great man to work for.

13. I think of the defining moments of The Game of the Century in 1971. NU was behind (28-31). There was 7:10 left to go and Tagge started our last drive. One of

defining moments of that whole drive was third down and we had 8 yards to go and Mr. Johnny Rodgers went out and squared to the left and came back falling down and caught that pass that gave us the yardage we needed for the first down. If Johnny had not caught that pass, 4th down would have been coming up. Not to take anything away from Kinney and Tagge, but if Johnny had not caught that pass that would have been lights out right there on that drive. [Editors' Note: Coach Devaney later said that NU would have gone for it on 4th down. He did not want to give the ball back to OU]

14. We were over in Hawaii playing Frosty Anderson at wide receiver, and Dave Blackwell was one of the wittiest guys I have ever met in all my life. He was quick with comebacks, and we were trying to move the football. Frosty went out to the left and the pass went over to him and he caught it and a flag was thrown on the play. And the flag was thrown by an official who was way back in the end zone. He had to run about 25 yards downfield towards the play to actually see what was going on. So Lyell was on the air and he said "I did not see anybody in the area" and clipping was called. And he looked over to Blackie and Dave says "Lyell, the only way I can figure it out is the official decided that had a Nebraska player in the area and he probably would have clipped anyway." It was a pleasure to sit with Dave and Lyell.

15. The most remarkable offensive plays I witnessed were the run JR made against OU in 1971 and the crucial catch JR made in that game.

16. It was important for Bob to beat the Bear (Alabama's Bear Bryant). I took a great load off his shoulder. I think it was a fitting climax to a great career. It had to be satisfaction. Bob went out in a blaze of glory.

17. I remember in 1971 Oklahoma's excellent quarterback Jack Mildren. NU went in there Number One and OU was Number Two. After we scored and led 35-31, they still had a minute and some to go. Glover and Jacobson were terrific at the end of game. How many times are you going to get talent like that to step on to a college football field? It seldom happens. It was a tremendous collection of talent on both teams.

18. At the airport in Oklahoma City. We were checking our baggage, and we had 8 big boxes of equipment. This guy checking us in asked "Are you guys in a band?" I said "Yes, we are known as "Bremser's Bombastic Bozos." He said "I have never heard of you," and I said "well, I have not heard of you either."

*"You shall judge a man by his foes
as well as by his friends."*

Joseph Conrad (1900)
"Lord Jim" ch. 34

*"To set the cause above renown,
To love the game beyond the prize,
To honor, while you strike him down,
The foe that comes with fearless eyes;
To count the life of battle good
And dear the land that gave you birth;
And dearer yet the brotherhood
that binds the brave of all the earth."*

Sir Henry Newbolt (1925)
"The Island Race, Clifton Chapel,"
Stanza 2

MEL GRAY

MISSOURI RECEIVER (1968-1970)
ALL-CONFERENCE; ALL-AMERICAN (1969)
BIG 8 CO-CHAMPIONS WITH NU IN 1969

UPDATE

Pro Football (St. Louis)

Married to Rhonda; 6 children

Works in Special Education; also in speed conditioning program; coaches girl's track and boys football

Lives in Rockford, Illinois

REFLECTIONS

1. When I first met Coach Dan Devine I was being recruited by a lot of colleges. He came to Santa Rosa, California to watch me play football and run track. I told him I would love to visit with him but I wanted to go see my relatives. And he said "bring them along." I brought about 8 people to eat. After a while I told him "Coach Devine, those were not my relatives" and he said "I know, but I wanted you." He treated me real nice. He knew I came from a large family and that I was a loner.

2. When I got to Missouri he used to pick me up off campus and take me to his house and just leave me there. He would say "I've got a banquet to go to so just stay here and shoot some pool and watch TV." He was always nice to me. The whole staff took me under their wing because I they knew I was a long way from home.

3. The first time I played Nebraska in 1969 we were co-champs. You guys beat us up so bad in 1968 that some of the guys were coming off the field and they were playing like they were hurt.

4. All the red in the Nebraska stands was just frightening. Nebraska and Oklahoma dominated the Big 8 back then.

5. When Coach Devine recruited me, he told me that he had an offense just for me. My first year there I sat on the bench, I ran back a few kickoffs. And Coach Devine said, "well son, we got some seniors here that need to play and you are just going to have to wait your turn." He did tell me that I did not have to play spring ball. I could run track and that was a blessing.

6. They wanted me to be a running back and my first year at the University I can remember playing Kentucky and I came out of the backfield and snuck through the line and I went 75 yards for a touchdown. And I said "man, this is easy." Then after that they put two linebackers on me and I don't think that I ever got across the line of scrimmage. And that was when they put me at wide receiver.

7. What made the NU teams tough to play against was that NU's defense was tough. They had Rich Glover and that dude was everywhere. The defense was awesome. NU's special teams I could not get over. I would say "man, there ain't no way." I thought we were pretty awesome, but NU's defense used to wear us out.

8. I wanted to go the Olympics and run. Football was not my first love, track was. Missouri did not throw the ball that much. I ended up going to the Olympics in 1968 as a fifth man on a relay team. It was awesome. I saw Bob Beamon long jump 29 feet. We trained together in Lake Tahoe.

9. My greatest thrill playing for Missouri was in my second year. They started throwing passes and I scored 9 touchdowns. I scored three against KU in 1969, and we were selected to go to the Orange Bowl.

10. The most important reasons for the wins were (a) The coaching. (b) And the personnel. The guys were determined not to lose. We practiced hard and Coach Devine ran us to death. He would say "you guys are going to run until I get tired."

11. To get us ready to play Nebraska, the coaches would tell us "you guys have the attitude and the formula to beat NU. It is just up to you to do it." They just told us "They are going to hit you, They are going to hit you." They always said we were Tigers and Tigers can always catch a rabbit and Nebraska is just Cornhuskers and we will knock the corn off of those guys. Playing Nebraska was always a dog fight. The boosters and rivalry and the fans. It was awesome.

2. Our Missouri fans to me were the best in the world. If opponents came into Faroux field they were not liked. They were out for blood. I remember playing in one of the last games against Kansas (KU) and one of our fans got up with this big old sign that said "Mizzou goes to the Orange Bowl and KU goes to the Toilet Bowl." The rivalries between all the Big 8 teams were very big, (the Purple Pride from K-State, the Cowpokes from Oklahoma State, the Cornhuskers). It was the best conference at that time.

3. To be considered the best is an honor. They have my picture in the locker room and the Hall of Fame. I made the Hall of Fame for football and track. They invite me back for a bunch of the games and occasionally they ask me to help them do some recruiting.

4. My biggest challenge was trying to make it through school. When I got to the University of Missouri and I went to class the professors were saying "Mr. Gray, just because you are an athlete you get no special treatment here." I would say "I really did not ask for any." I majored in psychology.

5. There were not really any big disappointments.

6. The most important reason that made the team work so well together was coaching. Coach Devine was a great philosopher and he got us ready to play. Clay Cooper, Hank Coolman, John Cadillac, Ana Frio, Vince Tobin. They got us ready to play. They told us what to expect. Our practices were hard. We would practice live punt returns, 11 on 2. The punt returner only had one blocker and he got the hell knocked out of him several times. And they stopped that because guys were getting hurt.

7. My most talented opponents, were Johnny Rodgers, Cliff Bryant and Oklahoma's Pruitt. Mac Herron from Kansas State. John Riggins of Kansas. When we talked about John Riggins we said that we were not going to let this guy run over us. We had pictures of George Fountain on his back and John Riggins had his foot in his chest and was breaking away. George was hanging on for dear life.

8. The NU fans and all that red was scary. I will tell you one thing, Nebraska had some ugly uniforms. They had those hips pads. In the long run I probably wished I would have had one because I got a hip pointer.

19. In my best game against NU I scored one touchdown and I caught about 3-4 passes for 1st downs. But I never did run back a kickoff against N.U.

20. My biggest game overall in football was always playing against KU. We played against Notre Dame and Joe Theisman was the quarterback. He threw a pass behind his back to Thomas Gatewood for a touchdown to beat us. It was unreal.

Mel Gray and Johnny recreate the "pose".

"Playing Nebraska was always a dog fight... NU's defense was awesome."

RUSSELL HARRISON
KANSAS STATE FULLBACK (1967-1971)

UPDATE

Married to Renee

Played high football in Omaha

Owns an herbal company called Russell Herbal Company. In business for more than 37 years. I've worked with hundreds of people and a lot of well known celebrities like Dustin Hoffman, Kevin Bacon, Kyra Sedgwick, George Dukes, Sammy Clarks, Stevie Wonder and Coretta Scott King.

After sports, herbs & diets and other things that are used to maintain health, promote health and longevity. And that is where my focus has shifted.

Lives in Los Angeles

REFLECTIONS

1. Nebraska was after me like fleas are after a dog. The reason I did not go to Nebraska was because they did not have a veterinary program.

2. In 1968 we flew down to Lincoln and that was the first time I had a chance to play in Lincoln. I had a chance to run track at the coliseum when I was in high school but there is nothing like coming out on the field with 70,000 fans. This particular day it was snowing and we spanked Nebraska 12-0. Mac Herron, Lynn Dickie and Larry Brown were our star players.

3. In 1969 when we were ranked 3rd in the country and NU was 4th. And Nebraska came down to Kansas State and we led the game until the 4th quarter. We got beat by 3 points in 1969 but it a great game. They basically put their best linebacker on me and he followed me everywhere. Ken Geddes and I will never forget the game because he is an outstanding athlete. I had a very rough time that game but it was all fun. I often think about a lot of the guys that I played ball with and what they are doing now.

4. The best offensive game I had in college was Penn State in 1969. I rushed for a 115 yards in the first half and I never carried the ball in the second half.

5. My sophomore year we played Colorado State. Larry Brown, who went on to play with the Washington Redskins, played the first 3 quarters and they put me in the last quarter. I carried the ball 8 times for a total of 97 yards which led the nation in yards per carry.

6. You have to understand that Kansas State was more of a passing team. There were a lot of negative things that went on at Kansas State, but once you sign for 4 years you do the best that you can. I learned and improved my life and it gave me a chance to see how people really are. It also gave me a chance to grow and I would not change one minute of anything.

7. The leaders on my teams were Lynn Dickie, Mac Herron, Larry Brown, Clarence Scott, Ron Dickerson, Mike Montgomery, myself, John Stuckey, Manuel Barrera, Orson Powell (defensive tackle from Atlanta) and Joe Colquitt. There was a long list of great ball players that went to Kansas State. They believed in the team and themselves. They were very hard workers. I think that if they would have played in a more rounded fashion, we would have been more successful than we were.

8. We were not a close unit. There was a lot of separation and discrimination on the team and even with the coaches. It was a rough time during those years because the whole nation was going through a transition with the death of Martin Luther King and Bobby Kennedy and people standing up for their rights. And there was a lot of hard nose old school people that were at Kansas State. Even some teammates kept themselves separated. A lot of that came from people being ignorant but it went on then and it is still going on now.

9. My personal goals in going to college were (a) to run the ball (b) and to be a veterinarian.

10. I always took the sport in fun. I moved to Omaha from Harlem, New York when I was in the 7th grade so I never had the experience of following Nebraska. The Big Red was not even in my thinking until my senior

year. My senior year Coach Devaney visited me about 10 times during the year. I was what you would call a "man-child." I was big and fast. I just went with raw power and ability but was never really taught the finer points of playing the sport.

11. To motivate myself before the game I would go off into a quiet corner and I would visualize the whole game. I remember times in high school the night before the game that I would actually dream about the game. I did not watch a lot of backs when I was young with the exception of Jim Brown. I just based my game on his particular style.

12. I never had grade problems and always had a 3.8 or 3.9 average. When you are known as a running back but you go to a school that has favoritism going on and it all about passing, you get a little discouraged. At the same time you still give 100%.

13. My biggest disappointment was the fact that I don't feel that I was understood when I young. I had a problem with stuttering and there were a couple of instances where in meetings that the head coach would crack a joke about my stuttering. Coach Vince Gibson was not the ideal person who took time to sit down and to talk to me and understand who I was. The assistant coaches were good people. There was a lot of things going on with the coaches that I did not care too much for. Sometimes you would see a coach kick one of the players in the ass. And I did not go for that. That was the biggest disappointment. I just lost my desire at Kansas State.

14. We had good team chemistry in 1969. That was the closest that most of the ballplayers got. We were a very tight team in1969 and did end up being Number Three in the nation.

15. My most talented teammates were Mac Herron and Clarence Scott. Clarence Scott was a defensive back that went in the first round with the Cleveland Browns and he played 12 consecutive years with them and was All-Pro for 6 years. He was also my roommate for 3 years at Kansas State.

16. The most inspirational teammate was Mac Herron.

17. Coach Vince Gibson was very arrogant. He really did not take time out to talk to all of his ballplayers. I don't think that he should have been a head coach.

18. It was a great feeling to run on the field for the 1st time against NU. It was feeling that you don't get day-to-day. You cannot help but hear the noise and see all the red. It was quite a thrill and especially if you can perform well in front of that crowd.

19. Kansas State had great fans but not on the same level as Nebraska. We had some great alumni. I had a chance to meet a lot of great and decent people. They helped us outside of the game. We had tickets that we could sell or give to family members. I had a couple of farmers that allowed me to come out and hunt pheasants. It was always good to get away from all the day-to-day rituals and do some thinking on your own.

20. I don't keep in touch with my teammates. I had a chance to talk to Clarence Scott a few years ago when I did a seminar in Atlanta. It was great to see him

21. Kansas State does not embrace former players. I went back to Kansas State to finish up on my studies and they acted like they did not know who I was.

22. Life is great. I have loved every moment of my life. I have great kids and a lovely wife. I have a place in Canada where I live part time, and the rest of the time I am in Los Angeles. Business is going great, but the most important thing is that I am helping people to improve their health. There is nothing more rewarding than that.

"It was a great feeling to run on the field against NU and to see all that red. It was quite a thrill."

JACK MILDREN

OKLAHOMA QUARTERBACK (1969-1971)
ALL-AMERICAN (1971)

UPDATE

Pro Football

Married to Janice (34 years)

Banker with Regional Banking Group

Daily Radio Show

Former Lt. Governor of Oklahoma

Lives in Oklahoma

REFLECTIONS

1. The Game of the Century in 1971. I think there are about half a million people in Oklahoma who went to that game or say they did. It has taken on a life of its own 35 years later. It was a game played between two teams that tried to win. Nobody played not to lose. Both teams led not once but twice. There were very few penalties and the referees did not control the game. The players played the game.

    There were so many big plays starting with Johnny Rodger's punt return. It was clearly a game that stood the test of time. President Nixon called Devaney in the locker room, and Chuck Fairbanks was doing his coach's show after the game up in the press box. I am sitting there and by gosh the phone rings and it is the President's office. So Chuck on his TV show takes a gracious call from President Nixon. I remember the players on both sides.

2. Rich Glover had a wonderful game on defense in 1971. It was not too long ago that Rich called our house because he was recruiting for New Mexico State, and I had a son in high school. We had a nice chat. Johnny Harrison, our wide receiver, had a wonderful day beating Billy Kosch. John and I went to high school together so that was wonderful for me to see. But the entire NU defense was great – John Dutton did not even start, and he was a first round draft choice a couple of years later. How great could a defense be? Jacobson was a good player. When I went to the pros I played with Doug Dumler and Dave Mason. We got to know each other better. We were all saddened when we heard that Jerry List had passed away. A very tragic event.

3. When I was Lieutenant Governor of Oklahoma, Maxine Moul was Lieutenant Governor of Nebraska. Maxine asked me to come up for a nighttime roast and do another one the next day at noon. One in Lincoln and one in Omaha, and Ben Nelson was the Governor. I came to Nebraska and did the roast. I got hammered pretty good but I had a lot of fun with some of the Nebraska players.

4. Both OU and NU had great players who were very similar. Guys that thought they could do it. We were trying not to be cocky. We had a rivalry with NU that was born out of respect. Coach Devaney and Coach Switzer used to kid each other a lot. Even Coach Osborne loosened up as time when by. I am not sure that Coach Callahan understands it because he has made a few comments down here that he will have a hard time living down. Two years ago when the Sooners just hammered him he called us "hillbillies."

5. I was a kid from West Texas and highly recruited. I wanted to win a national championship. I was fortunate that I got a great degree that has served me well. I majored in Petroleum Land Management.

6. The most important reasons for the Oklahoma wins were (a) great speed (b) ability to recruit great players. We had guys like Greg Pruitt who in the Game of the Century did not carry the ball as much as normal, because of the way Nebraska was playing. When we argue about the top five running backs in OU history, Greg is as good as any of them. He came from BC Elmore High School in Houston, a teeny, tiny high school. He did not have all the bells and whistles like some others did. And yet, he worked his way through college and got a college degree and played pro football for a long time. He has a business that is doing very well. He is the epitome of what should happen when a guy works hard and does well. Pruitt is a role model. He is a fun guy to be with. He could do anything. If you put him at cornerback, he could have played cornerback.

I came to Oklahoma as a highly recruited kid, and you have to deal with that. I enjoyed my OU experience and I could not have gone to a better place.

Staying in touch with former players is important to the Athletic Department. There has been at least one event every year even back to the 50s. The older I get it becomes something that I do not want to miss because I will see someone that I have not seen in a year or two. I am 56 and we are losing some of our teammates and that is sad. You want to take advantage of being around old teammates.

After we played Nebraska in 1971 I was in New York for a banquet and Alabama's Johnny Musso and I were roommates. Musso was going to play Nebraska in the Orange Bowl, and we were going to play Auburn in the Sugar Bowl. So Johnny and I are kidding each other and he made some statement that "we are going to hammer Nebraska." And I said "yeah, and we are going to kill Auburn and beat them by 60 points." Somehow it all got quoted in the Norman paper. And Coach Fairbanks let me hear what he thought about my big mouth. I had to apologize to Auburn's Coach.

0. Coach Chuck Fairbanks and Coach Barry Switzer were different personalities. Barry is much more open. Barry was the offensive coordinator when I was there and I am a big fan. Folks in Oklahoma tend to like him. He was always known as a great recruiter, but he does not get the credit for being the excellent football coach that he is. He is one of the few guys that won the Super bowl as a head coach and also the College National Championship. Chuck was a quieter guy. When he spoke, people listened. Chuck had the ability to delegate to his assistants and he got the maximum out of everyone involved. Fairbanks was a dynamite football coach, but he and Switzer went at it differently.

1. My biggest disappointment was a period in my career when I did not play as well as I wanted to or should have. Fortunately, it was so long ago that folks don't remember.

2. I appreciate Nebraska fans because of the way they treat opponents with respect. At other places, like the Cotton Bowl, you don't get that treatment. I went to the game last year in Lincoln and sat in the stands and listened to the fans. They are very knowledgeable as far as football is concerned, and they are very respectful toward the opponents.

"I appreciate Nebraska fans. They are very knowledgeable and very respectful toward the opponents."

STEVE OWENS

OKLAHOMA ALL-AMERICAN RUNNING BACK (1968-1969)
HEISMAN TROPHY WINNER (1969)
Pro Football (Detroit Lions); All Pro 1972

UPDATE

Married for 39 years; 2 children; one grandchild

Insurance and Financial Services

Lives in Oklahoma

REFLECTIONS

1. I was recruited by NU in 1966, my senior year in high school. I went to visit NU in the Fall of 1965 and it just so happened that they were playing Oklahoma. OU was on the downside. It was a tough year for them. I will never forget because Devaney was the head coach and Frank Solich was playing fullback. And they had those two big running backs, Ben Gregory and Lighthorse Harry Wilson. I was on the NU sideline and this was Thanksgiving Day. Bud Wilkinson had been the coach at OU and he was a TV commentator at the game. I was on the sideline and they introduced me to Bud. They said "this young boy is from Oklahoma and his name is Steve Owens" and he said to me "What are you doing here?" and I said "sir, they are recruiting me." And he said "Well, you need to go to Oklahoma. They need your help."

2. I always wanted to go to OU. I remember playing NU in 1967 at in Lincoln. They had a nose guard named Wayne Meylan. He was one of the best players I played against. He was incredible. He was a short stocky guy. We had a hell of a time blocking him. Meylan hit me so hard during that ball game.

3. In 1968, we had a hell of a team. We played NU at OU and we beat the hell out of them (47-0). I had 5 touchdowns. I think Devaney might have said we were the best team he ever played against. Of course, in 1969 my senior year, Nebraska came here and beat the hell out of us (44-14). I had rushed for 17 straight games for a hundred yards or more, but I only had 75 yards that day. They shut me down.

4. My personal goals were to get an education and to play on some great football teams. Have a chance to go to Bowl game. My dream as a kid was to go to OU.

5. The most important reason for the OU wins was that we had quality players. In 1969 we had three first round draft choices (Zabel, Jim Fowls, and myself). And we had probably 8 or 10 other kids that were drafted so we had great talent here. We had great coaches like Coach Fairbanks and Switzer. We just had great tradition like NU. We had a great tradition of winning. We had a 47 game winning streak here at OU in the 1950s. I came to a university that knew how important the sport of football was not only to the school but to the state

6. I was called upon to carry the ball so many times. I only played half the time my sophomore year and played full time my junior and senior year. If you go back and average the number of games that I played, I averaged carrying the ball 35 times a game over my career. I set an NCAA record my last year. I carried 55 times against Oklahoma State. I carried it 40 plus times against NU and 50 times against Iowa State.

So when you talk about preparation, I had to prepare myself certainly physically to be able to carry the ball. But I think the mental aspect was just as important. People used to ask me "How can you carry the ball 30-50 times a game" and I said "It's easy because in practice I carry it 100 times" Switzer was my offensive coach and he made sure that I was physically conditioned for it. Then it just became the mental aspect of getting myself prepared because Switzer used to tell me "you might get tired of running it but they are going to get tired of tackling you too" And they did in third or fourth quarter. Because we had great offensive lineman. We did not throw a lot. We had two great quarterbacks. Bobby Warmack was a hell of a QB in 1967-68 and of course Mildren came in 1969. Both had the ability to throw. But we were an I-formation team and we would just attack people. We did not make mistakes and we did not have penalties. When we got in the red zone we scored. We were well conditioned both physically and mentally. We were disciplined. We did not have any injuries. I was lucky physically. But I kept myself in shape. I worked out all the time and could run all day. I started working with weights when I was in high school so when I came to OU I had a background in lifting weights. I played at about 218 pounds so I was a pretty good size running back. I ran the forty in 4.6 seconds. I was the State Champion in high hurdles, won the high jump and broad jump and finished second in the low hurdles. I did not have the type of speed that Johnny Rodgers had but I had pretty good speed for a guy that was close to 220 pounds. The thing that I probably did best that was a gift was I could run to daylight. I could find the soft spot, the hole. A lot of times back then we scramble blocked so I just had to find the hole.

My biggest challenge was my freshman year because freshman were not eligible to play. I was high school player of the year at Oklahoma and I came to OU and I found out real quick that I was just another player. We had like 60-70 players on scholarship. So I really struggled my freshman year and thought about quitting a couple of time.

So a funny story, I called my dad and I am one of 11 kids and I told him "Dad, I think I am going to quit and come back home" and he said "Where are you going to stay?" and I said "I am just going to move back with you" and he said "We don't have any room, you need to keep your ass right there at OU". That was great advice. He was telling me I needed to suck it up and stay there. And I did.

My biggest disappointment was the fact that I wanted to play longer in the NFL. I felt that if I stayed healthy I was the type of player that could play 10 years in the NFL. But I got injured my rookie year, I dislocated my shoulder and had to have a shoulder operation and missed most of the year. I came back the next year and had a 1,000 yard year and I was All-Pro in 1972. It is tough enough to play the game when you are completely healthy.

The most important aspect that made the team work so well together was that we loved each other. We cared for each other. I am still very close to my teammates and the guys that coached me. We were truly a family.

Sometimes I think the word "family" is a little over stated or overused, but we knew that the only way that we were going to reach the level we wanted to reach was to be extremely close. When I think about my football career I think about my teammates and coaches first because the relationships I built with those guys were lifelong relationships and we would die for each other. That was the greatest part of playing football for me. The victories were great and winning the Heisman was great but the best part was my relationships with my teammates.

10. My most talented teammate was Eddie Hinton, a great wide receiver and wingback. He could do everything. He was a tremendous athlete. He made everything look easy. Also, Steve Zabel because in 1968 we were short on defense and he played both ways. Steve was a decathlon track guy. He was a great athlete and could absolutely do anything.

AN ERA OF GREATNESS: COACH BOB DEVANEY'S FINAL FOUR SEASONS (1969 - 1972)

11. My most talented opponent was Nebraska's Wayne Meylan. We had a good offense and I think that he shut it down personally.

12. In 1968 after we beat NU badly, I was at the midfield with Coach Devaney and Coach Fairbanks. I think they coached together at Michigan State. I remember that Coach Devaney told Coach Fairbanks that this was the best team he had ever played against. I had great respect for him as a coach. I later went on a NU-OU cruise with Switzer and Devaney, and I got a chance to know him. We were together about 7-8 days. What a wonderful guy. He was such a gentleman. And I think his coaching speaks for itself. Great football coach and guy.

13. I think NU fans are the top in the country. We have great fans here at OU but I am still impressed when I go to Nebraska. I came up there this last year for an OU-NU game and every time I walk into Memorial Stadium it is just a special place with special people. I have to say this to Nebraska people – of all the teams we played in the Big 8 or out of conference, Nebraska fans were the best people to play in front of. They treated us with great respect and appreciated good football and expected good football not only from NU but OU. After the game everybody shook hands and were still friends.

In 2005 it was a tough game and close, but after the game we sat there and visited with the Nebraska folks and it has been the same since the first time I played there in 1967. I made a lot of trips to Lincoln and I think I speak for all Oklahomans that it is a special place in Lincoln. I think Oklahoma and Nebraska have a great kinship and mutual respect for each other's fans and players and coaches. It was funny when Coach Osborne was running for Congress we had a fundraiser here for him at Oklahoma and Coach Switzer hosted it. We raised a lot of Oklahoma money for him because we have great respect for him.

Nebraskan and Oklahoma have the best relationship. After that 1971 game, for the next 20 years that became the big game. It comes down to mutual respect. It is my favorite place to go see a football game. If I am not rooting for OU, I am rooting for Nebraska. It is just great venue for college football. I cannot say enough great things about them.

"NU fans are the top in the country... They treated us wtih great respect and expected good football now only from NU but OU."

"Nebraska and Oklahoma have the best relationship. It comes down to mutual respect. I cannot say enough great things about Nebraskans."

TINKER OWENS

OKLAHOMA WIDE RECEIVER (1972-1975)
ALL-CONFERENCE
Most Valuable Player in Sugar Bowl vs. Penn State (1973)

UPDATE

Married for 33 years

Sells insurance to banks and finance companies

Lives in Norman, Oklahoma

REFLECTIONS

1. In the Nebraska game in 1972 I caught 5 passes and was Sports Illustrated's Player of the Week. More people bring up my freshman year playing NU (1972) in Lincoln than any other game I played at OU. Oklahoma won in an upset (17-14). I guess I started out with a bang and went downhill from there. Fortunately my freshman year (1972) Dave Robinson became our quarterback after Mildren left. He was a 5th year senior out of a California Junior College and he could throw the football. Most of our quarterbacks at OU could not throw the ball but they could run like crazy. I was lucky to have him one year.

2. We were typically a running team and the wishbone did not throw the ball very often. I was not expecting to play against NU because I was behind John Carroll at receiver. But John hurt his knee during warm-ups and I ended up playing the game. Nebraska had us down 14-0 and it was cold, but we ended up winning (17-14). Johnny Rodgers was supposed to be the star of the game but he got hurt. Greg Pruitt was supposed to be the other star but Pruitt did not play. And that is why Joe Washington played. It was a heck of a game.

3. OU football changed my life. People know me and in business it is easier to get into certain doors. Professionally it has really helped me. I almost signed with the University of Arkansas coming out of high school but my brother Steve (Heisman winner 1969) said he was going to kick my rear if I went to Arkansas.

4. I think our four year record was 43-2-1. The back-to-back National Championships (1974-1975) mean more than anything. We were on probation in 1974 so we could not go to a Bowl game but we could win the National Championship. We were 11-0 and that would not happen in these times. That was a great accomplishment because I think the 1974 team was the best team I had my four years at OU. In 1975, we kind of backed into it because Ohio State was Number One and they got beat in the Rose Bowl. We defeated Michigan in the Orange Bowl.

5. Coach Switzer was a great coach to play for because he was such a player's coach. Fairbanks was a great guy but he was not close to the players and Switzer was. Everybody wanted Switzer to be the coach once Fairbanks left, and that all worked out and the rest is history.

6. My greatest memory of Coach Switzer was in the locker room. His speeches were really good before the games. He always believed in me as a player. Billy Brooks came in the spring of my freshman year and Billy was a great athlete. He was drafted in the first round and I was drafted fourth. But even though he was a heck of a player, I always started. What I respect the most about Coach Switzer is that he cares so much for his ex-players, and they mean so much to him. When we had an alumni game he introduced each player and he did not have a script. He knew what high school they went to and what they did, their whole career, and it is amazing that he remembered all of that. Back in those days we had 45 scholarships a year and now you have 25. He has helped a lot of players that needed help after they got out. He would loan them money or find them a job.

7. We were a very tight and close knit group of guys. I was really fortunate when I came to Oklahoma, because the Selmon brothers came in the same year (Leroy and Dewey and Lucius). And Joe Washington, Elrod and bunch of other guys. We had a heck of class.

8. We played Miami my sophomore year (1973) and Miami had us down at halftime. There was about a minute left in the game and I caught a post pattern against Ernie Jones for a touchdown to win the game. To me that was probably the biggest play that I ever made, but nobody ever talks about it. In fact Switzer

told me after the game that I was getting the game ball, but I never did get it.

9. One of my scariest moments was my senior year against Michigan (1975) in the Orange Bowl (14-6). I was punting. We were backed up and it was late in the game. I was kicking out of the back of the end zone and I did not have much room and we did not have a good snapper. I got a good snap and I kicked it about 30 yards. I knew that our defense was so good that Michigan was not going to score and they did not. The defense stopped them and we won the National Championship.

10. Steve Davis, our quarterback, was a great leader (1973-1975). Joe Washington was a quiet guy, but he was a leader by the way he played. Joe Washington is the best running back that I ever played with. The guy was phenomenal with the runs that he made. Greg Pruitt was a great player. They made things happened that other players could not do.

11. I was a skinny kid. I was 161 pounds when I came to OU. And I did not know if I was going to play any position. My freshman year we were playing Oregon and John Carroll got hurt, and they hollered for me to go in the game. I did not expect to play and I could not find my helmet. I finally found my helmet and ran out there. We had one running play and then we had a pass play. They called an out pattern and I dove and caught it. The announcer did not know who I was because I was not in the program.

12. I never lost to NU in my four years (1972-1975). But we always knew that NU was going to be tough. We always had great respect for NU. Fortunately for us our offense was good but our defense was even better. NU and Texas were our big rivals.

13. I always practiced hard and did the best that I could. I gave 110% on the field. I was always prepared and studied the films.

14. My biggest challenge was making sure that I worked hard and Billy Brooks did not take my position. That was my biggest motivator. I knew that I had a guy behind me that was very talented.

15. My biggest disappointment was the 1975 season. We lost to KU in Norman and we turned the ball over 11 times that day. I was the punter and they blocked a punt. We lost 20-3. They had a good team but it was a game that we should have won. We then played

Missouri the next week and we are down 27-20. It is 4th and 2 and we ran an option play to Joe who runs 72 yards and scores a touchdown. Then we scored a two point conversion and won 28-27. We did win the national championship by defeating Michigan in the Orange Bowl (14-6).

16. Joe Washington was the most talented player that I ever played with, including those in the NFL. He could do so many things.

17. I did not get to know the Nebraska fans until after I was through playing. A few years ago I went to Lincoln and OU won. I have never been around fans that said "hey, you played a great game and you deserved to win." They are great fans.

18. Oklahoma fans are pretty fickle. We have great fans, but they expect to win every game. I will never forget the KU game when we were down at halftime and we came out to warm up a little bit and our fans were booing. And Steve Davis asked "Are they booing us or the other team?" And I said "the other team is not out here yet." Here we had won all these football games. We had not lost a game at home and we tied USC at the coliseum, and they were Number One in the country. I could not believe our fans were booing us, and it got worse the second half. But overall we have good fans and a good following. Kind of like NU, football is king in Oklahoma.

19. Playing for OU helped me phenomenally in the after football life. Getting into doors and people know you. I can call people and they know my name. I can get in the door.

20. I feel appreciated by the University for the time I put in. We try to help as much as we can. They keep the alumni very involved.

GREGORY D. PRUITT *(the "D" stands for dangerous)*

OKLAHOMA RUNNING BACK (1969-1973)
ALL-AMERICAN (1971-1972)
HEISMAN TROPHY RUNNER-UP (1972)

UPDATE

Married to Mary for 22 years

Drafted in the second round by Cleveland Browns and played 9 years with them and then 3 years with the Oakland Raiders

Shaker Heights, Ohio

REFLECTIONS

1. All of the OU-NU games were exciting. They could have gone either way. And both teams lived up to the billing. That is what made that 1971 game so different - we lived up to all the hype in the Game of the Century.

2. I had a shirt that said Hello and Goodbye. We were going to play USC which would was ranked Number One at the time. And Switzer created this shirt "hello/goodbye" and he gave it to me and told me that he wanted me to wear it. Before I could get to the dormitory I was surrounded by TV reporters. They are taking pictures. Later on that   day we go to practice and he calls everybody up and showed every-one this t-shirt and showed a picture that the people had taken and they were going to put it the paper. And he said "Pruitt, it better be hello goodbye because I know it is hanging in the locker room at USC by now." USC was a great team, but when they crossed into that Big 8 territory it was a whole different scene.

3. The Big 8 conference at that time was the toughest conference without question. There is no dispute about that. I mean one, two, three in that nation and no conference had done that before. The only teams that beat us was among us. No one else beat us.

4. Our best leader was quarterback Jack Mildren. He was definitely a coach in a football uniform. I don't think the wishbone would have ran as well as it ran without Jack playing the way he played. We called a timeout so he could get his head together because he would take licks. In order for the option to work, when you flow right along left the defense flows with you. If you don't do anything to make them hesitate, stop or react, then their flow is going to stop the play. We had fast enough guys so that all we needed was that second hesitation to get beyond the line of scrimmage and Jack provided that because he would always challenge that last guy.

5. My personal goal was to play in the pros. I guess around my junior year I started to think that I may have had a chance to play pro. My size was always a question mark.

6. Our team goal was to win the National Championship. I have always kidded and told people in the Big 8 if an OU coach wanted to keep his job and only win three games it would have to be Texas, Nebraska and Oklahoma State.

7. The most important reasons for the wins was that we were very knowledgeable. The one thing I remember when I came out of high school and went into college and it helped me also in the pros was as a running back we were always taught "even to the right, odd to the left, zero hold 2, 4, 6, 8, 1, 2, 3, etc." When we ran the wishbone and Jack got involved with it we started getting into the game in terms of "not 2 hold not outside." We started to read defenses. So we knew based on defensive formations what they could or could not do. I think that was our special aspect of the wishbone. We were all like quarterbacks because we read defenses.

8. Because of how the coaches made us prepare and read defenses (to take what they gave us) we had a tremendous amount of confidence. It was an unusual confidence in that we thought we could beat anybody. But when we played Texas and Nebraska, we knew they were good teams and we did think they would be close games.

9. In the Game of the Century when Nebraska beat us (35-31), that could have gone either way. I think NU had an edge defensively. We could not hold Nebraska, and I missed a tackle on a punt return.

10. I believe that the two best teams ever played in the Game of Century in 1971. Those were some great times and games. It is great tradition. OU fell off for a minute with Stoops coming in, but they regained it. But tradition was real important to schools like NU and OU and Texas.

11. It was disappointing when the Big 12 eliminated the annual NU-OU game. They should have made an exception where OU and NU could continue to play each other every year.

12. To motivate myself before a game, I had a routine. When I ate or slept or whatever my habits stayed the same. Maybe I was superstitious but I felt if I did the same thing week in and week out, I would get the same results.

13. For conditioning I used to run the stadium steps hundreds of times. Football is in 30 seconds recovery periods. You have to run full speed and then in less than 30 seconds run full speed again. So you have to condition yourself the way that you are going to play.

14. My biggest challenge was that I was a pass receiver coming to OU. I went from starting to second team running back. I told my Momma I was going to leave, and she told me I couldn't.

15. Iowa State had not beaten OU in 30 years and they had us 21-0 at halftime. Edward Marshal was the guy that started in front of me and he got hurt in that game. I came in and ran for a touchdown and the rest is history. He never got his job back.

16. In the 1971 NU game OU wanted to catch NU by surprise. Everybody knew we were going to run the football. So, we decided we would pass. I was totally disappointed with that move, but I understood the strategy. They told me that "they are going to be keying on you, Greg, and that is why we are going to throw the ball and use you as a decoy."

17. If I could go back and change one thing it would be keeping my lane on Johnny's punt return in 1971.

18. The most important aspect that made the team work so well together was Coach Switzer. He really was the brains of "the wishbone." He did things with the wishbone even more than Texas and Alabama. No one ran it like us. The incredible thing about the wishbone was on paper it was not hard to defend it. What people did not realize was how fast we were.

19. My most talented opponent was NU's Rich Glover. One of the mistakes we made was trying to let Brahaney handle Glover by himself. That was a big part of the outcome of the game. Brahaney needed help with Glover.

20. My most talented teammate was Joe Washington. The most inspirational was Joe Willey. He was a running back and a good kicker.

21. Fullback Leon Crosswhite surprised me the most with his toughness. When I hit Leon Crosswhite, I thought I hit a telephone pole. And he got up and helped me up. I quit playing defense because of him. He really played a big part in the wishbone because the fullback has to take so much punishment.

22. Barry Switzer was a players coach. He had a personality where players were very relaxed around him. He was not a tough guy who can't get close to you.

23. Nebraska fans had great fans. The OU and NU colors were so close I would just imagine that NU fans were our fans. Once the game started I was focused on the game.

24. After the game we would go to meetings and break down the game films. Switzer would watch every play 25 times. After a while you would just close your eyes and count. By 20, you opened your eyes and you would only have to watch it 5 more times.

BARRY SWITZER

ASSISTANT COACH, OKLAHOMA (1966-1972)
HEAD COACH, OKLAHOMA (1973-1989)
COLLEGE FOOTBALL HALL OF FAME

UPDATE

3 National Championships; 12 Big 8 Championships;

4th winningest coach in college history (.837)

Head Coach, Dallas Cowboys (4 years)
Super Bowl Championship

Lives in Norman, Oklahoma

REFLECTIONS

1. My favorite story of Coach Fairbanks (OU Head Coach 1966-1972). Chuck Fairbanks and I came as assistant coaches in 1966 when Jim McKenzie came from Arkansas. I was on the Arkansas staff and McKenzie was the Assistant Head Coach and got the Oklahoma job. And Chuck joined us from Houston. Chuck became the Head Coach and I was the Assistant Coach.

   We talked to him about changing the offense and switching to the wishbone. The fans had all those "Chuck Chuck" bumper sticker all over because we were struggling and people wanted more than that. Things were not going very well and I said to Chuck "I am sick of looking at those "Chuck, Chuck" bumper stickers." And he says "Hell, if you were the head coach it would be "Bury Barry" bumper stickers. We then went to the wishbone and turned it around and they got rid of those bumper stickers. I got a patented trademark on "Bury Barry" bumper stickers so no one could ever use that one. Chuck Fairbanks was a good football coach and he shocked me when he took the pro job. He asked me to go with him to New England but I told him that I would rather stay here and have an Oklahoma job. I see him about once a year.

2. Coach Bob Devaney was great and fun to be around. We would go to Big 8 Conference meetings, and Bob and I would be the last ones to leave the parties. Most of the coaches would leave and Bob and I would still be drinking a beer and laughing. The greatest story I think about Bob is back in 1980 when I called Tom Osborne and tried to get Tom to hook up with

Oklahoma either in an Orange Bowl or Sun Bowl tie up. They did not want a part of the Sun Bowl. There was a lot of stuff in the papers about Nebraska was Orange Bowl or bust and if Oklahoma lost we would go to the Sun Bowl and if we won we would go to the Orange Bowl.

But Nebraska would not go for it and come Friday night we are in Lincoln to play the game and I ran into Dick Janna down there at the TV station. I am doing a feedback to Oklahoma City and I see this set and I ask Dick what is this for? And he said Bob Devaney does his show live on Friday nights. And I said "really, what time?" and he said "10:30." I sent one of the stage hands down to Taco Bell to get me a sack of tacos and I said "I will be on your show but only if I can surprise Devaney and come out during the show." And I did that and walked out on the stage and shocked Devaney. And then I handed him a sack of tacos because he made the statement "Where Switzer is going he really is going to love Mexican food, and where we are going we are going to eat a lot of seafood."

Fortunately, the next day we were able to win the ballgame and we got to go to Miami and Nebraska went to the Sun Bowl. So, the next year Devaney gets even. We are doing a live feed from Oklahoma into Nebraska from Oklahoma City and I am doing a show with Dean Blevins and Dean does not tell me that Bob has set up something. Well in the middle of this live show all of a sudden this girl walks out there with this boom box and sets it on the desk in front of me and starts playing this Gypsy Rose Lee music and starts undressing down to a stripper's outfit. Then she drops in my lap and starts hugging and kissing me. All of a sudden I look around and I said "You know, I don't see you anywhere, Bob Devaney, but I know damn well you have something to do with this." Bob was always a great guy. He came around win or lose. I always have fond memories of him and Don "Fox" Bryant and cared very much about both of them. He was Nebraska football to me.

3. Coach Tom (Osborne) is totally different from Bob. He is a great football coach and I always remember that game in 1978 when he beat us and we were ranked Number One in the country and undefeated. That is the year Billy Sims won the Heisman and we lost 17-14. And I am walking out there to shake hands with Tom, and Tom and I have laughed about this since. I stick out my hand and about this time a wave of red fans just swept me away and I go tumbling to the ground and Tom disappears in a sea of red. Tom always talks about that and laughs that I disappeared in a sea of red, and he never saw me again that day. That it something that sticks out vividly in both of our minds. Tom and I have always had good conversations through the years. We always had a fine professional relationship and mutual respect for each other. I never did have any beer drinking stories with Tom.

4. The most remarkable play at OU `69-`72 was in 1972, when we won in Lincoln. The best play was knocking Johnny Rodgers' ass out of the game. Also, Tinker Owens making those catches because we won the game (17-14) and he made a bunch of big receptions to keep drives alive.

5. The biggest offensive play that NU made in 1971 was when OU's Raymond Hamilton had Jerry Tagge in his grasp on 3rd down and 8 to go and Tagge got away. Nebraska was in desperation, and Johnny Rodgers received the ball for about a 9 yard gain. That was the biggest play because if Tagge did not get that pass off, Raymond tackles him and we get possession of the ball and we would probably win. It was the biggest because it won the National Championship for Nebraska and kept OU from winning one.

6. The best defensive play NU made in 1971 is difficult. They made a bunch of them. Rich Glover was a dominate player up front. It is usually a group that makes a play.

7. The best leader for Oklahoma was QB Jack Mildren.

8. Our team goals were to win the Big 8 and contend for national. NU and OU were the two teams and everybody knew that. They had tremendous respect for our programs. We brought out the best in everybody. Our goal was the same as NU. That is why the Orange Bowl had more national championships than any other bowl game. OU and NU are the ones that did it. Won 13 of them because of NU and OU.

9. Nebraska was the most dominate team during the 1969-1972 period. We had a down year in 1969 even though we had a bunch of good players (3 first round draft picks in 1969). We did not do a good job offensively and I don't think I did a good job that year. I look back on that era as NU being the best program. But we were a close second.

10. NU and OU had an honorable rivalry and one of the reasons is the distance that separates us. We never recruited against each other. We were isolated from each other. We did not have bordering states. The only time we came into contact with Nebraska is when we played at Lincoln or they came to Norman. We constantly competed against Texas and we fought for the same players. We are bordering states in closer proximity. Our media created a closeness that made it more competitive here with those other schools in the Southwest Conference. But Nebraska was a program that was further removed. And we never really had any controversy with NU. Both schools and teams had great admiration and respect for each other.

11. The secret to being a "players coach" is that I cared about our players. And the players knew I cared about them and that they could count on me. I loved my players. I loved some more than others not because they were first team but because of who they were and how they represented themselves and the choices they made along the way. We had a closeness. They believed in me and that I sincerely cared for them. That was probably one the keys to my success.

12. The biggest challenge was trying to the right things for the team. Trying to keep focused. You never can do everything right, but you always tried to present the right option for your team and to present the right picture for them. My goal was to present an attitude of confidence and belief in being successful and striving and paying a tremendous price for the goals we set for ourselves. Football is nothing but a game of physical and mental repetition. Doing certain things over and over is how you get good at it.

13. One of my biggest disappointments in the Game of the Century was not throwing the ball a little bit more. I think if Jack Mildren had thrown the ball 4-5 more times (play action or wide out) we might have won the ball game. But I had more pluses than minuses. I had a pretty good run.

4. The most important aspect that made the OU teams work so well together were that we had a good staff and good players, just like Nebraska did. Nebraska and Oklahoma had better talent than other teams. Opponents did not have a Johnny Rodgers or a Gregg Pruitt. What separated us in the era was talent in all positions. It was not that Tom is a better football coach or Barry Switzer is a better football coach. We played against a lot of good football coaches, but my teams and Tom's teams were more talented most of the time. If we made the fewest mistakes with our talent level, we won the football game.

5. The greatest defensive football player I coached was Leroy Selmon. On offense it is hard to say. I had some great backs (Pruitt, Joe Washington, Billy Sims). It is a toss-up. Little Joe was probably the most evasive and the hardest to tackle. He was like a Barry Sanders and Johnny Rodgers. I have always said this many time publicly "in my career, (my years of 60s, 70s, 80s, 90s) looking at football players that played in the Big 8 Conference (before the Big 12 in 1996) there were three players that I saw in my tenure that made your heart jump in your throat when they were in the open field. Those 3 were Johnny Rodgers, Joe Washington and Barry Sanders. Those 3 guys struck fear in your heart when they got open space because they are going to score."

6. NU had a bunch of great defensive players. Rich Glover was the dominate player in that era. He was the hub of the defense.

7. NU fans were the greatest fans in the world. I have always said that I hope our fans are as good as the Nebraska fans, but I don't think we are. Nebraska had the greatest reception and warmth and hospitality that was given to an opponent and it has always been that way. I don't know if it is in the water or innate or breeding or whatever it is. But NU fans have always treated opponents with such class and dignity. Win or lose, they were always that way.

8. Currently, I am involved in a bunch of different things in investments. I live here in Norman right by the campus.

9. Bob Devaney brought Nebraska football to greatness. And Tom Osborne maintained it.

"NU and OU had an honorable rivalry... both schools and teams had great admiration and respect for each other."

"Coach Bob Devaney was great fun to be around..."

"NU fans were the greatest fans in the world."

JOE WASHINGTON *(aka "Little Joe")*
ALL-AMERICAN RUNNING BACK AND KICK RETURNER
[OKLAHOMA (1972-1974)
Pro Football (San Diego)

TODAY

Stockbroker for Wachovia

Married 30 years (to Meadow Lark); daughter (Brandi, 23)

Lutherville, Maryland

REFLECTIONS

1. Greg Pruitt and I missed the bus to the game when we were playing Kansas State. We had to call the State Police to take us to the game and we got there before the team did. And Coach Chuck Fairbanks called Greg and I in to talk, and Greg told me "let me do all the talking." And I said "Sure, you are the senior and I am just a little old freshman." So he called me " a jackass freshman" and I called Greg "a horseshit Heisman Trophy candidate." I thought I would die laughing.

2. Coach Chuck Fairbanks used to have a problem with the way I carried the ball and holding it in one hand. When I got there no one was doing that. By the end of the year at practice everybody was grabbing the ball like that. He wanted me to tuck it in so as soon as I tucked it no one touched me and it just flew out of there. He never said anything to me afterward.

3. My first memory of Coach Barry Switzer was after that Kansas State game and we were watching film on Sunday morning. He said "Look Joe, what are those damn things on your feet?" And I said "Those are my silver shoes, coach" and he did not say another thing. He said "okay" and just kept running the film back and forth. My junior year we were in the process of preparing for Colorado and their Coach Malrey was talking about Barry and how the players were undisciplined and had no control. Malrey made the statement that "just to show you how undisciplined they are, anybody that would let a kid wear silver shoes tells you a whole lot about that program." So, Barry called me over and said "Look, Joe, god damn it. You got my ass in trouble with those shoes." And I said "what do you mean?" Then he told me the story and I said "Coach what do you want me to do?" and he said

"put a couple of hundred on them" and at halftime I had a 190 yards against Colorado.

4. With Barry I could go on for days and days. I used to baby-sit his kids, and he would always tell folks that he paid me 100 bucks. Well, I don't remember it that way. I thought it was a chance to make a little money. I am a little freshman and I am getting a chance to baby-sit the kids, I am going to make a few "dead presidents." So I said "Coach how much I am going to make?" and he said "I am going to pay you like I pay all my other babysitters." Man, Coach paid me a $1.35 an hour. I probably made $3.70. He said in his book that he paid me $100. Who are you fooling.

5. I watched the Game of the Century in 1971. As a kid I wasn't sold on the wishbone. And I am watching NU run that I and running those little inside handoffs. I was really rooting for Nebraska but when it got tight and Nebraska went ahead I started rooting for Oklahoma. I always had a lot of respect for Devaney and Osborne and I never got the chance to meet them. That really stands out because we had such fierce battles and I admired them from afar.

6. You always knew each year that OU and Nebraska were going to play for Big 8 Championship. I don't remember any trash talking. Nebraska just came out and whether you won or lost you were going to get a physical beating. I never could block Willie Harper. He was big and tall and used his hands real well. He used his feet real well and kept you off of him.

7. I played against NU my freshman year in 1972 (17-14 OU win). I made a couple of good runs and actually scored the final touchdown for us to go ahead for good. Nebraska had Rich Glover and Willie Harper, and all these other guys that don't give up much yardage defensively. So that was probably the first true highlight in my career at OU. The whole world is watching because you have the two challengers for the Heisman trophy (Johnny Rodgers and Greg Pruitt).

8. It was tough when we lost to Kansas in 1972, but you could tolerate a loss to NU. You don't like losing to NU but you know if someone is going to beat you it is going to be NU. Nebraska has an unbelievable tradition of good football teams. There was a certain respect. You know if you walked on the field and are not ready, it's "Good Night Irene." They are going to "tear up your shoelaces."

9. My freshman year (1972) everybody always looked for Greg Pruitt to set the stage. Like with Johnny Rodgers at NU, everyone basically started with something from him. That symbolized transition.

10. Coach Barry Switzer would come by and say "gentlemen, you have never experienced a game until you experience playing against Texas and Nebraska." And if you come here half stepping you are going to get your butts kicked. These guys will hit you. He would always tell everybody to look out for Rich Glover because he covers the field. Everything Coach Switzer would tell you was the gospel. Playing Nebraska was always something that you looked forward to.

11. 1972 was the first year freshman were eligible. I am from Port Arthur, Texas. I just wanted to play in the same backfield with Greg Pruitt. And when I got to OU I was probably 15th on the depth chart, and everybody could fly.

12. The most important reasons for the Oklahoma wins were: (a) that Coach Barry Switzer did not care who got the credit for winning. He delegated things to his assistants and that made a difference. We were a good group of guys and respected each other. (b) But the key to us winning was the Selmon brothers on defense. Leroy Selmon was gospel and they were all good guys. During those years, we could do anything we wanted on offense, (throw the ball on the ground, drop it, kick it) and you did not have to worry about the opponent getting six points. If they were lucky, they might get three.

13. Motivating myself before the game all started during practice. Being a coach's son, it was instilled in me that was the way you got ready for football games. Your motivation was just making sure that every time you touch the ball in practice you imagine going the same way you would in a game.

14. My biggest challenge was blocking. I thought I was a good blocker in college, but I did not know what blocking was until I got a chance to watch Greg Pruitt.

15. My biggest disappointment was losing to Kansas. And not being able to have the type of stats my senior year. I was hurt the whole year. I did not miss any game but I was really beat up. I was wearing a metal plate in my football shoe. And that was tough because everybody was promoting and pushing me for the Heisman and I was not able to play on television (OU was on probation by the NCAA).

16. The most important reason that made the team work so well together was talent. Going into my senior year (1975) we were probably not as good as we thought we were. But we worked real hard in practice and that made a huge difference.

17. Coach Stoops has embraced the Old School. Also, the Athletic Department has enough respect that they want them to come back. They want to keep these ghosts around. If you do not embrace the past players who created this situation, they will be the first ones after your ass when things are not going right. But if you embrace them and bring them into the family when things are not going right, they will be the first ones to support you and surround the wagons. And a lot of other universities don't do that. Stoops and Stigleon make sure that they have a lot of events where they try to get players back. And that has been huge.

18. What was it like to run on the field for the 1st time in front of NU fans? To come and see a crowd in red like that (and it was not your red) was very intimidating. There is nothing like it. NU fans were very respectful of good football. In contrast, I remember at Iowa State I got hit with a 6 pack of beer in the end zone and thank goodness I had my helmet on. And we were taunted at other places. But at NU there was always a respectful environment that you enjoyed being in.

19. I feel appreciated by Oklahoma University for the time I put in. To this day it is one of those warm fuzzy feelings. You know that the people still think about you and hold you in high regard. It is one of those amazing things when a little kid about 8-9 years old will run up to you and say "Little Joe, Little Joe" and here I am 900 years old. That is a real good feeling with things being perpetuated. OU fans are unbelievable to this day. They make me feel as if I had never left. They remember everything, and it is bigger than it was.

STEVE ZABEL

OKLAHOMA TIGHT END; DEFENSIVE END (1967-1969)
Pro Football (6 years) New England

REFLECTIONS

1. In 1967 we were the league champs. Undefeated in the conference. We lost one game to Texas. We beat NU at Lincoln 21-14. Nebraska really had some good players. Wayne Meylan was an absolute terror on defense. He was an All-American nose guard.

2. My senior year I primarily blocked for Steve Owens. When I got into pro football they did not have any rules. There was not a 5 yard cushion on pass interference. So I got kicked out of 3 games for fighting my rookie year. And at the end of the year my coaches came up to me and said "Steve you don't have the appropriate aptitude or perspective to be successful on offense." So they asked me to switch to defense which I loved more anyway. I was fortunate to have played both ways my junior year at OU.

3. I went to kindergarten in Nebraska at the Winnebago reservation. My mom's family was from Winnebago – back to the 20s. I have fond memories of Nebraska and I had the ultimate respect for Nebraska. People in Oklahoma wanted to talk about what a great rivalry Texas and OU was but to me it was not even close. Nebraska was the rivalry.

4. I got recruited by Oklahoma and went there and loved it from the very beginning. My favorite moment from the Nebraska games would have to be in 1967. The score was tied 14-14. And we ran an option and my job was to come down and be the lead interference for Eddie Hinton with the pitch. I made my block and very luckily ended up getting both the cornerback and the safety and Eddie ran it in for a touchdown.

5. My cleverest memory would have to be in 1969. For some strange reason we played Nebraska at our place two years in a row. It was Friday afternoon and we were just getting ready to come off the field and Coach Devaney showed up with his team. And Coach Fairbanks called him over and introduced us to Devaney and he seemed like such a great guy. Devaney said "Now you boys embarrassed us on television last year. So please go easy on us. We are still not very good." And they beat us 44-14. He suckered us in.

6. The toughest offensive player I faced playing for NU was Joe Orduna. He was damn good.

7. The best defensive player for NU was Wayne Meylan. Wayne Meylan was super tough.

8. Our best leader was our captain, Jim Files. Jim was the 13th pick in the first round by the New Giants in the 1970 draft. And of course Steve Owens was a leader. Bobby Womack was a great quarterback `67-68. And he and Eddie Hinton could run that option to a T. It was pretty amazing. Eddie Hinton was unbelievable during that year and he was a first round draft choice with Baltimore (1969). In 1967 we had a tremendous defense. Our defense gave up under 7 points a game. We had four shutouts and ended up winning the Big 8 and playing in the Orange Bowl beating Tennessee. This was a time when they did not vote for the National Championship after the Bowl Games. I think we might have won it but OJ Simpson and Southern Cal were Number One before the Bowl Games were announced.

9. It was a great experience for me through my association with Oklahoma. The rivalry we had with Nebraska and the ultimate respect that we had for NU. It gave me a chance to meet guys like Johnny Rodgers and Mike Rozier.

10. My personal goal when I showed up was just to survive. Our era was so much different. We were the tail end of coaches still being able to kick you in the ass. Switzer said "we looked at you guys as a group and there were only a couple difference makers in this group. And so we are going to make it as hard as we can and see if we can't develop some difference makers so we can win some football games." We had 4th quarter classes and 2-a-days and guys were leaving in droves. My senior year we only had 7 seven guys left in our entire junior class out of 75. That is how tough it was.

1. Before we started the 1968 season our goal collectively was to help Steve Owens win the Heisman trophy. That is the respect we had for him. And we were successful in that endeavor. Because of Steve's abilities and him winning the Heisman trophy he was very gracious and included me in the festivities. I cherish that relationship.

2. The most important reasons for the wins were (a) we were a tough team. We were coached tough. Our coaches were so demanding. We would run the same play sometimes 30 times in a row (b) we had some really underrated players that were overachievers that rose to the occasion. We won two Big 8 Championships while I was there. We could have gone to a Bowl Game when we were 6-4. We were bowl eligible and we voted as a team not to go because we were embarrassed about the season.

3. OU football helped me succeed since my football playing days. I had a coach named Elden Holly and he was from Alabama. One time I got knocked down and he hollered "Zabel, get off that damn ground boy. That ground is your enemy." And I learned early on that life was a series of games. There are going to be good times and there are going to be bad times and how you handle good and bad is going to be the judge of where you go in life. I learned how to compete and be responsible and do the little things right.

4. My biggest challenge was overcoming a series of injuries.

5. My biggest disappointment was never getting to the Super Bowl. Never winning a national championship. I was close with both with the Patriots and Oklahoma.

6. When you think Nebraska you think football. When you think Oklahoma you think football. Tom Osborne and Bob Devaney are kings down here. And Switzer could probably run for governor in Nebraska.

7. The most important aspect that made Oklahoma's team work so well together (coaches, players, talent, attitude) was that cocky confidence that was on the field. The first minute I met Switzer, he grabbed my hand and said "We want you to come here. If you come here you will be an All-American and we will win a national championship and we will win the Big 8. What do you think?" I said "Where do I sign up, coach?"

18. From the moment you get on campus at Oklahoma you are indoctrinated into the fellowship and we have always had a very active O club. We started about 10 years ago our Football Letterman's Association. We developed that when I graduated from OU after my eligibility was up. I actually played in the Annual Alumni Game in 1970 and back in those days it was really competitive. Full contact football with no holds barred.

19. During my football career I came back for games and you would show up on Tuesday and it would run until Sunday. It was all the guys back together and playing in golf tournaments and drinking beers and having fun.

20. When I was playing pro football I was still living back in Oklahoma in the off-season. The coaches could have luncheon for recruits and invite key alumni to come and mingle with the kids. The first one that I went to Switzer was addressing the recruits about why they should come to Oklahoma. And Switzer above everything is a "what you see is what you get kind of a guy." He put it on everybody so hard that by the time that you left I wanted more eligibility. Switzer because of his background and his upbringing and his relationship skills had an ability to create a trust factor with people. He is a fierce competitor and is as sincere as the day is long. He has got the biggest heart and the most compassion.

SALUTING THE
ILLUSTRIOUS NEBRASKA-OKLAHOMA RIVALRY

There is one thing that all Nebraska fans and all Oklahoma fans can agree upon. And most college fans in general would concur. The NU-OU game should be played *every year!*

When the Big 12 Conference began in 1996, it was structured so that OU and NU would play for 2 consecutive years and then take a break for 2 consecutive years. That is a shame because the rivalry has been one of the finest in all of sports. It has been respectful, clean and classy. It has elevated the level of the college game in general. It has been a model for good sportsmanship and mutual respect.

It also produced more National Championships than any other college rivalry over the past 56 years (5 by Nebraska and 7 by Oklahoma).

The overall record of NU against OU is very close (1912-2005):

(1)	15 - 3 - 3	. . .	Era One (1912-1940)
(2)	3 - 17 - 3	. . .	Era Two (1941-1961)
(3)	19 - 20 - 0	. . .	Era Three (1962-2003)
(4)	0 - 2 - 0	. . .	Era Four (2004 . . .)
	37 - 42 - 6	. . .	**Total**

In the 56 seasons from 1950 through 2005, NU and OU have played 52 regular season games, and this illustrious rivalry has produced a combined total of the following championships:

(1) **44 Conference Championships** (85%)
(Big 7, Big 8, Big 12)

(2) **12 National Championships** (23%)

"Courage; Generosity; Fairness; Honor;
In these are the true
awards of manly sport."

Memorial Stadium, inscription in stone on the
northwest corner (1923), written by Hartley Burr
Alexander, UNL Professor of Philosophy.

■

"The spirit, the will to excel,
the will to win, they ENDURE, they last forever.
These are the qualities that are
larger and more important than any
of the events that occasion them."

Vince Lombardi (1967),
The most successful pro football coach of All-time.
("When Pride Still Mattered," Maraniss, 1999, p.402)

■

"And if, by mischance,
you should happen to fall,
There are worse things in life
than a tumble on heather,
And life is itself but a
game of football."

Sir Walter Scott (1815)
(Stanza 5 of a song, in England on the lifting of the
banner of the House of Bucceuch at a great football
match at Carterbaugh)

AN ERA OF GREATNESS: COACH BOB DEVANEY'S FINAL FOUR SEASONS (1969 - 1972)

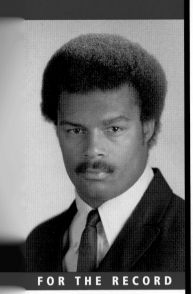

JOHN ADKINS, JR. *(aka "Spider")*

LEFT DEFENSIVE END

HUSKER HIGHLIGHTS

1. To me NU seemed like a perfect machine in 1970-1972. Coach Devaney was like a general. Coach Osborne was very intelligent. Coach Kiffin really knew defense. I think we were destined to be Number One with that coaching staff. With the players we had we could not miss.

2. Nebraska fans were incredible. They were totally behind the team. After we beat Oklahoma in the game of the century (1971) when we landed at the airport in Lincoln there were 30,000 plus people. It was amazing.

3. Knowing our players was a wonderful experience. We had a bunch of guys from different backgrounds and areas and we got together as a team. We felt like we were a family. The best thing about it was that everyone got along.

4. Our opponents were tough. During the second championship year (1971) we were so confident in the team, but we never disrespected an opponent. I always went out there and thought that we have to play our hardest. Later I would watch guys in the pros like John Riggins running over people and realized that we stopped this guy. I remember a later interview with John Riggins (All Pro Fullback) who said "Nebraska's football team could be a professional team". That is a hell of a statement. Coach Tom (Osborne) later became a hell of a head coach. Then Coach Kiffin later became one of the top defensive coaches in the NFL. Selmer could have been a head coach. Corgan was good. Fischer too. Powers and Thunder Thornton. They played in the pros, and then came back to NU. Anyone of them could have been a head coach. I think Devaney was smart because he let his coaches coach.

5. I remember that I got dropped down to second team and I said to myself "man, I got to get back on the good side of Devaney". I remember talking to him and he said "look, you are a good player but you can't be skipping the films". True to his word, he said if I worked hard I would get my position back, and I did.

6. The NU experience was wonderful for me because we had a top team, with a bunch of guys I liked, and having a school that is good academically, was the best of situations. NU is so well known for its football team, but it is also an excellent school academically.

7. The most remarkable offensive play I witnessed was Johnny Rodgers' punt return at Oklahoma in 1971 in the Game of The Century. During that run I was getting ready to block an OU player and he turned his back. I hit him and I thought "man, this is going to be a dog-gone clip". Years later I was at a bar in Denver, Colorado and they were playing these old highlights. One of the highlights they showed was Johnny's run. They showed the part when I was getting ready to block one of these guys and he turned his back. This guy next to me said "Oh, man he got clipped" and I said "No, it wasn't a clip. The guy turned his

back so it can't be a clip." He said "no, no he got clipped" and I said "No, no, I was the guy".

9. If you get a touchdown being a defensive player it is always memorable. One time I got a touchdown. Willie Harper came one way and hit the guy and the ball was in the air, and I caught it and ran for a touchdown.

10. One of the funniest games was going to Hawaii. Roasting the pig on the beach was the best.

11. Playing football prepares you for life because it is like a job. You have to show up on time, have to practice, and on and on. Once you have been on a National Championship team it's a tremendous confidence booster. Working on a team has helped me today in my career as an emergency room physician. There is teamwork. I am dependent on techs, nurses, x-ray techs and other physicians. It is a team effort and a lot of it I learned from playing football.

12. I often think about the Game of the Century with Oklahoma in 1971. We were the two top teams. My hat is off to Oklahoma because they had some incredible athletes. Just to be part of that was a great experience.

13. There were so many guys who were so strong in their particular positions. There was not just one guy who was the leader. Everyone stepped up. We had out-standing talent at every position.

14. My father was a garbage truck driver, and I was the first person in my family to go to college. To my parents the fact that I was going to college was great. I just wanted to get a college degree. In high school I always had good grades. My goals actually changed after I graduated from UNL. I took zoology and I got a very high grade in the course. There were a lot of pre-med people in there, and they said I should go into medicine and I did.

15. During my sophomore year (1969), we had a good team but no one was thinking national championship. When we won the Sun Bowl against Georgia (45-6), people started to think that we had a pretty good team. We did not really think we were great until we went out to Southern California (1970) (21-21). And we tied them. Then people thought we had the potential to be a great team.

16. The 3 most important reasons for the wins were: (1) The talent of the coaches and players; (2) Putting that talent together. A lot of teams have great talent but someone has to put it together; (3) Confidence and hard work. I don't think we would have beaten Oklahoma (1971) if we did not have the confidence to think that we would beat them. OU was good enough to beat us, but we won strictly on confidence.

17. Winning the National Championship instilled confidence in me for the future. When I went back to school pre-med, I had to take all those tough pre-med classes. I had the brains to do it, but there is a confidence aspect that you also have to have. The confidence from playing football carried over – the confidence that you would succeed.

18. It is an honor to be considered the best. I look back and I have no regrets. Being a National Champion is one of the best feelings ever. I appreciated it then, but I appreciate it even more now.

19. My biggest challenge was making sure that I did not get distracted from school. It was hard to practice for 2-3 hours a day and then study, but I stayed focused.

20. I never thought about quitting except when I was a freshman. When I first got to NU I was skinny. I was about 185 pounds, and I was a track star. And they told me that I was going to be a split end. I could not catch the ball, and they realized that after about a week. I went from 1st team to 4th. I actually went down to the Army recruiter. The recruiter said to me "Go back to school and stick it out for a couple more weeks and then come and see me again". He must have been a football fan.

21. I had no disappointments playing at NU. I felt that maybe I could have played pro ball as a linebacker.

22. Our team chemistry was like a family. Daddy Devaney was the chief and you knew he was your daddy. The other coaches were your uncles (like coach Kiffin). Then you have all your brothers who you were playing with. A challenge to team chemistry can be having mega superstars with big heads. That can destroy a team, but we didn't have that problem.

23. My most talented teammate was Johnny Rodgers on offense. On defense it would have to be Willie Harper or Rich Glover.

24. I learned so much from Coach Kiffin. He was a players coach. He felt he was one of the guys, but you still respected him as a coach. When you messed up, you would feel like you were letting him down.

25. Practices were hard work. Like a job, it was serious. The part of practice I hated the most was running the stairs. After we started winning, practices did not seem that bad because we had a goal and we had to practice to reach our goal.

26. The fans clearly affected our efforts in the game. When you are playing for a state or community that is that supportive of a football team, you know that you have to give everything you have.

27. It was amazing to run on the field for the 1st time. There are all these fans in red. There is an excitement and electricity in the air.

28. Playing for Nebraska helped me in the after football life. It goes back to confidence and being Number One. You take the same things that made you work hard in football and apply them to life.

29. I feel appreciated by the University for the time I put in – more appreciated now than I probably did then.

30. My greatest memory is graduating and having that degree.

"There was not just one guy who was the leader. Everyone stepped up! Our team chemistry was like a family."

John Adkins runs down LSU quarterback Bert Jones, in the Orange Bowl victory.

Frosty and DeEtte

FROSTY ANDERSON

PASS RECEIVER

HUSKER HIGHLIGHTS

1. Nobody knows this one: Coach Devaney was at Michigan State when my dad was the head basketball coach at Michigan State. Devaney was coaching on the football team with Duffy Daugherty and so I knew all those guys when I was a little kid. Dad eventually takes a job at Hiram Scott in Scottsbluff, Nebraska. My junior year in high school I missed my flight from Lincoln to Denver. So my dad said "call Devaney and tell him to come and get you." I was like Oh, Okay. So, I call and it was a Sunday afternoon. I say "Coach Devaney, its Frosty Anderson and my dad told me to call. Can you take care of me for the afternoon" so he comes and gets me and we go to his house. I remember this distinctly. I had cold leftover chicken and I hung out for the next 3-4 hours until the next available flight. And he took me back out and I did not think two thoughts about that.

Then my senior year in high school I get a letter stating that they would like to offer me a scholarship to play football at UNL. I ended up at NU. That was funny. Talk about a personal connection with somebody. He never used that in the recruiting process, and he never allowed that to become part of the relationship when I was at the University. He kicked my rear just like anybody else's rear.

2. Bob gathered us together before the 71 season. UNL was the defending National Champion. We were starting out Number One again and we had the whole season in front of us. Devaney says that he wants us to remember this story: the big joke and local prank used to be to take some dog crap and put it in a newspaper and then set it on a person's front porch, light it on fire and ring the doorbell and run away. Devaney said when he was young he did it all the time, and would watch the people stamp out the fire and get dog crap on their feet. And he said "what's the moral of the story, boys? Watch out for the crap in the newspapers." That was his story. We all broke out in laughter. He told us that on the 50 yard line at Memorial Stadium. It was a good reminder that we could not rest on our laurels.

3. We were running pass patterns at a regular practice. There was a long pass and I missed it. Devaney is nowhere to be seen and out of the blue I hear this "God, Frosty, catch the ball" and it is Devaney. I have no idea where he was. There he was like a ghost hovering. I guess every play counts. The message was loud and clear.

4. Coach Corgan and Coach Clete Fischer would crack me up. They were great. They were the old school. They were men's men. The things I distinctly remember about Corgan was that he always wore a long sleeve sweatshirt no matter how hot it was and he had a cup of coffee with him out on the field. That always befuddled me.

5. Coach Kiffin and Coach Powers were the young guys. We dearly loved them and Kiffin, being the defensive coordinator, was just driven like a mad man. He led by example. He ran those defenders up and down those steps and he was right there with them.

During my sophomore year. We ran a play and Bruce Hauge, the linebacker, just unloaded on our running back. I said "Jesus Christ" out loud. And time,

Kiffin just skewered me. He said "What the hell is wrong with you. We all got pads on. You don't bitch about that. You play this game" We were all going half speed and Hauge was at fault.

6. One day during practice Terry Luck and I were playing catch. I had a bad arm and we are playing catch maybe 30-50 yards away from each other. So, I loft one out and it is way off course and he starts to move but Ozzie is coming toward him and Terry does not say anything. And Wham! it hits him right in the face and drops him, Ozzie, the head coach. I sprint up there and I get there right as Luck is helping him up. Osborne is saying "Dad gum, that about knocked me out." And he says "Dad gummit, who threw that?" I said "I don't know." The next day, I am at my locker and into my view comes the Oz, and he says "Frosty, did you throw that ball at me, yesterday?" Now, I am freaking out. And I say yeah and he says "Why didn't you tell me?" And he shook his finger at me and said 'I am going to get you for this" and his eye was totally bloodshot and he had a black eye. I know to this day it was Runty who ratted me out.

7. My greatest college moment was when I got in on a great play of Johnny Rodgers'. I am sitting on the sidelines at the Orange Bowl in 1973 against Notre Dame. Coach Selmer goes "what about that halfback pass?" And Devaney says "okay, we are going to run the halfback pass." I went out there and broke to my left and that was a perfect pass Johnny Rodgers threw. Two weeks before at practice we ran that play and Johnny said "yes, we are going to score on that." Who thought Johnny could predict the future.

8. Early on with Devaney it was a little louder group. We had Satch, Carstens, Chi-Chi Jamail, Terrio, Sloey. Those guys were wild. At that time, it was more acceptable to go down and hit the bars at night. It was fun. Those guys were my closest friends in college. Jeff Hughes, Johnny Rodgers, Rich Bahe, me, Jeff Hill, Kenny Adkins, Tim Brown from Boystown, Woody Cox, Revelle, that was our group. I was always singing or playing air guitar because I loved music.

9. I have fond memories of "Country Club" during practice (break time with orange slices and salty water). We used to look forward to that. That was heaven. George and Schnitzy were in charge of that.

10. The most remarkable offensive play I witnessed was the opening play of our freshman game against Oklahoma State down there. Johnny Rodgers did a kick off return for a touchdown, and he came back and threw up. He went out and won that game for us too.

11. In the Game of the Century in 1971 Tagge rolled right on an option. We did not do the option when he was there. And he faked the pitch and went down to the 2 yard line. That was a stunning play because we never did that before. He ran the option and ran it great. And we scored after that.

12. I learned that you have to completely throw yourself into something because it was a team deal. What I was doing was not for me. It was for everyone involved. You were part of a group. I learned to respect Devaney because that is how he sold the program. We get out there and we will do this. We all are in it together.

13. I would like to relive the UCLA game Devaney's last year (1972) because we lost (17-20) and should have won.

14. The most important reasons for the wins were that we were always prepared. We knew what the competition was capable of, but we approached those games with the mindset that we will do this. We never changed anything because of what an opponent did. We also never felt we were too good.

15. My senior year (1973) we thumped UCLA in Lincoln. Also, in that year, I won the scholar/athlete award where I am one of 11 athletes nation wide and we go to New York to the Waldorf Astoria for this big deal. I met Mark Harmon, the quarterback for UCLA. We talked about our game. He brought up the fact that we really stomped them. He said "We were scared of you guys. We go out there and all that red, I am surprised we even scored at all." We never thought we were going to stomp any team, but we were always ready for battle.

17. We had a great inspirational leader in Devaney and maybe that was the difference. We did what we were supposed to do.

18. My best motivation during the game was performing for the coaches. That is how you won your spot. Do what you are supposed to because you will be held accountable.

9. My biggest challenge was maintaining that college athlete schedule because my grades were really my biggest priority. I had to have my scholarship to stay in school and I needed to get an education that would help me in the future. I was disciplined about that.

0. I never thought about quitting.

1. My biggest disappointment was being dropped from the starting lineup my junior year after that UCLA game (1972).

2. The most important reasons that made the team work so well together were the coaches and developing the winning attitude. Devaney put together a winning group of coaches and we all focused on the same thing. They were able to convince us that we were of the highest caliber.

3. My most talented teammate was Johnny Rodgers. We counted on him to win games for us and he did, period.

4. The most inspirational teammate was Doug Dumler. I respected him and he had a smooth demeanor. If he was saying something that he thought was important I was going to listen.

5. What effect did the fans have on my efforts in the game? Consider this, you break into the opening and there is a long pass coming your way. You are trying to concentrate on it. As the ball gets closer all of a sudden you hear this collective crescendo as the ball got closer. The fans made situations hairier at times.

6. My greatest memory was winning that Game of the Century in 1971. I kind of stalked the defensive back and BAM! Kinney runs right over him. This was 3rd and 7, and Kinney runs right over him for 10 yards for a first down. That game meant the most for all of us.

7. Playing for Nebraska helped me in the after football life. It really helped me grow up a lot faster. Having to deal with the press and people who adored you for reasons that they shouldn't have. It was just a game but somehow the leadership all came together and, man, we had it all. It is important to be humble, but I was able to talk to adults and to interact in business situations without being intimidated. That gave me a big leg up in the first five or ten years out of school.

28. I definitely feel appreciated by the University for the time I put in. It's easy because (1) my name is easy to remember because it is different (2) and I caught that touchdown pass from Johnny Rodgers in the Orange Bowl. A big play really solidifies things for a person.

Frosty Anderson catches a touchdown pass from David Humm.*

"Nebraska fans were incredible. They were totally behind the team."

"We had a great inspirational leader in Devaney."

FOR THE RECORD

JIM ANDERSON
1969-1971

6'-0" 180 lbs.
Green Bay, WI

All Big 8 Defensive Back
Co-Captain 1971

NOW

Married (wife Karin),
1 daughter (Abby 22)

`74-`76 backfield
coach at New Mexico

Currently working at University
of New Mexico in the
banking department

Albuquerque, New Mexico

Jim and Karin Anderson

JIM ANDERSON

DEFENSIVE BACK

HUSKER HIGHLIGHTS

1. Coach Devaney used to yell at me a lot when I would screw up. My favorite memory is when he would get mad and chew us all out on the sidelines. One time at that first Orange Bowl vs. LSU (1971) I gave up a touchdown pass to put us behind (10-12), and he was screaming at me when I came to the sidelines. Bob would get mad sometimes, but he had a great sense of humor and was a great psychologist. I enjoyed his all around demeanor.

2. Coach Warren Powers was my position coach. Coach Ross was my coach when I was a red shirt.

3. The great support from Nebraska fans was the main reason that I went to NU from Green Bay, Wisconsin. I used to go around and give speeches at the high schools in Nebraska and the people in the State of Nebraska were just diehard and lifelong fans. Our football team, and the guys were about the most important thing they had to rally around. They would just be in awe and it was really fun to be around them because they were so proud of the team. They reminded me of the Green Bay Packer fans – loyal, diehard, lifelong fans.

4. My most memorable play was in 1970 when we played Oklahoma in Lincoln. We won 28-21. On the last play O.U.'s quarterback Mildren threw the ball down into the end zone to Greg Pruitt. I jumped up over Pruitt and snatched the ball. I got the interception and ended the game and saved the win. I got my picture in Sports Illustrated jumping up over Greg Pruitt and stealing the ball. That was pretty cool.

5. I learned from sports in general and playing on our team at NU that you really learn the value of hard work. We were really a tight team. Our offensive and defensive teams epitomized teamwork, and unselfish play, and our schemes were all teamwork schemes where everyone worked together to do their assignment for the good of the team. That is a great lesson to carry on life as you go into society. The lessons of hard work and camaraderie help to develop leadership skills.

6. I would like to go back and relive the play in the 1971 Orange Bowl where I fell down and LSU got a touchdown. We came back and won but at that point that touchdown put them ahead. They had a poor crummy turf called poly-turf. It was the only one in the country and it was very slick. I would like to take that one back. It made for a dramatic finish because of my blunder.

7. The best leader was Jerry Tagge for the offense. He kept things together on offense. On defense, we had a lot of good players. Richie Glover never said a word, but was probably as good a leader as we ever had just by him keeping his nose to the grindstone and doing his job. In the Game of Century he came up huge and helped us win the game. He handled Oklahoma's center Brahaney,

nd he saved our butt. Everyone liked Richie. He was a cool guy.

. My personal goals were to play with a great team, and to be on a team that went to Bowl games and won. My dream came true.

. The most important reasons for the wins were unbelievable teamwork and camaraderie. We had great chemistry.

0. To be considered the best is huge and an enormous source of pride. I grew up in a football town in Green Bay, Wisconsin where football is really important. It is satisfying to know the high place our team has in history. We just went out and played hard.

1. To motivate myself before the games I would go over all my assignments. I would practice in my mind whatever could come up. I was motivated to do a good job for my teammates. I went to NU to win and my motivation was to be a winner.

2. My biggest challenge was to be smarter, tougher and better prepared because I was not the greatest athlete out there.

3. I had few disappointments during those times. I was hoping to be an All-American which I never achieved. But I was very successful, All Big 8 and set a couple of NU records, (most passes broken up for a defensive back in a career and the number of starts for a 3 year eligibility (1971) until JR broke it the next year).

14. The most important reasons that made the team work so well together were (a) Good coaches; (b) such great teamwork and camaraderie and chemistry. We had good players but so did other people, so there had to be something different about our chemistry and teamwork.

15. Winning solves a lot of problems. The players are happier and work better together.

16. My most talented teammate was Johnny Rodgers. Pound for pound Johnny was the greatest I have ever seen.

17. The most inspirational player was Jerry Murtaugh because of his toughness. He was a tough guy on and off the field.

18. Joe Blahak was just crazy. I really liked him, and he was fun and helped keep everyone loose.

19. Coach Warren Powers was a good coach because he had played in the pros with Oakland. He knew a lot of the techniques the pros were using. We had confidence and believed in him.

20. Coach George Kelly, the defensive line coach, recruited me in Wisconsin. He was slick and a smooth talking recruiter. Coach Devaney came up once and he was the ultimate smooth talker recruiter.

21. I was always concentrating hard on what I was supposed to be doing. I am sure the fans helped motivate us and intimidate the other team, but to be real honest I was just concentrating so hard on what I supposed to do.

22. I graduated on time in 5 years because I was red shirted. My Major was Mathematics out of Education. I was going to be a Math teacher and coach.

23. Playing for Nebraska helped me in the after football life. It helps you to work with people and to get to know them. Because we did so well, it is still an interesting topic that people like to talk to you about.

24. I feel appreciated by the University for the time I put in, but it's hard for me to gauge that because I have been away for so long down in Albuquerque, New Mexico for (33 years) and have not been back much. I think the fans always remember and appreciate our teams.

Orange Bowl Bliss with Jim Anderson and NU President Woody Varner (38-6 over Alabama, January 1, 1972).*

Joe Armstrong

JOE ARMSTRONG

OFFENSIVE LINE

HUSKER HIGHLIGHTS

1. During the preseason camps it was always so hot in August and Coach Devaney always liked to have his hair done. And usually it was a reddish color but on one of those 100 degree days he must have been at the parlor because it had turned slightly green. And everyone got a big kick out of it.

2. The University of Washington game in 1968 was unusual because Coach Devaney had me play all 5 positions in the offensive line. I never did that again and I think I was the only lineman in modern history to play all those positions in one game.

3. At TCU in `68 – We used to do a Friday walk-through at the opponent's stadium. We had a play called a boot leg pass where the guard pulls out, and as I pulled out in that practice session the ball was right there so I just took it and went on out to throw the pass. About 15 years later a TCU alum who was also at that practice said "you know that night we were scouting and watching for that play all the next day. How come you never threw that pass?"

4. The 1st game I played was in 1966 – As one of the four sophomores who was not red shirted. I was the punter and before I went in Kelly Peterson, who was a 5th year senior, said "If you screw this punt up, don't come back to this sideline". So on the snap from Kelly it sailed over my head about 15 feet and I went back and retrieved it and kicked it out of the end zone. As soon as I got back to the sideline Coach Devaney said "Good job, but next time take the safety".

5. The Nebraska fans were always very supportive. To see all the red was just amazing.

6. Stand out players were Bob Churchich quarterback; Dee Tapman, fullback; Larry Walcholtz; Guy Ingles ; Tom Penny; Dick Davis; Mike Green; Melbur Houtcheck; Joe Buda.

7. Oklahoma was always tough. They were the team to beat. And we did not beat them in my 3 years (1966-1968). Colorado was starting to get tough. Steve Owens of Oklahoma in 1968 ran for 200 yards against us and everything he did looked fantastic. He was the Heisman trophy winner that year.

8. In the mid 60s Coach Devaney was also Athletic Director, and I think that had some impact on our record. He had a lot of responsibilities.

9. NU football was a tremendous personal experience for me. We had lots of really good people from around the country. The work ethic that Coach Bob always taught – "winners never quit and quitters never win." A lot of it carries over into your life.

10. Oklahoma State had an outstanding middle guard, and Coach Bob told me that he always shoots the gaps and will never hit you head on. So what I had to do was wait one second, instead of charging off the ball to see which direction he went, and just take him out of the play and it worked all day. And we kept running right in his hole. It was a little unusual for someone to do it the whole time. They never changed it.

11. If I could change anything it would be to win more games. It would have been fun to play on Astroturf. It did not come until 1969 or 1970. That really dates you when you are one the guys who never played on Astroturf and who wore the 3 quarter high shoes (one of Bob's big

inventions was bringing them from Wyoming. He thought they helped prevent twisting your ankles).

2. The best leaders aside from the coaching staff would be Ernie Siegler and Dick Davis. Both of them had an ability to build confidence among the players and to get us aroused emotionally.

3. My goals were to get an education and play football. In those days recruiting was much more wide open than it is today. Coach Eddie Crowder from Colorado tried to take at least 20 of us on one plane and I do not think anyone went including Dick Davis. It was something that you thought maybe you could do as a little kid, and once you got the opportunity to play for NU you did not even consider anywhere else.

4. Our team goals in 1966 were to win the Big 8 which we did. Then we lost the Bowl game to Alabama. `67 and `68 were bad years – 6-4 and 6-4.

5. The most important reasons for the wins was that we could play best as a team. We seemed to hit a lot of teams that were good at the time, but have not had success since then.

6. We always thought we were going to win. Coach Bob was great at building confidence.

7. NU football helped me succeed since my playing days. You have to put it in perspective, but being able to win at that level gives you the confidence that you can win at any level if you work hard enough. It is a competitive game and business is competitive. A lot of it carries over.

8. You could not take too many of trainer George Sullivan's sleeping pills because that would not get you going the next day. He would give those to you down at the center and guys would fall asleep in the hall. You take one of those things, and you would not make it back to your room. George Sullivan and Paul Schneider were excellent trainers. They really were the backbone for many years of NU football. You always felt confident that they would do a good job and get the team prepared. They were kind of father figures to the whole group.

9. My biggest challenge was trying to match the academic requirements with the athletic requirements and the time commitment it took. It is a big adjustment going to college.

20. We received great personal attention from our coaches. When you would come in as a freshman, you would walk in and Bob and Coach Ross would look at your academic schedule and make some comments about it. I remember going up to Bob's office as a freshman and he looked at it and said "What are these advanced courses you are taking? You don't want to take all these advanced courses. You want to take the regular courses and that way you will do better and adjust faster, so change those". That was good advice.

21. One big game and challenge for the team was in 1968. We opened with Wyoming and that had a special sentiment because Coach Devaney came from Wyoming. Paul Rogers kicked the winning field goal with about 10 second left.

22. I would have liked to have won more games. But other than that I had no other disappointments.

23. The most important aspect that made the team work so well together was that Bob had an excellent group of assistant coaches. He brought many of them from Wyoming. The coaching staff was just outstanding as a group. Bob's personality and disposition carried through the coaching staff.

24. The most talented player I played with was in the East/West Shrine Bowl when I played with O.J. Simpson. I would also say Joe Green. The most talented opponent was Steve Owens from Oklahoma.

25. The most inspirational player was Ernie Siegler. Everybody trusted his ability and he was very thoughtful and deliberate. He was a leader.

26. The most outrageous teammate was Crazy Carl Quinn, defensive back in 1969.

27. Almost everyone played hurt. A lot of people would need surgery but they would wait until after the season. I had 2 knee surgeries in those 4 years. Jim McCord had pretty serious knee damage. The routine was to have them after the Spring game.

28. The hardest worker in practice when I was a graduate assistant was Barry Alvarez (later Head Coach at Wisconsin). Also, Dick Davis and the players that were not on scholarship. Also, Red Baron – that kid worked his tail off.

29. In 1969 Barry Alvarez and I were graduate assistants, Coach Bob had given us a group to work with and he let us have a homecoming for them to play the freshman. And we wiped the freshman out. And then Bob said "Okay, since you beat the freshman bad, I will let you hold dummies against the 1st team" – I will never forget this. You know how everyone on the 1st team is not moving too fast and just going though the motions. Tagge took the ball from center and dropped it. And Barry had this drill where all these kids had to hit the ball no matter what happens. The whistle blows and we had a 11 guys on Tagge, and Devaney was going nuts. The ball was on the ground, and they threw their dummies down and just took off after the ball. Bob never let Barry and I live that one down.

30. One good memory is All-American Wayne Meylan, who was number 66. I was 65 which meant we lockered next to each other. As a sophomore there only 4 of us that played. I did not get to sit on the bench until Wayne said I could sit on the bench, and I appreciated that.

31. Coach Carl Selmer taught me a lot. Carl was a lot into technique and knowing the plays inside and out. And he tried to prepare everybody thoroughly and we always felt we were well prepared for whatever was coming. He believed in details.

32. Practices were spirited type practices overall. In contrast to today, we had a lot more people at the practices.

33. The part of practice I hated the most was running the stairs or wind sprints after practices. And Sunday morning.

34. I think the crowd at Nebraska was just tremendously supportive and it really was an added boost to your adrenaline to be playing at home and the idea that most of them would be wearing red or white. It is just an exciting stadium to play in. It was extremely exciting to run on the field for the 1st time. We came out of the North Stadium from the field house and that is where the new entry is going to be in 2006.

35. My greatest memory is the overall experience. Just being able to participate in a competitive sport and get an education out of it.

36. Playing for Nebraska helped me in the after football life – mainly in the mental discipline you learn playing competitive sports. Also, when I played football, a lot of the kids that played were from working class families. Some were poor and there was a lot of commonality there. There are a lot of kids who probably would not have received an education without football.

MIKE BERAN *(aka "Red Baron")*

OFFENSIVE RIGHT GUARD
HUSKER HIGHLIGHTS

1. Coach Devaney was a great coach. He assembled a great staff of assistant coaches with Osborne, Selmer, Fischer, Thornton, Melton, Kiffin, Powers, and on down the line.

2. My favorite Devaney story is when I was a sophomore in high school. Our hometown basketball team at Ord, Nebraska made it to the state championships. I was walking down-town with a group of friends and Coach Devaney was coming out of the barber shop. He saw us and said "Hi, how are you guys doing" To me that was the ultimate compliment by such a famous coach, and he's actually paying attention to a bunch of high school kids. That just struck me as something terrific about him. He really did not have to do that but he did it anyway.

3. Coach Devaney had a good sense of humor, but was stern when he needed to be.

4. The Nebraska fans were always very supportive and courteous. They were not the typical Southeast Conference fans who are rabid beyond belief. They stuck with Coach Devaney when there was some rumbling in the `67 and `68 seasons. Some questioned Bob's ability as a coach, but they started to realize the national recognition he brought the team and the state. He put Nebraska on the map. Back in 1963 I visited my cousins in Washington and they thought people in Nebraska still rode around in covered wagons and fought off the Indians. They realized differently once we started winning football games.

5. I thought the players got along famously. A good work ethic and camaraderie.

6. Oklahoma was always a big rival and Missouri was always tough. Missouri physically was always the toughest game. It was always what you call "smash mouth" football.

7. UNL was a good positive experience. I ended up lettering 3 years. Winning 2 National Championships just sweetened it that much more.

8. The most remarkable offensive play I witnessed was Johnny Rodgers' punt return against Oklahoma in the 1971 Game of The Century. In the `70 game against Missouri, the biggest hit I ever heard was when Dave Walline, at defensive right tackle, hit Joe Moore who was an excellent running back for Missouri. They ran a trap against Dave, and the guard did not get over there to trap him in time and he just clobbered Joe Moore. A clean hit which unfortunately separated his shoulder, and you could hear the hit all over the stadium.

9. I learned that hard work and perseverance can pay off. I came to UNL at 186 pounds. I was not that gifted as an athlete and I worked hard and built myself up to 235.

10. I would like to relive a bad play on my part when we were playing UCLA out in Los Angeles opening the `72 season. We had a 4th and short yardage play and they put their middle guard in the gap between center Doug Dumler and myself. I did not come down as quickly as I should have and he ended up getting the tackle and stopping the drive.

11. The funniest situation I was ever in was with Dave Walline. We were playing Kansas and John Riggins was there. Dave was a defensive right tackle and they faked a dive to Riggins to their left and the play actually went to the right. And I just happened to watch Dave and he tackled Riggins and got up very quickly and Riggins was still on his hands and knees and Dave just kicked Riggins right in the butt. I will never forget that as long as I live.

12. A humorous off the field incident was the boxing match between Bob Jones and "Earthquake" (Jim Carstens). Doug Jamail got dressed up in a tuxedo and he was the ring announcer. The fight was staged in the old pit in Schulte field house. They built a little ring with ropes and got a fake microphone and they had judges and staged it just like a real boxing match. I think they went 3 rounds with 3 minutes per round but they both were so tired they did not last that long.

13. Another fun story is when we were in fall camp and Jim Carstens had that Harley Davidson. And he loaded it on the elevator and brought it up to the 6th floor of Harper hall and started it up. It raised quite a commotion.

14. The best leader is `69 was Jim McFarland in a quiet way. In 1968 it was Dick Davis; 1970 Jerry Murtaugh because of the way he did things. He did not say much but he did most of his talking on the football field. In 1971 Tagge, Dumler, Glover, Jacobsen, and Rodgers. In 1972 all of the above in 71 and Bill Janssen. They all led by example. They did great things on the field and you just wanted to emulate what they did.

15. A funny story about Coach Kiffin: When we were still in the Schulte Field House for our locker room, they had a steam room. Kiffin would go in there after practice with that rubber suit and take a steam bath and of course he was smoking cigarettes.

16. Coach Fischer had some sayings that I will never forget: Whenever the play would start, he would say "You are all the way, you are all the way, get up the field, get up the field" and he would tell the lineman to "get in there and root hog".

17. My personal goals was to play football. Despite my lack of size I wanted to be a member of the team.

18. I talked to an Oklahoma player at Coach Devaney's funeral. He told me about all the functions and get togethers the Oklahoma team alumni have. I was amazed that we don't do stuff like that. When UNL players do get together we just get along so well.

19. Our team goals were to win our games. To do the best we could. To win the Big 8. To win a national championship, especially the following year after we won in 1970.

20. The most important reasons for the wins were (a) great coaching, (b) the team was very cohesive – not a lot of big egos. Guys put the team in front of themselves. We had good chemistry.

21. In `71 we were very confident NU would win National Championship. We had been Number One since the preseason poll. Until Oklahoma, we were not challenged that much. That game was a tough challenge but we were able to overcome it. Against Alabama in the Orange Bowl I was very confident that we were going to win that game.

22. NU football helped me succeed since my football playing days. It allowed me to realize if you work hard and persevere you will succeed at what you are trying to attain.

23. It means a lot to be considered the best. Very few guys get the opportunity to play for one national championship, let alone two. I was fortunate to be on the teams that did win 2 national championships and came close to a 3rd one. It has been very rewarding and a self satisfying feeling to be a member of those teams.

24. We were well prepared for the opponents by the coaches. We watched films and studied their tendencies. I would always wait until just before we went out on the field before psyching up so I did not become over psyched and run out of "mental gas". I did not lose that edge before we started the game.

25. Before the game lots of guys listened to music. A few guys would yell and scream. Everyone did their own thing getting mentally ready for the games.

26. Coach Devaney was not that much of a yeller or screamer. He would mainly motivate us in a positive way. By telling us what we needed to get done and telling us we were capable of getting the job done.

7. Coach Selmer and Coach Fischer really were opposites. Selmer was more the cerebral type and did not say a lot. Fischer was more talking and yelling. But they complemented each other very well.

8. My biggest challenge was my size. I needed to make myself bigger and a better athlete in order to perform at that high level. But I always had a good work ethic and it enabled me to succeed. I never thought about quitting.

9. The `71 Oklahoma game was the biggest challenge for the team. I still remember the bumper sticker that said: "1, 2, 3 = 8 (meaning Big 8)"

0. My toughest opponent was my teammates during scrimmages. Rich Glover, John Dutton, Larry Jacobsen, Bill Janssen, Willie Harper, Jimmy Branch, Jimmy Pitts, Bob Terrio. Oklahoma State had a terrific middle guard when I was a senior named Barry Price. He was really quick and tough. Darrela Moore, Lucius Selmon (Oklahoma) were tough football players. U.S.C. had a guy that went to the pros by the name of Ron Yary. And he was tough and difficult to block.

1. My biggest disappointment was not winning a third national championship (1972), especially since it was Coach Devaney's last year as head coach.

2. The most important aspect that made the team work so well together was that the players got along so well and maintained a good attitude. Coach Devaney assembled a coaching staff that was just terrific.

3. My most talented teammate was Johnny Rodgers. He is still the greatest all time college football player. My toughest opponent was Barry Price. He was just an animal.

4. The most inspirational teammate was Rex Lowe – for what he was going through at that time. Rex was diagnosed with Hodgkin's disease. For someone with that type of disease to try to come out for football was just very inspiring. It really was debilitating to Rex. He did not give. I will never forget when Johnny Rodgers gave him the game ball from the Orange Bowl. It will always be etched in my mind. It was such a terrific thing that Johnny did.

5. The players who played hurt the most were running backs and receivers.

36. I learned from Coaches Selmer and Fischer just how well two individuals with different personalities can work together.

37. I was a walk-on and then I got a scholarship after my red shirt year. My first 2 years I was not on scholarship.

38. I had the mindset of a walk-on: I felt that I could play at that level. I just always wanted to be a part of NU football. I grew up idolizing the `63, `64, and `65 teams and knew all of their names and where they were from. I went to a couple of game and I went to the Kellogg Center before the game just to see the players. Fortunately at that time Boyd Eppley was just starting weight training and I figuratively lived in the weight room, especially my freshman and red shirt sophomore year. When I went from 186 to 225 pounds by the spring of my freshman year. I think the coaches analyzed me and said it must be working and lets get behind this weight training program that Boyd set up. It took off there and NU was one of the first ones to have a strength training program and they built it up until it was the premier strength training program in the country.

39. The practices were not that long. Tuesdays and Thursdays were the long days. Fall camp was really tough, simply because it was so hot and humid.

40. The part of practice I hated the most were sprints after practice.

41. The fans inspired our efforts in the game. You always wanted to do your best for them.

42. It was terrific to run on the field for the 1st time against Wake Forest (1970). No other feeling like it. The sea of red is a sight I will never forget.

43. Playing for Nebraska helped me in the after football life. It gave me a work ethic and realization that you can succeed through hard work and perseverance.

44. I feel appreciated by the University for the time I put in. But I wish they would have more functions where we could get together like we did in 2003 and for Coach Devaney's birthday. I still go down and work out. I get to meet the new players. The intimidating thing about it is these guys are so huge and I am a boy among men.

Joe and Diane Blahak

JOE BLAHAK *(aka "Airhead")*
SAFETY

HUSKER HIGHLIGHTS

1. My most memorable play was in the Orange Bowl against LSU in 1971 (17-12). LSU had a 3rd and 33, and I bit on a hook pattern. They threw it over my head and they gained 34 yards and got the first down. Billy Kosch tackled him. When I came off the field, I ran down to where the defense was. Murtaugh came up to me and says "Airhead, God damn you", and I am sitting there and all of a sudden I noticed that the players are parting, and here comes Coach Devaney. He walks up to me and grabbed my facemask and pulled me right down to his face and says "You stupid God damn Polack. If you ever do that again, you will never again touch the field at the University of Nebraska". Coach Melton was standing there and says "He meant it". God, I was scared. In spite of all that, I would do anything for Coach Devaney. He taught us to be committed.

2. In the Fall of 1969 I came to the University of Nebraska for my freshman year. I am sitting there in the north locker room. Dave Walline and Larry Jacobson came walking by, and I looked up at these guys and I thought "God, what did I get myself into here". They were huge. The biggest people I had ever seen in my life. I was not sure I really wanted to play football at UNL.

3. I drove Coach Warren Powers crazy. We were getting ready to play the Game of The Century against Oklahoma in 1971 (35-31), and we are downstairs in the field house going through plays on the blackboard. Coach Powers is going through plays. I am back there sound asleep and he says "Joe, what did you do here?" and I looked up and said "cover 3" because that is all I ever did. He got mad and threw an eraser at me. He said "It's the biggest game of your life and you are screwing around." That poor man. When I first got there he did not drink or smoke, but when I left he drank and smoked. I drove him crazy.

4. The very first game that I started was in 1970 against Southern Cal. in Los Angeles (21-21). I remember we are in the entry way on the way down to the field. All of a sudden we heard this rumbling and Southern Cal. ran out on the field and we heard a loud roar. Then we run out and there is an even louder roar. I looked up and the entire stadium was red. I was in awe over how many Nebraska fans came to support us.

5. I became very close with certain teammates – Dave Goeller, Randy Butts, John O'Connell, Bruce Hauge, Phil Harvey, Bob Terrio and Bill Kosch. I remember Bob Wolf used to talk like Donald Duck.

6. I played against a future teammate in my very first home game in 1970. It was my sophomore year and it was Oregon's Bobby Moore (aka "Ahmad Rashad"). We later played together at the Minnesota Vikings.

7. The most remarkable offensive play I witnessed was Johnny Rodgers' punt return in 1971 against Oklahoma.

8. The most memorable played on defense was Dave Walline's hit on Joe Moore from Missouri. He separated Joe's shoulder.

9. The biggest thing I learned from Coach Devaney was to believe in yourself. He instilled confidence in us.

10. I would like to go back and relive the UCLA game my senior year in 1972 in Los Angeles (14-17). The touchdown pass to Brad Lieman from Mark

Harmon. The sad thing is that I had that played perfectly. I cut in front of him and put my arm out and the ball glanced across my forearm into Brad Lieman's hands, and he caught it and ran for the touchdown. We were rated Number One and we lost our first game.

1. If I could change anything, it would be to work a little harder and study a little more. To lift more weights and stay in better shape.

2. The best leader was quarterback Jerry Tagge on offense because he held everything together. This became clear when Dave Humm came in 1972 with no experience. On defense the best leader was Jerry Murtaugh.

3. My personal goal was simply to play. I did not have a lot of confidence coming in. I was lucky I came in at the right time. We had lost Dana Stevenson, Randy Reeves, Al Larson. We lost a lot of defensive backs by graduation my freshman year.

4. The three most important reasons for the wins were: (a) We had tremendous talent. (b) We believed in ourselves. We never thought about losing. It never entered our minds that we could lose. (c) The most important aspect that made the team work so well together was the feeling of family. We took care of each other.

5. I was fairly confident NU would win the National championship in 1971. I felt that we had a great team.

6. It is an honor to be considered the best and to be surrounded with the kind of talent that we had.

7. I thrived on pressure. I wanted the ball. When the going got tough, I wanted to be part of it.

8. My biggest challenge was school. It was tough being a student athlete.

9. I never thought about quitting

10. The game that was the biggest challenge for the team was the Kansas game in 1970 with John Riggins running. Iowa State was a tough one our senior year (1972) when they tied us. That field was a mess (wet and slippery). Guys just kept making mistakes.

11. My biggest disappointment was not giving Coach Devaney a National Championship that last year (1972). I wanted him to go out as Number One.

He deserved it. But we did finish strong. We demolished Notre Dame in the Orange Bowl (40-6).

22. One time we were in the locker room. Devaney had a big thick oak clipboard, and he threw it against the wall and shattered it. People were scattering and just running for cover.

23. My most talented teammate was Johnny Rodgers. The most inspirational teammates were Dale Ditter, Phil Harvey, and Rex Lowe. Woody Cox surprised me the most.

24. Playing for Nebraska helped me in the after football life. It provided a lot of opportunities. The fans of Nebraska are incredible. They are the best in the world. They always provide opportunities. It has opened doors. Your name is out there and years later I will introduce myself to people and they say "Oh, you are the old football player."

25. Sometimes I do not feel appreciated by the University for the time I put in. I think they could do a lot more for some of the old UVs, the extremely old veterans.

26. Coach Warren Powers is the man who allowed me to play five years in the N.F.L. (Minnesota Vikings) with what he taught me about the game. It was based on fundamentals. He stressed footwork so much. Coach Powers taught me what it took to be a defensive back. It took repetition, repetition, on footwork. No wasted steps.

27. One day in practice we were back and forth with the defense and the offense hitting each other. And Coach Osborne decides he is going to run a pass pattern against us. So, he made me get out there and he ran a pattern against me. It was like a three yard out. He caught the pass and his chest was all puffed out proudly, and I said "Yeah, No one is going to win a game with three yard outs."

28. Coach Monte Kiffin was quite a leader. All the defensive guys just loved him as a coordinator. He would run the stadium stairs with us. He got the guys to do things they would never do on their own. He used to get those great big guys to run the stadium steps after practice. I did not have to do it, but I did it with them.

JIM BRANCH

LINEBACKER

HUSKER HIGHLIGHTS

1. I did not have much contact with Coach Devaney. Most of what he said at half-time was inspirational. He always made a halftime adjustment which put us over the top. Our halftime adjustments were really critical.

2. Coach Kiffin used to run the stadium steps after practice and the defense was in super condition. Coach Kiffin was fun and was always joking around. He would always say that if you got knocked down, you were to scramble up, scramble up. One time in practice he slipped and fell and I told him "Scramble up, coach, scramble up." It was funny reversing it on him. Kiffin was more of a personality guy and Coach Melton was more standoffish.

3. We had a lot of super players. Think about Bill Olds and Ralph Powell. What if they had those two guys in the same backfield?

4. Nebraska fans were really great. It made you feel like "Why are they asking me for my autograph?" The fans put us on a pedestal. It was a sea of red at the stadium with Roman gladiators. They were fanatics. Nebraska was the biggest game in town.

5. Watching Rich [Glover] was remarkable. Willie [Harper] stands out in my mind. The LSU game when Willie took the ball from the running back. That was a critical play. Rich was a dominate factor.

6. Sports in general teaches us a competitive spirit and a stick-to-itive-ness and teamwork philosophy. It is an approach to life to dig down deep and come back against adversities. Sports give you that attitude where you never give up. In some of the games that we played it seemed like all is lost and then we came back and won. I can see why people still talk about the Oklahoma game in 1971.

7. Currently in 2006, NU needs to get some more speed to open up the game a little more.

8. We were so dominate. I don't see much I would change. That last year (1972) it would have been nice to get that third national championship. In the UCLA game (17-20) Johnny Pitts and I sat out that second half and I don't know why they pulled us out. They had Tom Ruud and Nelson in.

9. The best leaders were Johnny, Rich, and Willie. Tagge led by example. When you played with these guys they were inspirational and that raised the level of play of the other guys. And Coach Kiffin would tell the defense that "We bend but we don't break." That always stuck with me. People may drive on you, but you are not going to let them score.

10. At first, I just wanted to play football. As I got a little older, I really started to concentrate on the books. I graduated with a psychology degree.

11. The 3 most important reasons for the wins were (a) the preparation was outstanding. Watching films and being prepared for what teams would do. Preparation was almost like a game, and especially what keys they would give us. We knew what the other team was going to do before they did it. Teams had a pattern. It made it simple and easy. (b) we were in good condition. Sprinting at the end of practice gave us that extra wind, where you did not get fatigued. We were stronger in the 4th quarter. They called it the "Big Red

Jim Branch

Machine" because it seemed like it was unstoppable. At halftime I would stuff my helmet full of orange slices because they seemed to reenergize me and give me that little burst of energy. (c) It did not hurt to have great players. You can scout and give them preparation, but they have to be able to execute.

2. The biggest thing I remember about Coach Osborne was one time he had a flat tire. Then he jogged to school. I thought he was crazy. I thought "This man had a flat and he just took off and ran to the campus." That was the kind of guy he was.

3. I was confident NU would win the second National Championship in 1971. I was really confident that we could win a third title in 1972. It was disappointing when we lost that first game at (UCLA). The main reason was that Humm was inexperienced. He became more comfortable with the quarterback position later. He eventually was a good quarterback.

4. It means a lot to be considered the best. You always carry it with you.

5. When I first came to Nebraska from Chicago, I would come home and I would try to get people to come to Nebraska. You would have thought that I was talking about a foreign country. They asked, "where is Nebraska?"

6. I had this love to play football. I did not think much about the game until I got on the field. On the field I was in a zone. I really enjoyed away games more than home games because I liked going to different places. I would look up at the opponent's crowd and see them cheering for their team, and I would think "It is not going to happen today."

7. Coach Bill Thornton helped build my confidence. I missed him when he left my junior year. He would always say "You have to make believers out of them." We had some good heart to heart talks and he kept me motivated.

8. My biggest disappointment was 1972 because I thought we were going to win the third championship. At that time if NU lost one game we had a "bad season."

9. The most important reasons that made the team work so well together were a combination of coaches, player's talent and attitude. You have to have a combination of coaching and players that are coachable. I helped a few teams here in Chicago and the kids are a lot of different now. They look at you and they are not really paying attention.

20. My most talented teammates on defense were Rich and Willie. Willie was an all around athlete and could play it all. Rich was just outstanding at middle guard.

21. The most inspirational was Red Baron. He was a walk-on. I thought Red Baron was crazy. He would be in a weight room and he would say "The more it hurts, the better it is!" I could not grasp the philosophy at that time because I did not know how to lift weights then. I would go in the weight room and stay about 5 minutes. I would lift and then get a headache and walk out. He was a guy that worked hard.

22. Another inspirational guy was Ken Geddes. He worked and after practice he would lift. He moved to the next level just through hard work. It was inspirational to see guys who pushed themselves beyond what I thought they could do.

23. One time we went to Omaha and Johnny Rodgers gave a speech. He said "whenever you think that you have gone as far as you can go, take one more step." That was inspirational and he had his mind together at an early age. Johnny was taking care of business.

24. Gary Dixon was a funny guy. I always called him the "Little Munchkin Man" from the Wizard of Oz. Tom Robinson was always making jokes and was funny.

25. Coach Kiffin was like a surrogate. On the way to the game Kiffin would take the linebackers to the back of the bus. Then he would go over strategies because Coach Melton was always cracking jokes but he was not that much of a fundamentalist or into strategy.

26. Playing for Nebraska helped me in the after football life as far as attitude and preparation. Most people have a competitive spirit. It is part of being an athlete.

27. My biggest game was against Colorado and I got the Chevrolet Award. But I got more satisfaction out of the Oklahoma game in 1971. That was just a great, great, great game. It was an emotionally high game. It seems like the team that makes the least amount of mistakes wins when the teams are so close in talent.

Van Brownson

VAN BROWNSON

QUARTERBACK

HUSKER HIGHLIGHTS

1. My most vivid memories of Coach Bob Devaney are his mannerisms and his way of handling people. You could do something out of line that was not even associated with football and he would shake his head. And he would say "You know what, we have to make it right." In other words, you were going to have to run stairs. He did not say it with any animosity.

   Of course if you threw an interception you did not want to come over to the sideline. You tried to see where he was and to hide in the crowd because he did not hesitate to get into your face and let you know about it. It just amazed me that he could do that and in the next minute pat you on the back and encourage you to forget about it.

2. In practices Coach Tom Osborne ran the spread station and Coach Mike Corgan ran the quarterbacks and the I station. As far as coaching the quarterbacks it was 75% Tom and 25% Mike.

3. Coach Corgan was the gruffest man in the world, but we learned over the years that he could help your performance.

4. NU's greatest game was probably my Junior year down at Kansas (1970). We got behind 14 to 0. They had John Riggins and Connelly, the two big backs that were fast. We came back and beat them 44-20.

5. The two most remarkable offensive plays I witnessed were (a) Johnny Rodger's punt return at Oklahoma in 1971; (b) a catch that Guy Ingles made at Kansas in 1970.

6. The biggest factors that changed my life were the amazing athletes and fans that I had the opportunity to meet. The best lessons that I learned from the football experiences are dedication and that hard work can overcome most obstacles.

7. I would like to go back and relive one play against Iowa State in my sophomore year (1969). I rolled out on a 51 and I saw the cornerback come up on the split end. So I immediately went to the crease. I tried to guide the ball and I threw it right into the chest of an Iowa State player that was trailing him.

8. If I could change anything, it would probably be my lifestyle in college.

9. Doug Dumler was one of the best leaders on our football team. He wasn't "rah-rah." He was the type of individual that Tom Osborne was and is. He led through example.

10. My personal goal was to play professional football. I reached that goal and I was drafted. But because of my lifestyle I lost interest my senior year in improving (1971). My senior year I did not play much because I separated my shoulder in spring ball.

11. The most important reasons for the wins were (a) we had a lot of great athletes and (b) the leadership of Devaney and his ability to delegate responsibility to probably the most effective coaching staff ever assembled. We had a lot of great coaches with tremendous imaginations and commitment to the program.

12. I had tremendous respect for my teammates. I got along with everybody.

3. After the Sun Bowl in El Paso and defeating Oklahoma 44-14 my sophomore year (1969), I knew we were going to be a national contender. I did not realize it was going to be two national championships. I knew a lot of the pieces were in place with the athletes, coaches and the dedication.

4. I was definitely focused on playing. I might not have been the best practice player in the world but at game time I was ready.

5. UNL football taught us persistence and an understanding of what it takes to succeed. Some of our players did not have the most talent in the world but because of their desire and their heart they succeeded.

6. To motivate myself before the game I visualized different scenarios and opportunities that could happen. As far as throwing or running with the ball most of time I had already done it in my own mind.

7. My biggest challenge was my lifestyle. I don't know that I ever overcame it while I was in college.

8. I never thought about quitting. My biggest disappointment was injuries.

9. The most important reasons that made the team work so well together were (a) the coaches (b) team chemistry was great. We knew we had a great offense and a great defense, and they fed off each other. It was the encouragement you would get from the other side of the ball. It was a total team effort.

10. My most talented teammate was Johnny Rodgers and the most talented opponent was John Riggins of Kansas. The two most talented athletes that I played with were the two receivers who were catching passes, Johnny Rodgers and Guy Ingles. They sure made life a lot easier for me. Fullback Bill Olds was tough and fast.

11. I enjoyed watching when we would get into the spread formation and the fullback would stay in as the lone back. We would run an option and they would pitch that ball to Bill Olds. Here is a 230 lbs. fullback and the defensive backs would take an angle on him and Bill would just shift gears and pretty soon they did not have an angle on him. I was amazed at his speed and strength and quick acceleration. He was just a tremendous athlete.

22. Three guys who were inspirational were Wes Maven, a tremendous individual, Johnny Pitts and Rex Lowe. What made them inspirational were their battles. Johnny because he had that quiet leadership ability and I felt that he overcame a lot of odds. He was a tremendous linebacker. Rex Lowe overcame problems in his life and eventually lost the medical battle, but he stayed as positive as any individual could.

23. The most outrageous teammate was Doug Jamail.

24. Doug "Hell Man" Johnson and I ran the stairs the most. I would miss a meeting or be late to practice. Coach Corgan would come to me and say "you owe me some stairs."

25. The fans created the atmosphere to make you want to do well. They had a big influence on the things I did on the field. The crowd noise would increase the rush of adrenaline that led to success.

26. There is probably more recognition from being a former Husker than the association with the best team ever. People talk to me more about playing on the two national championship teams.

27. My greatest memory of Coach Tom Osborne is the selfless commitment that he displayed in teaching us and trying to set a good example for us. We got along very well. I respected him for his lifestyle.

28. The one thing that I remember about Coach Corgan was when I ran the ball in the Sun Bowl. He was always saying "get under their pads and lift." And I actually got under a defensive back's pads as he came in to hit. I can still remember Corgan lifting me up off the ground and saying "that's the way to do it. That's the way to deliver a blow."

Jim Carstens

JIM CARSTENS *(aka "Earthquake")*

FULLBACK AND DEFENSIVE END

HUSKER HIGHLIGHTS

1. My best memory of Coach Bob Devaney was when I was going to quit in 1971 Coach Jim Walden wanted to move me to defensive end. I was discouraged. So, I went to Coach Devaney's office and I let him know that I was done.

   And Coach Devaney said something to me that epitomizes NU football. He said "Jim, I can't think of anybody that's more valuable to my program than you". Whether it was true or not, he did his magic once again. He got me to turn around and go to the field house and put on my uniform. He put that spirit right back into me. What inspired all of us was the motivation we got from one another. That all started with Devaney.

2. There is not a day that goes by that I do not think about the people at the University and how they touched my life. And the example they set for me. The reserve players who never would step on that game field when it was going to make a difference. It never fazed them and there were moments when they shined at that practice field. They brought out the best in all of us.

3. The team spirit all started with Devaney. I can remember walking through the coliseum in the basement one day and he had the assistant coaches in a classroom. Erasers were flying and he was telling them what he wanted done. It was a defensive meeting and it was unbelievable how they responded to him. Coaches Kiffin, Powers, Selmer, Osborne.

4. It was a thrill working with Coach Kiffin.

5. Coach Corgan had a saying that I will never forget and it has helped me so much through my life: "Jimmy boy, move your bowels or get off the toilet".

6. I remember Coach Osborne and the winter workout program when we would run around that indoor field house. He was behind us running and he said: "Earthquake, if I pass you, you are running again". The coaches loved us, and we truly loved each other.

7. In 1969, we were hosting USC and it was the first opportunity I had to see that crowd in red. It was most overwhelming and magnificent. The whole program starts with the fans and they put the spirit into the participants. We are on the field but they are inside of us.

8. Against Southern California at the Coliseum in Los Angeles (1970), they had a middle linebacker named Greg Slaw. Danny Schneiss and I were the only fullbacks and Dan came off the sidelines and he had blood all over the front of that white jersey. I said "are you alright?" and he looked at me and pulled his shirt and said "you mean this?, it belongs to the linebacker".

9. We played Kansas State in 1971 with QB Van Brownson. It was late in the game. Van is in that huddle and he looks at all of us and he goes "We are getting Earthquake in the end zone". At that moment I woke up and realized what the game was all about. And he gave me the ball three straight plays in a row. I didn't quite get in but it was a thrill to know my teammates wanted me to score.

10. In the Spring game my last season I carried the ball and I got tripped up and came down on the ball. It knocked the wind out of me. After the game my father said to me "I have been watching seven of my sons play football all my life and I saw something on that field at Nebraska that I have never seen before, and it was the biggest thrill. I said "What was that?" He said "When you had the

wind knocked out of you both benches emptied onto the field to make sure you were alright. That sent a very clear message to me". And he got to see why Nebraska was the place for me.

1. Gibbs and Bill Shepard were guys that expressed humility and they were such an important part of the program. Every single person touched that program. Don Bryant. Ursula Walsh. They were leaders and left such an impression on me. They had such a sincere concern for us beyond football.

2. It taught me love and humility. You go into that huddle a boy and come out a man.

3. I would like to relive any block I missed. They always say that you have one hit left in you.

4. If I could change anything, I would like to have used the opportunity to touch more people lives. To be more like Brook Berringer, who had the foresight to see kids who are sick in the hospital. I would bring a helmet and just see them smile.

5. The best leader was Dan Schneiss – a very quiet leader. He led by example. He was such a perfectionist. And he did it with such expertise and finesse.

6. God gave Johnny Rodgers so much talent. He developed it and took it to the extreme and won the Heisman Trophy. It did not get any better than JR. And everybody that knows college football agrees.

7. I changed my outlook to what I could do for the team. It changed my whole life in a positive way. If you work together, you can reach the top.

8. Mike Beran is the best example of someone who worked and worked. He earned his spot on the team.

9. The most important reason for the wins boiled down to one thing – the love we had for each other. It made us do things that we did not think we could do. Together we could do anything.

10. I was confident NU would win the National Championship in 1970 and `71. I saw the determination in people's faces, John Adkins, Willie Harper, Jerry List, and the list goes on. They were so confident in each other. List used to say "Earth, I am coming down on you" and he would. It was like trying to hold back a freight train. He was unbelievable.

21. It is every athlete's dream to play against the best possible competition. You could see Oklahoma had the best offense in the country in 1971. We had the best defense. We met the challenge week in and week out. I can't believe the guys we played against who went on to play professional football.

22. I didn't need to motivate myself before the game. My teammates did it for me. It was contagious. Coach Monte Kiffin was in the corner having a smoke. You knew the guy was going to explode. Coach Clet Fischer could not even go on to the field. He went to the press box he got so excited.

23. The Oklahoma game of `71 was the biggest challenge for the team because the teams were so well balanced and equal, offensively and defensively.

24. In 1970-1971, the coaches realized that the teams were something special. Our team chemistry was special. You could spell team N-E-B-R-A-S-K-A. The love is hard to describe in words.

25. My most talented teammates were Richie Glover and Johnny Rodgers. They responded to the talents that God gave them.

26. Who inspired me more than anyone was Dennis Morrison. He came from to NU from Omaha as a quarterback and ended up being an All Big 8 tight end. He was my graduate assistant on the `68 freshman team. He taught me how to believe in myself. He gave me a chance, and he is very special to this day in my life. After 2 weeks of practicing he looked at me spitting out sunflower seeds and he said "I don't know where you are from but you are my fullback".

27. The most outrageous player was Doug Jamail. He was funny and crazy. The boxing match: he was the announcer, and I have it on video, I was boxing in the field house in the lower level. Paul Rogers, Rex Lowe, Bob Tavis were the commentators.

28. The hardest workers in practice were Eddie Periard, Bill Olds, Janssen, Rodgers.

29. Coach Corgan taught us toughness and no nonsense. Coach Jim Ross recruited me and he impressed my parents. A very kind man.

30. I feel appreciated by the University for the time I put in.

FOR THE RECORD

WOODY COX
1970-1971

5'-9" 167 lbs.
Grosse Point, MI

NOW

Single

General Manager of the
Pro Sports Club

Racing bicycles is a hobby.
In the Masters (30 and up)
earned 9 world championships,
22 national championships,
and set 5 world records.

Redmond, Washington

*"I was motivated
because I didn't want
to let my teammates
down."*

Woody Cox

WOODY COX

WIDE RECEIVER

HUSKER HIGHLIGHTS

1. One interesting thing I remember was that on the back of Coach Devaney's clipboard it said "Nebraska Track."

   It was humorous because on the field at practice Coach Devaney would have his clipboard and he would say "Okay, offense 1 and 2, over here and defense over there." He probably had the sheet from 2 days ago, so we all just listened to Coach Osborne and the others and went where we needed to go.

2. When I graduated and went into the coaching offices, I saw that Devaney was an amazing manager. To this day he affects my management style because on the field he trusted all the assistant coaches. The second he got up in those coaching offices he knew exactly what was going on. He delegated and let his coaches take authority.

3. The players were able to relate to Devaney more than Osborne because he was like a Grandpa. He was funny and you knew he cared. He was also amazingly perceptive. If Newton screwed up he would tell Newton "I am going to kick your ass and take away your scholarship." Whereas if I screwed up he would say "come on. Woodrow, I know you can do it." He knew that I was already hard enough on myself and I just needed support. He knew immediately and instinctively how to motivate each individual player, and everyone did not get motivated the same.

4. Coach Tom Osborne was very honest and dedicated. "Judas Priest" was about the worst word you would get out of him. I remember him during the summer practices and he would just be running and running around the field. Just amazing dedication. I remember being home some nights real late after a football game party and you would see the lights on and his car parked at the coaching office looking at films for the next week. I have seen him a couple of times at booster events here in Seattle and Hawaii and the man's memory is just amazing. He remembered things about me that I could hardly remember. With all the players he coached he is an amazing guy.

5. My senior year Coach Osborne asked me to show some recruits around and I said "sure, I'll show them around." A couple of players were from California and were black and they asked me "how many black kids are on the team?" I did not know because I did not think of anyone in terms of black or white. I had to stop and think because we were just a team. It was more geographic – from Chicago, California – where you were from.

6. In 1971 we were playing Colorado and we were doing okay but we were not scoring. Near the end of the 2nd quarter we were down in our own end zone and Tagge had his back to the end zone but the rest of us were all facing the end zone. Keith Wortman looked up in the stands and told us that there was a pretty girl four rows up in the stands. So here we are on national TV in a huge game and we all were looking up in the stands. Tagge turned around and said "hey, we have to get going." Jerry got us focused. We just marched down the field four more times after that.

7. Before some of the games Doug Jamail would come out in a boxing outfit. He would dance around and he broke the tension and got us excited. Things like that were the difference for us.

8. In 1971 we played and defeated the Number Two team 3 different times – Colorado, Oklahoma, and Alabama.

Everybody was well prepared by our coaches. Missouri always blasted us pretty hard. They had tough defensive backs.

0. It was inspirational when our teammate, Rex Lowe, came down to the Orange Bowl even though he had Hodgkin's disease.

1. A fun memory is when we were playing in Hawaii (1971) and I caught a pass. Johnny Rodgers was in front of me and I started to have a little fun. Johnny was trying to block for me and I was jamming all over the place. It was fun to think "Here Johnny, take some of your own medicine."

2. Johnny Rodgers had eyes in the back of his head. I saw some replays and he was running down the field and two guys were converging behind him. There is no way he could have seen them but just out of instinct he ducked and the two of them hit each other and Johnny ran off and they missed him completely. There were times I would be trying to block for Johnny and trying to guess where his crazy legs were going to take him.

3. Somehow I knew when I was playing that it was just "a moment in time." It was not as really as big or as important as we thought.

4. What I learned from NU football was that you have limited time and resources. It taught me to be accountable and prepare and to hire the best staff I can. It is important to surround yourself with people that care and have a sense of teamwork and camaraderie. It helps me everyday.

5. I would not trade or change any of my experiences. Playing at UNL was a great experience.

6. There were a bunch of leaders in different ways. And that is why we were so successful in 1970-1971.

7. Doug Jamail was a tremendous leader in his own quirky way with some of his antics. He was second string and I never heard him complain about that. Jerry Tagge had a leadership role at quarterback. "Fig" Newton had amazing character and discipline.

8. I never thought I was going to play football at NU. I was just happy to have a scholarship and play. I was so small and I transferred from a Junior College. I thought that if I could just be part of the team that would be great.

19. The 3 most important reasons for the wins were: (a) Incredible preparation. Even back then Coach Osborne was breaking down percentages; (b) winter conditioning and working hard (c) there were a lot of good athletes. Jerry was a multi sport All-American and we had a bunch of multi-sport All-Americans. There were not any major superstars, until Johnny won the Heisman. But he was just part of the overall team and was a team player. We went to him a lot but there were others we went to as well. We were close and had no tensions.

20. NU football helped me succeed since my football playing days. My support staff must be smiling and happy in dealing with the members. That support of the front line people effects my management style everyday. I respect and appreciate everyone of the staff that I work with. That is what Coach Devaney and Coach Osborne did for us. They pushed us so we were prepared to do well. What we did was for the team.

21. I was motivated because I did not want to let my teammates down. When we first ran into the stadium with all that red it is blinding. The noise was deafening. But an amazing thing is once you got to the line all that became background noise. It was this focus from the repetition that we did over and over of all those plays. It would get quiet behind me, and I would focus on Tagge calling the plays.

22. Identifying my most talented teammate is a tricky one in that a lineman can be a tremendously talented in their position but they only have to blast out two yards and hit somebody. Overall as an all around athlete, Johnny Rodgers could play any sport he wanted to. Guy Ingles was a good athlete and a good basketball player. There were a lot of great athletes – Tagge and Runty. All of us had some athletic ability.

23. Two things differentiated us: (1) our winter conditioning program, which was good and that kept us focused during the winter; (2) the racquetball we played had a big effect for agility and quickness and camaraderie.

24. Doug Jamail kept the locker room the loosest and Jim Carstens. Also, Satch was a big character. You need those humorous elements. You need people to break up the monotony and to keep it fun and light.

25. I honestly do not feel like I deserve any appreciation from the University. I got a free education out of it, both in the classroom and also on the football field.

MAURY DAMKROGER

FULLBACK

FOR THE RECORD

**MAURY DAMKROGER
1971-1973**

6'-2" 215 lbs.
Lincoln, NE

NOW

Wife, Kristy
2 children: Andy 26, Alison 24

Salesman for
Corporate Express

Omaha Nebraska

Andy, Kristy, Alison and
Maury Damkroger

HUSKER HIGHLIGHTS

1. After The Game of The Century in 1971, I rode next to Coach Devaney on the bus from Norman to Oklahoma City to catch our plane back to Lincoln. Jim Carstens was also sitting next to me. Coach Devaney was just wired. He was so excited. First, he told old stories and just reminisced because it was an hour bus ride. Then he mentioned over and over again what a great game Jeff Kinney had. He said it was the greatest display of running that he had ever seen. That was the neatest memory I have of him.

2. Coach Corgan was rough and tough, but he was an honest guy. He would do anything for you and help you anyway he could. He had a bunch of sayings, some of which you could not put in a book. He was a great guy to play for. You go back and talk to Roger Craig and some of those guys, and they always bring up the fact that Coach Corgan was a great guy. He was "old school."

3. The most remarkable offensive play I witnessed was Johnny Rodgers' punt return against Colorado in Boulder in 1972. Johnny had about a 15 yard punt return but there were eight guys that missed him on the sidelines. That was incredible.

4. Playing for NU changed my life from the standpoint of knowing the loyalty that the State has for the players. It is incredible that this State supports the program the way they have. Back then it was real strong. It's the State's following that amazes me the most. It's in the newspapers everyday and whether its football season or not.

5. If I could go back and relive one game, it would be the UCLA game in 1972 in Los Angeles. We lost (14-17). We just gave that baby away. If we would have won that one, I think we would have a chance to win a third consecutive national championship.

6. That same year (1972) I had a motion penalty in the game against Iowa State (23-23 tie). We went for it on a 4th down, and my motion penalty nullified our 1st down. They called it back and we kicked a field goal. Then Iowa State came back and tied the game.

7. Jerry Tagge was a tremendous leader. Also, Johnny Rodgers, Jeff Kinney, Doug Dumler, Bill Janssen. The upper classman in those two years were not only great football players but great people.

8. My personal goal was to play pro football. I got that opportunity. It was not an illustrious career but I got to find out what it was like.

. The two most important reasons for the wins were (a) Coaching. We had excellent assistant coaches and many of them went on to be Head Coaches in college. (b) The quality of athletes, both from an athletic standpoint and from a personal standpoint. There were some unbelievable people on those teams.

0. We were confident NU would win National championship in 1971. When I first got there I really never thought about it. But then we got in the Game of The Century and with the talent we had on that team I was pretty sure we would win. We had leadership and great coaching.

1. It is fun to be considered the best. If you Google that, like I did last summer out of curiosity, they still list us as the best team ever. It's a neat thing to be a part of it. You can argue about it until the cows come home, and no one is ever going to win.

2. My biggest challenge was just making sure on the `71 team that I did not make any mistakes.

3. My biggest disappointment was not winning a 3rd straight national title in 1972. We had as much talent on that team as we did on the 1971 championship team.

4. The most important aspects that made the team work so well together were coaching, players and attitude. It was all three. The coaches and attitude obviously. The 1971 team had one hell of a chemistry. The older guys just got along great. As a sophomore on the team I just watched. The guys were incredible. When Saturday came everyone was focused. They knew what had to be done.

5. My most outrageous teammate was Doug Jamail. Doug and Satch kept the locker room loose.

6. The fans had a positive effect on my efforts in the games. To walk on that field in front of 70,000 fans is just incredible. My dad played for Nebraska in the late 1940s. He told me "The opening kickoff when you are on the field, you will be so nervous you won't believe it." He was right. It is scary.

17. Playing for Nebraska helped me in the after football life. There is name recognition and it has opened some doors.

18. NU was a lot of fun. I can't think of a better place to play. I am sure that all the Tennessee, Southern Cal, and Oklahoma players also think that their place was the best.

"Playing for NU changed my life. I knew the loyalty that Nebraskans have for their team."

Dick and Sharon Davis

DICK DAVIS

FULLBACK

HUSKER HIGHLIGHTS

1. Some of us were having lunch and teasing each other and doing the "chicken man Pock!, Pock!, Pock!" routine at the lunch table. And Coach Devaney saw us and he got a little perturbed. So he came over and jumped on us and said "You are laughing and having a good time now but if you don't win this game your ass is walking back to Nebraska." We won the game and we did not have to walk back to Nebraska.

That is the difference between coaching and playing. Sometimes you don't really understand the humongous pressures of coaching and the pressures to win. The man always had a noticeably quick wit, and that was one of his best traits.

2. Coach Devaney was furiously competitive. He connected to each player in the way that made the player respond most positively. Coach "Iron Mike" Corgan would tell us "go hit that cement wall" and some of players would say "okay, coach" and go hit that cement wall. Others of us would say "wait a minute, explain the rationale for hitting that cement wall," so he would motivate me to do so. Different players have different motivations, and Devaney was able to read that extremely well.

One time I was not living up to his expectations and he had a conversation with me. He was reasonably rough at the beginning of the conversation and I think he saw my demeanor, and he automatically changed to more of the counseling kind of conversation. He understood that I was getting it when he approached me differently. He was able to figure out the psyche of a young person and get the best out of that person. That was one of his best gifts.

3. We were playing Kansas State and it was my junior year (1967). It started to snow heavily with humongous snowflakes, and we came out. It was tight game. For a moment we stopped playing football and looked around the stands and nobody had left. It was not a blizzard but it was heavy snow. And we said these people are crazy. You can't have better fans. I was fortunate to play in other stadiums including pro stadiums and there is really no place like Nebraska. Just first class in how they embrace their players. They want you to do well not just as players but as human beings.

4. The relationship among the players was always very good. When you have two 6-4 teams, (1967-1968), you sometimes thought there would be finger pointing or criticism. I did not see any of that. The team always was very cohesive and connected when I was a junior and senior (`67-`68). At Nebraska we always had fun and it was a strong and positive environment. Our coaches were enormously serious. They took the games very hard and as you walked past coaching offices late at night after you partied you would still see the cars there. We really had some strong dedicated coaches.

5. I broke some records as a fullback at NU and still have some of them. I had some good running games as a fullback but the one play that always stands out to me is a fullback swing pass. After you swung you went straight down the sideline and the quarterback would throw the ball to you. I think I caught 27 passes and for a back that was pretty good. We were playing Colorado and Frank Patrick was our quarterback and his claim to fame was that he could throw it 70 yards. So it was the first half of the Colorado game and it was a fullback swing out and up

pass. And the pass hung there forever. When the ball comes right over your head it is a lot tougher ball to catch. I saw this ball and it was in the air forever. It is coming down and I was thinking "my goodness, I am not going to be able to catch this ball because it is at the wrong angle." And so I just put my arms out and it fell into my hand and I said "Wow!" For some odd reason I was a flanker that day. I still get tickled about it because it was an unexpected benefit.

The experience of NU was a life changer just for the fact that I became assistant principal at my old high school at North High School at age 24. And I was a principal at McMillan Junior High School at age 30. The name recognition helped, but also the relationships that you built. Harold Reeves was my principal when I was at North High School. Harold said "Dick, I think you can go back to your old Alma Mater (North) and do this." I did not have my Master's or my Doctorate at the time but by the time I went to McMillan I had both my Master's and Doctorate. He very frankly said "I knew you as a student here at North High and you played with my son at Nebraska. I got to know you better and based on the fact that who you are and how you handle yourself. I thought you were the best candidate for this position." And for the next 7 years I tried to prove him right and won some national recognition for that.

My experience at Nebraska allowed me to broaden my experience outside of my old neighborhood and exposed me to a broader set of folks. Life is awfully good and I am blessed. When I sit down with recruits I always say to them from a practical standpoint "I don't know if you are going to be a great football player at Nebraska, but very frankly if you understand the Nebraska environment and it is a love affair with it's football players, you will be successful. You can become even more successful outside the gridiron because of the respect and admiration that Nebraskans have for their football program and their players.

I would always try to work harder and longer. As you continue your life there is always an element of hard work. Through Nebraska you learn that and you hope that you can be a better pro football player. That extended to OPS and to my business now. Hard work and focus and discipline and understanding are what you are trying achieve. Nebraska taught me that because Nebraska was a national program and needed

to step up my game. I appreciated Nebraska allowing me to play on a national level.

8. I don't think that we had one "best" leader. We did not have what I call dynamic motivating in your face kind of leadership on our teams.

9. My personal goal was to graduate. When I was a Junior in high school I came into my own. I figured out that I couldn't be my brother Ricky Davis or Gale Sayers, but I had to be myself and I had a successful career after that. My goals were always to be the best I could be. All I wanted to do was be a starting player and contribute to the team and do the best I could with the abilities that I have.

10. The most important reason for the wins were (a) the system was a good system. The organization structure allowed players to mature and be as successful as they could be. That is very important to have a great organization. When I played pro football, Cleveland was a great organization and New Orleans was a very poor organization. And it is night and day for an organization regarding when you win or when you don't win.

11. To motivate myself I would play the game in my mind. When I went to bed the sheets were nicely tucked and the blankets were appropriately placed. By the time I got up from that morning nap, the covers were off the bed, the sheets were crumpled, etc. I would play the game repeatedly in my mind. So by the time I got to the game it felt second nature to me.

12. I don't think that I had any big personal challenges. But from a team perspective sometimes we were just outgunned at various positions. In the Big 8 when a guy outweighed you by 30 pounds, there are some things that you had to compensate. Sometimes you can compensate and win the game, and sometimes you can't.

13. I did not really have any disappointments. Did I want to be the quarterback rather then the fullback? You better believe it. Did I want to play both sides of it offense and defense? You better believe it. I was also sharp enough to know if I played both sides they might stick me on defense forever. But when you look back that was such a wonderful experience and led to so many more opportunities as I grew older.

14. The most important aspect that made the team work so well together were coaches, player's talent, and attitude. A combination of all of that. There is never just one factor. Each team developed it's own personality. And that personality will win you two more game or lose you two more games. I never saw any hostility between players. I did not see any of mean spiritedness at Nebraska.

15. My most talented teammate from a back perspective was Ben "Pope" Gregory. Ben never made the record books and never had any great statistics, but Ben is what I call a "complete back." There are some backs that run well. Some block well. Some backs catch well. Ben was the most complete back that I played with. "Greatness" is not raw talent but the completeness of the player. Ben was able to do all of those functions very well. He was a complete athlete.

16. There were so many outrageous players, and that is why we were so fun. Buster Yannon and Sherwin Jarmon were all around crazy guys. The storytelling was just marvelous. Mike Green always had an enormous amount of wit and humor and intellect. He has always made me laugh and I have known him since he was 4.

17. My position coach was Mike Corgan. He was crazy but I learned an enormous amount of discipline from Coach Corgan because I believe in reason, logic, and rationale. He would inspire me and he would say "You go out there and kill them." I was able to be pro competitive by the various disciplines that he taught. He taught an enormous amount of fundamentals.

I remember playing for Denver and I was 207 pounds. I was on Lou Saban's T.V. coaching show and on the phone he asked "Why are you as tough as you are and block the way you do?" Coach Saban liked his fullbacks at 230-235 pounds, but if you could do it the same way at 207 pounds and still be quick then that was fine. I basically said to him on the TV show "It was the background that I had at Nebraska. The basic techniques of being a complete football player are taught at Nebraska and taught very well." Frankly I did not appreciate that as a freshman and sophomore, but Nebraska taught us to be a "complete back" I appreciated that more after I left Nebraska. Coach Mike Corgan was a great teacher.

"One of Devaney's gifts was getting the best out of a person."

RICHARD DUDA

CENTER AND LONG SNAPPER

HUSKER HIGHLIGHTS

1. Coach Devaney demanded that we never make a mistake in the "red zone," and he meant it. Once in the red zone, we scored a touchdown, PERIOD! Heaven help the player who blew a red zone scoring opportunity with a false start penalty.

2. My favorite memory of the staff was Coach Monte Kiffin singing "Sherry" on the bus on game nights. Coach Kiffin kept us "loose" in the locker room.

3. Husker fans were and still are the best and most loyal college football fans in the nation.

4. I had a great experience at UNL, and I'm proud of my alma mater.

   What I learned from playing football at UNL was this: "Because of our days of never giving up on the field, we can never give up in life." My football experience made me mentally stronger for the challenges I undertook in life after college. It also taught me how to perform under tremendous pressure.

5. The most remarkable offensive play I witnessed was how Johnny Rodgers dominated the 1973 Orange Bowl. His five scores versus Notre Dame were mind-boggling. I remember most vividly watching Johnny sucking oxygen from a mask on the sidelines after his 77-yard punt return against Oklahoma the year before (1971)!

6. The three most important qualities that accounted for our wins were: (1) The confidence instilled in us by our coaches through exhaustive practice and preparation. (2) The shared trust among all team members - each of us knowing the great abilities of the other team members. (3) When all is said and done, and you have that red N on your helmet, you simply owe it to your teammates, your coaches and your fans not to blow it.

7. The best motivation for me during the game was the fear of making a bad snap (in front of tens of thousands of people) on a punt, FG, or PAT that might result in a lost scoring opportunity or, worse yet, give our opponents the opportunity to score on us! When you are an offensive lineman or a long-snapper, your actions are largely unsung. Your identity is rarely mentioned unless you make a mistake.

8. The Oklahoma teams during those years were by far my biggest night-mare. They were very tough hitters, and their fans in the "Snakepit" were frightening. They hated us.

9. My biggest disappointment was the fact that I never played first string. Still, I cannot complain because I was second to two All-American centers - Doug Dumler and Rik Bonness.

10. Coach Devaney retiring before the `72 season was a big change. Devaney and Osborne had very different coaching styles, but the team adapted.

11. The most important factor that made our team work so well together were the coaches. They set the stage. They expected perfection. The high expectations of the fans also motivated the team.

Richard Duda

12. The most inspirational person on the team was Coach Tom Osborne. He was an excellent offensive coordinator. He was so inspirational because of his intelligence and professional demeanor.

13. My position coaches were Carl Selmer and Clete Fisher. They taught us to run plays, to know defenses in my sleep and execute, execute, execute!

14. Coach Monte Kiffin recruited me. I was the only recruit who Monte tested in a 40-yard-dash because of my knee injury in high school.

15. I snapped every punt, PAT and field goal for three years. Fortunately, I never made a bad snap.

16. One of my claims to fame in Nebraska Football is that I am a second-generation Nebraska player. My father, Charles, played guard on the 1941 Rose Bowl team. In my tenure with the Cornhuskers, I played in the Orange Bowl, Cotton Bowl, and Sugar Bowl. I doubt many families can claim representation in each of the four longest-standing college bowl games. Unfortunately, I was unable to convince my daughter to play offensive line when she was in school for the `93, `94, and `96 Orange Bowl teams or the 1995 Fiesta Bowl team!

17. The fans affected our efforts in the games because there was definitely the feeling that the team couldn't let down the fans. The fans were and are extremely loyal.

18. I was nostalgic about playing football for Nebraska in bowl games because of my dad's experience in the 1941 Rose Bowl. In 1993, I felt honored to accept an award on behalf of my father who was inducted into the Nebraska Football Hall of Fame. My father passed away in 1977, but my mother, brother, wife and two children also attended the event at Memorial Stadium.

19. I was scout center for Richie Glover during my "red shirt" year. It was my job during that year to prepare him for weekly opponents, and Coach Monte Kiffin made sure I did. Richie was a great guy. I loved that year, even though I didn't play.

20. Playing for Nebraska helped me in the after football life. I learned how to be a team-player, push myself toward goals, and not give up easily. I also learned the importance of exercise and mental stamina, which was especially important in dental school. Unfortunately, as I have gotten older, my hips and joints have experienced the negative effects of those many years of football.

21. I very much appreciate the once-in-a-lifetime opportunity the University gave me to play football with some of the best players, coaches, and fans in the history of college football!

"My football experience made me mentally stronger for the challenges I undertook later in life."

DOUG DUMLER
1970-1972

6'-3" 230 lbs.
Melrose Park, IL

2nd team All Big 8

Pro Football
New England &
Minnesota Vikings
played in Super Bowl 11

had 5 years in the NFL and it
was a wonderful experience.

NOW

Attorney at Law

*"We had a special
chemistry. The players
bonded with
each other."*

Doug Dumler

DOUG DUMLER *(aka "Goose")*

CENTER (CO-CAPTAIN 1972)

HUSKER HIGHLIGHTS

1. When I was first recruited Coach Devaney came to my house in Chicago and that was a great honor. I was recruited as a tight end and I went into his office on a recruiting trip and he said "Doug, I think you can start for us as a sophomore." And that blew my mind. I thought it was designed to get me to come to NU. Bob was a great recruiter and a great massager of a person's ego. He was able to read your mental attitude and say the right thing.

2. Nebraska fans were remarkable when Bill and I would first walk out for the coin toss when we were captains. The people would pat you on the back as you made your way toward the field. It was awesome that these people would come from so far away in Nebraska every Saturday in the fall to just come watch us play.

   When we came back from beating OU in 1971 it was Thanksgiving Day evening and it was dark and we land at the Lincoln airport. I am trying to figure out why we didn't come to the terminal. There is this waving in the darkness. All of a sudden I realized it was people. There were 30,000 people at the airport and they spilled out onto the tarmac and onto the runway. That was another classic example of NU fans that cannot be repeated anywhere in the country. It was unbelievable.

3. The fans were great but the camaraderie that you develop as a team is really something. We had a special chemistry and the players happened to bond with each other. Black and white, young and old, seniors and sophomores, we just got along.

4. The 3 times that we played OU were high points. We were able to beat them 2 out of 3 times. The Game of The Century was probably the highest point of my career. The first time we beat OU I was a sophomore and it was at home (28-21) and we won the Big 8 Championship. In fact I have a picture of us carrying Bob off the field and it is one of my cherished mementos. Oklahoma has to be the top opponent. But we also played Southern Cal. in the coliseum in 1970. We are out there in the coliseum where OJ Simpson played. You think about the history in that place and we are playing the Trojans, one of the storied programs of college football. We tied them and we really should have won.

5. I got a great education and I am today what I am because of my education and my experiences at NU. I met my wife and she is a native Nebraskan and as red as you can get and her family is the same way. It is just a big family there. I grew up in Chicago but Nebraska is my second home.

6. I remember recovering my only fumble ever at Iowa State. I looked down and the ball was there and I fell on it. That was a big deal at the time. The Jerry Tagge's quarterback sneak to make the winning touchdown against LSU was huge. Whenever you see a picture of Tagge stretching his arms out to get the ball over the goal line, I am the guy at the bottom of the pile.

7. I remember watching JR's punt return against OU. It was maybe Nebraska's biggest touchdown ever. I was not on the field but it was just a thrill. Also Joe Orduna scored on the 70 yard touchdown run against Southern Cal

in 1970. I think I threw a halfway decent block on that play.

8. I think of Bill Janssen as the ultimate teammate. He and I were roommates and seniors and co-captains. The guy knew everybody on the team by their first name and I think that he knew all their parent's names. He was one of those guys that knew where you were from, what you were doing, what was making you happy. He was just one of those teammates that was absolutely indispensable to a team.

   I finally learned that lesson about 10-12 years after I left Nebraska. You need to be part of the team whether you are in the employment situation or in a school or whatever. We were all cogs in the same wheel and to the extent if one of us got chipped off that would make the whole machine skip a little bit.

9. I would enjoy greatly to go back and play that last offensive series in 1971 at Oklahoma where we drove down 65 yards for the winning touchdown. It was 3rd and 9 and Jerry made a nice play to make a scrambling pass to JR for the first down. He had to scramble because I missed my block. I would like another shot at that one.

10. Bill Janssen led by the fact that he was the genuine all American nice guy who was a friend to everybody. Johnny Rodgers led with extreme talent on the football field. Willie Harper was a guy that I looked up to and led by example with consistent play all the time. Spider Adkins was that same way. Spider was more reserved and quiet but get him on the football field and that man was a leader. Joe Blahak and Doug Jamail were cutups. Doug never really started as a player at NU but was one of indispensable guys on the team that just kept us all together. There were many aspects of leadership that team exhibited throughout those years I was there. Rich Glover, I played against him in practice and he never said 2 words but get him on the field and he just dominated. How can you not follow a guy like that?

11. The most important reasons for the wins were (a) teamwork was by far the number one quality (b) we had great talent throughout the team. We had quality people who not only had physical talent but were smart and dedicated. The thing that stirred the whole pot was the coaching staff. Bob Devaney is in the Hall of Fame. Tom Osborne is in the Hall of Fame. Monte

Kiffin is now with the Tampa Bay Buccaneers. We had a number of coaches go from there to the pros.

12. In terms of confidence and being the best team on the field at any given time, I don't think there was any doubt. For example, before that final drive against OU in 1971 we are out there at the 35 yard line and it is a TV timeout. And we are all talking to each other like hey guys this is it, our last chance, if we pull this off. And during the TV timeout I look over to the sidelines towards the OU side and I see my brother in the stands. And out 75,000 people I pick out my brother, are you kidding me? And he was looking right at me and I gave him the number 1 sign. All 11 of us on that field knew that Oklahoma was not going to stop us and we were going to go down that field and score. We had confidence in ourselves and in each other.

13. The idea of teamwork is something that you carry with you throughout your life. It is a life lesson that NU football taught very well.

14. It was a great honor to be considered the best. And as years go by it is a bigger honor.

15. Before the games I got quiet. I turned inward and prepared myself mentally. I remember my roommate Jim Carstens would get really frustrated with me because I would not answer his questions and I would not talk to him on Thursday and Friday before a game.

16. When you think about it every Saturday was a challenge when you faced OU and the Selmon boys. Those kind of people forced you to rise up against a real top notch player. You just had to elevate your game.

17. I never thought about quitting. There was too much excitement there. Even if I had never started. Just to be on that team would have been a great honor.

18. The whole drive against OU in 1971 to win the game was a great challenge. Also, the quarterback sneak that Jerry Tagge scored against LSU to win the first national championship. We had worked our way down and it came down to one play.

19. My biggest disappointment was losing to OU as a senior in 1972. Johnny Rodgers caught a touchdown pass that they called back because they had pushed him out of bounds before he even caught the ball. I would have loved to beat OU all three times we played.

20. We had three things that led to success: (a) teamwork. We had 100 guys that believed in each other and then (b) we had the great talent and (c) great coaching. That combination is death to the other team.

21. My most athletic talented teammate was Johnny Rodgers. Nobody that I can ever remember could stop and start like he did. All you have to do is look at the punt return against OU where he caught that ball and got nailed immediately, bounced back, took 4 steps to his right full speed and stopped and cut up the field full speed. It was physically impossible.

   In terms of going beyond pure athleticism to being great football players I think of Jerry Tagge and Jeff Kinney. Not the fastest guys and not the strongest but intelligent smart football players and knew what they had to do. They got the most out of their talents. Joe Blahak. Rich Glover was unparalleled in the defensive line. Too small to play in the NFL but terrorized the offense with his penetration and quickness and his uncanny ability to stay on his feet and knock the guy down. Bill Kosch at safety may never had been out of position in any play in his career. Bob Newton and Keith Wortman would not be great athletes on the basketball floor but the two of them played 20 years in the NFL between them. You cannot get much better than that.

22. My toughest of opponents were Herb Orvis of Colorado and Matt Blair Iowa State. The Selmon brothers were always a challenge.

23. Herb Orvis was a 25 year old senior because he had been in the Marines. And he broke my facemask with one forearm.

24. One thing I will tell you when a person comes up to me and says "I hear that you played football?" I always say "yeah, I played for Nebraska." That is where I had the greatest experience and learned the most and had the best time.

25. In a quiet sort of way I looked up to Jerry Tagge. He was the general and ran the offense. The guys in the offensive line like Bob Newton and Keith Wortman. I learned a lot from them when I was a sophomore. It was a joy to play with them because I was scared to death out there and next to me is Keith knocking somebody's helmet off. You fed off that. Rich Glover was inspirational because he was so steady and so dependable.

26. The hardest worker in practice was Mike Beran. He was a walk-on and deserved to start as a senior. You look at his work ethic and then you are not surprised because you knew that anybody that worked that hard and was so dedicated was going to be successful. Frosty Anderson was a guy that did not have great speed but he was a starter and played very well and caught some big touchdown passes for us. There were a number of guys that overachieved.

27. Once the game gets going your adrenaline and training takes over and you just do the job that you were trained for. In 1970 we were coming into our own as a national power. It was a nervous time but it was a very exciting time because of that frenzied crowd of 75,000 people. It was just great.

28. I am a lawyer and I recognize that there are lots of lawyers that are far better than I am. You learn from the mistakes you made and you follow the good example set by people around you. I learned that from playing on a team like Nebraska.

29. I feel appreciated by the University for the time I put in. I get invited back from time to time to participate in an event or reunion or most recently the Breakfast for Champions. Nebraska does a very good job of tapping its heritage of student-athletes who have made Nebraska great. They do a very good job of bringing people back and showing that their contributions to the university are appreciated.

30. One more story about our game against OU in 1969. I was a sophomore. We beat them 28-21 in Lincoln to win the Big 8 Championship. And before that game and during the week the coaches had spotted something in the Oklahoma secondary when the team lined up in a certain offensive position their secondary did a couple things. And they thought that we could take advantage of this. We would audible into a post pattern that Guy Ingles would run.

   During that week at practice every time we audibled into that play it went for a touchdown. And sure enough we get down to the 30 yard line against OU and Tagge calls that audible and I was just inches away from telling Lucius Selmon across from me "Lucius, touchdown coming up." I wish I had said it. And sure enough it was. He threw to Ingles and it was a touchdown and it was the winning score.

FOR THE RECORD

**ADRIAN FIALA
1967-1969**

6'-2" 210 lbs.
Omaha, NE

Academic All-American
(Baseball)

NOW

Married, no children.

Omaha attorney and Sports
Commentator for UNL games
on Pinnacle Sports Radio.

Omaha, Nebraska

*The NU fan support
and admiration stays
with you a
long, long time."*

Adrian Fiala

ADRIAN FIALA

LINEBACKER

HUSKER HIGHLIGHTS

1. My best memory is winning the Big 8 Championship my senior year (1969) because I played on both of the earlier teams when we were 6-4 (1967-1968). There was a lot at stake in `69 and we won the Big 8 that year. This provided the engine for success in later years.

2. One of my personal greatest memories was watching Wayne Meylan throw a water bag out of a hotel window. He was a piece of work. Also, stopping Oklahoma's Steve Owens my senior year. He was such a great football player (Heisman Trophy `69).

3. My favorite memory of Coach Bob Devaney was the time we played at Kansas when I was a sophomore (1967). We got beat 10-0, and I think that was Devaney's first shutout as a Head Coach. We practiced that Sunday morning after the game. A lot of guys were hung over. Christ, if you got behind the wrong person you could get drunk off the smell of their breath. Our practices were usually about a half an hour, but that time we practiced about one hour and fifteen minutes. Devaney just looked like somebody had kicked him around all night. He was up all night watching film.

   Then that afternoon, we went over to the coliseum and watched film, and instead of an hour session it was about a 2 hour session. He had a comment for each player who walked into the room. The one he said to me was "Fiala, you should have bought a ticket to get into the ballgame yesterday" (laughter). It destroyed me, but I took that comment and wrote it down and taped it to my locker and my closet door, so I would see it everyday. He always had a way with words. I probably should have purchased a ticket to that game.

4. When we went to the Sun Bowl in El Paso, Texas in 1969, some guys went over to Mexico and got drunk and thrown in jail. Some of the Sun Bowl people went out and got them. Everyone sobered up except "Mr. X", and he is laying there in the bed half drunk. Coach Kiffin came in and Monte was livid. Then all of a sudden Devaney shows up and Devaney sees "Mr. X" drunk. "Mr. X" looked up at Devaney and used some profanity. Devaney went berserk and was ready to rip his head off but Monte gets between them and says "Calm down, Coach". "Mr. X" is a doctor now so he probably does not want this story printed. You did not hear it from me.

5. Defensive line coach George Kelly left in 1968 and went to Notre Dame. He was very nice but he would get excited. We were in scrimmage one time when a defensive guy came up in the hole. He just whiffed (grabbed air) and missed the tackle. We got in the huddle and Kelly walked in and looked at this kid and said "Next time that guy is coming at you, hit him with your purse".

6. Regarding Nebraska fans, day after day, year after year, the majority of our fans are very loyal. I am truly amazed at times when people walk up to me and hand me things when we played (pictures, programs, mementos). I just got a thing in the mail from a lady who is about 80, and she said "I have had these things from when you played and you autographed some things for me and I am getting on in years and I thought you might like to have these". The fan support and admiration goes a lot deeper than when you are playing. It stays with you a long, long time. It is amazing and quite refreshing. It succeeds because it gets into the blood and stays there.

Marv Mueller from Columbus and George Buckler were both sophomores when I came to NU and they showed me around on my recruiting trip. When I finally came down to play both of them looked after me and gave me advice. My bond with Marv became even stronger. He was really important in giving me stability in terms of school and career and football. He still is my friend today.

Bob Best from McCook and a lot of guys from smaller towns gave me an opportunity to make friends with people from small communities. I came from South Omaha and most of my friends were city guys. Bill Dice from Grant was my roommate. Mike Green and Dick Davis from North Omaha. Dick and I took recruiting trips together and have stayed friends.

When we played Alabama in the Sugar Bowl (1967) (7-34), I was a red shirt sophomore. It was Bear Bryant's team. "Snake" Stabler was their quarterback and they had a great team. We were just getting ready to go out there and play, and Coach Ross and Devaney got together with all of us and said "Now watch out the first play because we all know that Stabler likes to go long early." First play they go deep and beat our secondary. Bob and Jim are going crazy. Devaney said "what the hell happened here," and we said "Well, we just didn't think Stabler would do that, coach."

10. The next year (1968) I started my first game against Washington in Seattle (17-7). I was so excited I could not stand it. We went out on the field on defense and Barry Alvarez was the linebacker and he called the defense. They snapped the ball so I just went across the line of scrimmage and right through the blocker and made a tackle for a loss on my very first play. That still sticks in my mind.

11. Beating Oklahoma 44-14 my senior year was memorable (1969). It set the stage for the winning streak and national honors.

12. I was able to meet Bear Bryant. He and Bob were talking and I really wanted to meet Bear so I went up to him and introduced myself. There I was with two college football legends. It was an amazing moment for me as a young kid.

13. I finally finished law school and got my law degree. I felt a great sense of pride because of that.

14. We played Missouri at Columbia in my sophomore year (1967) and Barry Alvarez and I had watched a lot of film together. So they lined up in a formation that both of us quickly recognized. I looked over at Barry and said "I am going for the ball" and sure enough it was the play we thought was coming and nobody blocked me. I knocked the ball loose and Barry was able to recover that fumble. Barry is a great guy and great player. (Alvarez just retired as Wisconsin University's head coach).

15. I learned at UNL the benefits of hard work and discipline. How to manage your time and work together as a team. How to respect others and their individual progress. Without goals you do not achieve. Mental toughness. If you make a mistake or get knocked down, there are two things you can do: (1) stay down or (2) get up and fight again. Quitting is not an option. The first time you quit is hard, but the second time it is a little easier and so on. I always tell the young kids not to measure someone when the times are good but measure them when times are tough and how they come through those times. That is the true measure of an individual.

16. The key to the comeback season in 1969 was Kansas. We had to win that game. If we did not, we were pretty much done, because of our earlier losses to Southern Cal and Missouri. We were 2-2. It was the turning point not only for the season but for Bob as well. Fortunately, we won (21-17) and that was the start of 32 consecutive games undefeated.

17. The best leader as a Coach was Jim Ross. None better. The best leader as a player was Bob Liggett. He would stand up and say what needed to be said. Dick Davis was a leader.

18. Devaney was straight forward honest and not a phony ounce in his body. Good sense of humor. Great teacher. Someone you felt like you could talk to without restriction.

19. My personal goals were to do well in school and get my degree. I became honorable mention academic all American, and Second team academic all American in baseball.

20. Our team goals in 1967 were to carry on the tradition, to win the Big 8 and go to a bowl game. Coach Bob used to say "You win the big 8 championship and the rest takes care of itself."

21. The most important reasons for the wins were that we never thought about losing. We had great confidence in Bob and his staff and that we would be better prepared than our opponents.

22. We were confident NU would win the Big 8 championship in 1969. We could see a great improvement in the offense. We played USC in the first game and gave them a great tussle. We lost (21-31), but we still played well. That built our confidence.

23. What I learned that helped me succeed since my football playing days is mental toughness. If you get turned down in the business world, you get back up.

24. I thought about quitting early in my career when I first arrived. Fortunately, my parents were understanding and supportive and gave me good advice. Quitting in my family was never an option. You start something and you finished.

    In 1968 I had a tear in my lower intestine called a fissure. I lost a bunch of weight. I missed 4 or 5 games. And I was pretty down and thought maybe I should give it up. During the off season I had a surgery and I came back in the spring. Everybody has a period like that.

25. The biggest challenge for the team in 1969 was that K.U. game when we were down and we had to come back in the 4th quarter and score. We did and we won (21-17).

26. The most important factor that made the 1969 team work so well together was that we were all focused on the two previous 6-4 years and Devaney's status. We were extremely committed to getting the job done.

27. Our team chemistry was great. Everybody on defense played together as a unit. Everybody respected each other and that had a lot to do what we all accomplished (9-2; Big 8 and Sun Bowl Champions).

28. Jim McFarland was a little odd but was a great guy. He marched to a different drummer. He and Van Brownson were the only ones who voted not to go to the Sun Bowl game.

29. My most talented teammate was Dana Stevenson, a great athlete. The most talented opponent was Bobby Anderson from Colorado, a quarterback and running back. Tough kid, great football and baseball player.

30. The most inspirational player was Ben Gregory. He was a good solid guy. There was no "foo foo" about him. He played the game tough. He was a good person and as hard a working guy as there was. He was not a rah-rah guy but in he instilled confidence in everyone.

31. The hardest worker in practice was Glenn Patterson. He was a center and he worked his rear off all the time.

32. Randy Reeves surprised me the most. He played safety from Omaha Benson. He was a high intellectual and for him to be playing this violent game was a big surprise to me, but he played very well.

33. Practice was a treat. Practice under Bob's plan was highly organized. I was surprised that we would take a break in the middle and have a glass of water or a piece of orange. It was such a revitalization. Practices were intense and difficult, but come Saturday you were very well prepared. In some respects the games were easier than the practices.

34. The part of practice I hated the most was getting dressed and taped. Putting all that stuff on and taking it off.

35. I heard the fans pre-game and at breaks but during the actual action my concentration was so intense that I did not notice the fans.

36. Running on the field for the 1st time was like floating in the air. I was oblivious to everything.

37. Playing for Nebraska helped me in the after football life. All the preparation we went through to achieve what we did. It created a trust and a bond between us. You have to perform. People remember you. It helped open doors for me.

38. Do I feel appreciated by the University for the time I put in? The answer is double edged. There are parts of my activity and relationship with the University where I feel appreciated. There are parts where I don't. I mainly get a great deal of appreciation from people outside the university with fans and working with the Alumni Association. But when we get directly in the athletic part it is a different story.

39. I want to add this advice to all young people: Never give up. Just keep going!

*"Nebraska fans are
the biggest reason
that Nebraska football
is world renowned."*

Pat Fischer

PAT FISCHER

DEFENSIVE BACK

HUSKER HIGHLIGHTS

1. Bob Devaney and his coaching staff were very stable people with a lot of common sense. Players could clearly communicate with them.

2. What can you say about Nebraska fans that has not already been said? They are the biggest reason that Nebraska football is world known and world renowned.

3. Nebraska players always played with class. I do not remember any dirty players or hot dogs on the `70 and `71 teams.

4. We had respect for all our opponents. They gave us their best shot.

5. UNL was a terrific place for a football player to go to school. I cannot imagine a better campus on Game Day.

6. The most remarkable offensive play I witnessed were Johnny Rodgers' two punt returns for touchdowns against Oklahoma (1971) and Alabama in the `72 Orange Bowl.

7. I learned to be a productive member of an effective organization. I did not have to be a top dog to make a valuable contribution. That is the essence of team chemistry.

8. I intercepted a pass and scored a touchdown against Kansas in `71. That was a great moment for me and my family.

9. We had great leadership from guys who did not talk a lot. People like Jerry Tagge, Rich Glover, Goose Dumler, Bob Terrio. And we had more vocal guys like J.R. and Doug Jamail.

The characteristics that made them the best leaders were consistent behavior and performance and a good work ethic.

10. My personal goal in coming to Nebraska was wanting to play. I wanted to contribute to the best program in the country.

11. Our team goals were always to win the first game, then the Big 8 and finally the National title,

12. I do not remember any coach talking about specific goals before a game. I do recall the talks about great effort and what we had to do to win.

13. The three most important qualities that accounted for the wins were: (a) We were very confident. Coach Devaney and staff conveyed an aura of confidence. (b) We had super talent, (c) we were well prepared. I believe we were better prepared than our opponents.

14. I was confident that NU would win the National Championship in 1971. As confident as you can be about anything. It was a shock when we did not get that 3rd consecutive title in 1972.

15. NU helped me succeed since my football playing days. I try to bring the same attitude and effort to my job. I am a coach and have been since 1974. I wish my players can obtain the same benefits of playing that I did.

16. I am flattered to have my face in the National Championship team picture. Living in Texas the last 23 years made me realize how much other people respect Nebraska Football.

17. I did not have to do anything to get motivated before each game. Saturday morning I was ready to go! I love the game. I was motivated by wanting to contribute to a victory and not let the team down.

18. NU had the best team in the country when we were there. It was a huge challenge for me to actually play on that team.

19. I learned to persevere. I once thought about quitting, but thankfully not for long.

20. The games I remember as being the biggest challenge for the team were 1971 Oklahoma (Last Drive) and 1971 LSU (Orange Bowl)

21. If I could go back and change one thing I would train differently. With all the advancements in training techniques, I could have been better prepared.

22. Coach Devaney's decision to retire before the `72 season did not affect me to much, but I know it had a huge impact on the coaching staff. We lost some of the continuity we had before.

23. The most important aspects that made the team work so well together were: (a) Devaney and his staff brought us together. (b) We have guys with real positive attitudes. (c) we had super talent.

24. We had super team chemistry. Everyone wanted to win. I don't remember any back biting.

25. The most talented athletes I played with were Johnny Rodgers, Willie Harper, Van Brownson. The most talented opponents were Joe Washington and Greg Pruitt

26. The most inspirational person on the team was Mike Beran "Red" Baron, the hardest working man I have ever met.

27. The most outrageous teammate was Doug Jamail.

28. Bill Olds worked the hardest in practice. Bill was a tireless worker but most of the players worked very hard.

29. Who kept the locker room the loosest were Doug Jamail and Paul Schneider (trainer).

30. My position coach was Warren Powers. He taught me many of the techniques that I still teach to this day.

31. I enjoyed practice. During the season we seldom had any tough contact drills. Devaney believed in saving it for Saturday.

32. I did not hate any part of practice.

33. I got into all the games my senior year. My Sophomore and Junior year all Home games, all Bowl games and a few road games. It was being part of something great.

34. It meant everything to me to be part of the team. I played three years of Varsity Football at NU and played in the Orange and Cotton Bowls.

35. Nebraska fans brought out the best we had to give. My feet did not touch the ground when I ran on the field the 1st time (1971).

36. My greatest memory was after winning the 1974 Cotton Bowl. The Texas coach, Daryl Royal came into our locker room and congratulated the whole team from my locker. That was a class act.

37. I live in Beaumont, Texas. I have been a resident Texan since July 1982.

38. Playing for Nebraska helped me in the after football life. So many life lessons were learned. I am a coach now, so Devaney, Osborne and my dad Cletus Fischer are my role models.

39. I always felt appreciated by the people in the State of Nebraska. I don't know what to say about the University itself. In '95 we had a reunion planned but Brook Berringer was killed in a plane crash and most of that was put on hold. When Tom Osborne retired that was the single greatest night for former players and coaches. Guys from all the way back to 1962 were there. That was the true "Husker Nation". The only draw back to the evening was Bill Bryne charging us $40.00 to get in. It seems $ is on top of everything that happens at the University. I know Tom was not happy about that. Bill Bryne was the Athletic Director and if Bob Devaney was in charge a lot of things, it would have been done differently. I still miss Bob and Tom and for that matter Frank. People with ties to the "Old" Cornhuskers seem to be disappearing from the Athletic Department.

LARRY FROST

RUNNING BACK AND WINGBACK

HUSKER HIGHLIGHTS

1. My best memory is the 1969 OU game. We beat them (44 – 14) and got our share of the Big 8 championship.

2. Coach Bob Devaney never held grudges and always was so jovial. One time in practice I got knocked out by a little cornerback, Tony Dvorsak. I went through the entire practice and did not remember any of it. Bob was yelling and one of the coaches told him that I was out of it and probably did not even know where I was. At the end of the practice it was time for sprints. I remember that Devaney came over and tapped me on the back and said "You know, Larry, this is probably the best practice that you have ever had". Wonderful man. He cared about his players more than any other coach ever.

3. During my red shirt spring, four linebackers all got hurt at the same time. Coach Melton came over to me, put his arm around me (which he had never done before or after) and said, "Frost, how would like to play linebacker?" I said "no thanks". And he said "Tomorrow you are on the Blackshirts." I started out at linebacker with the Blackshirts for about a week. In the second practice I had no idea what I was doing. I went running at Ben Gregory and he hit me right in the stomach with his helmet and lifted me off the ground. I flew right over the top of him. Coach Ross came up to me and asked "who in the world taught you how to play that position". And I said "coach, no one taught me anything". They thought it was funny, and I thought it was painful.

4. Our players in 1969 were a very solid football team offensively and defensively, but we did not have a big breakaway threat like Johnny Rodgers (who would begin play in 1970). I-back Jeff Kinney was a sophomore and was pretty solid. Devaney was masterful using both Van Brownson and Tagge at quarterback. Our closest thing to a homerun hitter was Guy Ingles as a receiver.

5. I enjoyed playing Oklahoma. They were classy players and always polite. I can't say that about a lot of teams.

6. Since I was age 5, I wanted to go to UNL. I was in heaven. UNL was the best 5 years of my life, aside from having my family. They treated us like royalty.

7. The most remarkable offensive play I witnessed was Guy Ingles catch against Oklahoma State in 1970. My best play was a 39 yard run against USC in the opening game (1969).

8. I learned so much. To this day I still catch myself saying stuff that Coach Osborne and Coach Devaney said. They were a huge influence in the way I coach.

9. If I could change anything, I would not be so "uptight". I used to throw up before every game. I just needed to relax and let my natural abilities take over.

10. The best leaders were the group of Seniors we had. Offensively – Mike Green and myself and Guy Ingles. We had a lot of solid leaders without yelling and screaming.

Larry Frost

11. I reached my goals – to play and become a teacher and coach for 30 years.

12. Our coaches talked about specific goals before a game. Devaney was a master motivator. We had a camaraderie on the `69 team.

13. The 3 most important reasons for the wins were (a) loyal players; (b) a good coaching staff; (c) motivation from the time we started from Coach Tom Osborne.

    There were differences between Coach Tom and Coach Devaney: Bob's and Tom's lifestyles were very different.

14. Coach Devaney cared so much about the players. After my Senior year I was trying to decide what job to take. I went to Bob's office and he was on the phone with the Big 8 Commissioner. Bob told him that he would have to call him back because he had a player who needed to talk to him. I was not a star but that was the type of man he was. He really cared.

15. In 1969 our confidence grew. We had to win 7 in a row and we did. By the end of the year we got more and more confident. There was no doubt in my mind playing Oklahoma that we were going to win, and we did (44-14). Then we defeated Georgia in the Sun Bowl (45-6).

16. Watching and learning helped me succeed since my football playing days. The people at UNL really prepared us for life. I owe them a lot.

17. It is wonderful to be considered the best. In 1969 we did not win a National Championship, but what we accomplished was great – the Big 8 title and Sun Bowl victory. I knew that the teams that followed us were going to be very solid and on top for a while.

18. I could motivate myself before the game. I gave everything because I can't stand to lose. I just sat alone and thought.

19. My biggest challenge was that I was different physically. I was born with a birth defect and some people at first did not like me because of my double cleft palate. The first couple of years were rough but it got easier after they saw I could play.

20. The biggest challenge for the team was Oklahoma in `69. My challenge was to keep my position. It was me vs. Mick Sigler. Kinney and I for I-back my senior year. But Joe Orduna got hurt and Jeff took over for him. I always wanted to be a running back.

21. If I could go back and change one thing, I would spend less time worrying about football and spend more time enjoying college.

22. Camaraderie was the most important aspect that made the team work so well together. We were mostly Nebraska kids. We all knew each other and in`69 we were close knit. The out-of-state kids fit right in as well

23. Alternating quarterbacks is always challenging to a team. But it worked out for us and Devaney handled it great with Tagge and Brownson.

24. My most talented teammate was running back Ben Gregory – a great football player and man. My most talented opponents were the Quarterback and I-back at USC in 1969.

25. The most inspirational teammate was Mike Wynn – Defensive end. He was a quiet guy but a great motivator with a strong work ethic. He had a classy attitude and approach to the game.

26. The most outrageous teammate was Langston Coleman. I once saw him come into our huddle and tackle a teammate because he was mad at our opponent. Scary.

27. The hardest workers in practice were Mike Green, Guy Ingles and myself.

28. What surprised me the most in my senior year (1969) was Jerry Tagge. He did not really look like the prototype for a quarterback, but he played super in the games.

29. Bob Liggett kept the locker room the loosest. He kidded with everyone. He listened to the Supremes everyday and he would sing their songs. Lots of laughs in the locker room but no one laughed at him in the games.

0. I learned from Coach Osborne to have confidence in myself. Coach Corgan would yell and scream and cuss, but I did better under Osborne.

1. Practices were not bad. You made the schedule and then you followed it. With Devaney you always knew when you started and when you ended (usually 90 minutes). During practice I hated sprinting the most.

2. It meant everything to be part of the team, My claim to fame is being a small town kid and coming from an 8 man team. In the Shrine Bowl I won the outstanding Player Award and I think I am still the only 8 man player who ever won it.

3. The fans were great. After the 1st huddle I would notice all the red. In running on the field for the 1st time I don't think my feet touched the ground. I floated out there. I loved it when they played the "Hail Varsity" song.

34. The first game I played away was Washington in Seattle in 1967 (17-7). It was my first plane ride.

35. My greatest memory was feeling like I was accepted by most of the players, and they felt like I could help the team. It happened my sophomore year.

36. I graduated on time with a 3.4 average. The last year I had to take crazy courses because they did not let you take graduate courses.

37. Playing for Nebraska helped me in the after football life. I became head coach at Gothenberg high school right after I was done at UNL. I feel appreciated by the University for the time I put in. The last 2 years have been a little different, but before that I felt very comfortable and appreciated. I am proud that my son Scott performed well and made it into the NFL. [Editors Note: Scott Frost was QB on the 1997 National Championship Team].

AN ERA OF GREATNESS: COACH BOB DEVANEY'S FINAL FOUR SEASONS (1969 - 1972)

Ken Geddes

KEN GEDDES
LINEBACKER 1967-1968; MIDDLE GUARD 1969

HUSKER HIGHLIGHTS

1   I became interested in NU because I went to high school at Boys Town in Nebraska. I narrowed my choices down to Notre Dame, Wyoming and UNL. Notre Dame, because it was a catholic institution and it would be similar to Boys Town.

The Director at that time of Boys Town, Msgr. Wagner, said "if you go to NU, you would be closer to what we consider home, and if you need anything you would not be that far away". When Father Wagner mentioned that part about being "close to home," it solidified my decision.

The most important thing to me was when Coach Devaney said "When you come to Nebraska, we are interested in you getting an education," and "if you need extra time, an extra year or whatever, we will pay for that". That was really important, and that happened with a number of other athletes.

2.   Coach Bob Devaney was a great guy. The one thing I vividly remember about Devaney was when I was moved from linebacker to middle guard my Senior year (1969). I was All-Conference my Junior year (honorable mention All-American) and I would have been a shoe-in for All-American my senior year. It did not phase me because it was a team decision. I came back down about 4 years later for a banquet and I ran into Devaney and I said, "You know, you owe me about a million dollars. It cost me about a million dollars when you switched me to middle guard". And we chuckled.

3.   Coach Kiffin was great. Always there for support. When I first got there he was a

big guy, and he started to lose weight. Everyday when I would come into the sauna he would be in there running in place and smoking a cigarette. I could never figure out how in the world he did that.

4.   We were at the Sun Bowl (1969) in El Paso and some people went over to Juarez, Mexico. A linebacker got drunk and Devaney went to his room because he missed practice. The player cussed Devaney out. People had to hold Devaney back, and Devaney sent him home.

5.   During my time at NU (1967-1969), we never beat Missouri. And at the Senior Bowl Coach Devine from Missouri was the coach of the team. When I was in high school I wanted to go to Missouri but they never offered me a scholarship. So, during this game I went up to him and told him the story and he said "How was I supposed to know you could play football?". That was funny and we had a laugh.

6.   The support of the Nebraska fans is the one thing I will always remember about NU. Even to this day no matter where you go there is always a sea of red. There is nothing like a home game at NU. They talk about places like Michigan that have more seating capacity, but they could not have any better fans. Whenever you mention that you are from NU, the first thing people mention are the fans. How gracious and nice they are.

7.   Players I remember are Tom Robinson, Kidd, Miner and people who did not play a lot in the games. I hung around with them and we stuck together. I just enjoyed my whole experience. My lifelong friends are Bob Liggett and Willie Harper.

. I prided myself on playing my best games against the best opponents. For example, the middle guard from Oklahoma was the best in the country.

The game I dreaded the most was Iowa State because it was always a blowout and in the second half you did not want to continue. When you do not want to be in the game, that is when you get hurt.

. We were pretty much celebrities on campus. People treated us with respect. We wanted for nothing. Tutors were always available. If you were interested in getting a good education, you could.

0. The only touchdown I got at NU was an interception, my junior year, against Missouri.

1. NU football taught me how to deal with life and all the adversities and hardships. How to accept success and overcome setbacks. Life is like a game, and it is how you play the game. You play with passion and you are always looking to win. When you don't win, you accept that and move on.

2. I could relive beating Oklahoma in 1969 (44-14) and the victory over Georgia (45-6) in the Sun Bowl.

3. The best leader was Coach Devaney. He knew how to treat young men. He gave you responsibilities. Coach Kiffin was great and he took over that defensive line and molded us into a Championship unit. Coach Melton taught me a lot.

4. The coaches had the ability to relate to people in all kinds of situations. They treated everyone fairly and with respect. They delegated duties and allowed you to do it. If you made a mistake, they did not get on your back. They used it to teach you. All great teachers.

5. My personal goal was to be a chef. I had taken baking as a trade in Boystown and before NU I had the opportunity to go to France to cooking school. At NU my major was Home Economics. I enjoyed working with kids when I went to Elementary Education. My goal was just to get an education. I was the first in my family to graduate from high school and get a college degree.

6. Our coaches talked about "one game at a time." The rest of it would take care of itself.

17. The 3 most important reasons for the wins were (a) the coaches were together (b) the team was cohesive (c) hard work. Coach Monte Kiffin was great.

18. My senior year (1969) I thought we were one of the better teams in the country. We were in the Top 10 in 1969.

19 NU football helped me succeed since my playing days by knowing that if you set your mind to something you can do it. With hard work and perseverance it can happen. And it has.

20. Everyone wants to be the best and to be recognized for it. So when people do recognize it, that's rewarding and it feels good.

21. The hardest part was the practice. I looked at the games as a release of all that preparation. People do not always realize how much preparation it takes.

22. Playing against the best motivated me. I wanted to beat that guy, and I knew at the end I would beat him more often than he beat me.

23. My biggest challenge was to play my best when we were not playing the best teams. You need to play every play like it is your last.

24. Oklahoma was the biggest challenge for the team because they were always contending for the Big 8 Title. In retrospective, Missouri was also a big challenge.

25. My biggest disappointment was not making All-American. If I had not been moved to a different position, I am confident that I would have gotten it at linebacker. But I do not dwell on it. I truly loved playing middle guard. We were all so close-knit and together. We were like a family.

26. My most talented teammate was Bob Liggett, a talented athlete for how big he was. They used to call him the most agile man over 250 lbs.

27. My most talented opponents were Center Tom Brahaney of Oklahoma (1969-1971 All-American) and Kansas' John Riggins and Oklahoma's Steve Owens (Heisman winner `68)

28. My most outrageous teammate was Tom Robinson (did not play with him but we hung out a lot) or Liggett. Out there and fun. Liggett and Sherwin Jarmon kept the locker room the loosest.

29. No one worked harder than I did in practice, but everyone worked hard. Coach Kiffin worked us hard but did not overdo it.

30. Who surprised me the most was wide receiver Guy Ingles – being so small and having the talent that he did.

31. I learned from Coach Kiffin and Coach Melton that hard work and perseverance would overcome any deficiency that you may have. That you can win if you are willing to pay the price. It was a team sport and you worked together with your teammates in order to accomplish the goal. Hardwork would pay off in the end. We worked hard, but we had fun too. Practice was long and hard. Intense.

32. It meant so much to be part of the team. There is nothing like being part of a winning tradition.

33. The fans had a big effect on my efforts in the game. When something good happened, you knew you could count on the fans to be there. Even when you were down, you could count on them for support. When something good happened, they would be even louder. The one thing that is always consistent at NU is the fans.

34. Running on the field for the 1st time on game day was exhilarating. A big rush. Nothing like it.

35. My greatest memory was the first day I got to practice. I had to wait a week because of my physical exam. Putting on that equipment and running out there and being able to hit someone was a thrill.

36. Playing for Nebraska helped me in the after football life. It started it all. It afforded me the opportunity to get an education. Football prepared me for life. The most important thing about Devaney was that he was really interested in people getting their education. He said it and meant it. It was not idle talk. That impressed me. That is what I remember about him more than anything else.

37. I feel appreciated by the University for the time I put in. They have asked me to return and have given me a number of awards, such as the Hall of Fame. It feels good.

"The best leader was Coach Devaney. He knew how to treat young men." – Ken Geddes (2006)

Rich Glover

RICHARD GLOVER (aka "Richie")

NOSE GUARD

HUSKER HIGHLIGHTS

1. In the Game of the Century (NU 35 - Oklahoma 31) in 1971, I had 23 tackles. The guy that was playing in front of me was All-American center Tom Brahaney. And I told him right there "you just don't know what you are doing." It really added more to the fire of the game when he just laughed at me. He would not shake hands after that game, but we later shook hands when we were in the N.F.L.

2. Coach Monte Kiffin was like a dad. He was a good coach, friend and a motivator. He took time and pointed out important things. We were watching films and he said that Oklahoma in 1971 was coming off the ball so hard and so fast that the other lineman did not have a chance to react, and so with my quickness and speed I needed to play as tight as I can to him. That way I could get off of him quick enough.

3. The `72 Orange Bowl vs. Alabama (38 - 7) was another tremendous game for us because we were playing Alabama and "The Bear". I remember coach Devaney saying "hey I don't want to lose this game. I want to beat Bear Bryant and Alabama".

4. Coach Devaney was the best coach ever. He was more of a father figure, too. He let his coaches coach and let his players play. He met all of us said that he only had two rules – 1. You go to class. 2. You don't get in trouble with the police. If you can follow those rules you will have a great career, if you can't, you're going home soon.

5. Devaney was a good coach and he took care of business. Everything he said was confidence. . . before we went on the bus he said this is a business. We are here on a business trip. We are going to take care of business. And even when we played the great game in 1971 when we came back from half-time we thought he was gonna holler and scream at us but he just said "go sit down and everyone go get some water, some orange juice or whatever you need, we're gonna win this game – all we got to do is make some adjustments". He was always positive and said we are never ever going to lose. He always said we were gonna win. He was a great man!

6. We had a great group of guys both black and white. We all came together when it was time to play football. We had a great camaraderie where everybody respected everybody. I am still friends with John Dutton, Bill Jansen, Larry Jacobson, Joe Blahak, Jerry Tagge and Jeff Kinney and JR.

7. Winning was part of it, and the respect that we had for each other.

8. The Big Eight back then was the toughest conference, hard nose, smash mouth, football. We played against some of the best players in the country. Every week you had to get ready. Against Missouri you definitely better get padded up because they're gonna hit you.

9. Attending Nebraska was the best thing that ever happened in my life. They were serious about your education. You had to work for everything. The coaches helped you out. You had the academic people to help you study.

10. I learned from playing football about how to communicate with people.

How to get along. If you fall down, get back up because football is a game of life. I learned about life and goals and to get my education. I just think of football as life because you have to have a game plan and you have to adjust. You have to work hard and have discipline.

11. I currently work in the New Jersey Public Schools as a Physical Education Teacher for 6, 7, 8 graders. Also, I am advisor for high school football for 4 public schools. I enjoy working with the coaches and the players and helping them get in shape so they have opportunity to go to the next level.

12. My most memorable play was 4th down in the OU game of `71. Jack Mildren had that ball and we had to get to him. Larry Jacobsen missed him and he was spread out of the pocket and I got off my block and he getting ready to throw. I batted the ball down and knew the game was over and we had beaten them (35 - 31).

13. I would like to replay the 1972 UCLA game (17 - 20) our senior year. We were going for our third national championship. We had the longest winning streak in college football. Our quarterback situation hurt us. Q.B. Steve Runty was a senior too. He was used to the offense. He had a little more confidence than David Humm. I just think that game hurt us. That first game. We probably would have won the rest of our games.

14. My 1st personal goal at Nebraska was to graduate. At that time pro football was down the line but my number one goal was to get my education. My number two goal was to play. My number 3 goal was to be the best linemen in college football because when I left Jersey City I was the best linemen in high school.

15. When I was a sophomore Coach Kiffin said you are number 8 and go to the end of the line. I had 7 guys in front of me. Right there you knew if you want to play for Nebraska you've got to go to practice everyday.

16. I was motivated to play the game because I liked playing football. Some people have a zone, and football was my zone. It was just all fun to me. The most important aspect that made our team work so well together was the coaches and their game plan and their toughness on us not messing around. The system that they had the different teams on defense, like blackshirts and goldshirts. When you got a blackshirt that was pride. There was a lot of pride.

17. The most talented athlete I played with on defense was Willie Harper; on offense, Johnny Rodgers, because all the different positions he played.

18. The most talented athlete I played against on offense was for Kansas and went to the 49ers. Deven Williams. Also, John Riggins of Kansas – you had to get him before he got some steam. Oklahoma's Greg Pruitt was real fast, quick and shifty.

19. Our offensive lineman always were hurt but always came out to play. You did not hear about a lot of injuries because once you went out you might not get back in.

20. QB Van Brownson did not get to play a lot, but when he did get in there he did a good job. He should have played a lot more. I thought he was very valuable on offense.

21. I learned from Coach Monte Kiffin that you had to play hard every play and you had to study film so you knew your opponents. You had to know your assignments in order to get on that field. He looked at everything so you had to hustle.

22. The fans were great. The best fans to have. To run out of that tunnel and see all the fans dressed in red and to hear that noise it was like "Wow". We would have a big crowd when we traveled. But when we won that Oklahoma game in 1971, I never saw anything like that when we could not land the plane because there were so many people on the runway. They were lined up on that street from the airport all the way back to the stadium. That was one of my greatest memories.

23. Playing for NU helped me after football. I have my degree. I have my education. I earned that and that helps me today to teach and coach.

24. Our teams in 70-72 helped to start a dynasty. Nebraska was known as three yards and a cloud of dust. But when we came we changed the whole thing – winning, going to the bowl games, winning National Championships.

25. I'm glad to have had the opportunity to go to Nebraska. To have met all of the guys. Today we are the best of friends. I could call any of them for help and they would try and help as much as they could. It was the best time of my life going there and making friends and the experiences I had, not just for me but for my family.

DAVE GOELLER
1971-1973

5'-11" 188 lbs.
Pilger, NE

NOW

Married to Cindy; children

The University of Nebraska
Economics Department
transitions specialist working
with farmers and ranchers)

Lincoln, Nebraska

riends still today –
eated, left to right:
oe Blahak, Bill Kosch,
Dave Goeller and standing,
heir wives.

DAVE GOELLER

RUNNING BACK

HUSKER HIGHLIGHTS

1. Coach Bob Devaney was influential in my life. When my wife and I wanted to get married, I sat down with Bob and we were talking about a scholarship. He said "could you wait a year on a scholarship?" I said "We want to get married and we would really like to have the scholarship so we could make ends meet. Otherwise I am going to have to work in addition to playing football and that could be pretty tough." And Bob said "let me see what I can do." They had an extra track scholarship and he gave it to me. Bob went to bat for me and made things happen. That was the kind of guy he was. He would go way beyond and get things done.

2. I was a walk-on as a freshman. Steve Runty and I and Brent Longwell were the 3 guys that ended up getting scholarships out of that walk-on group.

3. Coach Jim Ross set up a program after we were done with practice running wind sprints. Coach Thornton would take all the walk-ons off to the side for what they called "opportunity sessions." The basic idea was that you ran wind sprints until

everyone dropped out. That was the one that I always won.

4. The axe handle. Coach Monte Kiffin was a wild man and a great guy. He has a great memory. I saw him a couple years ago at a reunion and I did not even have to introduce myself. He remembered me and that really impressed me.

   Monte would get a group of 20 players on the handball court. They had wrestling mats on the floor and 2 guys would get down on their hands and knees. They literally had an axe handle with tape on each end. When Monte blew the whistle your job was to get the axe handle from the other guy and everything is legal. It was a great drill and it separated a few guys out.

5. Nebraska fans are tremendous. I came from the little town of Pilger. And they had a Dave Goeller Day on one of the last games my senior year. There were less than 400 people from Pilger and they brought a whole busload down with probably close to 100 people. That was nice for me.

6. Walking out of the old locker room hitting that horseshoe and there is no way to describe the emotions that are going through you – the anxiety and excitement, is tremendous. It is similar to going out of the tunnel and hearing that round of applause. It makes you work harder.

7. I fumbled my very first carry in a varsity college game. Coach Mike Corgan got me to the side and grabbed me under the shirt and said "don't do it again." And I didn't. That was the last fumble I had.

8. I learned that you can do about anything you set your mind to. I always tell my kids "you might not be able to do everything that you want but you can do anything that you want." You just have to decide what is really important. The other lesson is how important a team is and that the whole of the team is worth a lot more than what 11 guys can do individually. It is satisfying to look back and see what our teams accomplished.

9. We were playing some team and we should have been kicking their ass, but we were barely ahead at halftime. Coach Devaney came out and says "Guys, we've got to keep getting better. You don't stay the same. You are either getting better or you are getting worse. Right now we are getting worse. We have to get better by a lot this half." We came out the second half and scored right away. You may not realize it in any field but things are either getting better or they are getting worse.

10. Against Wisconsin (1973), I got dinged a couple of times and I probably should have left the game but I didn't. I was woozy. Dave Humm was the quarterback and he changed the play at the line. I couldn't hear Dave's audible and so I went the wrong direction and Humm made nothing and we had to punt. We still won the game but it wasn't by much.

11. The best leaders were Tagge and Murtaugh. Dutton did a lot his last year or two. They earned the respect of other teammates. And they were not afraid to give the extra effort.

12. Our team goal was to win the conference. I did not dream that we had a chance for the National Championship. It was not even on my radar screen.

13. The most important reasons for the wins were belief in ourselves and in our teammates. We had confidence that we are going to win. Belief in our coaches was also huge. We had all the confidence in the world in Coach Devaney and Coach Osborne and our other coaches.

14. The lessons from UNL football helped me succeed since my football playing days. I still to this day don't think I am going to lose. There is a fine line between being confident and cocky.

15. It is an honor and a privilege to be considered the best. It was a blessing to be a part of it.

16. The first smack that you get either in warm-ups or in a game motivated me. That would always get my adrenaline going.

17. My biggest challenge was injuries. I broke my arm one year and then I had knee surgery between our sophomore and junior year. I had total reconstructive knee surgery. And I got to fall ball in August which is only 2 months after the knee reconstruction. During that whole fall ball I had my knee aspirated taking out blood 17 times during fall ball. And cortisone shots.

18. I never thought about quitting.

19. My biggest disappointment was my senior year in 1973. Coach Osborne and I did not see eye to eye as much as we could of. Towards the end of my senior season I did not play a whole lot.

20. The most important factors that made the team work so well together were (a) talent (b) great attitude (c) the coaches would show you how to do things. They are probably more influential on attitude than on anything else. They can develop the scheme and draw the Xs and Os and Ozzie and Kiffin were really good at that. But it was the attitude in fall ball every year. They would do those up and down grass drills, and Kiffin would do them with us. It was 100 degrees out there, and Kiffin was just as mentally tough as anyone.

21. The most outrageous player was Bill Sloey ("Dirty Red"). He was crazy. Jerry Murtaugh also was a wild man. Coach Kiffin would get us in the huddle and would say "you knock him (Murtaugh) on his blanky-blank. I don't care what you do." And I got out there and I would hit him just as hard as I could and Murtaugh would say "What are you trying to do? Be All-American scout team?"

22. The hardest worker in practice was Mike Beran. He is a great guy and he just never quit. He stayed at it and worked hard. Johnny Pitts is another guy that worked really hard on defense. He was tough.

23. Playing for Nebraska helped me in the after football life. I travel the whole State for the University and I work with farmers all over the country. Every couple of weeks someone will recognize my name. That is nice.

24. Do I feel appreciated by the University for the time I put in? It could be better, but it is not bad. I think some of the things they have done in the last few years have really helped a lot.

MIKE GREEN

RUNNING BACK

HUSKER HIGHLIGHTS

1. We lost my junior year in 1968 year to Oklahoma (47-0). The next year we were going back to Norman, and I was team captain. The night before the game Coach Devaney was debating on whether or not to show us the game film from the previous year. I told him "I don't think anyone wants to see that. You are going to get everyone down." And he did not show it. So the next day we went out and beat them (44-14). And Coach Devaney came up to me and said "I am glad that I did not show that damn film." Then we threw him in the shower.

2. One day in my sophomore year (1967), it was raining like crazy and we thought we were not going to have practice. About 1 o'clock Devaney came out of the coliseum and as soon as he came out the door it stopped raining. We said "That isn't Devaney, that is God."

3. When I first came in 1966, Coach Corgan smoked like a fiend. Two or three pack a day. So he went to the doctor around my sophomore year and the doctor told him to stop smoking cigarettes and to smoke cigars. But he started smoking cigars and inhaling them. It was hot in August and the doctor told him to stop smoking all together and to chew it. So he is standing right in the middle of us and he pulls out some ragged ass looking tobacco and stuffs it in his mouth. We almost threw up looking at that sorry mess.

4. The first big impression I got of Nebraska fans is when we got back from the 1967 Sugar Bowl and Alabama had just kicked our rear in the Sugar Bowl. We got back late at night and the whole airport was crowded with fans. It was unbelievable.

5. The most memorable play I witnessed was in 1969 against Texas A&M in Lincoln. We punted to them and I was a safety. This dude took off and it seemed like our whole team went to the middle of the field and watched this guy run around the end. And I went and got that player. He was not going to outrun me on national TV. And Coach Corgan said "Great play, great play."

6. It was not a spectacular play, but in 1969 we beat OU. We used to run that Iso when I was playing fullback and Jeff Kinney was running halfback. Van Brownson called that Iso and I stuck that OU linebacker who was tough. And I ran back to the huddle and said "call that again." And we did it again and I stuck him again.

7. Guy Ingles was always making good plays at wide receiver. I used to love watching him stretch out and go flat out to get a pass. He was not fast, but he was a really fantastic receiver.

8. The lessons I learned from football are (1) persistence; (2) not allowing defeat

to define you (3) the ability to learn from defeat. Devaney's process of coaching taught us to look at things and analyze what you did, instead of defining who you are in terms of defeat. Even in victory, you don't assume that you were that good. That process of critiquing ourselves taught me that you should never take yourself too seriously. There is always a lesson to be learned either way. In losing it is highlighted more. People tend not be critical of their performance when they are winning, but they look harder at what they did when they are losing.

9. If I could go back and relive, it would be 2 games. My senior year (1969) the two losses against Southern California and Missouri. By the end of that year we were number 9 in the country. And most people knew (except for those two early losses) that we were one of the best teams in the country. If we could have defeated both those teams or either one of them we had a possibility of playing for the national championship that year. In 1969 the Sun Bowl was kind of a second tier Bowl, but we demolished Georgia and that returned us to national prominence.

10. In 1969 the defensive front five were seniors Mike Wynn, Sherwin Jarmon, Ken Geddes, Bob Liggett, and junior Dave Walline. All those guys were leaders. They were strong. All the guys behind them played harder because when they got in the game to substitute they did not want to give any slack. Those 5 guys as a unit were one the best front defense lines NU ever had as far as the way they played together.

11. My personal goal was to graduate. I realized that my mother could not afford to send me to college on her own and I could not afford it by just working and pay for it myself. My main thing was to get my degree. My major was Business with a concentration in Economics.

12. The 3 most important reasons for the wins were Devaney, Devaney, Devaney. He was a hell of a leader. He had a loyal coaching staff around him. Osborne's staff were also loyal to each other. You will never see that again in college football where you have a staff that stays intact for over thirty years.

13. In the early games of 1969 we were shaky. We played hard against USC but did not have it all together. The defense did not play up to its potential in that game. We gave away a cheap fumble and that set USC up to win the game (31-21). After Missouri, which was the 4th game, we were rolling.

14. What changed in 1969 was our group of seniors. We had a determination that we were not going to go out with another 6-4 record. We thought we would win the Big 8 championship. By the end of the year when we went down to Oklahoma we knew that we could beat them. And after we beat OU, I thought to myself if we would have beaten Southern Cal and Missouri, we could have played Texas for the national title, and I know we would have kicked Texas' ass.

15. To motivate ourselves before the games we would just talk each other up. We were all so close knit because the seniors on the team had all come in together as freshman. One of the things that motivated us was we would have been the first class that would not have gone to a Bowl game. It was not like today when you can go to a Bowl game with a 7-5 season.

16. The biggest challenge as a student athlete in general was just keeping up with the class work during the season. There were many days that you would come back from practice and be so damn tired.

17. My senior year in 1969. I had a case of fumblitis the first couple of games and I was angry at myself. Corgan and Devaney were not too hard on me. Ironically, Ben Gregory had the same problem the year before. I fumbled against Missouri and we lost that game because of that fumble.

18. My biggest disappointment was the two games that we lost in early 1969.

19. The most important reasons that made the team work so well together were the coaches, players, talent and attitude. All those things. We were a close team.

20. My most talented teammate was Ken Geddes. The most talented opponent was Gene Hughie of Wyoming

21. The most outrageous teammates were Ken Geddes and Bob Liggett. Geddes was a clown and he would made you laugh. We always made fun of Ken because he was scared of bugs. We would catch spiders and he would be getting taped and we would throw the spider on him. Liggett was a jokester. He was always looking for stuff to do to Geddes.

22. Playing for Nebraska helped me in the after football life. It has been helpful in making business contacts.

23. I feel appreciated by the University for the time I put in. People around here are very loyal to former Huskers.

Willie Harper

WILLIE HARPER

LINEBACKER

HUSKER HIGHLIGHTS

1. When I was a freshman, Coach Ross always had nice things to say about my abilities, and that meant a lot to me.

2. When we went into our sophomore year (1970) Coach Devaney was walking out the door to the practice field during summer camp and he said "Willie Harper, I have been watching you and you have been doing a really good job, and the kind of job. That you are doing can push some of those players. You have a great opportunity to become a starter depending on how bad you want it and how hard you push yourself". I thought "why in the world did he tell me that?" I was seventh on the depth chart and he's telling me that I had an opportunity to play. And by the time the season started I had worked my way up to third on the depth chart behind John Highland and John Pitts. Pitts had a stringer and Highland went in and something happened, and then I got called in. Then Pitts came back in and something else happened, and I went in again and I was there to stay.

3. My position coach was Jim Walden. Jim was always easy to work with. He would always challenge us to see basically if we knew what we were doing. Jim and I got to a point where he never pulled me over to see if I knew my responsibilities. He just knew I was going to be prepared.

4. Our opponents are a big blur for me. The Big 8. Oklahoma was great in 1971. Oklahoma State was always tough, and we did not give them enough of credit. Iowa State always played us tough.

5. There was wonderful camaraderie among the players. Rich Glover and Johnny Rodgers especially. The relationships really maximized our abilities on the field. We were all team oriented. And we understood it was a team effort. Branch and Pitts were smart ball players. They could play.

6. My most memorable play was sophomore year in the Orange Bowl (1970). We came back and held off LSU and won the National Championship (17-12). The last series I stole the ball from their running back. We stalled on offensive and LSU got the ball back again and was marching up the field, and I caught QB Burt Jones and put him out the game. I can see that in my head like it was yesterday.

7. I learned a lot at UNL. As a youngster, before I came to NU I had never been anywhere. I am a ghetto kid. At UNL I was around so many other people beside black folk. That was a great experience for me. It taught me how to deal with other people. A lot of life skills. You have to have people skills to make it in the next level in football. I did not grow up with a lot of mentors, but I got them at UNL.

8. I remember playing Kansas State, and I had that endzone sack. And another time we were playing and I made an interception and I ran it back 15 yards. Man, I made a cut upfield like Johnny Rodgers. It was on a dime. There was no one between me and the goal line but I slipped and fell.

9. One of the most memorable things that comes to my mind is on the NU campus there was not a real black presence even though we had black

athletes. My Junior year (1971) we got together and started the Black Student Union.

10. The best leaders were Johnny Rodgers and Jerry Tagge. A lot of guys were outspoken. Rich Glover was quiet. James Branch stands out in my mind. Bob Terrio and Branch on defense. Myself and Glover always practiced like we were going to play in the Orange Bowl. Our work ethic was focused with no fussing or down play.

11. My personal goal was to get an education and then get out in the workforce. Football opened some venues for me and made my life more comfortable. My degree was in Education with a minor in Industrial Education.

12. Our team goal my Sophomore year (1970) was to beat USC in Los Angeles because SC came to Lincoln and beat us in 1969. They tied us in L.A. with the help of some penalties (21-21).

13. The most important qualities for the wins were (a) the best athletes of that era, not only in ability but we were smart, (b) Coach Monte Kiffin did a tremendous job in getting us ready defensively. Monte had the uncanny ability to get us to believe not only in ourselves but in each other. When you allow yourself to believe in your teammates, you become more of a team. There is no "I" in "team", and you will be more successful because everybody understands their role. I know that you are doing your job, so I don't have to step out of my realm. When you step out of your realm, you are more likely to make a mistake.

14. In 1970 and 1971 we were confident NU would win the National championship, but we took it one game at a time. I always thought we could beat every opponent for the simple fact that most of our opponent's key players were renowned running backs. Rich [Glover] is not going to let anything come up the middle and Sugar Bear and Terrio, Spider and I were definitely not going to let anything get outside of us. We wore running backs down. Ahmad Rashad (alias Bobby Moore), we ran his tail in the ground. Joe Moore from Missouri was killing folk, but we ran his tail into the ground. John Riggins of Kansas had that good first half on us, but he did not gain a lot the second half. Our level of confidence rose with each game, and we did not care who the running back was. His butt was ours.

15. NU Football helped me succeed after my football playing days. I am in the ministry now. Its work ethic is similar. Putting forth the effort and doing your homework. Preparation for everything. It carries over into what I do.

16. I had an uncanny ability to see portions of a game before I played it. I could daydream it. I would dream aspects of that game. Like dejavu, and I did that throughout my pro career. I would always envision it before it happened. It gave me a mental insight.

17. My biggest challenge was not getting a "big head". One of my greatest fears was becoming successful and then becoming a flop. That is where my work ethic came from. What was intimidating were those summer 2-a-day practices. 100 monkey rows that we worked up to every year. I felt like "man, I am going home today". Not even in the pros did I ever think that I was going to quit. Coach Monte put us through it. He knew how to get the best out of an athlete. If Monte tells you that you can do something, then you can.

18. The biggest challenge for the team was in 1971 and the last drive by Oklahoma that stalled and we won (35-31). That was one of greatest challenges mentally for me. I had that role and could not afford a mistake. I had to have the discipline to do my role. Rich Glover did a great job in the inside that game.

19. I had no disappointments playing at UNL. My disappointment came later because UNL does not always recognize former players, and especially players who helped open the door to that dynasty. When you came back, the players were always treated like strangers. Even though there was a changing of the guard, it still should have been prevalent that these are the guys that actually got us started. What makes a successful future is understanding your history.

20. I love the "west coast offense," but you should not put something that has worked for us for so long on the shelf. You do not just stop taking your medicine. You wean yourself off of it.

21. If I could go back and change one thing, it would be that Devaney would have been the only head coach that whole senior year (1972) without Osborne being the second head coach. It caused some confusion. I loved Osborne, but they were two different coaches.

22. Coach Monte Kiffin did a tremendous job on defense, and he was my captain on defense and called my shots

Monte had such a complete handle on his defense. Our problem in 1972 was that offensively we found

3. The most important qualities that made the team work so well together were the Coaches, player's talent, and attitude. We had to buy into what our coaches were saying. We had to believe that we had the opportunity to accomplish what they thought we could do. Secondly, they had to properly prepare us to have the ability to utilize our abilities and to overcome all the obstacles. We played some tough teams in the Big 8.

4. Our front seven had unbelievable chemistry. We just believed in each other. John Dutton had the worst feet and did not have great mobility, but he was smart and we could always count on Big John Dutton being there. Somebody who does not get a lot of credit was Bill Janssen. You could always bet that he was not going to make a mistake.

5. We had team chemistry because we bought into the teachings of Coach Monte Kiffin. He was a crazy maniac, but you could trust and believe him. He went to bat for you. He went through a great deal to make sure that we were ready and prepared. He took time out, explained things to you and broke it down. You could understand all the surrounding components. He knew that blackshirt defense.

6. My most talented teammate was Johnny Rodgers. Regarding our opponents, I can't remember his name, but in 1970 we played against Minnesota and they had a great offensive tackle. I made some tackles on their quarterback, but that tackle made it tough.

7. I did not have a lot of problems with the tight ends. It was the tackles that I had to deal with. And most teams then were right handed and running to Spider's side. Spider would always hold them up, and I would come with the pursuit and make the tackle because Spider was not going to let them outside. My problems with those big tackles was that I only weighed 205 pounds.

8. We had so many inspirational players: "Sugar Bear," Branch. Pitts. They were all inspirational. Richie Glover after he made a tackle had that big smile.

9. We all worked hard in practice. No one worked harder than Pitts and Spider, not only during practice but after practice in the weight room and off season. Every single guy was focused.

30. The biggest surprise was when we lost our final home game against Oklahoma in 1972 (14-17). How could Joe Blahak let that freshman (Tinker Owens) beat him? That was my biggest disappointment.

31. Walt Jackson from Detroit kept the locker room the loosest. Westbrook was also the life of party. It was funny just to watch him crack up at his own jokes.

32. Defensive ends ran the stairs the most. They were rough but they were ready.

33. Fullback Bill Olds, if he got a good shot on you, would hurt you. Bill Olds outplayed that Oklahoma State linebacker that weighed 250 pounds. He treated him like he was a little boy. Bill Olds was no joke.

34. Coach Kiffin taught us how to approach the game. It takes more than just ability. There is a certain level of skill that you have to have in order to play the game, but you have to know your abilities and to know your role.

35. Coach Thunder Thornton recruited me in Toledo. Thunder brought me to Lincoln on a trip. To tell you the truth I could not see myself going to Nebraska when I came out there. But they treated me like a king. Branch had me and got me anything I wanted. I drove out with Thornton when he left Toledo because he was my high school football coach. I said this is longest ride in the world. It was pitch black with no light anywhere.

36. Practice was fun. Monte made it fun. It was a serious kind of fun. We had a team that looked forward to practice. Except in bad weather we would practice beyond the time that was scheduled.

37. Regarding Nebraska fans, I don't think you could find any greater fans anywhere. To see that many people in all that red was such an intimidating factor. With that kind of fan support, we had to play well.

38. It was awesome to run on the field for the 1st time. I can't explain it. I was saying "My goodness, is this a dream, is this me?"

39. Texas A&M was running all over our tail in 1969. That is how I got a chance to play. When I got my opportunity I said "hey, I'm not looking back."

40. I graduated on time and playing for Nebraska helped me in the after football life. It played a very important part in shaping my character, my level of confidence and my ability to be able to perform at a certain level. The University had high expectations in its program. And to excel in that program gave me tremendous confidence.

41. I do not feel appreciated by the University itself for the time I put in. But at the same time, there were some tremendous individuals that I remember who were very pleasant. I enjoyed being around them and I feel that they were real. Don Bryant was real and Schnitsy [Paul Schneider] and George Sullivan. They have been long lasting in my memory. Also, Boyd Eppley who actually talked me into lifting weights. Lifting weights was not mandatory, but I give Boyd a lot of credit. He had a tremendous influence which carried through my professional career.

Don Bryant, Jerry Tagge and Willie Harper bringing home the Orange Bowl Trophy (1972)

Bruce and Cheryl Hauge

BRUCE HAUGE

LINEBACKER

HUSKER HIGHLIGHTS

1. What I remember most about Coach Devaney are his halftime talks. He always started out in a nice monotone voice and as the speech continued it increased in volume and inflection. No matter if we were winning by 30 or losing.

2. We were having a scrimmage. I slanted and put a hit on Van Brownson (quarterback) and hurt his arm. Coach Devaney grabbed my helmet. He held on to that helmet all the way for 40 yards telling me about that hit I put on Van.

3. I think that tie at USC in 1970 (21-21) put Nebraska on the map as a national powerhouse. We never trailed and USC came back to tie us. When we ran onto the field in Los Angeles the USC fans did not know where Nebraska was.

4. John Melton was my linebacker coach. He had a unique wit and still does. When Monte Kiffin came as the defensive coordinator his intensity and excitement motivated everybody.

5. Nebraska fans are like no other fans in the country. I am originally from Minnesota and the loyalty the Nebraska fans show the team is unimaginable.

6. My most memorable defensive play was in Minneapolis, my hometown. I made an interception. And Melton yelled at me for carrying the ball in one hand. They knocked me out of bounds on the Minnesota sideline. I was recruited by Minnesota's Murray Warmath. The Minnesota players and

their coaches did not make the best remarks about my interception.

7. I learned about a winning tradition. I learned that 36 years later people still recognize that I played at Nebraska which just blows me away. Several years ago Jerry Murtaugh called us to come and sign some footballs at the Regency in Omaha. The reason was to get a strength coach for the Omaha Public schools. I said "Jerry, we are 50 some years old. Who in the world is going to care that we are there?" And he said "no, this will work." When we got there the band played and they had this auction. They hired two strength coaches. That blew me away.

8. During one of our practice sessions we were working on isolation plays. Bill Olds and I hit on an isolation play during the scrimmage and we were both knocked out. They told me that we both woke up in the student health center.

9. I had no disappointments. I don't know how it could have gone any better. We won two consecutive National Championships and did not lose a game (1970-1971).

10. There were several good leaders but the ultimate was Coach Devaney.

11. The most important reasons for the wins were (a) teamwork (b) the attention to detail in preparing for our opponents. The coaches studied the films so we knew what to do.

12. When I came in 1968, the National Championship was never discussed. I thought that at as long as we stayed focused on the next game, the rest would take care of itself.

13. To be considered the best has affected my life forever. When I am in a crowd or in a golf tournament, I never bring it up but someone always comes up and says "you played at Nebraska."

14. My biggest challenge was trying to tackle Johnny Rodgers in practices. I only got him once or twice. The other biggest challenge was making the mile and half run during two-a-days.

15. The most important reasons that made the team work so well together were the coaches, player's talent and attitude. For a team to work you have to have it all. The only question was by how much we were going to win.

16. My most talented teammate was Johnny Rodgers. We had a lot of good athletes but without Johnny and some of his moves who knows if we would have done as well.

17. Coach Monte Kiffin was inspirational because of his personality and his knowledge of the details of the game. He lived and breathed football, and I think he still does to this day.

18. The most outrageous teammate was Doug Jamail. Who kept locker room the loosest was our trainer, Paul Schneider.

19. The hardest worker in practice was Mike Beran (Red Baron").

20. I feel appreciated by the University for the time I put in. They put me on the Beef Club Board and I have been there for many years.

21. I had Johnny Rodgers' Heisman trophy for about 6 weeks in the early 1990s. We had Johnny out here to Sidney as the Grand Marshal of the Parade. I had to lug that heavy trophy to 6 or 7 schools all over Cheyenne County. I was so glad to give that trophy back to Johnny.

"That tie with USC in 1970 (21 -21) put Nebraska on the map as national powerhouse."

"The most important reasons for the wins were (a) teamwork (b) and the attention to detail in preparing for our opponents."

FOR THE RECORD

**JEFF HUGHES
1969-1971**

5'-11" 196 lbs.
Burlington, VT

NOW

Married to Linda

Radio and Broadcasting

St. Petersburg, Florida

*"In offensive strategy
we were light years
ahead of
everyone else."*

Left to Right:
Dakoda, Roco, Linda, Jeff,
Niko, Dylan (grandchildren)

JEFF HUGHES

I-BACK, WINGBACK AND PUNTER

HUSKER HIGHLIGHTS

1. I remember Coach Bob Devaney running around at practices in his Cushman cart. When the cart came, we kicked into high gear. He got tremendous leadership from his assistant coaching staff, and especially Corgan and Osborne.

2. I could not believe the Nebraska fans. It was like playing on a pro team and everyone knew who we were on and off campus. We used to sneak off campus for beers at Misty's bar. There were also Pioneer Park parties with grain alcohol and fruit juice.

3. Against USC in Los Angeles in 1970, Joe Orduna had a super game. USC's Tody Smith gave me a clothesline and almost took my head off. Al Larsen did it in Spring game. Those 2 players gave me the worst hits.

4. I remember the 2 National Championships and the respect that everyone had for each other. There were no racial divisions. Everyone on the team was the same color.

5. The most remarkable offensive play I witnessed was the 1971 Johnny Rodgers Oklahoma punt return. I was the first person to run up to Johnny and he said "hold on" and he threw up. Also Johnny's run against Alabama in the 1972 Orange Bowl. Rich Glover controlled that `71 Oklahoma game. Dick Rupert against the Selmon brothers. How fast Mel Gray was. Jerry Tagge had something wrong with his knee and he still threw the ball 75 yards. That just blew my mind.

6. I have good feelings and life long friends from my UNL experience. I just clicked with everyone and the camaraderie is still there now.

7. I could go back and relive that TD that I ran against Minnesota. If I could change anything, I would have worked harder in the weight lifting program.

8. The best leaders were Jerry Tagge, Joe Blahak and Johnny Rodgers who led by example. Larry Jacobson got everyone fired up. On the field Tagge. Off the field Rodgers.

9. Coach Osborne was cool and collected in calling the plays. He had confidence in Tagge and Rodgers.

10. My personal goals were to start and then play pro football and to get my education. I got the degree.

11. Devaney was brilliant in offensive strategies. We were light years ahead of everyone else.

12. The 3 most important reasons for the wins were (a) Talented players (b) Attitude – believing that we could win; (c) Coaching. The most important 26.

aspect that made the team work so well together was the players and their respect, unity, closeness to each other. We had nicknames and joked with each other. It was a unique band of guys that all clicked together.

13. We were confident NU would win National Championship in 1971. But Oklahoma's John Harrison scored right before the half, and I thought "we have a game here."

14. Playing at NU helped me succeed since my football playing days. A car accident prevented me from playing pro football. But I got into broadcasting and radio. I am happy and successful. I don't ask people to do something I haven't done, and that goes back to football days.

15. I am proud to wear my championship ring.

16. I was motivated before the games. With punting, I was always ready and alert. I was always on the sidelines, and not sitting on the bench

17. My best motivation was Coach Devaney's speeches and watching him get upset which did not happen often. He knew what he was doing.

18. I never thought about quitting football, but I thought about transferring after they moved me from running back to wingback. I talked to Devaney and he said that they needed someone good behind Johnny.

19. The biggest challenge for the team was in 1971 and that last drive against Oklahoma (Game of The Century) when we had to score. And we did.

20. My biggest disappointment was getting hurt in the Minnesota game. I had a real good Spring and it was between me and Kinney. I helped teach Jeff the position at running back.

21. My most talented teammate was Johnny Rodgers. My most talented opponents were Anthony Davis (USC), John Riggins (Kansas), Mel Grey (Missouri), Greg Pruitt (Oklahoma).

22. My most inspirational teammate was Johnny Rodgers. JR had flashy ways and confidence and everyone took off from there. JR was humble and everyone listened to him.

23. The most outrageous teammate was "Dirty Red." He was off the wall and kept everyone loose.

24. Teammates who played hurt the most were Larry Jacobson, JR and Jeff Kinney. The hardest workers in practice were Eddie Periard, Dave Mason, Jim Anderson, and Joe Blahak, a competitor who always wanted to win.

25. Who surprised me the most was Bill Kosch with his interceptions that turned some games around. Also Jim Branch and Bob Terrio.

26. My position coaches were Cletus Fischer, Corgan and Osborne. I learned from them to keep my head when I blocked and ran. Mike Corgan was a tough guys coach. Coach Osborne was ahead of his time. Some pro teams never heard of the moves Tom taught us.

27. Spring practice was the toughest when I was a running back. The level of hitting was a whole other ball game.

28. The part of practice I hated the most was running in that heat. I was from Vermont and not used to that heat.

29. The fans had a motivational effect on my efforts in the games. I never saw so much red in my life. Running onto the field for the 1st time (Wake Forest) was amazing and a rush.

30. Playing for Nebraska helped me in the after football life with a winning attitude. You think you can accomplish everything, but you know you cannot do it alone.

31. I feel appreciated by the University for the time I put in, but I think they should do a little bit more for their former football players, like Notre Dame and UCLA do If I want to come see a game, I should be able to get tickets.

GUY INGLES *(aka "The Fly")*

WIDE RECEIVER AND KICK RETURNER

HUSKER HIGHLIGHTS

1. My best memory of Coach Bob Devaney was when I was a Junior (1969) and we went back down to OU after getting beat 47-0 the year before (1968). We beat them (44-14) and Bob was happy. Some of the guys on the first team got a little upset because he took us out, but then the second team went right down the field and scored. It was less then 26 months later from the 47-0 loss and we won the whole thing. That was my most satisfying victory in beating them after they ran it up on us the year before. OU kept the first team in there the whole day and Don Bryant told me that Steve Owens carried the ball for the 33rd time with 17 seconds left in the game.

2. When we beat OU my senior year in Lincoln (28-21) the Nebraska fans were really good (1970). It was for the Big 8 title and it was an important game. I caught a touchdown pass in the north end zone and then Schneiss scored on the swing sharp at the south end zone.

3. Before the 1970 season Jerry Murtaugh said that he had no doubt that we were going to win it all. His prediction happened. At the end of the season we were going to the Orange Bowl undefeated and we found out Notre Dame had beaten Texas. I thought Eddie Periard was going to kill the bus driver because he would not get the bus parked so we could get off at the stadium. We did not find out until pre-game warm-ups that Ohio State lost and we were the last undefeated team.

4. Rex Lowe was a split end so we were together all the time. He was such a nice guy. He was a good split end and a good colleague. When the medical adversity hit he handled it with a lot of class.

5. OU was always the team to beat. Missouri hit hard and I was always sore after we played Missouri. But it always meant more when we beat OU.

6. My catch in 1969 against Oklahoma State was the best catch that I ever made. Tagge scrambled to his left and I was running a post. I turned the post into a flag and he got out in the flat and just let her go for about 50 yards and I caught the ball and landed on my back. I had 5 catches for 163 yards that day. JR's punt return against OU in 1971 that was the best play that I have ever seen.

7. NU football helped me meet people easily. In a way we were forced into learning how to deal with people outside of football either in class or with other students. It helped us learn how to interact with others.

8. Out of all the guys we played with I probably could not tell you more than 2 or 3 that I did not like. Guys like we

Richie, Kinney, Tagge, JR and Van were pretty easy to know and like. And their performance led by example. Most of the leaders were pretty quiet. Murtaugh and Schneiss were quiet solid types. And the other captains Tom Penney and Jim Hawkins were the same way. I thought Jim Hawkins was a hell of a guy, and a great captain and defensive cornerback.

9. It was a unique time. We were in the right place at the right time and with a wonderful coaching staff. My junior and senior years (1969-1970) I cannot imagine anything better. I had a wonderful school with my friends and my family got a big kick out of it. The coaches treated us like human beings. They cared about us as people. It was a good environment. And that came straight from Bob (Devaney) and Tom (Osborne).

10. My goal was to play at a big school. I did not want to go to Wayne State or Kearney which were the only other chances I had. There were not a lot of people beating down the door for a 145 lbs. running back.

11. The most important reasons for the wins were the coaching staff's ability to motivate us and to make decisions on how the game was going to go and how we were going to practice. Everybody was pulling together and worrying about team goals.

12. It means a lot to be considered the best. I think about those years not longingly but remembering how lucky we were. I can't think of any team that had more fun than we did.

13. At the Orange Bowl in 1971 the team went to see the Temptations. We had a blast. We got to see the Temptations about 15 seats from the stage.

14. It was different when Bob took over in 1962. It went from negative to positive overnight. It went from being negative where they worked the hell out of you and scrimmaged the day before the game and practiced for 3 hours. Suddenly practice was only an hour and 15 minutes and it was positive.

15. My biggest challenge was trying to put on weight. Also a big challenge was trying to fit in and be a good team-mate and a good player. I tried to do the best I could do.

16. My biggest disappointment was not having a very good season when I was sophomore (1968). We really did have a pretty good football team but we were not very strong at quarterback. Tagge and Van were freshman and were not eligible to play. Ernie Siegler was a good quarterback but not good enough to win in the Big 8. We ended the season on a lousy note and we had to live with that 47-0 loss to Oklahoma the whole winter. In a way it was a blessing.

17. The most important reasons that made the team work so well together were a combination of coaches, player's talent and attitude. We had a wonderful coaching staff. We lived through that 6-4 season in 1968 and the next season we are thinking "yeah, we can turn this thing around because now we got some football players." There were guys like JR, Willie, Jacobson, Kinney, and all the Junior College lineman like Newton, Rupert and Wortman.

18. The most satisfying thing was being there when the streaks of 9 wins per season began in 1969. It extended for 34 seasons, a national record.

19. The most talented opponent when I was a sophomore was John Riggins. He was a load and a great player. I remember looking at him and thinking "there cannot be a back bigger than him." He was only about 215 but at that time that was pretty big.

20. With our coaches common sense normally prevailed. The most efficient way to do something is usually the best. If you were prepared it was a pretty easy game. About the middle of my junior year a light bulb went off in my head and I thought "we can win because nobody is going to be better coached than we are".

21. Playing for Nebraska helped me in the after football life. People don't forget. The woman that cuts my hair said that she met somebody in Phoenix and they were talking about Nebraska. My name came up and the lady said my nephew is named after Guy Ingles. The guy's name is Guy Riley, and his dad thought you were great and was a Nebraska fan. My best friends still call me "Fly." Given our shortcomings demographically and population-wise, Nebraska is a pretty special place. There is not another one like it. 35 years later they still think we matter. *People care.*

#75 Larry Jacobson

LARRY JACOBSON

DEFENSIVE TACKLE

HUSKER HIGHLIGHTS

1. Coach Devaney gave discretion to the assistants. On Saturday he made the important decisions.

2. The Nebraska fans were always behind us and always bought our tickets.

3. That Oklahoma game in 1971 always replays on television. The most remarkable defensive play I witnessed was the last series against Oklahoma in 1971. Rich and I. I got him (QB Jack Mildren) one time and Rich [Glover] got him the next time on fourth down to end the game.

4. I learned to just keep trying no matter what. Just keep on plugging and something good will happen. UNL Football gave us an education, and I took advantage of it.

5. The best leader in 1969 was Larry Frost. If Larry had not stood up and given his talk to the team, we would have never gone to the Sun Bowl. Coach Devaney asked if anybody wanted to go and about half the guys raised their hands. And Larry Frost got up and said "Let me talk to the team" and all the coaches left. Larry gave his talk about how we were getting better and we needed to keep it going. He got everybody all riled up and the coaches came back and we voted to go to the Sun Bowl.

6. The main reasons for the turning point in that era (1969-1971) was that they recruited a lot of better players. There was the same coaching staff and same defense that they always ran, but better athletes made the difference.

7. My personal goal was to graduate in four years. I got my degree in accounting in 4 years. And luckily I got to play pro football after that.

8. We tried to win every game.

9. The 3 most important reasons for the wins were good players, coaches, and luck. Everybody played together as a team and that is why we were good. In 1968 and 1969 Devaney had two really good recruiting classes and they got the best out of everybody else. They also got a bunch of excellent junior college transfers.

10. To be considered the best makes you proud. It is nice to be remembered.

11. My biggest challenge was trying to stay on the first team. There were so many good players playing behind me that it just motivated me to get better. I worked hard and never thought about quitting.

12. The biggest challenge for the team was in 1971 in the OU game.

13. I did not have any big disappointments. We won almost everything. We had good coaches and players and we had a lot of fun. It was a good time.

14. The most important reasons that made the team work so well together were talent and everybody played together as a team. Nobody really tried to stand out. There were not any big stars on the defense. Everybody just played together.

15. We had excellent team chemistry. Everybody got along, had a good time, worked hard, respected their coaches. The coaches worked their butts off and so did we.

16. My most talented teammate was Rich Glover.

17. The most inspirational teammate was Bill Janssen. He came from North Dakota and he did well.

18. The hardest workers in practice were Eddie Periard and Billy Janssen.

19. Who surprised me the most was Jimmy Branch. He was not very big, but he played really well.

20. I learned from Coach Kiffin how to work hard.

21. I feel appreciated by the University for the time I put in. Every time they have a get together they always invite me and it is nice to be remembered.

22. Coach Monte Kiffin was a freshman coach and my sophomore year he moved up to varsity. He had a bunch of high school coaches watching him at one of the practices and he just worked our asses off. As soon as the coaches moved over someplace else, Monte let up and goofed off again. Also, we used to do these grass drills every fall camp, and we would add one or two every year. At the last day of camp we would do our record and Coach Kiffin would get out in front and do them with us. He did them and Coach Thunder Thornton did all of them too.

"There were so many good players behind me that it motivated me to get better."

BILL JANSSEN
DEFENSIVE TACKLE (CO-CAPTAIN 1971)
HUSKER HIGHLIGHTS

1. I came to UNL in `68 as a freshman from Grand Forks, North Dakota, Red River High School. After that spring (1969) I became a right defensive end.

2. The memory that makes me the proudest was being elected co-captain and the defensive captain. Another great memory is walking off the field after beating Alabama in the 1972 Orange Bowl (38-7).

3. Coach Kiffin and everyone were crying and happy. Two days before the game we were in a restaurant in Miami. Dave Mason was at the table with a bunch of players, and one of these guys from Alabama said "You know, I have been to all their games and I just don't see how you guys can beat them." Dave said "Don't bet against us. I have watched them on film and on a man to man basis we are better at almost every position". When he said that everyone at the table puffed up a little bit. We believed that we would prove Dave right. Mason was usually a quiet kid.

4. Bob Devaney was a great salesman. When I was a senior in high school I was down there on a recruiting trip.

It was grass in 1968, and Devaney and I walk out to the middle of the football stadium and he says "Bill, I want you to look around here for a while. I have to go use the telephone and I'll be back in a little while" and he takes off and leaves me standing there in the middle of that field. And I thought this guys thinks I can play here. It was a pretty good trick.

After that trip and we are leaving Lincoln and as we get to the airport he goes around and opens up the trunk and gets my suitcase and carries it. And I said "I can carry it." Devaney says "Bill Janssen, I know you can carry your suitcase but you better enjoy it now because it is never going to happen again". And it never did.

5. Devaney had a way of getting you excited about what you were doing. He was also a good teacher. He came into our first freshman meeting and he said "How many of you have heard your high school coach say after you lost a game that you played a good game and it is too bad you lost". And all the hands went up. Devaney said "Did you ever think about that? That's bullshit!" If you played a good game, you would have won. You actually made more mistakes than they did, and therefore they won. The team that makes the least mistakes wins. Football is a game of mistakes." He taught us to eliminate mistakes.

6. Coach Kiffin was so focused on football that walking across campus he used to smoke and he would look up with the cigarette in his mouth and you would say "hi coach," and he would not acknowledge who you were. He was in a zone his whole life. He used to do a slide in the mud during .

practice and we loved it. He always maintained a player – coach relationship.

7. Coach Clet Fischer was the toughest man I have ever seen. He would look you in the eye and you knew that he could whip you.

8. Oklahoma's team always had class. They always seemed to have cookie cutter type players. They had offensive lineman who could be receivers, etc. They seemed to have this shape, these outstanding athletes, who could interchange positions and never miss a beat. They also had great sportsmanship.

9. Some teams we played just quit before they got started. They did not believe they could win. They would be tough for a quarter and get tired and quit.

10. NU has the best fans when it comes to support and sportsmanship. I remember in 1982 when Bobby Bowden and Florida State came to Nebraska and they whipped us. Our fans gave them a standing ovation when they left the field. That is class. When you come to "Our House" and whip us, you are the better team and we congratulate you.

11. In 1969 Devaney and the coaches focused on junior colleges and realized that we needed the experience of 20 and 21 year olds, instead of just 18 and 19 year olds. They were eager to get that experience and they got it with Rupert, Workman, Johnson, Newton, and Dumler. A tremendous group of JC players.

12. The most remarkable offensive I play witnessed was against Notre Dame (`73 Orange Bowl) and Johnny Rodgers got hit so hard when he went up for a pass. It was high and behind him and he went and extended himself and the defensive back came up and cut him in the sternum up in your chin. I was very impressed because I thought that Johnny is done playing tonight. He went to the sidelines and flipped on his stomach and put his knees up. And then he came back. I have seen people hit like that and they do not come back.

13. Some important things you will not see on the films. One of my jobs as a defensive lineman was to fill up the holes with as many bodies as you could. Make a wall. Jim Branch was not very big, but you could feel him when he hit the pile. He was a big time hitter. Also, when Joe Blahak would hit the pile, he would hit it like a car. He would hit people and they would look like they had been shot because he hit them so hard.

14. I enjoyed watching the offensive line play. In practice Dick Rupert put a bunch of stitches in my chin. He would unload like springed steel, like a big sledge-hammer. Every time he sees me he says "Bill, let me see that scar on your chin". He was a great player. He hit Mercury Morris when Devaney coached in that Senior Bowl when the Miami Dolphins played the college seniors, and he hit Mercury so hard he took him out of the game.

15. I am very proud of my affiliation with the University and what it has afforded me. People remember you. The fans love to see you win.

16. Coach Kiffin never allowed us to spin. We always had to keep our eyes up field and not turn our backs to the quarterback.

17. The best leaders were (a) Ernie Siegler who was so sincere and nice spirited (b) Mike Wynn had this presence about him and smile and handshake and heart. He was just a strong great person. Not a rah-rah guy. (c) Bob Liggett was an entertainer and a great football player. He was able to make you laugh and he worked when it was time to work. (d) Donnie McGhee was a great football player. "Floater" was his nickname. He was as serious and as ominous as the day was long, and you loved him for it. I have a lot of respect for these guys. I watched the way they treated me, and I tried to emulate that when I was senior .

18. I wanted to get my college degree. My dad had focused that goal on all of us.

19. Coach Kiffin was our defensive line coach. His philosophy was "If you can't win the first one, you can't win them all". Kiffin stressed mistakes and not making them. He always has been a student of the game.

20. The most important reason for the wins was the respect that the coaches showed each other and every player. They made you feel important. They valued you as a person and as an athlete. They earned our respect.

21. We were confident NU would win the National Championship in 1971. I really believed that we could beat everybody. I did not see anybody in the films who could beat us. OU was going to be the test. I did not have the same concerns about Alabama.

22. NU football helped me succeed since my football playing days. I am an investment broker and manager.

I have 18 people under me, and I know the focus that was placed on discipline. I believed that we represented the University 24 hours a day and that stayed with me.

3. I feel very fortunate to have played on a team that was considered the best (1971). One of the blessings that cannot be taken away is that we happened to hit at a time in Nebraska's history with talented a bunch of men and a bunch of recruiters who got us together.

4. I hold myself to a high performance level in my life and activities, and I am very serious about what I do. I knew in football that I would let a lot of people down had I not worked as hard as I did.

5. The biggest challenge was the academic side. Being a student came first. After I got married my grades went up because after practice I went straight home and had a place to study. I wanted good grades because my brother went to the Air Force Academy, and he graduated second in his class and he played football.

6. The game that was biggest challenge for the team was in 1972 against UCLA after winning 32 games in a row and then going to Los Angeles. When I missed that tackle against McCallister, I let myself down and Kiffin and my teammates.

7. Max Linder from Plattsmouth was the Nebraska high school athlete of the year in 1968. He came in on our freshman team, and this is not a criticism of Tagge or Brownson but if Max's back had stayed healthy, he would started for 3 years. He was one of the best quarterbacks I have ever seen. He hurt his back our freshman season and that was it. He became a doctor and eye surgeon.

8. I don't know if I would change a whole lot. I would have liked to have won those 3 games my senior year and NU's third national championship.

9. The most important aspects that made the team work so well together were the coaches, players, and talent. Look at Jamail, Dale Ditter, Willie, Blahak, Rodgers – the talent they brought to the table. We had a lot of intelligent men on that offensive line. They did not make mistakes. They had the confidence of the coaching staff to call a lot of "audible" plays from the line of scrimmage.

0. My most talented teammate was Johnny Rodgers who had moves that other people will never imitate. He

took hits that would have eliminated other players. He caught balls that should not have been caught. Johnny had a special talent that made me very thankful that he was on my team.

31. My most talented opponents were (a) Dean Unrue from Oklahoma my senior year. He was excellent, disciplined, tough and he gave me a challenge every time. (b) Ben Gregory from Iowa State was a tough individual. (c) George Almandson, the quarterback for Iowa State was a good all around athlete. He was tough to tackle. Big, strong and fast.

32. My most inspirational teammate was Rex Lowe. When he got cancer in the Sun Bowl in 1969. They spotted it when he showed George Sullivan this big lump in his armpit. And George knew what it was right away. I remember coming into the training table one time and Rex would wear a wig because he was on the chemo treatments and was so sick. He was on crutches and guys would help him through the food line. His attitude was right out of the book of Lombardi: "God never forgives a quitter." You never lose. Time just runs out sometimes.

33. My most outrageous teammates were Jamail and Sloey.

34. Jerry List played hurt the most. He was fast and tough and a good blocker. Mike Beran work hardest in practice. He was a crazy man. He would sprint the 12 minute run. And he would lap you 2 or 3 times during the first couple laps, and then he would die and we would catch up.

35. Jimmy Branch surprised me the most. I would never want to be on the defense without him. He was a little fire plug of a person with little arms, legs, and torso. But he just had this way about him. When he hit someone, he brought the wood.

36. Jamail kept locker room the loosest. People laughed the hardest at him. Dutton our senior year was a lot of fun. He used to hide in lockers when fan or coaches would come to gawk at us and then they would turn around and see this huge man in the locker. That was funny.

37. Coach Kiffin taught us the discipline and mental gymnastics of football. That you have to be thinking all the time. Keep in shape and keep your teammates in mind. Play clean, tough and go 110% all the time. Coach Selmer was the intellectual side of the game.

38. Coach Kiffin got excited in practice over grass drills. He would always do them with us. The sprints were tough and the stairs were tougher. After you got in games, you realized this guy across from me is sucking gas and is about to die, and I feel crisp and ready. You realize there was a reason for those drills.

39. The fans had an exciting effect on our efforts in the games. They made you feel excited before, during, and after. As soon as you walk out there to flip the coin as co-captain and the place goes crazy. Dick Perry and Chuck Stevens from KFOR Radio used to hang outside. I told Dick Perry every time I went out and stretched my right arm up during, before, or after the coin toss, I was saying "hello" to my grandma who lived in Omaha. He would always say "Mrs. Singleton your grandson, Bill, is saying hello today and is thinking about you." That meant the world to me.

40. Playing for Nebraska helped me in the after football life. It is a given in this state. People remember that I am a competitor and I want to make sure that my customers win.

41. I feel appreciated by the University for the time I put in. Steve Pederson has done a better job including former players in the things that are happening at UNL. I think Callahan is spinning that way too with the invitations to practices and different things that are happening. I feel that the Athletic Department appreciates the blood, sweat and tears we gave them.

42. People need to realize that in football these are 18-22 year old young men who make mistakes. There are consequences to bad decisions, choices, behaviors, but we were all 18-22 at one time and we want to give them the benefit of the doubt and have patience with the coaches.

43. You are looking at a stadium full of people, including myself, who are spoiled rotten, because we had a run like no one else in the country. With the number of wins that our coaches put together back to back to back, Devaney and Osborne, all those years, and we are students of the game. I know a lot of fans that know football inside out. I think the new coaching staff was surprised and I were not prepared to have this astute fan base that understands football as they do. The fans are as intellectually advanced as they are when it comes to the game itself. And we have expectations. We are not patient. The old "win or tie" is still alive and well. I think Bill Callahan and his staff will do very well.

"We were confident NU would win the National Championship in 1971...The fans had an exciting effect on our efforts in the game."

CARL JOHNSON
1970-1971

6'-41" 252 lbs.
Phoenix, AZ

Pro Football

Majored in Business
Administration

Married to Kathy,
3 children, 1 grandchild

Owns a commercial real
state company (since 1981).

Tempe, Arizona

Carl and Kathy Johnson

CARL JOHNSON
OFFENSIVE LINE

HUSKER HIGHLIGHTS

1. My strongest memory of Coach Devaney was when I was a Junior in Spring ball. I was blocking and I was not doing a very good job. He got in my face and here I am 6-4, 260 lbs and Bob is 5-8, 165 lbs. He got in my face and started yelling at me and poking his fingers in my facemask. He almost brought me to tears. He was so fiery and so strong and on the other hand he was a guy that we all loved. We all related to him in a way that I don't think is typical with coaches. He could get in your face but deep down you knew that he liked you. It was a combination of the strength of his personality and his character and the love and compassion and feeling that he had for all of us.

2. Coach Carl Selmer was a hard driving, detail oriented coach. And Coach Cletus Fischer was kind of like a good cop, bad cop deal. Selmer was the bad cop and Cletus was the good cop. Cletus was the gravelly voice yelling guy. He was always laughing and having a good time. We loved him. And we worked with Iron Mike Corgan too. He was always in the huddle and having a good time. Iron Mike and Cletus were a lot alike in that regard. They were both tough but we loved them. Tom Osborne was the straight shooter of the bunch. I would not had been there if it weren't for Tom. I love that guy.

3. The highlight of my career at Nebraska was when we played Colorado my senior year in 1971. Colorado was undefeated at the time and they were the first big test for us. I had to block a guy named Herb Orvis. Herb was back from Vietnam. He was an ex Marine and he was just killing everybody. He was All Big 8 Player the year before. My first big test was to block him. Mom and Dad were back there and I had a really good game against Orvis. I just dominated him and Colorado ended up being number 3 in the nation. They were a good team and he was a good player. Orvis played in the NFL for a long time. At the end my Dad was in the locker room and I picked my Dad up and swung him around. We were all happy.

4. Playing at NU changed all of our lives. We are all proud of being Number One. It was the best years of my life frankly. I learned a lot. They treated us so well. I am happily married to a Nebraska girl, and the Lord has blessed me. Those years at Nebraska are at the top of list with the learning and forming lifelong friendships.

5. The best leader on offense was Jerry Tagge. On the defensive side I have a lot of respect and fond memories of Willie Harper. He was a leader. Jerry Murtaugh and Dan Schneiss and Rich Glover were leaders by example. Rich was a quiet guy. We were all serious and confident. Not many teams had winter training programs like we did or guys in the weight room on their own on Saturdays and Sundays. We were ahead of our time in that regard. We all had a shared goal. In 1970 we won that first National Championship, and we had guys like JR, Dutton, Tagge, Kinney, Harper. All of a sudden we had all these stars. From that junior year forward there was no question we were going to win that second national championship in 1971.

6. We all played as a unit. We all worked and played hard to get the job done as a unit.

7. One of the most important reasons for the wins would fall on Tom Osborne's shoulders because our offense was cutting edge. We had more of a pro style than Nebraska did for many years after. We threw that ball better than they did 15 years later. We were running the "I" type offense and a pro set. Bob Devaney gave Tom free rein to run it.

    Secondly, I would give a lot of credit to Monte Kiffin who has proven to be a defensive genius over the years. Third, Bob held it all together. We all had a shared vision. There was no fragmenting regarding what we were trying to achieve. Finally, we had talent because they did not have the restrictions on scholarships like they do today. We happened to be at the right place at the right time.

8. NU football helped me succeed later. I learned to work hard to achieve a goal. Team sports are great for character. I learned to play with people and to be tenacious and aggressive. Nothing comes cheap. Camaraderie and friendship and relying on your "brother."

9. I am proud to be considered the best. Our 1971 team has been voted the greatest college football team of all time at least a half dozen times over the last 25 years. It was a special place. It was a special bond.

10. To motivate myself before the game I started studying films. I would know my opponent. I would get my mind set on the person I was going to be playing.

11. The biggest challenge was The Game of The Century against Oklahoma in 1971. I wrecked my knee in the Kansas State game 12 days before. And I was not going to let them operate on my knee because I wanted to play in that Oklahoma game. By game time I was taped and they had been draining my knee. The coaches came to me the night before the game and they said they were going to start Alan Austin and see how he does. I totally understood because my knee was kind of wrecked. Probably the biggest disappointment of my life was not being able to play in that game. I buried it for years and years. I would not even watch films of that game because it hurt so much standing on the sidelines.

I had to start coming to grips with that disappointment. When ESPN filmed a documentary on that game about 5-6 years ago, they came out and interviewed me. He sent me a tape of the actual TV game including commercials. I sat down and watched it and it was almost like an exorcism. I am 56 years old and now I can deal with it.

12. The most important aspect that made the team work so well together had to be Bob Devaney. It all starts at the top. We had wonderful players, but a lot of teams with wonderful players do not go very far because they are not all on the same page. Coach Osborne was a critical part of that. But you cannot outscore every opponent, and our defense was a key part of it. I leave it on Bob Devaney's desk. The biggest reason was his guidance and personality and setting the tone for us in every way.

13. We had fantastic team chemistry. I loved not only my teammates but my roommates Keith, Fig, Rupert and Woody. I had friends like JR who cared enough about me to call me his friend. And Johnny took time out of his life to help me learn how to run faster 40s for the NFL scouts. I had friends on the whole team and I loved my time at NU. We were all was bonded through blood, sweat, and tears.

14. The best player I played against was Rich Glover in practices. Rich ate my lunch regularly. He was plowing his way to the quarterback and using me as the plow.

16. On my screensaver I have that picture of Jeff Kinney at the OU game in 1971 running through the line with his jersey torn. Jeff was a fantastic player. And Tagge was a great college quarterback. JR was the most talented overall.

17. The most inspirational teammates was Mike Beran. He had nowhere near the talent of most guys, but he made it through determination.

18. The most outrageous teammate was Glenn Garson. And "Earthquake" was outrageous in a different kind of way. Doug Jamail was entertaining. He was made to be a talk show host.

9. We all believe that there are no better fans than NU fans. Kansas State was playing us in Lincoln in 1971. It was really cold and there is a little old lady sitting in a wheelchair on that area where K-State came out. And a K-State player looks down at her and she looks at him and said "We are going to kick your ass." Nebraska fans certainly have a reputation for being polite and not being rude like that but they believe in their team. No better loyalty than NU fans.

10. I came from Phoenix Junior College where we were lucky if we had 15,000 people. To run out from on to the Nebraska field with 65-75 thousand people was a major thrill.

11. Playing for Nebraska helped me in the after football life. You learn a lot of life skills about teamwork and tenacity and goal setting. Also, in my business people like to talk about football. I don't wear my ring often and I am in the industrial real estate business, which is mostly men, and so when I am meeting new people often times I will wear that ring. They will ask about the ring and want to talk about NU football. It is an icebreaker. And it is just as effective today as it was 30 years ago.

12. I feel appreciated by the University for the time I put in. I think they have gotten better in terms of treating ex players better as years have gone on. All schools have to embrace their former players and bring them back in the fold because it is a wise business decision.

13. One factor in being number 1 was that we had such an advantage because of Boyd Epley and Tom Osborne. Tom kept feeding Boyd money when he was setting up that weight lifting program up. And we all ate it up and that gave us an advantage.

14. I met my wife Kathy at NU. I made some wonderful friends. I never lost a game and had 2 National Championships. It does not get any better than that.

"NU was a special place. It was a special bond. We had a fantastic team chemistry."

"The best player I played against was Rich Glover in practice. Rich was plowing his way to the Quarterback and using me as the plow."

JEFF KINNEY
1969-1971

6'-2" 210 lbs.
McCook, NE

All-American 1971
Academic All-American 1971

Pro football with
Kansas City Chiefs 5 years

Married and 3 children

Sale of investments and bonds
20 years (FTN Financial)

Overland Park, Kansas

*"One of the most
intangible but great
factors was the way the
fans responded..they.
were just great fans..."*

JEFF KINNEY

I-BACK

HUSKER HIGHLIGHTS

1. I remember Georgia coach Vince Dooley at the 1969 Sun Bowl saying that they should not have been there. Nebraska should have been in a better bowl and Georgia should not have been in a bowl. I also remember at that time there were a lot of things said racially by Georgia players and that fired us up. Some things they said at the bowl game really helped motivate us.

2. One night Johnny Rodgers, Jerry Tagge and I went to Omaha to this hypnotist at a club. The next day Coach Bob Devaney came up to us at practice and said "I got a phone call last night from some little frightened lady in Omaha. She said that she saw you guys at a bar." And Bob said to us "cool it" until the season is over. I remember that because the media today would have slammed us and kicked us off the team. But it was just somebody calling in and saying "boys were being college boys." We handled everything internally, and it seemed to work. We had so much respect for Bob because when he said that, that is all he needed to do.

3. I loved Coach Mike Corgan to pieces. He had some of the funniest sayings that I had ever heard in the world, and none of them made any sense. For example, "you could not knock a whore off a piss pot." I never knew what that meant and I still don't. But Coach Corgan put his stamp on Nebraska football, and until Frank Solich left that was mainstay stuff for running backs. He made the fullbacks of Nebraska. He created the mold for anyone that ever played there.

4. In 1969, there was a great bunch of players like Danny Schneiss and Bob Liggett. They were seniors as we were coming in as sophomores and they

provided great leadership. They embraced the younger guys and helped us come together. And they wanted to finish strong. I had a pretty good junior year in 1970 and there were some great leaders like Jerry Murtaugh and Schneiss and a lot of those people. We knew we were a part of something special, and we began to win and it was fun. It was fun to go out there every Saturday and show some of the greatest fans in the world what we could do. That was really motivating.

5. I know that the game that probably gets the most recognition is NU vs. OU in 1971. But there were probably several other key games in my career in my sophomore and junior seasons. When we played Colorado in 1971 in Lincoln, we manhandled them pretty good. As a sophomore I also felt good about developing even though I made some mistake early on. The coaches showed a lot of confidence and I had a good season as a sophomore both receiving and running.

6. The era of 1969-1971 will always be very very special and important to me because of the things we accomplished and the people that we were with. Also because of the support that we got and just the way the fans responded. But I also know how fleeting fame can be and it is amazing that people to this day talk about things back then. It had an impact not only on the State of Nebraska but on fans all over the country. It was a good game we played in 1971 against an excellent OU. We were very well balanced.

7. I know that there are some critical mistakes that I made as a sophomore that I would like to take back, but it was a part of the learning process. I had like 3 fumbles in one game against Oklahoma State, and Coach Corgan did not like fumbles. But he hung in there with me.

. The best leaders my Sophomore year (1969) were Mike Wynn, Jarvis, Bob Liggett, Periard, Ingles. Guy was an inspirational person. Dana Stevenson and Al Larson were also inspirational.

. My first personal goal was to play quarterback. When I was recruited they recruited 7 quarterbacks. I got moved to receiver and then to running back. The overall personal goal was to play at Nebraska, but we were there at a critical time when they just came off two 6-4 seasons. It was important to turn things around.

0. The most important reason for the wins was "the team". The coaches coached us well and we were prepared well. By "team" I mean everybody was really unselfish and everybody played hard. One of the most intangible but great factors was the way the fans responded. They were just great fans and you were really proud to run onto that field and lay it on the line. You wanted to do the very best you could.

1. I don't know if winning the National Championship really even entered my mind until it was upon us. We were always in the Top Ten and we worked our way up. In my senior year (1971) we came off that win against LSU in the Orange Bowl and then everybody was aware. Everybody knew where we were and what we had to do. We mentally took on a different approach. It was more of "let's go out there and get the job done" every week. It was not playing to a certain level. It was "let's get the job done and do the best we can" and move on to the next week.

2. It was not difficult to motivate myself before the games. Every week it was just such a thrill. We knew we were getting a lot of media attention and the fans were great. There was a lot to live up to. It was a challenge that everybody really relished. We all made the commitments that you need to make in order to perform.

3. My biggest challenge was my Senior year in 1971. I may have gotten some food poisoning and I lost a lot of weight. So they were running all kinds of tests on me. It took me a while to get things cranked up and be at full speed. It was not until the Missouri game that I really started to play at full speed.

4. My biggest disappointment was that we did not beat Southern Cal and Missouri my sophomore year (1969). Those were the only games we lost in our 3 years (1969-1971).

15. What were the most important reasons that made the team work so well together (Coaches, players, attitude)? I don't think you can answer that question with one definitive answer. If you look at what makes a team special, it is all those things. It is coaching, good preparation, attitude and talent. All of those factors made us a very special football team.

16. We had a special team chemistry I remember how much our offensive players respected our defensive players.

17. In my senior year (1971) there were 6 to 8 games where at the half Devaney would say "you guys take the ball and score the first time you get it and we will let you rest." We would have a 28-0 lead starting the first series of the second half, and Bob pulled us out and played a lot of people. That was good because it gave the guys that were practicing hard all week a chance to play, and it made us better. That created a great atmosphere.

18. My most outrageous teammate was Keith Wortman. Dick Rupert surprised me the most. He was only 210 pounds, but he was a ball of fire and did a great job as offensive guard.

19. Tom Osborne recruited me. McCook at that time had a pretty good Junior College team so Tom would come out and recruit both at the high school and the Junior College. Tom was straight up and honest.

20. The fans had a tremendous effect on our efforts in the games. They gave us inspiration to unite and play hard.

21. Playing for Nebraska helped me in the after football life. Name recognition has always been a big plus. Having been a kid that grew up in Nebraska, I had always watched Nebraska football and could not wait to read the papers and see the pictures of the football team. Having played and been at the right place at the right time helped me in my career and provided a public platform for speaking. It was awesome and a good positive experience.

22. What I remember about Coach Bob Devaney is the tremendous amount of respect we had for him and his position and what he was doing. You had a certain affection for him because he was that type of guy. Bob taught me a great deal about respect.

23. I don't know if I feel appreciated by the University for the time I put in. It really does not make any difference to me. The fans are what I appreciated.

Bill and Linda Kosch

BILL KOSCH

DEFENSIVE BACK/SAFETY

HUSKER HIGHLIGHTS

1. Coach Devaney was the ultimate sales-man, a great storyteller and captivating speaker. He shaped the lives of young men whose lives needed to be shaped for the good. Bob had a knack of knowing his players and when to punch you in the gut or pat you on the back. Sometimes that is a fine line. Just the perfect coach.

2. Nebraska fans are very knowledgeable and loyal and respectful. It is amazing how they want to keep hearing the stories of the past.

3. NU football players came to NU in 1968 (30-40 guys) and we were just a micro-cosm of society. We have a huge cross section of personalities. What I really enjoyed about being in Nebraska was going over to Selleck Quadrange to eat lunch and just sit at a table and listen to guys who came from Chicago and New Jersey or Florida. I was just a little guy from Clements, Nebraska and I didn't get exposed to a lot of things. The way they expressed themselves was always enter-taining. Every noon was a riot.

4. Once I got interviewed after the `71 game of the century. One of the sportswriters told me that he just interviewed Oklahoma pass receiver John Harrison. John gave me a hell of a bad time in the `71 game. And the sportswriter gave me his phone number and I still have that number in my desk and I am going to call him one of these days. He was telling me that John still has nightmares about the game, and said that he should have just made one more catch. One of these days I will call him up and let him know what nightmares really are.

5. I totally enjoyed college life at UNL. It was 4 years of bliss.

6. The 2 most memorable defensive plays I witnessed were in the 1970 USC game in Los Angeles. USC was down on our 3 yard line and we had a goal line defense. I was probably two yards deep in the end zone and "Slam Bam" Cunningham (fullback) ran a fullback draw and the line opened about 5 yards wide and all of a suddenly everything went into slow motion. Cunningham looked at me with wide eyes because I was a scrawny guy in the end zone. My eyes were open wide because I saw this monster coming at me with the football. I just put it into high gear and we met right at the line of scrimmage. My right shoulder hit his right thigh pad just as he had planted his foot so he did not have any momentum and it was just a perfect flip and I nailed him.

Well, as the game went on they ran a similar play out on mid-field a full back sweep and they kicked John Adkins out and they took Jimmy out and crashed down on the linebackers and Slam Bam turned up-field, and there I am again. I thought it might work twice. I think I hit him just the opposite and my head came down and his size 99 knee hit me right smack in the forehead and I went cold turkey. It was the first time I had ever been knocked out. I think I slowed him down just enough so Jimmy could and tackle him.

7. Bob Hahn and Kent McCloughan were defensive backs and I really admired them. Both of them were always in the top 10 sprint chart and had track speed and ability to play football. I wish I could go back try to do something to Bob Hahn's genes so he would not get the crippling disease that eventually killed him. Gary Holstein and Rex Lowe as well. My last memories of Rex were of him sitting in the locker room at the

Orange Bowl in a wheel chair after we won the game. It was the last time I saw him and it was emotional. I would like to go back and try and do something to help these men. Rex died shortly after. Gary is still sick but very weak.

8. For the best leaders in 1970 – 1971, you could not go wrong with any of the starters. There was total quality on the team. On Defense it was Jerry Murtaugh. He instilled such fear including the defensive coaches. We did not want to disappoint him and lose. He could fight hard as an old mule, and I don't know how you would take him out. I don't think he ever felt pain.

9. I was a small town guy who did not have any huge expectations. I was just happy to be on scholarship. I wanted to be a defensive back. It all worked out well for me. I started for two years and played quite a bit my sophomore year. I exceeded my goals.

10. Our team goal my sophomore year (1969) was to "stop the bleeding" because people were growling about the record and the coaching staff. Get the program on the ramp back up. The goal my junior year (1970) was to win them all and we did. Senior year (1971) to repeat as National Champions and we did.

11. On defense we talked about tendencies and strategies to win the game.

12. The 3 most important reasons for the wins were: (a) Talent, just amazing. (b) Pay attention to detail. Very precise tactics. We did not make mistakes. (c) We pretty much stayed injury free.

13. We were confident NU would win National championship. In 1970, we were only 3rd going into that game and LSU was a formidable opponent and we went out there and did our thing. In the middle we kind of relaxed but we still won (17 – 12). My Senior year (1971) there was no question that we were going to knock Alabama off the face of the earth (38-6).

14. NU football helped me succeed after my football playing days. The lessons translate over to the business world. You have to do your homework. You have to know your opponent. Prepare, be confident, and have plan "B" ready to go if plan "A" does not work.

15. It means a lot to be considered the best. I'm still amazed. The older you get, the more you realize what happened. College football has been going on in the United States for about 140 years and they still single us out as one the best or the best team ever. Think about the thousands and thousands of games that have been played and they still pick us. It is awesome and so special.

16. I did not motivate myself before the game. I am not a guy who gets real high or real low. Pretty monotone. I did not need radios or music or hand-slapping or that stuff. All I really wanted to do was get out of the locker room.

17. I am glad they had freshman football. It helped me adjust to the speed of the game and size of the guys. Recruits in `68 – `69 were of the smaller size. We were lean and thin and fast compared to the guys before us many of whom were pretty large and slow.

18. The challenge was overcome by perseverance and familiarizing yourself with the coaches and the guys you were playing with and against. I absolutely never thought about quitting.

19. The biggest challenge for the team was the `70 USC game in Los Angeles. We tied it in the coliseum in L.A. (21 – 21). We should have won it. It was a spring board and they were ranked high. Just by tieing that game put us back in the national focus and pulled our ranking up.

20. The most important factor that made the team work so well together was that our group was almost instinctive. We knew what to do. Almost like a society of army ants. Everyone did their thing and everything just flowed. I was impressed with our business-like attitude. We were very efficient.

21. Our most talented opponents were Dan Fouts (Oregon) and Bert Jones (LSU).

22. My most outrageous teammates were Jim Carstens, Bob Jones, and Chi-Chi Jamail. They were all right guys but they were all crazy. They even set up a boxing match. These are the guys you wanted to sit by at lunch. They were always cutting it up and keeping you entertained.

23. The hardest worker was Red Baron (Mike Beren). Talk about perseverance, he always ended up starting. When he came, he was my size. When I left I was 170 lbs and he was about 246 lbs. He worked hard. He could eat a large Valentino's pizza for a snack.

24. Middle Guard Richie Glover surprised me the most. He seemed like an uninspired kind of guy on campus, but you put a helmet on his head and he turned into a 50 caliber attack dog. He was truly an amazing person.

25. Joe "Airhead" Blahak kept the locker room the loosest. He had that personality that just got you going.

26. Coach Clete Fischer came down to Columbus to recruit me. We were having basketball practice and the coach came up and said Clete wanted to talk to me. He took me back to the coaches room and asked me if I wanted to be a football player for NU, and I said yes and that was it. He never came back again. He sent Don Bryant back on signing day and that was a 5 minute ordeal. My mom wanted to know if they had washing machines for my clothes. It was funny.

27. The part of practice I hated the most was wind sprints. It was something that you did not look forward to but you knew the value of it. That really would take the juice out of me.

28. The fans did not affect my efforts during the game. When I was on the field I blocked out the external effects. I did not hear a thing. We had our hand signals for changing coverages, and I never really heard the fans. After the game I really appreciated their noise and support.

29. To run onto the field for the 1st time in 1969 was awesome. About 70,000 fans were there. It was even fun during my freshman year when about 5,000 were there. I heard them then because it was before the game.

30. One of my greatest memories was my last home game (1971). When you go out as a Senior they announce your name. That was fun.

31. I graduated on time in 1972 Spring Major: Mathematics B.S.

32. Playing for Nebraska helped me in the after football life. If someone finds out that you were on the team, it is a good icebreaker. It has opened doors. The fans don't forget.

33. All of us starters from the 70-71 teams get a lot of ink and publicity. I would just like to give some credit to the reserve players who pushed us. The green shirts and the scout teams and the guys that took all the hits getting us ready. And I would like to name a few names like: (a) Johnny Pitts, a wonderful man. I still see him today on the streets and he is a policeman; (b) Johnny Decker, I really like the guy. These guys never got to start. My good roommate Mike McGuire, Bruce Hoggie, Pat Morel, Phil Harvey and Wes Maven. Those guys pushed us and made us good. They all stuck it out and they were an important part of our team.

"I would like to give some credit to the reserve players who pushed us... They were an important part of the team."

PAT LAHEY

DEFENSIVE TACKLE

HUSKER HIGHLIGHTS

1. Coach Devaney told me during recruiting that if I gave him 100% in school and in football, he was sure I would get through school with a degree and the team would win a lot of games. We did both together

2. The Nebraska fans are so great. In 2000 NU played in South Bend, and Notre Dame fans still talk about how great NU fans are.

3. The Nebraska players were a total cross section – poor - rich - big - small- funny - and all had heart, with a will to win.

4. If you don't play the best teams, how will you ever know how good you are. Our opponents made us #1.

5. Every year had different leaders on the team, but it always looked to me that the team was so determined. We all went in the same direction with a one goal in sight – to win.

6. My personal goals in coming to Nebraska were education - play football - make friends - be the best I could be and still remain the person I hoped to be. I achieved all of my goals. I reached my goals at UNL: Wife of 36 years from UNL - son a doctor - daughter graduated from UNL and went on to further education. I have done well in my life, and still have friends from school.

7. We won a lot of games in that era. The three most important aspects or qualities that accounted for those wins were:

   1) Heart;
   2) Hard work;
   3) People - involved players and coaches and fans.

8. The most important aspect that made the team work so well together was the mix of the personality of the players and coaches. Our team chemistry was the best.

9. Practices were very hard, but we all did it together so we got through them together. I hated 2-a-days.

10. I never started a game, and that was a dream I never achieved. The team was my family and I knew I was going to start the next game. I just ran out of games.

11 The fans had a huge impact on our efforts in the game. Big Red when you ran into the game put it all in perspective. How could you let that many people down?

12. I can remember everything. My greatest memory is when a small player (JR) was hurt on the field and the game was stopped and he was taken out on a stretcher. As they took him by the rest of us he looked over and said "How are the fans taking it"? That's the kind of men we got to play with.

13. I feel appreciated by the University for the time I put in. Just last year they asked, and I represented NU in a commencement at Notre Dame.

Jim McFarland
Photo courtesy of the Lincoln Journal Star

JIM MCFARLAND
TIGHT END

HUSKER HIGHLIGHTS

1. My best memory is beating Oklahoma 44-14 in Norman (1969). The previous year (1968) we went down there and lost 47-0. Steve Owens scored 6 touchdowns. We played a miserable game. In 1969 we went back to Norman, and we were very worried that the same thing would happen again. They kicked off to us and there was a strong wind in our face. We did not make a first down. Dan Schneiss punted and it went about 20 yards into the wind. OU had the ball at our 30-40 yard line, and the first play everybody tackled Steve Owens and nobody remembered that Jack Mildren, the quarterback, pulled the ball out. And Mildren went right in and scored a touchdown. So right off the bat they were ahead 7-0. Everyone, including myself, was thinking "Oh no, not like last year."

   But we starting moving the ball. Van Brownson started that game at quarterback and OU tried to blitz Van a lot. They were rushing 8 guys and I remember at least 3 times where he evaded the rush and got outside the pocket and starting running down field. He made several good 20-30 yard runs. It really hurt them and we started scoring and did not stop. Before we knew it the game was 44-14, and it was the only game that I was disappointed that it ended. I could have played all day the way we were running up and down the field. I think the comparison between the 1968 and 1969 games showed the turnaround that happened in 1969.

2. The victory in the Sun Bowl (1969) was a very good memory to close out my career. We beat Georgia 45-6.

3. In 1969 Coach Devaney called me into his office and wondered why I had not voted to go to the Sun Bowl game. We had not gone to a Bowl game in two years and the Sun Bowl game against Georgia started our national record of 35 consecutive bowl appearances.

   And then Mike Green said "Let us discuss it among ourselves, coach". Coach Devaney left the room and we starting discussing it. Then Coach Devaney called me afterwards and persuaded me because the guys wanted to go and we would have a good time. And he was right. The big benefit was that a lot of guys were married and their wives had really struggled to help support them through college. They did not have a lot of money to spend, and this Bowl trip enabled the players to take their wives and have a good time. I did not think about that because I was not married at that time.

4. Editors Note: Jim explains the reasons for "the turnaround" from 1968 to 1969 [see '69 season].

5. Coach Clete Fischer helped me a lot. And I really liked Coach Corgan. There were no pretenses about Mike Corgan. He got his message across very directly. He was very gruff and ornery. But he really had a good heart, and he liked the players even though he was not reluctant to criticize any of us. He believed in tough football, and when you really get down to it football is a tough, brutal game. You have to be disciplined and aggressive to play it well. He epitomized that. If you did a good job he would tell you, but if you messed up he was going to let you know.

6. I remember one time, we were practicing a spread option play where I had to release down field and block the cornerback, and the flanker would crack back on the safety who was supposed to be covering me. It was a cross blocking type of action. I was 6 foot 5 inches and 225 pounds and I was trying to block corners who were 5' 8" and very agile and speedy. So I had to take dead aim at them. One day in practice Corgan stops the practice and said "Mac, you are not doing this right, you are not buzzing your feet. You have to keep your feet wide apart. You have to buzz your feet and get into these guys". He then said "Here, Mike Green, you show Jim how to do this" and it was kind of humiliating for me. Mike comes and says "here, this is how you do it." And he released down field and Mike buzzed his feet and kept his feet right and man, did he give a pop on that defensive back. Corgan was right. Mike did it a lot better that I did. I concentrated on that and did much better.

7. We had great fans and still do. The great thing about Nebraska is that we have no pro team in our state, and we have no other major college football power like Kansas and Kansas State or Oklahoma and Oklahoma State. Nebraska is the team for the entire state. So there is a lot of loyalty.

8. In 1968, we lost to Kansas State (0-12) and there were a lot of people including the coaches who said that was the low point of Coach Devaney's career. As I am walking off the field, disappointed and dejected, two of my fraternity brothers came up and said "Jim, you played a good game. We are sad the way it turned out, but we watched and we know you played hard." It was comforting to me that those guys would take the time to wait for me and to go down on the field and shake my hand. I think there were a lot of fans that felt that way about our team. They were disappointed, but they were still loyal. And they showed their loyalty because we were sold out both in 1968 and 1969.

9. There were a lot of good players. I remember a guy who was a freshman (Johnny Rodgers) my senior year. I wished freshman were eligible because he could have helped us win a few more games.

10. There were really two guys that I admired for different reasons. One dear friend is Ernie Siegler who played quarterback in 1968. Ernie is now a faculty member at the Dental School. He was out every year and he played on the scout squad with me when I was a sophomore. He stuck with it and finally his senior year he ended up starting and helped win some games for us.

11. I really admired I-back Jeff Kinney. In 1969, Joe Orduna was a great running back and was scheduled to be our starting running back, but Joe got hurt during a scrimmage in Fall camp and was lost to for the year. So they switched Jeff Kinney to I-back from wingback and he had to learn all the plays and adapt to a new position. He and Frank Vactor were the I Backs. Jeff improved dramatically over the season. At the end of the year when we beat Oklahoma Jeff gained over a 100 yards, and he also led our team in pass receiving that year. He was such an all around athlete. He was a good blocker, runner, receiver. He threw some touchdown passes. A real student of the game and he recognized defenses when he went up to the line of scrimmage. He added so much because of his physical skills and also his knowledge of the game. He was like having a coach on the field. When it came to crunch time, he was the guy that made the big plays, key plays, big first downs.

12. In 1968 and 1969, the Oklahoma linebacker that played across from me was a guy named Jim Files, number 84. He was about my size. I had to block him in both games in Oklahoma. He was big and tough. He was the enemy. After the season I went to play in a North-South game in Tampa, the Lion's All-American Bowl Game, but Jim was on my side, a teammate. He came in and said "Hi Jim, I am Jim Files, glad to meet you. You may remember me because I played against you." He was such a pleasant guy. And he says "God Bless you, buddy, it is good to be on the same team with you" and he left. I thought that he was really a great guy. I later discovered that he played pro football with the Giants. He is now a Baptist minister in Arkansas. I realized that my opponents are not the enemy, and he in fact was a model guy. There are a lot of good guys on the field.

13. Playing in your home state is a big benefit. Nebraska players will stick with it. I admired Mike Beran because he came as a walk-on. He worked on weights and built himself up and finally his senior year (1970) he earned a starting position on a national championship team. Just through determination and hard work.

14. My professors were very helpful. If I could do it over I would try to spend a little more time on my studies. I still had a "B" average but with a little more effort I could have had an "A" average.

15. The one play that turned around the entire `69 season. [See '69 season pp 40-41].

16. I learned perseverance. Coach Osborne emphasized to go hard on every play. He wanted you to give your best on every play. Even if you don't win, if you are doing your best that is all you can ask of yourself.

17. I would like to go back and relive the Missouri game my senior year (1969) when we lost 17-7 at Columbia. Missouri put everyone up on the line of scrimmage, and they came at you with 9 rushers. Whenever they were in that defense and we had an option played called to that side, the quarterback was told to check out because it is tough to sustain a block on a line-backer. And if he blitzes inside he can be right on the quarterback and jar the ball loose or throw the quarter-back for a loss. The defensive end in their scheme on the option play would go to the outside and take away the pitch. Our offense that whole game was three plays and punt. One time Van called the option play to my side, and he did not check out of it and I was taller than the linebacker. When he came down the line I walled him off. Van then took off and he made about a 15 yard run, one of longest runs we had that game. In retrospect, I would have told Van not to check out of that play because I can handle that guy.

18. I think everyone was a leader in a different way and that is the great part about being on a team. Glenn Patterson was a quiet guy. One time we were scrimmaging and quarterback Jerry Tagge sprained his ankle because someone tackled him. And Glenn was yelling at the defense, and it really struck me that this guy is really on our side and he really cares about Jerry who was a sophomore on the offense. Glenn really expressed leadership.

19. In 1969 on defense our leaders were Jerry Murtaugh, Ken Geddes, and Larry Jacobson. Leadership comes in all forms. It is not magical. We talk about leadership too much and try to attach a messianic aura on someone. I think everyone is a leader at one time or another. For example, Coach Devaney and Coach Osborne were tremendously different people and personalities, yet, I looked upon both as great leaders because of the way they conducted themselves. They complemented each other and that is part of being on a team. You may be deficient in one area, but your teammate helps you make up for it.

20. At Nebraska the tradition established by Devaney was to have a top ten ranked team and go to a Bowl game. It was an expectation. We failed in 1967 to do it and in 1968 we failed again.

21. The 3 most important reasons for the nine wins in 1969 were: (1) Our defense was good and kept us in games. No one really scored a lot of points on us; (2) Our offense improved dramatically between 1968 and 1969 and, so we were scoring points; and (3) The patience and foresight that both Coach Devaney and Coach Osborne had when we came back in 1969. They said that they would ask the players to work hard, but the coaches would work just as hard. Making changes turned things around. After we lost early in the season to Southern Cal and Missouri, the coaches did not give up and were still positive and we won our final 7 games.

22. In 1969, Colorado upset Missouri, so both Nebraska and Missouri finished with 6-1 records in the Big 8. Missouri went to the Orange Bowl and NU to the Sun Bowl.

23. I learned from NU football. It conditioned me in a very public arena to realize that you are going to fail and make mistakes, but there is always a second chance. You can overcome your failures and mistakes. It also teaches you a degree of humility. It is easy to think when you are winning that you earned it and deserve it, but in playing at Nebraska or professionally over a period of time you realize you are not special. Whatever you have achieved, you had to work hard to get it.

24. I was very fortunate to be at U.N.L. at that time. It gave me a great perspective because I saw the down years when we were struggling in `67-`68. It made me appreciate how much progress we made in 1969. And when the National Championships were won in 1970-1971 I appreciated them more because I had seen how far the program had progressed.

25. The first game I played in 1968 was against Wyoming in Lincoln (13-10). I was really nervous and apprehensive. I was quiet and trying not to show my fear. And I got on the elevator to get to the bus, and

the door opens and who is standing there but Coach Devaney. As we are riding down, he said "Jim, this is your first game starting isn't it." and I said yes, and he says "Probably a little nervous about that, right" and I say yes again. And he says "Jim, you have been practicing really hard and you have earned your spot on the team. You just go out there like you practice and you will do just fine." And I walked off that elevator with such a sense of calm and satisfaction because he was right. Coach Devaney instilled confidence. I was very calm before the game.

6. My teammates were the best motivation during the game. I would see them do a good play and it would inspire me. If Guy Ingles caught a pass and got knocked around really hard but still hung onto the ball, I thought, "hey, I can do that too." Jeff Kinney would get hit and still get 5 yards.

7. My biggest challenge was when I was on the scout squad in 1967 and we were having a losing season. I felt unworthy to suit up for a home game. After one practice I came in and most of the people were gone, and I was sitting there with my head down and having self doubts. And Coach Devaney walked by and poked his head in and said: "Jim, you know, I have been watching you practicing out there. You are doing some good things. You keep at it, and you will play a lot of good football for us." And then he walked by. It was the first time he had talked to me in weeks and it was like he sensed my feelings. He knew how I felt. When he made the effort to provide some encouragement to me it made me think that I am not just a spare part, and he appreciates that I am trying to do my best. It was a great incentive and encouragement to me. That one isolated moment was very important.

28. A few times I thought about quitting, but I had a lot of good friends on the team. And if a guy like Ernie Siegler, who was on the scout team with me, could do it so could I.

29. My biggest disappointment was not having another year of eligibility. Those 2 years at Nebraska were some of the best years I have had.

30. The most important aspect that made the team work so well together was the culmination of everybody's effort. Everyone played their role.

31. My most talented opponent was Mac Herron at Kansas State. I have never seen a guy accelerate so quickly, when I tried to catch him during a punt return.

32. The most inspirational player was (1) Junior year: Ernie Siegler (2) Senior year: Guy Ingles because he was not big but made tremendous plays and got tremendous performance out of his physical abilities. He was so meticulous with everything he did.

33. Coach Monte Kiffin was the guy who did things that made you laugh. I would listen to his pep talks because he was always so enthused about everything. He was quite a character.

34. No one worked harder in practice than I did. I had to because I did not have exceptional skills. Randy Reeves and Guy Ingles also worked very hard.

35. Practices were hard, but very organized. We were not beating up on each other.

36. When I got into a game, I was in a zone. I had full concentration on what was going on. It was exhilarating to run on the field for the 1st time. Seeing all that red made you think what an important event it was.

37. Playing for Nebraska helped me in the after football life. I feel appreciated by the University for the time I put in.

DONNIE MCGHEE *(aka "The Floater")*

OFFENSIVE LINE

HUSKER HIGHLIGHTS

1. Bob Devaney changed my life. Between my sophomore and junior year I was trying to make weight and I told Coach Devaney. When I come back after summer my goal is to be in the best shape possible." But it did not happen and I was overweight. And Bob said "McGhee, I expected you to come back here looking like a greyhound and you come rolling back looking like a MAC truck." He embarrassed me and motivated me to get to the racquetball courts and to lose weight. He made me feel as if I had let him down.

2. When we played LSU in the 1971 Orange Bowl, we were 3rd in the country. And Number 1 and 2 played during the day and lost. So we knew that we had the possibility of coming out National Champion. A couple months later President Nixon held a press conference at the University and the team had the opportunity to share the stage with him. Devaney got a bigger round of applause than Nixon and Nixon said: "Bob, you ought to run for office in this State."

3. The entire city of Lincoln, Nebraska prior to game day is just a sea of red. The fans are obsessed with the Cornhuskers. The teams brought notoriety to the area.

4. There were a few players on the team that were married – me and Bob Terrio and Bob Liggett. And at times we would get together and have little house parties. Every Sunday morning we would have to get up and run the stadium after Saturday's game. After the runs we would go out to the fields and do pheasant and rabbit hunting.

5. We were 11-0-1 my senior year in 1970. We tied SC. The one player I remember at USC was Bubba's little brother Toady Smith. He was a defensive tackle. I was in awe of the Bubba Smith name.

6. Things for me were great at UNL. It was the first one in my family to go to college. I came from an industrial environment in Flint, Michigan. Most of the people that I knew ended up working for General Motors.

7. I remember the Orange Bowl and the prominence of winning that game against LSU in January, 1971. There was a shot in the newspaper where I was on the ground and trying to root out for Tagge to score. I distinctly remember that last goal line drive. Wally Winter and I were saying "We have to do this." There was a lot at stake.

8. The biggest lesson I learned is good old teamwork. And knowing that individuals can collectively achieve a goal. A lot of things I learned back then I am applying now. I know that I cannot do it by myself.

9. Jerry Tagge was a leader. Eddie Periard was a leader. He was a little nose tackle and he epitomized the leader unexpectedly. You would not expect him to be a Big 8 nose tackle but he ran rings around those centers. He was quick and tough.

10. To be a leader you must have a plain old desire to accomplish. Lead by example. It is a matter of being dedicated yourself and trying to instill that dedication in others.

Donnie McGhee

1. The most important reasons for the wins were (a) the desire to win for Devaney because he had charisma and he made you want to win (b) the Big 8 conference. I wanted to make sure that the conference maintained national prominence. I came from Michigan which is the Big 10, and I wanted the Big 8 to be dominant.

2. In that 1970 season we started to blow out some teams. Each succeeding win gave us more and more confidence and we started to climb up in the polls. That 1970 championship was a springboard for a very good beginning for the 1971 team.

3. Those aspects helped me succeed since my football playing days. It made me set high goals. It instilled a level of confidence in me from a personal and business standpoint. We were the best in the nation collectively. In the business world I owe a lot of that to the confidence I gained from playing on those teams.

4. My biggest challenge was trying to be a student and an athlete and a father and a husband all rolled into one. Things were tugging on you from all directions. It was a matter of trying to prioritize. It was a struggle.

5. My biggest disappointment was not being drafted by the pros. I saw guys that I played against who were drafted and I remember that they were not better than me. But, then I remember Nebraska had afforded me the opportunity to go to college and to get a degree, and you put things behind you.

6. A combination of qualities made the team work so well together. Devaney had recruited coaches that gelled together and had the charisma to make their players want to perform. They were very confident in their skills and were tried and true veterans. They were good teachers. Nebraska was a special place for all of us.

From a defensive standpoint if you say the word "blackshirts," you stick out your chest with pride. If you say I am the starting offensive lineman from Nebraska you stick your chest out because that is the epitome of success. We had a conference which was the greatest in the nation and a school which was the toughest in the nation.

17. My most talented teammate was Richie Glover. From a strength standpoint and a hustle dedication standpoint he was a monster out there. In one practice Richie came with a forearm across my head and my helmet snapped. I still have that helmet. There is a patch that the equipment manager put on to hold it together.

18. The most inspirational was Eddie Periard because he did things that you would not expect because of his size. He was a small man playing in a big man's game.

19. Ken Geddes was a prankster. Bob Liggett is the one who gave me the nickname "the floater"

20. It was awesome to run onto the field for the 1st time for a game. We would always touch the horseshoe. To see 60 thousand people and the sea of red was a humbling feeling. To say you are a part of this team and these people are out here to cheer for us was an awesome feeling.

21. People from my hometown know I played at NU. Those Championship rings standout and their eyes will go to the ring. That enables me to start telling stories about Nebraska. And that means a lot. That ring is very prominent.

22. I definitely feel appreciated by the University for the time I put in. My thanks goes to the University for the opportunity they provided. The University changed my life.

"The most important reasons for the wins were (a) the desire to win for Devaney... (b) to make sure the Big 8 Conference maintained national prominence."

Jerry Murtaugh

JERRY MURTAUGH

LINEBACKER

HUSKER HIGHLIGHTS

1. After the 1970 season I went as a free agent to the New England Patriots. The 1st year I got hurt on a kickoff. I blew out my knee and had surgery. The 2nd year I blew out the same knee again. They said I was done. Short lived pro career.

2. I came from a family of 10 children where the girls were meaner than hell and you had to be tough.

3. Coach Devaney and I never did get along. We were both Irish and we always pounded heads. When they had his retirement party in 1973 at the Devaney Center, his wife called me and invited me and she said "I am tired of you guys still fighting." And I said "Mrs. Devaney, I am not going and I don't like your husband." And she said "By God, you will be there." And I did go for Mrs. Devaney.

   So, I get there and I'm hiding with a bunch of guys and all of a sudden someone grabs my ear and starts twisting it. It was Mrs. Devaney. She said "you come with me". And everyone is laughing at me and she has me by the ear and drags me the length of the Devaney center. In the corner is Coach Devaney by himself. She says "you go sit down next to him". So we sit there and we don't look at each other. And all of a sudden Mrs. Devaney says "You two talk, I am sick of this".

   And I will always remember that Coach said "How are you doing?" and I said "Fine, Coach". And Devaney says "You want a beer?" And I say "Oh yeah". We have a beer and she leaves. And for about 15 minutes he and I talked and he said "Our feud should end." And I agreed. We shook hands and he told me a couple of stories. And the greatest story he told me was when he said that everybody in the State of Nebraska thinks I am a great coach, but he said "I am not a great coach but I was smart enough to hire the greatest 8 assistant coaches in the United States". I wish I would have known him better. I actually knew his wife better. She was such a great lady.

4. Coach John Melton was like a father figure to me. Whenever I would get mad at Coach Devaney, Melton would say "now calm down". He always calmed me down when I would get angry.

5. Coach Melton always says I caused his first heart attack. In 1970 I was a Senior and Johnny Rodgers was a sophomore. Tagge was quarterbacking and he had his green shirt on, and you don't touch the quarterback when he has the green shirt on. I was a senior and co-captain and Johnny is running pass plays. The whistle blows and the guys don't stop. So, I grabbed Johnny and threw him down. And Devaney got madder than hell at me. And then he went after Coach Melton and said "can't you control that guy?" The next play was a blitz and I ran in there and hit Tagge and dropped him. Devaney went nuts. He went over and fired Coach Melton on the spot. And like Melton says, "he fired me that day and hired me back that night". It was funnier than hell.

6. The Nebraska fans are one thing you can always appreciate. They always were kind, but in 1968 they were not so kind. We were 6-4 two years in a row. They wanted to fire Coach Devaney. I got a lot of letters and hate mail. My Junior year (1969) we went 9-2 and the fans started appreciating us. Then my Senior year (1970) we won the National Championship and everyone was okay with us.

In 1968 a majority of the players were Seniors. I was just a sophomore. 1968 had a great bunch of guys, but not a lot of talent. My Junior year in 1969 created a great football team with guys like Ken Geddes, Mike Green, Tagge, Brownson, Guy Ingles,

Our toughest opponent was always Oklahoma and Steve Owens. He was something else. KU's John Riggins and Junior Riggins, Joe Moore from Missouri, Glen (Slam Bam) Cunningham from Southern Cal. These guys were 2-3 inches taller and 25 plus pounds heavier than me.

Eddie Periard was the greatest little defensive football player. And guys like Dave Walline and Willie Harper helped win the National Championship.

0. The most remarkable defensive play I witnessed was when Dave Walline hit Joe Moore from Missouri and broke his shoulder. That hit was heard throughout the stadium. It was a head on collusion. And Joe Moore's career ended right then. I hated to see that because he was projected as the number one draft choice. He was a great running back. Nothing illegal happened. They just hit head on.

1. I remember John Riggins (Kansas) and Steve Owens (Oklahoma) because I still have some football cleat imprints on my chest, and I hope they have a couple that I left on them.

2. On offense, I remember NU's Joe Orduna as a high stepping power runner. He had it all. Tough to bring down. He was key to the first National Championship in 1970.

3. I learned so much at NU. I never thought I would go to college. My degree is in Physical Education with a minor in English. My father was shocked. He thought I was the least likely out of the 10 of us to go to college. My parents were very happy. Devaney taught us that you cannot quit. Coaches Osborne, Melton, Powers, Kiffin gave us that one lesson that "when it gets tough you have to keep going." You have 10 other guys next to you and if you quit, you hurt the other 10.

4. I would like to relive one play against Anthony Davis of Southern Cal. in 1969. They beat us (21 – 31) and I missed the tackle on Anthony and he scored. And I think that is what beat us. No one ever remembers that, but if I would not have arm tackled him I don't

think he would have scored. I would love to take that one back because I was always taught not to arm tackle.

15. Our best leader was noseguard Eddie Periard. He died in a car accident about 5 years ago on Christmas Eve. He was against all odds. Nobody wanted him. Then Devaney let him walk-on, and the kid would not quit. He did not care how big you were. He kept pushing and pushing. He would go against guys much bigger and beat them. He was 5 feet 8 inches tall. Eddie would get excited, and he was inspirational.

16. I reached my goals – played a little pro football and got my degree. I have 4 kids and I have the greatest life. I have been blessed.

17. My Junior year (1969) is when it all came together. Everybody knew we were good and not too many teams were going to beat us.

18. Every game Coach Devaney would give his spiel on determination. You better not quit. You better leave it on the field because "Your soul belongs to the Lord, but your ass is all mine if you do not give your all". And boy did he mean it. If he thought you did not give it your all, he took it from you at the next practice.

19. The 3 most important reasons for the wins were (a) attitude; (b) aggressiveness; (c) determination. They instilled a winning attitude in us.

20. I was confident NU would win the National Championship in 1970. I made a public statement before Fall camp that "we were going to be Number One and no one was going to beat us." Coach Devaney made me run steps because the papers took it and ran with it. He said "you can't say those things". But I had complete faith.

21. Being considered the best is an honor. The `70 team started a dynasty. I am proud of that.

22. I was motivated before the games by my dad in the stands watching me. And my mother at home listening on the radio. I did not want to disappoint them.

23. My biggest challenge was learning how to study. But tutors really helped me overcome the challenges.

24. I never thought about quitting. My 9 brothers and sisters and my father and mother would have been disappointed.

25. My biggest disappointment was the `68 team: I could not believe that we could lose to Oklahoma (47-0) on national television and they took it off national TV at the half. We were humiliated.

26. The most important aspect that made the team work so well together was our coaches, who gave us the attitude to play well and succeed. In 1970 our team chemistry is the reason why we won the National Championship. On both sides of the ball we all got along. No bickering or fighting on or off the field.

27. My most talented teammates were (a) Joe Orduna – he had it all even with a hurt knee; (b) Guy Ingles – for being so little he could get up and go over the middle and catch the football; (c) Dan Schneiss – powering over people – Nasty – Aggressive, never backed away; (d) Dave Walline; (e) Eddie Periard; (f) Bill Kosch; (g) Joe Blahak.

28. The most outrageous teammate was Eddie Periard. Once I saw him jump in the air and grab a quarterback and bear hug him face to face. Eddie Periard kept the locker room the loosest. I can't say enough about him.

29. Who played hurt the most was Dave Walline. He blew out his knee, never complained, was always in the weight room, played hurt at all times

30. Bob Terrio surprised me the most. He became my partner on the defensive side at linebacker and he did a great job. He intercepted balls and was always in the right place.

31. I learned a lot from Coach Melton. He calmed me down. He used to say "you know, Murt, being a linebacker is not that difficult" and I would say "what are you talking about?" He would say "Well, what's your job? Your job is to go get the football. I don't care how you get it, just go get the ball". We got along really well.

32. Coach Devaney recruited me. I was going to sign with Oklahoma, and then Coach Devaney talked me out of it. He did a great sales job on me and my parents.

33. Practice was tough. You had a hour and a half and about 5 stations. You spent 10-15 minutes and you were on the goal at all times. If you walked, you ran steps and all hell broke loose. It was defined and set just right. The part of practice I hated the most was running into Dan Schneiss.

34. The fans helped our efforts in the game. Players like Eddie Periard thrived on the fans. It hyped him up.

35. Running on the field for the 1st time was chilling. Goosebumps. I thought "Boy, I'm in the big time". Quite a thrill.

36. My greatest memory was knocking down Oklahoma's Steve Owens in 1969. It was thrilling because we stopped him and he had 20 plus 100 yard games. I stopped him my junior year (1969) from reaching his goal and he was the Heisman trophy winner that year. It was a thrill because the year before he beat the hell out of me.

37. I still live in Nebraska and I am a Conductor for Union Pacific. I also run an organization called GOAL where I put wellness programs in the schools fighting obesity in our youth. Also, I am a volunteer linebacker coach for Creighton Prep high school.

38. Playing for Nebraska definitely helped me in the after football life. That is why I volunteer. I get a big kick out of watching a young high schooler develop and learn discipline and how to work hard and other things about the game.

39. I feel appreciated by the NU fans for the time I put in. People still come up and shake my hand and say "Wow, look what you guys did for us."

Bob Newton

BOB NEWTON *(aka "Fig")*

OFFENSIVE TACKLE

HUSKER HIGHLIGHTS

1. The starting offensive line in 1970 was Wally Winter, myself, Donnie McGhee and Dick Rupert at guards. The center was Doug Dumler. I was on that 1969 team too. I was a junior college transfer from California. After that 1968 season when Nebraska went 6-4, Coach Osborne went to Coach Devaney and said that we needed to get some junior college transfer to help us immediately and especially on offensive line. I was the first one to come and then Coach Osborne brought Keith Wortman, Carl Johnson, and Dick Rupert. So there were four of us in two years from the junior college ranks in California.

2. My greatest happiness for Coach Devaney was when we won the first National Championship in the Orange Bowl against LSU (January 1, 1971) and seeing how happy he was after the game. It was similar to the win that we had against Oklahoma in Norman in 1969 because that was the first time that Devaney had beaten OU in Norman. Those two victories were very gratifying and they made Coach Devaney happy.

3. My senior year (1970) against Missouri we won 21-7, but I had a very poor game. The guy in front of me, Rocky Wallace, was very quick. I probably did not prepare well enough that week. After the films Devaney called me over and he said "Bob, you know that you did not have a good game against Missouri, and do you plan on playing pro football?" and I said "Well, yeah, I really want to play pro football." Devaney says "Well, listen, if you have another game like that this year you

might as well forget it." That next week I was Big 8 Lineman of the Week and played well the rest of the year. That was just a typical motivational talk that took about 2 minutes, but he really touched me and motivated me with just that little simple fear of "you can't screw up like that again." Coach Devaney had such great respect from us and I saw him as a father figure. I really wanted to please him on the football field.

4. The most remarkable offensive play I witnessed was Joe Orduna's touchdown run for 67 yards against USC in 1970. It was a phenomenal run against a good football team. Also, Jerry Tagge's touchdown on a quarterback sneak to beat LSU. Those two plays that year were very significant.

5. My 2 years at the University of Nebraska were the most rewarding experiences of my life as far as having long time friendships with former players and coaches. I liked the friendliness of the Nebraska people and the sense of community. I just had deep respect for Coach Devaney and Coach Osborne. Being associated with those men has helped me tremendously.

6. I would like to go back and relive my senior year and the drive to score the winning touchdown for the National Championship against LSU (17-12). We were down 12-10 and it is the 4th quarter and we had to get down there and drive the ball. We had a very long drive and Tagge quarterbacked us. Everything was on the line, and we did it.

7. If I could change anything, I would study more and get my academics more focused. My major was in Community Health Education. I later got my degree while at NU in Physical Education. I got my Masters degree last summer in Psychology.

8. There was a real connection among the players. I did not see any hostility. I saw guys who were happy and doing things together after practice. There was good team chemistry, and that came from Coach Devaney and Coach Osborne blending that team together.

9. My first semester there I ended up on the 3rd or 4th team. When I went home I was going to transfer to another school. I told Coach Devaney and Osborne that I was not going to come back. It was a culture shock for me to go from Los Angeles to Lincoln. 12 below zero the first week that I was there in February. And Coach Osborne said "no, come on back." So my first goal was just to work myself up the depth chart. Coach Osborne put me on first team in the middle of the season my junior year (1969).

10. The 3 most important reasons for the wins were (1) we had a very explosive offense, especially with Johnny Rodgers' capacity to break out big plays; (2) we had an excellent running offense with Orduna and Kinney; (3) a tremendous defense. Jerry Murtaugh, Eddie Periard, Bob Terrio, Fiala, all those guys were tough nosed defensive players.

11. Playing at NU helped me succeed since my football playing days. The integrity of Coach Devaney and Osborne and my teammates gave me a special feeling of the whole experience. It motivated me and generated some of the good decisions I made in the future.

12. What does it mean to be considered the best? I feel very fortunate, and grateful. I had a lot of passion and I loved football with all my heart. It was a great opportunity to play for a program like the University of Nebraska.

13. I had to practice hard and lift weights and prepare myself mentally and physically. Playing at home at Nebraska was a fantastic experience. When we used to get off that bus and all the people would be lined up, and we would work through that lineup of people all dressed in red to get to the locker room. Then we would get dressed and come out. That whole scene was just exciting. Again, I wanted to please Coach Devaney

but I was also motivated by the love that the people of Nebraska had for the football program.

14. My biggest challenge was coming from Los Angeles and adjusting to the culture of the Midwest. And the weather and making new friends. I had a class around 8 a.m. and I walked about 10-15 feet from Harper Hall and I turned around and went back to bed because it was so cold.

15. I overcame the challenge because of my need to stay connected to the football team and my belief in Coach Devaney. We did the hard work that winter. Staying connected to the football team and the coaches kept me inching forward.

16. I got angry at times at the coaches or the situation I was in. About mid way into my first semester I thought about quitting and going home. I was really down and depressed. And my brother talked me out of it and told me to hang in there.

17. As I look back I can't really say that I had any disappointments. It took me a while to adjust to the system because in the junior college program the offensive systems were quite different.

18. If I could go back and change one thing I probably would have taken better care of myself. I would have trained even harder in the weight room and studied more.

19. The most important reason that made the team work so well together was the leadership of Bob Devaney. And the way the players bonded with one another on that football field on Saturday. When we walked on that field we played as a team. It all trickled down from Bob.

20. My most talented teammate was Johnny Rodgers. Even as a sophomore in 1970 I could see how his exciting and explosive skills could break a game wide open. That was real impressive. The next best was Jeff Kinney. He caught and ran the ball well. He was big and a hard runner and a good pass receiver. Jerry Tagge was very inspirational too.

21. The most inspirational my senior year was Danny Schneiss. Danny set a good tone of leadership. And of course, we lost Rex Lowe.

22. My most outrageous teammate was "Earthquake," Jim Carstens when he and Jones had the boxing match. That was quite outrageous. Those guys were in the ring just throwing haymakers at each other for 4 or 5 rounds.

23. The fans affected our efforts in the games because you would come into the stadium and hear 76,000 people all dressed in red. There is a psychological high that I would get from that to motivate me to become more intense and do the best I could as a offensive lineman to block for my teammates.

24. I feel appreciated by the University for the time I put in. I am part of the alumni. I am always invited back for golf tournaments. I still stay in contact with Boyd Eppley. With the change from Coach Osborne to Frank Solich to Bill Callahan there has been a little bit of a disconnection for me because I do not know any of the coaches like I used to. But I feel a strong connection to the University.

25. One of the happiest and funniest moments of my life was when we threw Coach Cletus Fischer into the showers after the OU game in Norman in 1969. We had never beaten OU in Norman under Devaney. After the game Cletus was just screaming and yelling and so we grabbed him and threw him in the shower. He got all wet and he was having a blast. Cletus was a great guy.

" ...I was motivated by the love that the people of Nebraska had for the football program."

John and Nancy O'Connell

JOHN O'CONNELL

DEFENSIVE SAFETY

HUSKER HIGHLIGHTS

1. It was fun in Fall football because Johnny Rodgers and I roomed together. We both were sore a lot, and Johnny got the corner room and I got the TV room.

2. We defeated Minnesota in 1970 in Minneapolis when we were sophomores (35-10). Bruce Hauge and I made a tackle in front of the Minnesota bench and Bruce was from Minnesota. The Minnesota coach chased Bruce all the way back to our huddle, and I said to Bruce "that guy sure does not like you or respect you." And Bruce said there are a lot of underlying circumstances because he was from Minnesota and they did not get Bruce.

3. One of my best memories was meeting Johnny Rodgers. We met at the Shrine Bowl in high school in 1968 and have been close friends ever since.

4. There is one saying that I have always used that Coach Devaney taught me, and that is "Mr. O'Connell, when I stop talking to you is when you want to worry." He came to my home and recruited me. He was such an icon.

5. I still have a great relationship with Coach Monte Kiffin. I see Coach Powers sometimes in St. Louis. Coach Fischer was a kick. Coach Melton is a good friend.

6. Coach Melton had such a great sense of humor. He always made fun of us. For example, "Nice tackle, I got kids younger than you that can tackle better." He always had a story.

7. I remember the story about how Coach Kiffin stole a milk truck when he was in college. My high school coach, Tom Ernst, and Monte and Warren Powers all went to school together at Nebraska. Before they went to the Gotham Bowl, Monte stole a milk truck as a prank. Those of us who knew that story used to say it to Coach Kiffin whenever he was giving us a bad time. We would say "how is the milk truck route going?"

8. Regarding my teammates: (a) Johnny Rodgers was elusive and had the best hands; (b) Jeff Hughes was very fast, and an all-around athlete; (c) John Dutton when he came to NU tall and slim. He went to the weight room and changed his whole physique; (d) I remember one time in study hall when Richie Glover was there with his girlfriend, and we were teasing him and he flipped the table. That is when I knew he was going to be a good football player. Richie Glover led by example; (e) Willie Harper really impressed me; (f) Bob Terrio became a Nebraskan from California.

9. Regarding our opponents, Texas A & M hit very hard. Oklahoma always played tough.

10. NU football taught me to never quit. It's a tough road but you can get through it. You will never have friends like we did when we played at NU. I fulfilled my personal goals. I did my best on and off the field

11. The best leader was Johnny Rodgers. People always looked up to Johnny even as a freshman. Jerry Tagge was an on-the-field leader and not a rah-rah guy. He did it by calling the right plays and following the script.

12. We achieved our team goals – to win but if we lost, lose graciously. We all patted each other on the back. You always acknowledged the team.

13. The 3 most important reasons that made us win were: (a) we did not make a lot of mistakes; (b) we were physical, and we wore the other team out; (c) we won with style

14. We did not think anyone that could beat us. I heard the comment that "the toughest team we played was at practice," and I believe that.

15. The biggest challenge for the team was Oklahoma in 1971, when it kept going back and forth in.

16. My biggest disappointment was not starting every game.

17. The single most important aspect that made the team work so well together was that our players learned how to work with the coaches. We were ahead of our time. We were always proud of each other.

18. My most outrageous teammate was Joe Blahak. He had about 7 different personalities.

19. The hardest worker in practice was Billy Olds. Our first year as freshman (1969) we were roommates. At 3 o'clock in the morning I hear this big "kaboom" and I thought that the building was falling down. I said to Billy "what the hell are you doing," and he said "practicing my blocking." I said you shattered the bathroom door, and how am I going to explain this to Coach Ross tomorrow. Billy said he was just trying to work his forearm shiver. I said, "Billy you are going to knock them dead so just get in bed." Coach Ross came in the next morning and said that he roomed me with Billy to keep him out of trouble.

20. Coach Warren Powers taught us to be smarter than the opponents. He had played pro ball, and he taught us stuff we never learned in high school.

21. If you made it through practice, you could make it through anything. Coach Devaney was smart about practice. He kept a lot of injuries off the practice field. He knew we would be hitting on Saturday, and he just saved it until then.

22. It meant everything to be part of the team – just to be part of the team and camaraderie. It was a dream come true to run on the field for the 1st time. My claim to fame is being on the National Championship team, and being one of Johnny Rodger's best friends.

23. The fans had a positive effect on our efforts in the game. At that time, we were in a new era and the fans had all the enthusiasm and they were first class.

24. I do not feel totally appreciated by the University for the time I put in. You cannot get tickets without paying a bunch of money and even if you lettered. You have to pay extra fees on top of the ticket price. The Athletic Department should have a better relationship with former players.

"NU football taught me to never quit. You will never have friends like we did when we played at NU."

FOR THE RECORD

JOE ORDUNA
1967-1968; 1970

6'-0" 196 lbs.
Omaha, NE

All-Conference (1970)

Pro Football
New York Giants and
Baltimore Colts

NOW

Wife Valerie (35 years);
3 children; 2 grandchildren.

A middle school
science teacher for
7th & 8th grade.
(just finished masters degree
to become a principal)

Irvine, California

Joe and Valerie Orduna

JOE ORDUNA

HALFBACK AND I BACK

HUSKER HIGHLIGHTS

1. I missed the season and the Sun Bowl in 1969 because I was injured, but I played on the first National Championship team in 1970.

2. In 1967-68 we were 6-4. We had two different quarterbacks: Frank Patrick, a big tall guy, and Ernie Siegler. I don't know what it was. We could not beat Oklahoma, and also we could not beat Kansas State, Kansas or Missouri. It was frustrating because we were good. We should have been better than that.

3. Coach Devaney walked around the field in those long khaki pants and a reversible jacket and a clipboard. He got mad at me one time and he used an expletive. He was so angry he said "Horse____." But in spite of that I just had a real love for him. The man did not say much to me, but he brought up that my parents are going to expect certain things of me.

4. Bob Devaney was one of the first adults that I learned to trust. And Coach Tom Osborne was another adult that I trusted.

5. Coach Osborne is the only coach that ever pulled me aside and taught me some skills. When I was a sophomore I was both a wide receiver and running back. He would keep me after practice and drill me on catching the ball. Many people don't know this, but I was a very good receiver. I learned how to catch a ball with one hand. They just never threw it to me and with the speed that I had I think that I would have been a very good wide receiver because I was not big enough to be a running back in the NFL (194 pounds). I still got to play running back in the pros but the problem was they put me at fullback (Giants and Colts). I definitely was not big enough to block people.

6. I loved Coach Corgan. I laughed at that man forever. He had some of the most vulgar funny expressions, but I never knew what they meant. His favorite expression was "When it gets down to nut cutting time, we will see who is the toughest." I was naive in those college years but I used to laugh at him. He talked about "looking like a dog on a hydrant" because you are blocking wrong. I look back with fondness on Mike Corgan. He was one of a kind.

7. Paul Schneider, our trainer, pampered me for 5 years. He gave me massages and leg rubs and treated my injuries. I have total respect for him. I talked to George Sullivan last fall when I was back, and he told me that Schnitzy had passed. I am sorry that I did not get to say good-bye to him and Devaney and Corgan.

8. Regarding Nebraska fans when I was a recruit, I walked into the stadium and I had never seen so much red. They were rabid fans and they embraced me and took me into their homes. I spent the night and shot their guns and rode their

horses. These fans were wonderful. And I still get asked for my autograph today and people write me letters 36 years later.

The players I remember the most are Guy Ingles, Dick Davis, Mike Green and Ben Gregory. In 1967 when we played Minnesota. Ben Gregory said to me after the game "I am sure glad we had you on our team today." Whoa, I will never forget that. A senior talking to a sophomore. I just loved Dick Davis. I thought he was an exceptional player with a lot of talent. He had speed and power. Mike Green was funny and kept us laughing so hard. People who I loved from a distance were Jerry Patton, Mike Wynn, Sherwin Jarmon.

Guy Ingles my senior year (1970) was really a motivator for me. He was always in my ears telling me, "you can do this, you can do that." I remember when we won the Orange Bowl in 1971. It was at night and Guy said "the sun is shining on us tonight." And then there was Coach Bill "Thunder" Thornton. We played USC out at the coliseum in 1970 and he said to me "You are going to break one tonight." And sure enough in the 3rd quarter I made that 67 yarder and he told me "I told you were going to do it." Those are good memories.

0. The biggest offensive play I made was a play a photographer snapped against Missouri my junior year in 1968. They handed the ball to me deep in the backfield and there was a linebacker standing in the hole, fully erect and had me dead to rights and without thinking I hurdled him completely over the top of his head. And the photographer caught that and you see this guy and he is leaning forward and he is still fairly erect grasping air and I am hovering above him with my legs spread apart and he completely missed me. I hit the ground and cut to the right and had a clear field to the end zone and I stumbled and fell. I think about that play all the time.

1. I remember Herb Orvis from Colorado, a linebacker in my Junior year. I am laying on the ground after someone tackled me and he jumped on my forearm with both feet deliberately. He was trying to break my arm. It angered me so much that I jumped up. I was going to spike him with the ball but I didn't. He got penalized. That is the only time I lost my temper in a game.

12. At UNL I learned that it does not matter how good you are. What matters is how well you discipline yourself and make the most of the opportunity that you have. I saw talent come and go. They were good but they did not have self discipline. I was able to focus and had the ability to do what the coaches asked me to do.

It took me a long time to know what I wanted to do in life. It was not to make money but to shape lives. I am looking at the next generation. I love being a schoolteacher because I am a preacher, actor and mentor. I am always on stage every minute of every day. And kids are coming back to me saying "I remember having you as a teacher. You were hard but you were good for us." Necessity makes people do what they have to do. You don't work, you don't eat.

14. If I could go back and relive one play, there was a 4th and one play when I was sophomore. I had to carry the ball and make one yard. And I did not make it, and the reason is that I did not understand that you don't dance on 4th and 1. You don't outrun people on 4th and 1. You just knock the hell out of them and get one yard.

And another was in 1970 when we played USC in the coliseum. It was in the 3rd quarter and we were driving. I fumbled and we lost the ball on that drive. If I had not fumbled the ball we might have kicked a field goal and avoided the tie (21-21).

15. If I could change anything, I would have been a better student. Fortunately I married the woman I did. She made me finish by correspondence, and I got my degree two years after I left.

16. The best leaders were Ben Gregory (1967) and in 1968 I looked to Dick Davis. I trusted him and fed off his confidence. In 1969 when I was injured, Jim McFarland stepped forward as a leader. In 1970 it was Guy Ingles.

17. The most important reasons for the wins were the conservative nature of the coaching staff. They were not looking for flashy players, but for solid consistent players. The coaching staff put together people that could be depended on and that mindset lasted for a number of years. Nebraska had a mystique with the blackshirt defense. You mention "blackshirt" and it was like saying a holy word that no one was supposed to mention. They chose people that wanted it and had discipline.

18. The player that had the greatest impact during my time at NU (1967-1970) was Johnny Rodgers. People were serious and conservative, but JR came along and he was outrageous. The way he dressed, talked and joked was great. His sophomore year (1970) it was like a disco in the locker room with the music that was being played (the Temptations) because we were relaxed. He had a lot to do with that. Dan Schneiss used to call him "Johnny R. Super Star." He wore sunglasses all the time and he broke the ice and loosened people up. I don't think that could be duplicated.

19. To motivate myself before the game, there is a place that an athlete goes to when he is alone. And he feels the energy and the power inside of him. I would focus on that energy. I would see myself moving quickly and powerfully and running over people. That was my first two years at the University (1967-68). But the year I played with Johnny Rodgers (1970) I was very relaxed and casual. I did not get nervous because I had so much confidence in everybody I was playing with. I was out there having fun.

20. In 1968 I thought about transferring to another school because Nebraska was so conservative in its offense. NU's offense was boring and not exciting. It did not emphasize speed. But Coach Devaney caught wind of it, and came to me and basically said "Don't transfer. It will be a big mistake." I listened and believed him and did not transfer. And I am glad I did not transfer because in 1969 NU changed to the Pro-I and spread formations, and that utilized speed.

21. Some schools featured one running back like Steve Owens and John Riggins, who got to carry the ball a lot. Nebraska did not do that. We spread it around. But it worked out okay and the coaches were wise. I see the value of everything that they did. I wish Tom Osborne would have succeeded in making me a wide receiver because I think that I would have been a great one.

22. The most important reason that made the team work so well together was cohesiveness. Monte Kiffin was a big part of the defense. We got along well and did not have racial strife. By 1970 we were a family and had fun and relaxed.

23. The most talented teammates were Johnny Rodgers, Dick Davis and for his size Guy Ingles. But my all time favorite was George Hicks. He came to NU but it did not work out for him. I played with him in junior high and high school. I always thought that he had a talent that went unrecognized.

24. The most inspirational teammates were Mike Green and Dick Davis in 1968. In 1970 Dan Schneiss and Johnny Rodgers kept us loose.

25. The fans definitely affected our efforts in the game. They are the reason no one could stop us on 4th and 1. The fans wanted it and willed it and you had to make it because the fans were there.

26. Playing for Nebraska helped me in the after football life. We achieved at the highest levels. In life the glories of men come and go and they tarnish. You can't live on those glories. Nebraska was such a successful positive experience. As long as you do your best, that is all that really matters.

27. Football isn't really all that important. What is important is life and the way we go about it. I have been married to the same woman for 35 years and she is the love of my life and the reason I am what I am.

28. I am glad for what we achieved at NU but I have to admit it hurts a little bit to watch Nebraska in these last few years. It seems like they don't know what we used to know. Showboating too much and not enough "Smash Mouth" football.

FOR THE RECORD

JOHN PITTS
1970 -1972

6'-1" 209 lbs.
Flint, MI

NOW

Married to Katie Glass;
3 daughters and one son
Police officer with the Lincoln
Police department
(Lead defensive tactics
instructor and firearm
instructor since 1986)

Katie is a health technician
at an elementary school.

4 children

Left to Right:
John, Katy, Tanya, Taylor,
Christie, Jay

JOHN PITTS

'70 DEFENSIVE END; '71 MONSTER BACK; '72 WEAK SIDE LINEBACKER

HUSKER HIGHLIGHTS

1. My best memories of Coach Devaney were his motivational talks during half time when we were behind. He had that way of getting you all excited and getting you to go out there and do the best you can. He knew how to get 110% out of you.

2. For the most part, I enjoyed Coach Devaney's coaching style. The only thing I did not enjoy was 1970. I started the Wake Forest game. Then in the second game of the season against USC, I did not really get to play even though I led the team in tackles that first game. So it blew me away that I did not get to play that second game. But, as a result Willie Harper got to start and that's history.

   I was thinking of leaving school at that point. I got hurt the next week in practice. After that year I changed positions each year. I thought I had the opportunity to start at monster back and I ended up on second team behind Dave Mason. Finally in `72 I started at weak side linebacker. It all worked out in the end, but it was trying times to get there.

3. Warren Powers was my position coach for monster back. John Melton for weak side linebacker. Coach Kiffin was the defensive ends coach.

4. Coach Melton had that real good sense of humor. He always had that cigar in his mouth. I remember him always getting on Jimmy Branch and wondering how such a small linebacker could make such big plays.

5. My last Orange Bowl game against Notre Dame (1973) I had some solid tackles. That was one my better games.

6. What I learned at UNL was growing up. I had the opportunity in a summer program to work for the police department, and I really enjoyed that. I learned a lot about people and behavior. Football is kind of those ups and downs. You have the good times and your hard times. I learned hard work from football. Do the best you can at every stage.

7. The thing I remember most about Coach Kiffin was 1970. He had the defensive team do 100 grass drills, and he did 100 grass drills with us. It took us about 10-15 minutes to get them done and we were all shot after that.

8. If I could go back and relive a play, it would be a play I did not make in the 1970 Wake Forest game. I had 10 tackles in that game, but I did miss one big one. I missed the quarterback.

9. I don't think I would change anything. Everything has a way of coming around. I hate to say "destiny" but everything has been arranged. All you can do is make the most of it.

10. Bill Janssen was probably the Number One leader for me. Also, Richie Glover and Darryl White because they always worked hard. They always made the big plays. I think Van Brownson was one of the leaders that I looked up to. The quiet leader of the bunch was Jimmy Branch. He just went out there and did his job.

11. I was the first one in my family to go to college and I wanted to get that college degree for myself and my parents. Football was the only way I would get through school. I came from Flint, Michigan.

12. The 3 most important reasons for the wins were: (a) a group of coaches who knew how to motivate ball players; (b) a talented group of people; (c) we all worked together to get our team goals accomplished. We all had the desire to excel and push the person in front of us. Our Number One and Number Two teams were interchangeable because we had such great talent.

13. Playing football at NU helped me later. It helped start our defensive tactics program at the police department. Staying in shape and working out, doing martial arts.

14. It means a lot to be considered the best. It is really an honor because we are still considered one of the best teams ever. It is an honor that comes from our desire to push each other and to excel in everything we did.

15. To motivate myself before the games, I was one of the quiet guys. I reached within my self and was not vocal. I tried to concentrate on what I needed to get done. We had such great people up front (Glover, Dutton, Jacobson, Janssen, Willie, and Spider). Jimmy Branch and I were really like brothers. We fed off each other.

16. My biggest challenge was probably my size. I came in at 6 foot 1 inch and 190 lbs. Probably the biggest I ever got was 220 lbs. I needed more weight and a couple more tenths of a second in speed.

17. My biggest disappointment was getting injured. I played a lot, but we all want to start if we can. What the coaches did worked out great.

18. The most important aspects that made the team work so well together were (a) unity and (b) the players' attitude. A lot of us on and off the field were pretty good friends. Even to this day you can still call people and they will try to help you out. Everyone came together as one team. What made us a great team was unity on and off the field.

19. My most talented teammate was Johnny Rodgers. I always wanted to get a good shot on him, but I could never get it. He always wiggled or stopped on a dime and made people miss.

20. Out toughest opponent was Oklahoma. They were all good athletes. Greg Pruitt was a terrific running back. Quarterback Jack Mildren was very tough.

21. The most inspirational player on the 1969 team was Ken Geddes. The most outrageous players were Shatch or Dirty Red. Doug Jamail as well.

22. I wanted to prove to everybody that I should be playing. So I worked really hard to get back in shape. I got into the weight room with Boyd [Eppley] and lifted weights and I got a lot stronger for my size.

23. When you look back you think "boy, we had a heck of a good time." We had a lot of talent and a great coaching staff. We were just destined to be together as champions.

24. Once you start playing you get into that zone where you don't worry about the fans. You just worry about what you need to do. It is great coming into the stadium. You know the fans are there and becoming very loud.

25. I graduated on time in 5 years. In Industrial Education with a teaching certificate.

26. Do I feel appreciated by the University for the time I put in? Yes and no. The staff and the coaches that we played for really appreciated us coming back and working out. But with the new staff I feel a disconnect. But yes, I did feel appreciated by the coaching staff and University for a majority of the years. With the "Husker Nation" Reunion in 2004 I saw a lot of people that I had not seen in years and that was nice.

27. Coach Kiffin loved Diet Dr. Pepper. We always raided the coolers and got his Diet Dr. Pepper.

TOM ROBISON

DEFENSIVE TACKLE

HUSKER HIGHLIGHTS

1. I had a terrible practice my first year. Coach Devaney told me "If you miss another tackle. I will make you a Javelin Catcher on the track team."

2. Nebraska players were tight as a group. We learned to never accept losing.

3. Coach Monte Kiffin was a tremendous leader. He never asked you to do something he didn't do. He taught toughness.

4. The most important reason for the wins were (a) lots of talent; (b) good leadership; (c) good preparation. We were confident NU would win the championship in 1970.

5. It feels great to be Number One.

6. My biggest challenge was injuries to my knee.

7. I got my degree, but I wish I would have studied more seriously.

8. Our team chemistry was special. We overcame diversity.

9. My most talented teammates were Willie Harper, JR, Glover, Adkins, Pitts.

10. Jim Branch always made me laugh. He kept the locker room loose.

11. Practices were tough but quick. They ended on time. I hated the wind sprints at the end.

12. I loved playing and the championship years. The fans had a tremendous effect on my efforts.

13. Playing for NU helped me after football. I got some jobs as a result of it.

" Nebraska players were tight as a group... our team chemistry was special."

"Coach Monte Kiffin was a tremendous leader. He never asked you to do something he did not do. He taught toughness."

Tom and Darlene Robison

JOHNNY RODGERS (aka "The Jet")

WINGBACK AND KICK RETURNER

HUSKER HIGHLIGHTS

1. One of my fondest memories is that Coach Devaney encouraged me to be myself.

2. We were allowed to relax and have fun at all of our Bowl Games. It was never an atmosphere of all work and no play. Coach Devaney arranged for us to go to Jai Alai games, to the tracks, to the Ike and Tina Turner concert and to the Temptations. He was really a player's coach, and premier players rally for a player's coach. If you treat them correctly, they will do anything in the world for you. We would rather slide bare booty down a razorblade than disappoint Coach Devaney.

3. Coach Cletus Fischer kept me fired up all the time. I always had the "green light" and that meant I could do whatever I wanted to do on kick returns. I did not have to fair catch. In the OU game in 1971 that was actually a right return which ended up going to the left.

4. Coach Osborne was like a big brother to me and he still is. I would run after practice because he would run with me. After practices I caught hundreds of balls on a daily basis and he would throw what we called "turnarounds" and "horseshoes." He was quite a motivator. And we had the concept that you did not come to camp to get into shape. You came to get the mental edge. Premier players push themselves. They are self motivated.

5. Our trainers were George Sullivan and Paul Schneider ("Schnitzy"). They were like trainer/coaches. They were delegated responsibility and power by Coach Devaney. They decided whether you practiced or if you were hurt. I very seldom had to practice the day after the game because I was generally in the room getting massages and whirlpools and ice because I took so many hits.

6. Coach Kiffin was a player's coach as well. He did the things we did. And he took it to another level. He was exciting and motivating. And he was tough as nails. He would run the stairs with us.

7. After the Oklahoma game in 1971, our plane landed in Lincoln. There were thousands of fans at the airport waiting for us. We were trying to fight through the crowd and Coach Devaney had this rich fan named Capper. Capper had a limo sitting in back of the plane. They took Devaney to another plane and they flew off into the sunset.

8. The most remarkable defensive play I witnessed was Rich Glover's play in the Oklahoma game in 1971. He had 22 tackles. Also, John Adkins and Willie Harper played equally as tough a game because they had the responsibility of guarding the pitch man. They had to have the discipline to stay with that pitchman or else at the last second Mildren would pitch the ball to Pruitt or Wiley and they would get a big play. We all played as a unit and maintained our responsibilities. That is what it took to win the game against an outstanding OU team.

9. I learned about teamwork. You really don't achieve anything by yourself. Teamwork makes your dreams work.

10. If I had to do it all over again I would be a geek. I would marry my childhood sweetheart and I would study all the time. I would want to go to the pros. But in the off-season I would come back and finish up on my masters degree and

continue until I got a doctor's degree. I really believe that education is life itself. We never stop learning and I am still learning now.

1. We had a team of leaders. All of our coaches could be head coaches at universities. Devaney was able to delegate all the responsibilities they needed. He also gave us the same power and freedom as individual players.

2. Before a game our coaches talked about the fundamentals which are the most crucial part of life and football. For instance, being able to read defenses so you can know what a person is getting ready to do before they do it. There are plenty of people with ability but they don't know how to apply their skills when the pressure is on. This is the same in life.

3. The 3 most important reasons for the wins were (a) The coaching. (b) Caring for each other (c) and confidence. We were treated like adults who were curious and trying to go take it to a higher level. The biggest motivation was not letting each other down. We believed in ourselves and in each other. It all came together in a masterpiece.

4. We were confident NU would win the National Championship in 1971 because we were well conditioned. We were very disciplined and had leadership and perseverance and teamwork. We did not have a weak area. Whoever gets tired first loses. We had that old fashioned Husker dedication.

5. It is prideful to be considered the best. You would never think that 35 years later NU would still be ranked by some as the best team of all time and NU-OU in 1971 as the biggest game in college history. We just tried to be just as good as we could be.

6. The Big 8 was the toughest conference in the country. Nobody played better football from top to bottom. There never again will be 3 teams in one conference that finish 1, 2, 3. We played Oklahoma when OU was number 2, and we played Alabama who was number 2. The Oklahoma team was so good and they had world class sprinters in their backfield.

7. Before the games I was self motivated. I did a lot of stretching and breathing. I did not do a lot of hoopla and I was not nervous before the games.

18. My biggest challenge was staying out of trouble. I was very wild and reckless at times. At the same time I was bashful and shy. Coming from my background in the ghetto of Omaha, I did not have the necessary confidence to always maintain some direction.

19. I never thought about quitting. I have learned more from my mistakes than from my successes.

20. The game that was the biggest challenge for the team in 1972 was our first game vs. UCLA in Los Angeles. It was the first game we lost in 32 games. We came to Los Angeles with the intention of winning a 3rd national championship. I really thought we had a better team in 1972 than we had in 1971, but in 1972 our coaches had been away doing some camps and they weren't as focused as usual. Also we had a new quarterback with Dave Humm. He eventually because a great quarterback but he was still a rookie in 1972. We lost to Oklahoma in 1972 for the first time in four years. So we learned how to win and how to lose. Those two games did not diminish our two national championships. But we did learn how to be gracious losers as well as graceful winners.

21. If I could go back and change one thing I would not get in trouble. I would not have a college prank and take a dare. We would also not lose that UCLA game because that would have put us on track to win another National Championship.

22. Coach Devaney's announced retirement before the 1972 season threw off us off a bit. When you are sharing leaderships between Coach Osborne and Coach Devaney people don't always know which direction to go.

23. The most important reasons that made the team work so well together were coaches, player's talent, and attitude. You can win a lot of games because of talent, but you have to have dedication and working together in order to win championships.

24. When you see that your coaches are committed that helps you be committed. When you are coming in from a dance at 1 o'clock at night and you see Coach Osborne or other coaches are still over at the office studying plays and looking at films, it helps you also become more committed. It gave us a chemistry of oneness. We were in this together and any weak link will break the chain.

25. We did not have any challenges to our team chemistry. We did not have any racial dissension or individual jealousy.

26. The whole defensive team was back there on punt returns which helped us take punt returning to a whole new level and to set college team records. We were like a family.

27. My most talented opponent was Greg Pruitt from OU.

28. My most inspirational teammate was Rex Lowe. He was a fun guy, but he became terminally ill. Watching him go from 180 pounds down to 100 pounds was such a sad experience. After the 1971 against OU he came into the locker room in a wheel chair. We gave him the game ball and two weeks later he was dead.

29. Our practices were not that hard, but they were intelligent. They were more educational and mental practices. It was a team of workers and thinkers who were trying to take their game to another level.

30. Who surprised me the most was Mike Beran ("Red Baron'). He wasn't big or fast but he was committed to be the best he could be.

31. Who kept the locker room the loosest was Glenn Garson ["Satch"] and JJ Hughes was a wild one too. JJ and Glenn and myself and Rex Lowe were all very close and good friends.

32. My position coach was Coach Tom Osborne. I learned about hard work from Tom and about catching techniques and conditioning and motivation. I learned to be a better person from Tom.

33. Coach Devaney recruited me. And also Mike Green and Dickie Davis and we are all still friends to this day.

34. I had fun at practice. We had the number one defense in the country and I had the opportunity to work against them and learn. I hated sprints the most. They made me better but they sure did hurt.

35. The fans helped our efforts. The yelling and the enthusiasm helped take our game to another level. We took almost 20-25,000 fans to every away game. We really never had an "away" game.

36. I still live in Nebraska and I still enjoy the fans and the people. It is remarkable that 35 years later that people are still talking about the Game of The Century and the things that we achieved collectively. The friendships forged over the years are gratifying.

37. Playing for Nebraska helped me in the after football life. I have high name recognition. People appreciate what we did for the state, for football and the University and for the fans. There is a statewide pride.

38. I feel appreciated by the University for the time I put in. The leadership has changed at the University but they still have us down for different functions. I am still asked to come down and speak to the players each year. Coach Callahan has made it very clear that everyone is welcome. It helps in recruiting to have former players still part of the program.

39. In the 1972 Orange Bowl, Coach Devaney wanted to beat Bear Bryant more than anything. The Oklahoma game was really his biggest win, but egotistically in his mind Bear had toyed with him in 1965-1966. Bear caught him a couple of times in those earlier Bowl Games where it was a mismatch.

40. The `73 Orange Bowl vs. Notre Dame was Devaney's last game and it sent Bob out on top. It was the first time I played I-back. I probably should have played I-back earlier in the year to give us extra quickness.

Rich Glover, Bob Devaney and Johnny Rodgers with the Outland and Heisman trophies.

Steve and Jeannie

STEVE RUNTY

QUARTERBACK

HUSKER HIGHLIGHTS

1. My senior year (1973) was Tom Osborne's first season as head coach. A couple of days before our first game our starter, Dave Humm, went down with a knee injury so I got to start at quarterback against UCLA in Lincoln. UCLA was supposed to win, but we did (40 – 13).

   What happened after that game was magical. I was player of the game and they were going to donate a scholarship in my name from Chevrolet. I looked at the sidelines, and there stood my Dad and he was sobbing and weeping. That was a special moment for me to see how proud and happy my dad was, and we were sharing that moment.

2. Coach Devaney was the type of individual who commanded respect. When you passed him in the hallway you did not know whether to say "hi coach" or "hi sir". But his greatest talent was surrounding himself with outstanding people and coaches. In the end Devaney always made sure that everyone agreed and was on the same page and unified.

   Secondly, Devaney had that Irish smile, and he allowed his players some freedom. He worked us hard but he allowed us to have some fun. Right before the Orange Bowl in Miami Bob said "alright, you guys, I have a surprise for you. I got you all front row seats for the Ike & Tina Turner Show and just behave yourself. You know what I mean by behave yourself – don't get too drunk". Players responded well to his style.

3. Tom Osborne was the most prepared coach. You believed in him.

4. Both Tom Osborne and Bob Devaney were street smart and understood which players were good and how to design plays around the best players.

5. The Nebraska fans are extremely special. The common man and woman in Nebraska who filled the stadium are just so special. They were fun to talk to afterwards. I and my father and mother were school teachers and we were in all kinds of small towns in Nebraska, – Milford, Plainview, Ogallala, Crescent and I had a good feeling in my heart about these people in Nebraska. They loved us and we loved them. When you would run on the field it was uplifting.

6. In the 70s I remember more student involvement. They were more vocal in the section behind our bench and I think they took a lot of their seats out. Today is materialistic and if kids get the tickets they will sell them, but back then they would not sell their tickets for love or money.

7. My favorite players were the offensive lineman. The big fellas had the best sense of humor and could get by with saying anything. They had the biggest hearts and would do anything for you.

8. Regarding our opponents, each week was fun because the Big 8 was such a great conference. My favorite was beating Colorado because their fans were so nasty and especially in Boulder. We would have to keep our helmets and jackets on at all times because they would throw snowballs and beer on us. 1971 was amazing when we had the 1st, 2nd, and 3rd best teams in America all in one conference (NU, Oklahoma, and Colorado). Oklahoma's Jack Mildren ran the option exceptionally well.

9. NU football changed my life because I was 18. We went to Nebraska and wanted to conquer the world. We had athletic talent. And we were molded by the great minds. It was just a great experience to go through. We grew through natural hard work and conditioning and not like today with all the enhancement supplements.

10. Life after football for me was easy because I learned about time management. That made it easy for me to transition into the business world.

11. I remember when we would finish practice and Coach Kiffin would take the defense over and have them run stadium steps. They had the QBs and receivers run patterns and we would throw. I respect the work ethic of the lineman because they worked so hard and were intense.

12. On the 2nd team, you would get a scholarship. When I got my scholarship, I called my dad and told him that he did not have to send anymore checks. My dad was speechless.

13. Our team goal was winning. In the business world everything is measured.

14. The 3 most important qualities for the wins were (1) Preparation over and above our opponents; (2) the desire to win; (3) the desire to serve our teammates. We had believability in our team and our leaders. We never second guessed and had confidence in our leaders.

15. In 1971, we were confident NU would win the National championship. No one was going to stop our team.

16. It meant a lot to be considered the best. The expectation for the rest of my life was that everything would be that great. Out of 1,400 people, I was "Rookie of the Year" salesperson for IBM. It just felt natural. My next job was with Modern Business Systems that had 30 branches. The Omaha branch was in the bottom 10% and my boss said that if I could move this branch from the bottom to the middle of the pack, there will be some rewards for you. I told him that we will be the top branch in two years. And it happened. Now I am in this clothing business that started with $800,000 in sales and we worked it up to

the $15-16 million range. We are going to be the best with the same thought process we used at the U of Nebraska. My second phase is going to be giving back (not proving myself), and I am looking forward to that.

17. Devaney had the ability to inspire like no other. Coach Monte Kiffin did also. Mike Corgan could in his own way

18. Coach Monte Kiffin was outrageous when he came to practice. He was so wired that no one could understand what he was saying. At Kansas State, we were flipping quarters to the goal line to see who was closest to the line. Coach Kiffin came running over there and I thought "Oh God, he is going to chew us out," but he grabs me and said that he had a quarter and he wants to beat us.

19. Wide receivers and wingbacks worked the hardest in practices because of the amount of running and sprints.

"The Nebraska fans are extremely special."

"Coach Devaney always made sure that everyone was unified."

Dick Rupert

DICK RUPERT

OFFENSIVE GUARD

HUSKER HIGHLIGHTS

1. One time Coach Devaney saw me after a game and I was at the Legion club. I had this Tom Collins drink in front of me, and it was during the season. He just walked up to me and said "Well, we will see you Monday for stadiums". That meant running the stadium stairs because we were not supposed to be drinking. I thought that was ironical. I knew that half the guys were out there drinking a six pack, and I am sitting here with my family with a "prom drink" in front of me. I just happened to be at the same place where Coach Devaney was. I had to run 10 stairs. I should have drunk straight whiskey.

2. Coach Osborne recruited me out of California. He gave me a call the day after my last junior college game. We picked a spot to meet for breakfast and I asked my mom for a couple of bucks in case I had to pay for the meal. Coach Osborne impressed me.

3. I saw Coach Osborne about 15 years ago. He did not know I was coming and even after 20 years he immediately recognized me and asked about my family. That was awesome. He is an amazing guy.

4. A fun story about Oklahoma fans: After the Game of the Century (1971) we were getting on the bus to fly back and some fans came up and said "Good job, guys, you gave it a good try and we still support you." And we finally told these 6 ladies that we won the game. They were so embarrassed because they were Oklahoma fans, and they thought we were the Oklahoma players. We all had our red blazers on. That was funny.

5. Regarding Nebraska fans, I was being recruited and I came to Lincoln. They took me out to dinner at the Legion club, and there was Husker memorabilia all around. I went into the bathroom, and again there is all this Husker stuff. I thought "Wow, these people are serious about this". That was impressive.

6. There were warm feelings among our players. One of the reasons for our success was that we got along. I enjoyed the guys. I feel sorry for the people who went to the movies when we were there because we would cut up and have a great time. Those were good times.

7. The Oklahoma game in 1971 was significant because of the press. We were very familiar with the guys that we were playing against. Oklahoma had the Selmon brothers on defense, and we had Glover, Jacobson and Harper on defense.

8. When we beat Alabama in the 1972 Orange Bowl (38-6), we had the dinner after the game and we were talking to some of the Alabama players. They indicated that they had no fun at all at the Orange Bowl, and we had a blast. They just worked all the time. We went to the Ike and Tina Turner concert, and we were down at the beach and learning how to body surf. They had a crummy time and we had so much fun. That is a tribute to Coach Devaney as far as seeing the big picture. He liked to have fun, which is one reason I liked the guy.

9. My most memorable offensive play was against Missouri in 1971 (36-0). I trapped in front of Jeff Kinney. There was a perfect hole except for

one Missouri defender standing right in my way. I caught him perfectly right under the chin with my helmet. I knocked him back into two others guys and the three of them fell down. Kinney walked into the end zone. That was the best block of my career.

10. I remember Dave Walline when we were playing Missouri in 1970 (21-7). A Missouri guy missed his block and Missouri had a big running back who was supposed to be All-World (Joe Moore). Walline came in and absolutely killed the guy. He was on a slant and Dave just caught him under the shoulder and unfortunately dislocated his shoulder. You hate to see a guy get hurt.

11. I was fortunate to get a degree. My dad was a factory worker and no one in my family had ever gone to college. It gave me the opportunity to get into the insurance business and do well. I learned discipline and staying with a program.

12. A little known fact about the Game of the Century against Oklahoma in 1971 was that there was only one penalty and it was my penalty. We had a third and four and it was in the 3rd quarter. Tagge says "we are going to pull them offsides because we usually go on two, but we are going to go on the third hut." We get up on the line and he calls "hut, hut," and I take off and smacked the linebacker.

What is really funny is 15 years later I am in Des Moines at a Rotary Club meeting. The speaker happens to be the official who did the Game of the Century. He proceeds to talk about what a clean game it was and to his knowledge there was only one penalty in the whole game. The guy next to me stands up and says "I would like to introduce you to the guy that did that penalty". That was funny. The Game of the Century is a funny thing because you go back and think "if we did this or that differently." But if you changed even one thing, it is not the Game of the Century anymore. It is not the same game.

13. On offense Jerry Tagge was the leader. Doug Dumler had leadership. They had it all together. They had a little more direction and saw the bigger picture. You knew that no matter how tough the situation was they were going to perform. Johnny Rodgers would fall into that category. I think I fall into that category.

14. My personal goal was just to play. I did not care where or how.

15. Our coaches emphasized where they thought we might have an advantage. My goal was to not miss a block.

16. The four most important reasons for the wins were: (a) tremendous talent; (b) as the season went on, especially the 1971 season, we had a lot of confidence. (c) the coaches utilized our talent to the best of our abilities. Some of the current teams try to fit a square peg into a circle hole, as opposed to focusing on a person who has special skills. On offense the coaches put in designed plays to get the ball to JR and to Kinney. We were well prepared and confident (d) the camaraderie we had as players really made the difference.

17. I was confident NU would win the National Championship in 1971. The Oklahoma game was going to be our National Championship game, and I never thought we would lose.

18. The NU experience helped me succeed since my football playing days. It helped me as far as business and reaching higher levels. Confidence and working hard in order to get something done.

19. I am totally honored to be considered the best. I feel lucky. How does a guy from California end up in Nebraska on two National Championship teams. I was a Junior College transfer and in 24 ball games we win 23, tie 1 and win 2 National Championships.

20. To motivate myself before the game I tried to find a quiet space and have some quiet time and reflect on what my task was.

21. Schoolwork was never easy for me. I had to discipline myself. Some guys could look at a book and take a test. I had to read everything and highlight it. They took good care of us with the training tables and the dorm rooms and tutors.

22. My biggest disappointments were when some of the guys got hurt. One of the rules of engagement was that you were only one play away from getting hurt.

23. You could see in the 2005 USC team that there were too many guys who were just individuals, instead of team guys. What made our 1971 team so special was

that everyone on the team liked each other, and we were not going to let down our teammates. The fact that we all partied together after games was a big factor in our closeness.

24. My most talented teammates were Johnny Rodgers, Jerry Tagge, and Willie Harper. Johnny had that unique ability to put his body in a position that would make people miss. Tagge was a natural athlete. He could throw with his right or left hand. Willie Harper had a physique out of a catalog. He was big and strong and just amazing.

25. The most inspirational player was Johnny Rodgers. The things he was able to do were amazing. He could go as fast sideways as he could forward. I remember my first spring ball and I told Johnny to line up about 10 yards from me and I said "you come at me like you caught a punt and I am going to see if I can tackle you" and I did not even touch him. Also, Rex Lowe, talk about inspiration. You think how fortunate you are.

26. The most outrageous teammates were Jim "Earthquake" Carstens and Doug Jamail in the boxing match.

27. My position coaches were Clete Fischer, who was the barker, and Carl Selmer, who was the brains.

I learned a lot from Coach Selmer as far as blocking strategies. Carl has all these intricate blocking rules.

28. Cletus Fischer was fun. If you were doing a drill, he would be barking at you the whole time and push you. I remember when I missed a block at the Colorado game in Boulder in 1970. Coach Devaney comes up from behind me and grabbed the arm by the triceps and says "Dick, if you ever miss a block like that again, you will be on a bus back to L.A."

29. We did not want to let the fans down. I did not want to let myself or my teammates down either. The adrenaline and extra energy that the fans gave us was indescribable. Unless you are down there on the field actually playing I don't think you can understand what that does. It is tremendous.

30. My greatest memory was the celebration after we beat L.S.U. in the 1971 Orange Bowl. All of a sudden we realized that we had done it and won the 1st National Championship. I played a good game that day. The LSU player came up to me after the game and he says

"You are the best guy I have ever played against" To me that was the best compliment someone can give you. Everyone was so excited and the crowd was on the field and guys were throwing their helmets into the stands. We knew we had arrived.

31. The second time (1971), we expected to win the National Championship.

32. Playing for Nebraska absolutely helped me in the after football life. The contacts have opened up some doors professionally for me. I was in my chiropractor's office a year ago and a guy says "Are you Dick Rupert?" I answer yes and he says "You played for the Huskers in 1970 and 1971?" and I answer yes and he says "I remember you" And I remember thinking "wow, how can he?" That is just indicative of how incredible the NU fans are.

33. I feel appreciated by the University for the time I put in. I wish that they would have given me a season ticket for a little longer time. I got one free ticket for 5 years and I could buy the one next to it. I got a college education and I did not get hurt. I had a blast.

34. To be Number One requires guys getting along. Teams get into trouble because they have some personality conflicts that will not work themselves out. That is a cancer that develops in some teams. We did not have that. I also think that it is luck that we kept people healthy.

35. The toughest guy I played against was Oklahoma's Derlin Moore in the Game of the Century (1971). He was 6 ft 5 inches. He was a good player. If I made a mistake, he made sure the running back knew it.

36. Possessing talent is not enough. You have to have talent and hone it to be as good as you can.

37. The funniest teammate was Joe Blahak. I used to sit on the bus with Joe. We were going down to play Kansas State in 1971. Joe was feeling some bad vibes and thinking we are not prepared. We went out and beat them 44-17. All I could do was laugh because Joe was worried, and we actually played one of our better games.

*"Everybody
performed at a height
that no one could
do on their own.
They could only do
it in a team."*

Bill Sloey

BILL SLOEY *(aka "Dirty Red")*

LINEBACKER

HUSKER HIGHLIGHTS

1. Coach Devaney had charisma and leadership. He "barked" and we would "bite." He had good coaches around him. He was a great leader because he was dedicated to the guys that were working with him.

2. We were running sprints after my first workout in pads and I did not hear Coach Devaney blow the whistle. As I went by him he was cussing up a storm. His cheeks puffed out and the whistle came out right after that.

3. In 1972 we tied Iowa State (23-23) and we are all getting on the bus. We tied it because we missed an extra point. Devaney was totally livid. He was biting his lip. And nobody wanted to be on the same bus that he was on. And damn if he did not start to get on the bus that I was on. And he threw his bag into storage on the bus and he missed. He went down to pick it up and he hit his head on the door. And it started bleeding, and we all thought that we were dead. And Satch and I were just sitting there shaking like "oh no, he is on our bus and he is really going to be ticked off at everybody." Nobody really said anything and he got over it. Coach Devaney showed a lot of class.

4. Devaney had a sense of humor. We used to have "rookie day" during fall camp just before we went to the training table. And Devaney is downstairs punching this speed bag and he said "Sloey, you are going to be impersonating me tonight." And I said "How do you know that?" and he says "I know everything." So he kind of put the fear of God in me. I got up and flipped my hair back and put on his uniform which was the shorts and the black shirt. And Satch was Howard

Cosell and I was Bob Devaney. I was kind of scared, but it started to lighten up and I saw him laughing. Devaney was laughing with us and that is part of leadership. You can laugh at yourself and at the same time have respect.

5. John Melton was my coach and John and I just did not get along. I was hurt. I had torn my ACL and PCL the first game against Oregon. John thought I was faking it. I was sensitive to his comments. We would have game films and he would be smoking a cigar and we were choking. Terrio and Morell were keeling over.

6. One quality guy was Coach Monte Kiffin. He was very dedicated and he had a loyalty to Devaney. He got the most out of everybody. Monte Kiffin could see the potential in people. And he got them in the right spot.

7. Coach Warren Powers was super. Everybody around Coach Melton was super.

8. Nebraska fans are incredible. We went back in 2002 to the Oregon State game. I went up to sit in my seat in section 21, and these two fans on both sides of me were telling me where I was from, when I got hurt, how I got hurt, and when I played or did not play. They were walking dictionaries of anybody that was there. It was awesome. You always hear about NU fan's sportsmanship. They really got behind us.

9. The NU players at that time were awesome. There were a few in the "world class" category. They played to their total ability because of the expectancy of performing for the team. I think that is what made us a team. Colorado had excellent athletes, but they were not coached right or handled right.

Oklahoma had quality coaches and ball players, but we surpassed them because we played as a team. We kicked ass for whoever had the ball. There was such a camaraderie. You could not let anybody down.

10. I got defensive player of the game at Kansas. I got an interception and 2 fumbles and about 7 tackles.

11. When I was out on the football field I was totally amazed at how everybody was working. What I learned the most was keep working and it is a day to day effort. We worked hard and we stayed together. We played together and partied together and we won together. The 1971 team was best team because of the total dedication and focus.

I liked how Jeff Kinney and Johnny Rodgers and all the big guys would party with the little guys, and everybody was part of the team. You look at OU, Colorado, and Texas and they were all fractioned out. They had their superstars and then they had the other guys. We had some superstars, but everybody played together and it was our amazing team effort.

12. I am in a company with 4 billion dollars worth of work and everybody talks about being a team, but the only thing they know about being a team is "I am the boss and everybody does what I say." That's the "team" to them. They don't have a clue about what a team is.

13. The most important reason for the wins was that we were well prepared physically and from a scouting standpoint. Preparation by Devaney and his crew got us ready to play.

The undying love that we had for each other all boiled down to "we have to win." The collectiveness of the team effort was very dramatic and that was second reason why we won. The third reason is everybody had that notion that they could do better than they did in the last game. Everybody performed at a height that nobody would do on their own. They could only do it in a team.

14. We were confident NU would win National Championship. I remember being on the sidelines during the Oregon game and I am thinking they have Dan Fouts and Ahmad Rashad (aka Bobby Moore) and I said "this is a good team." And Keith Wortman was next to me and said "Yeah, but we are not going to lose at home. We will never lose at home." I looked around and saw the Big Red fans and they are going nuts and I said "You are right. We are not going to lose at home." It was a confidence that was there by preceding juniors and seniors.

15. The greatest play that I ever saw in college football was Johnny Rodger's punt return against Colorado my junior year. We stopped and started that film and I counted 23 guys trying to tackle Johnny. There were only 11 on the field, so everybody got a couple shots. Only 3 touched Johnny and he ran 47 yards for a touchdown. He was like up and down the sidelines. I think he ran 158 yards for that touchdown. He ran 158 yards on a 47 yard catch. I tell everybody about that story.

16. One of the best catches I ever saw was a fluke against Oklahoma State my senior year when Satch was going across the middle. Hummer threw behind him and he reached back behind him and the ball stuck in his hands and had both hands on the ball on his butt and he could not move the ball around. He got hit and got knocked out of bounds and fumbled. He was running down the field about 13-14 yards with his hand on his butt hanging on to the ball. That was amazing.

17. To be considered the best means tremendous pride. All the effort that we put out, not only at Nebraska but through high school, junior college and then Nebraska. That was a payout to be Number One. When we beat Alabama (`72 Orange Bowl). I got on the bus and everyone was so quiet and calm. Everybody was so professional. We knew that we were going to beat them. There was a pride and a confidence that the whole team had. It was not a surprise that we beat Alabama 38-6 and were National Champions.

18. My biggest challenge was overcoming the injuries I had. I think my ego was involved and I learned a lot from that and dealing with disappointment.

19. The most important reason that made the team work so well together was the system that Devaney put in. You were always active and nobody was standing around. That type of proactive coaching is what really kept us together. He had everybody going at the same time. That was the dynamic of his strategy of getting the team together. And that kept us on an even keel.

20. There was one thing that scared me when I went to Nebraska and I have never told anybody. Ernie Britt. He was a tough guy. But we started to figure out that he did not like to get hit. And Thornton says "He does not like to get hit." And I said "Well, don't tell him that," because he might start hitting us. Could you imagine what would have happened if he did hit us. He was a monster.

21. The most inspirational teammate was Johnny Rodgers. When you see 23 guys try and tackle him and the undying effort of a guy who wants to win, that picks you up. Also, Jerry Tagge and the way he conducted himself. He was a low key guy but at the same time he was concerned and considerate to everybody around him. He was not a selfish person, and that was a type of inspiration. Also, Richie Glover was like 3rd team tackle and then he becomes Number One middle guard and breaks everybody. You wanted to stand behind Richie and watch the powder fly.

22. The most outrageous teammate was Doug Johnson out of Omaha. He never changed his bed sheets the whole time he was in school. He took them off at the end of the semester and I think they broke in 3 pieces. That was pretty outrageous. As far as being charismatic, Satch takes it. He was very charismatic and he would get everybody going. And everybody would know Satch was there for everybody. He was outrageous in a sense but he was not crazy and just liked having a good time.

23. Playing for Nebraska helped me in the after football life. I deal with a lot of government agencies. I am meeting guys that played at K-State, Texas Tech, Texas A&M, and we can relate. They can remember NU being Number One and that opens doors. It opens conversations which I try to handle with humility. I get a chance to talk about what it takes to a real team. That has helped my credibility in my profession.

23. Do I feel appreciated by the University for the time I put in? We all got honorary Admirals in the Nebraska Navy. They tried to highlight us and I think they did a good job.

"Coach Devaney showed a lot of class. He had a sense of humor."

"Coach Monte Kiffin was dedicated and got the most out of everybody."

JERRY TAGGE *(aka "Tags")*

QUARTERBACK

HUSKER HIGHLIGHTS

1. My best memory was our first National Championship in 1970 against LSU (17-12) in the Orange Bowl. We had to win it with our last drive. My picture on the QB sneak for the winning touchdown was later made into a place mat at Valentino's. I have signed that so many times. Also, Johnny's run back of the punt against Oklahoma (1971) was the pinnacle of my Nebraska career.

2. The times I basically remember Coach Devaney was when he was yelling at me. He never said a lot to me except when he was mad and upset. I was always with Coach Osborne and Coach Bob was always a defensive guy. The curious thing about Bob is, I think, that he always liked Van Brownson as a quarterback better than me. If you watched me in films I was slow and awkward and looked like I really did not belong at quarterback. But Osborne always had all those statistics, and he noticed that the team moved the ball and scored more when I was the quarterback. It was Tom's prodding that kept me at quarterback. I was always prepared and my biggest talent was being consistent. Once I gained my confidence, my game really took off.

3. We played Minnesota in 1970. We were watching the films before the game and the Minnesota defense would come up and the safety would tip off the blitz. Coach Osborne went over that at least thirty times. He said "Jerry, do not miss this." And Jeff Kinney was out there and I saw it. It was my first audible and I hit the pass on the post. It was not a touchdown but it was a fifty yard gain. Things

clicked for me at that point, and I thought to myself that I really understood the game and it was really fun and I can play. It was like a chess match where I won. If it was not for Coach Tom stressing that over and over, I would be sitting on the bench. It gave me so much confidence in Tom because he said things, and it happened. I started trusting and believing.

4. I think Coach Callahan's first year (2004), NU's average starting field position was the 22 yard line. I bet we started at the 40 yard line. Our defense was so good, and we had great punters and kick returners and special teams. Our field positions were phenomenal.

5. It was amazing how much of our strategy was around getting the ball to one guy, Johnny Rodgers. It made practices long for Johnny.

6. In 1969 Jeff Kinney was our I-back and we were playing Kansas at Memorial stadium. It was a hot day and Jeff had hay fever. I gave him the ball 4 or 5 times in a row, and he was in the huddle and gasping for air. Jeff said "Tags, give it to someone else and give me a break here". When we got in the huddle I called his number again and he went 35 yards for a touchdown. After that he never said another word in the huddle for the rest of his career.

7. Nebraska fans are tremendous. It always seemed that no matter where we went it was always a "home game." The only exception was at Oklahoma on Thanksgiving Day (1971), but it did not matter because of the electricity in the air.

8. The Big 8 Conference was the best conference back then. It was a great and tough conference. It was remarkable in 1971 because at the end of the season NU was ranked Number One, OU Number 2 and Colorado Number 3. OU was a great football team and they played so clean, with good sportsmanship. But Colorado would do anything. They would kick you and scratch your eyes. They were out to hurt you intentionally. I think Colorado would have been a better football team if they focused more on playing than hurting people. The OU players were always gentlemen.

9. The most important play of my career was 3rd and 8 at Oklahoma in 1971 in the 4th Quarter when NU was behind 28-31. I threw the ball between those two linebackers and Johnny Rodgers slid over and caught it and kept the winning drive going (35-31).

10. At UNL I learned how to push myself and to work hard. I still do things that Coach Osborne taught me. I am pretty thorough. He was a big believer that "the journey is more important than the game". Always be strong in the basics, and the game will take care of itself. He always had us so prepared. Some guys can wing it, but I can't. I have to be prepared.

11. I would like to go back and relive my sophomore year (1969) when I threw an interception at Missouri. We lost the game (7-17) and that was the last game we lost in my career. We were undefeated over the next 32 games.

12. Everybody was a pretty good leader. As a quarterback, I was in the position to be a leader and I respect that my team allowed me to be a leader. They believed in me and trusted me. My biggest attribute was my consistency. I would always play by the book and never gambled. I was never questioned in the huddle.

13. My biggest disappointment was freshman year (1968). My personal goal was to be the quarterback. There were 12 other quarterbacks when I got to NU. I was 3rd string quarterback in my freshman year. I played about 3 minutes that year and it was depressing. I was going to quit. When I went home to Green Bay, I talked to my high school coach, and he told me "Go back to NU. They gave you a scholarship and if nothing else get your degree and get on with your life". I moved up because a lot of people moved to other positions and there were some injuries and some players quit or dropped out. I stayed at quarterback because no one wanted me at another position. And after a while things started clicking.

14. The players just loved Coach Monte Kiffin. He would do crazy things on the football field. He would run into someone head first and that person had a helmet on and he did not. He would slide head first into big puddles on the field. He had more passion for the game than anyone I have ever known.

15. Coach Corgan was such a gruff guy. He was more interested in a good block than a guy carrying the ball.

16. I was anxious to play against Oklahoma for the National Championship in 1971. It was exciting to see Tom's game plan and how he planned on beating them.

17. It was a gift from God to be considered the best. It was a wonderful phase in my life. It was because of guys like Johnny Rodgers. Where would I be if I could not throw to him. At NU I had a good offensive line and receivers. Great protection and I could sit in the pocket. I feel humbly fortunate.

18. To motivate myself before the game, I would review the plays in my head. I would take a 10 play drive and try to picture in my mind what would happen. I went over my keys and audibles and last minute preparations.

19. The best motivation was getting off to a good start. Make a couple of 1st downs. The biggest challenge was staying focused, keeping positive and splitting time with Van.

20. The biggest challenge for the team was against Oklahoma 3rd and 8 in the 4th quarter in 1971. It was for all the marbles. It is amazing how many people remember that game. It was a clean game, and both teams played great and with class.

21. The most important aspect that made the team work so well together was the fact that we were good and we knew it. Another neat thing was the pride of being a defensive blackshirt. It was an honor to get a blackshirt on defense. Guys really worked hard all year round. You did not want to let your teammates down. It was a talented group of guys with good chemistry and camaraderie. Everyone had good attitudes.

22. The most talented opponent was Missouri's receiver Mel Grey. He was fast. Oklahoma's running back Greg Pruitt obviously was a good player (Heisman Trophy runner-up in '72).

23. The most inspirational players were some of guys who didn't play a lot, like Doug Jamail and Jim Carstens. These guys were so fired up and behind the team.

24. The most outrageous player was Dick Rupert. He was just a crazy guy. I remember Dick and Keith Wortman getting off the plane from California in 1970 and they had t-shirts on and cowboy boots and the temperature in Lincoln was 10 degrees.

25. The player who surprised me the most was nose guard Rich Glover because of his size. He got a lot out of his ability. No one could block him, even using double teams. He was just awesome. Red Baron was also very inspirational.

26. Playing for Nebraska helped me in the after football life. Getting into the business world where people already know who you are is really helpful.

27. I feel appreciated by the University for the time I put in. I have done a lot of banquets and signed autographs and stuff like that.

28. My favorite Devaney story is this. I remember his and my last game when we beat Alabama in the Orange Bowl (1972). I was going to go to the East West All Star Game in San Francisco. They were going to pay me $1,500 and Bob was the coach for the Hula Bowl in Hawaii. Bob says to me "I want you to come to the Hula Bowl". I said "I have already committed to the East West Game and they are going to pay me $1,500," and Bob said "B.S., you are coming with me and I am going to pay you $1,500". And he arranged for me to get my $1,500. I never had that much money in my life. I thought I was the richest man on earth and plus I was in Hawaii. I think I came back with $1,000.

The stretch for the 1970 National Championship, in the January 1, 1971 Orange Bowl (17-12 over LSU)

"My best memory was our first National Championship against LSU. We had to win it with our last drive."

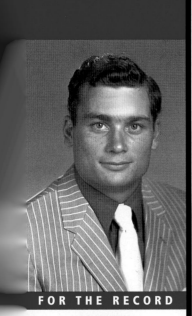

Bob and Dee Terrio

BOB TERRIO

LINEBACKER

HUSKER HIGHLIGHTS

1. I came from Fullerton California Junior College in 1969. Bob Newton and I came together. In my four years of playing football I lost only one game and tied one game. We were National Champion at Fullerton my freshman year. My junior year at UNL (1970) we were 11-0-1, when we tied USC. And the 13-0 my senior year (17-0).

2. I came to NU as a fullback. I red-shirted in 1969. The following year in 1970 Spring ball the coach said "We are going to try ten practices at linebacker then ten practices at tight end." Melton gave me the green shirt and I was on the third team stating weak side linebacker. After a scrimmage they threw the blackshirt at me and said "You are going to be a blackshirt" and I never left Linebacker. I don't regret it one bit.

3. My best memories are the Oklahoma game (1971), Alabama in the Orange Bowl (1972), USC (1970) and the overall program at the University.

4. Coach Devaney was a very passionate person. He was very considerate and strong. In 1971 the day my son was born was the day we played Oregon (34-7). We were playing against Ahmad Rashad. My son was supposed to be born the next day but my wife had gone to the hospital and she did not tell me. I thought she was at the game the whole time.

   At halftime Coach Devaney said "Bob, I just want you to know that your wife is doing very well and she sends her regards and that everything is fine, don't worry about a thing." He knew she was in the hospital. He said "I want you to go back at half and play your heart out and don't worry about your wife." It was not until after the game Devaney comes back up there and says "Okay, everything is still fine, but I think you better hurry up" and I say "Well, why is that?" and he says "What do you mean, why is that? She is having a baby" I rushed to the hospital and everything was fine. The nurses brought my son in a pink blanket with a little Go Big Red football on it.

5. I was a Southern California boy wanting to go to USC. Then Coach Osborne comes knocking on my door and said the University of Nebraska wants you, and I said "Where is the University of Nebraska?" They asked me to come out for a weekend and Dale Ditter, Bob Newton and I came out at the same time. That is when I met Bob Devaney. When we got there it was 1 degree above zero and I thought it is too damn cold for us California boys.

6. My very first Spring ball, (1970) the quarterback went back to pass and Willie Harper came up and hit me in the side of the head. My helmet spun around my head a few times. I was red shirted and the next year they put me at linebacker.

7. Coach Melton used to get after me. I could not do anything right at first. I guess that is the way you teach. Coach Melton was always there whenever I needed him. You could talk to him and he knew what was going on.

8. I am not the fastest person straightforward but I could run sideways very quickly. They put me on the weak side, and I had 6 or 7 interceptions that last year (1971). I had pretty good hands and I could read the offense.

9. Coach Corgan talked like a grouch but he knew what he was doing.

0. Our coaches were far and above the best coaches I ever had. They had their act together. They knew what was going on. It was tremendous.

1. In 1973-74 I did one year as a Head football coach in Sidney, Nebraska. Coaching wasn't difficult because I taught everything I learned at UNL.

2. Coach Devaney yelled at me once really loud but I deserved it. Just before we played SC, I got a stringer in my arm. I could not even put my hand in my pocket because my shoulder hurt so bad, but I did not tell anyone. We are out there scrimmaging and it looks like I am dogging but I my arm was hurting so much. He yelled up one side and down the other. When we started the SC game my arm had healed up a little bit. Coach Devaney knew what he was doing. He was a hawk.

3. Nebraska fans are so gung ho about football. They know who is what and who is where. They wanted to help you out in any way. They would say "hi, I know who you are and I appreciate what you are doing and keep up the good work." That just made your heart want to burst.

4. I try to give back with the Bob Terrio Golf Classic. A friend is a deputy district attorney here in California. So he called and said "I am a great fan of yours" Well, every year they had Western days in Western Nebraska and he would have the first annual Bob Terrio Classic. I came back to sign autographs, be in a celebrity soft-ball game and sell the copies of the Sport Illustrated where I am on the cover. The proceeds would go to the Western Fire Department in purchasing an ambulance. So I went back there and did that.

5. This year (2006) Nebraska is coming out here to USC, and we are trying to get something going where the night before the football game we are going to go on a harbor cruise at Newport Harbor with the Californians for Nebraska. And then have a tailgate party on Saturday before the game.

6. Our players were so close. All the players – Johnny, Tagge, Jeff Kinney, Wally, everyone. There were no racial issues. It's a team thing. It's a brotherhood.

7. The police department likes to hire people with military and athletic backgrounds because they have discipline. You have to rely on the player next to you,

behind you, and in front, all 11. Then the whole team. We were a very close knit group. All us married guys at the air base hung out together even on the off-season and weekends. We played poker and went cat fishing at midnight.

18. Regarding our opponents, I remember Ahmad Rashad of Oregon. The hardest guy that ever hit me was Johnny Riggins from Kansas. He ran over me like a tank. Oklahoma's Crosswhite and Pruitt and Jack Mildren and all those guys. That 1971 game was the game to remember. All the hype beforehand and Number One playing Number Two.

19. The most memorable defensive play for me was in the Orange Bowl (17-12) against LSU. I intercepted the last desperation pass by Bert Jones about 20 seconds before the game ended. I intercepted the Hail Mary pass and everybody could not believe that a linebacker is way back there.

20. In Los Angeles in 1970 I distinctly remember USC going for 1st down. It was like 4th and one and they run that iso on the left side. And Jerry Murtaugh and I ran up and we tackled the guy for about a one yard loss. It was great.

21. I learned discipline, togetherness, being considerate for your fellow teammates and friends. Be a team player. It helped me out a lot in my performance as a police officer and my handling of people. I rode a motorcycle for 12 years and basically all I did was write tickets. I never got one complaint from anyone in reference to writing a ticket. I actually got one compliment in the mail. I owe all this to the discipline and the teaching and coaching I received at the University of Nebraska.

22. I would like to relive the whole darn dream. I was there five years and I don't remember a disappointing moment even as cold as it was.

23. If I could change anything, we would beat USC by one point in that 1970 game (21-21 tie). Paul Rodgers would make that 30 yard field goal that he missed. But we still won the National Championship.

24. The best leaders would have to be Jerry Tagge and Johnny Rodgers on offense. On defense my junior year it was Murtaugh, and then myself my senior year.

25. The characteristics of leaders are ability, cohesiveness, and knowledge. The backbone is to be unafraid. If you are quiet and don't say anything, you cannot be a leader. You have be bold and you have to take your lumps too.

26. Our main team goal was to win. If you get your fundamentals down you will win the game.

27. The 3 most important reasons for the wins were (a) the ability of the players (b) the ability of the coaches to teach and instill what it takes to win (c) the support of the fans.

28. Playing at UNL helped me succeed after my football playing days. It helped very much in my family life. I am still married after 37 years. I have three wonderful kids who never gave me any problems. I have been blessed and I think it is because how I was taught at the University of Nebraska. It carries over to your family. You teach your kids and they grow up and teach their kids and you sit back and think "boy, I must have done something right."

29. What does it mean to be considered the best? I just happened to be in the right place at the right time. I was one little wheel in a big moving vehicle.

30. I did not have to motivate myself before a game because I was dry heaving as we ran out. After the first play it was good. I was so nervous every game.

31. The best motivation was running out on the field and   listening to those fans yell. It was tremendous. I went back there in 2005, and they honored me at the Missouri game. They had me on the tickets. I stood on that field before that game and I am looking at up in the stands and I was still motivated. I would love to put on a uniform and go out there. I can still do it in my mind, but the body is not able.

32. My biggest challenge was after being red-shirted they were moving me to linebacker. I told myself I am going to play my heart out. I had such a good spring that they moved me to the blackshirts immediately. I went from orange to black.

33. I never thought about quitting.

34. The biggest challenge for the team was in 1971 on the last defensive series against Oklahoma. We tackled the quarterback a couple of times and he did not have time to pass. We knew he was going to pass. We had to stop them. Whoever had the ball last was going to win. We decided that even though they got the ball last, they are not going to win. We are going to stop it right now.

35. I remember Bob Newton and I got to the dorm and it is January. And it is zero degrees out there the first day of classes. We got up at seven to go to class at 8 and Bob gets up and walks down stairs and all of a sudden he is back in 15 minutes and jumps back in bed. Bob said "It's so damn cold out there. I walked about three feet and the wind blowing in my face, and I am staying in bed."

36. The most important reasons that made the team work so well together were Coaches, players talent, and attitude. It is a combination of a finely oiled machine. Johnny was the spark plug and everyone followed after him. I mean Tagge and Kinney played better. It always seemed to pick up when Johnny got the ball in his hand. His performance made the defense work that much better. We were trying to make ourselves look like Johnny.

37. Out most talented opponent was Oklahoma's Jack Mildren. I was not at all impressed with Alabama's Johnny Musso.

38. Everybody inspired us. I looked up to Johnny Rodgers, Jerry Murtaugh, and Jerry Tagge. It was not just one person. Everybody spoke up at different times. If the defense was going down, it was Willie Harper or Adkin or Murtaugh or Kosch or myself saying something. On offense it was Johnny, Tagge, Kinney, Olds, Schneiss. Everybody knew what had to be done and took the initiative to say something.

39. The fans helped my efforts before the game. During the game I was just too busy enjoying myself.

40. Playing for Nebraska helped me in the after football life. It taught me everything. Respect and teamwork. Discipline and approach and safety.

42. Do I feel appreciated by the University for the time I put in? You bet. They send me all the alumni stuff. They know who I am if I have to call back for something.

PAUL TOPLIFF
OFFENSIVE LINE

HUSKER HIGHLIGHTS

1. When Bob Devaney first came out to recruit me, I had already signed an acceptance letter to go to the Air Force academy. After I signed the letter, Devaney came down and talked to my dad and I. Devaney said all the right things. I was impressed by him and my dad was even more impressed. He made all the right arguments. For example, he pointed out how you had to be strong in every area at the Air Force Academy, and I had a little hesitation about my math skills at that time. Then he let my folks know that my scholarship would be certain for four years.

2. In 1968 the Nebraska fans occasionally started booing for the very first time. We had played some lackadaisical games against Kansas (13-23) and Kansas State (0-12). Before 1967-68, nobody ever expected Kansas or Kansas State to beat NU. We played some poor games against those teams.

3. The most remarkable offensive I play witnessed was JR's runback against Oklahoma in 1971. Also, some catches by Jim McFarland and Guy Ingles when they laid themselves out and still caught the pass. Tom Penny, Ingles, and McFarland made some spectacular catches by giving up everything and going for the ball.

4. I learned how important hard work is. Part of that is an example set by Coach Tom Osborne, probably the hardest working guy I have ever known. I learned that a lot of hard work pays off. Devaney also believed in hard work, and he also had tremendous charm.

5. I vividly remember when recruits would come to football camp, and Bob would be cussing out the coaches in the coaching room. And as soon as a recruit or a mom or dad would walk in, Devaney would suddenly turn on the charm and a different face.

6. The best leaders were Jim McFarland, as one the older players; Quarterbacks Jerry Tagge and Van Brownson, as the sophomore players. When they came, it made a very big difference. The more they played and the more success they had, the more confidence we had in general on the team. Jeff Kinney played a big part. But Tagge and Van made the biggest difference.

7. My personal goals were getting a good education and being ready to hit the world with some skills to get a good job. I did not have any goals of playing professionally.

8. The 3 most important aspects or qualities for the wins were (a) protecting the passer was one of the biggest goals and we started doing that, (b) staying in shape (c) as an offensive tackle you always have to know where the play is going. If the play is going to go outside or inside of you and how to seal the defensive guy away from the ball carrier.

9. I motivated myself before the game by not wanting to fail.

Paul Topliff

10. Initially, I did not know if I was going to play as a tackle because I figured a lot of people were bigger than I was. I was 6'3" and 205-210 pounds. As a Senior I weighed about 225 pounds and I was lifting weights all the time in order to gain weight. Now I know I could have gained a lot of weight if I had tried to work on my legs. I could have gained another 20-25 pounds.

11. I never thought about quitting. I felt a little bit like I failed as a tight end, but being a starter at tackle was better then second string at tight end

12. The game that was biggest challenge for the team in 1969 was our loss (21-31) to Southern California. We didn't make that first and ten against them my Senior year. I remember that I did not make a good block against their really good defensive tackle and I felt bad about that. A lot of guys in those days were not much bigger than I was when we played Georgia in the Sun Bowl and some of the Oklahoma and Oklahoma State teams. I never felt too intimidated by size because at that time there were a lot of guys that were not much bigger than me.

13. There were guys that played like they would never give up, and those were the hardest to play. You would get a good block on them and somehow before the end of the play they would get into the tackle. They impressed me the most.

14. My biggest disappointment was not going to a Bowl game in 1967 and 1968.

15. The most important aspects that made the team work so well together were: (a) Players and talent, especially the 1969 year with Tagge and Van Brownson coming on. Also, a guy that made a big difference was Jim McFarland when he was a Senior. He played hard and was big, strong, and fast. (b) The receiving core was good and the backs ran well. (c) I think our offensive line my senior year was better than the two previous years. We made fewer mistakes. The offensive lineman in `67-`68 did not play as consistently as we did in 1969.

16. My most talented teammates were Tom Penney and Guy Ingles was a great receiver. Glenn Patterson at center was a strong and tough athlete.

17. I learned from Coach Osborne about hard work. It was hard to emulate Tom as far as work ethic. Coach Carl Selmer taught good techniques. Selmer added confidence and let us know where the receiver would be running, where the back would be going, and where the holes would be opening up, and knowing where the quarterback was and how to position yourself to protect him.

18. Playing for Nebraska helped me in the after football life. I moved down to Phoenix. My boss's boss when I first came down here was pretty impressed with the fact that I had played football at NU and he was a sports fan. He sent me off to Ohio State to get a Masters degree in Electrical Engineering. My third year I stopped because I was getting married. Not getting the Master's was one of the dumbest things I have ever done in my life. I was getting good grades those first 2 years.

19. Fundamentals are so important. We had great fundamentals because we had good high school coaches.

20. I never thought about being appreciated by the University for the time I put in. I always felt appreciated by the coaches. Osborne and Devaney were always great. The guys in the training room, George Sullivan and Paul Schneider, were always really friendly and nice.

"I learned how important hard work is. Hard work pays off. Coach Osborne was probably the hardest working guy I have known."

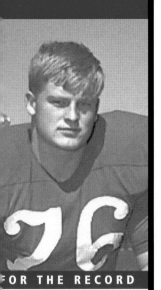

DAVE WALLINE
1968-1970

6'-2" 235 lbs.
Ypsilanti, MI

NOW

Married to Linda,
2 children, 1 grandchild

Dentist

Columbus, Nebraska

"Coach Devaney helped former players after they were no longer involved. He cared about his players as people."

Dave Walline

DAVE WALLINE

DEFENSIVE TACKLE

HUSKER HIGHLIGHTS

1. The 1969 season was successful. I think Kiffin and Powers made a big difference. Coach Kiffin had a lot of enthusiasm and he made a difference on the sidelines. He had a lot of energy and worked hard.

2. My favorite memories of Bob Devaney are the things that he did for former players after they were no longer involved. I know several people that were down and out and he was able to help them. That said a lot to me about Devaney. Beyond winning, he cared about his players as people.

3. Opponents that I admired were teams like Missouri and Oklahoma. They always brought out the best in me. I respect them because they played to win, played hard and they didn't talk or do extraneous things on the field.

4. NU football opened doors to a lot of opportunities. I could have gone anywhere in the country and still not have been on a National Championship team and that means a lot. I had good experiences and you can't replace them.

5. The best leaders were in the offensive line like Donnie McGhee and Wally Winter. They weren't necessarily praised every week in the paper but every Saturday they gave it their all.

6. My personal goal was to survive. I came from Michigan and I had just turned 18 and was a little immature. Being away from home was a little intimidating.

7. The most important reason for the wins was that a tradition had been established. The expectations were there so the team tended to meet the expectations. Also, the strength and conditioning program aspects were important because that was back when a lot of people did not do that.

8. I have always had a work ethic. And that is more from my family. When you set out to do something you finish it and I think that is the same with football. You don't go out for football and decide to quit because the conditioning is hard. You follow through no matter what.

9. It means a lot to be considered the best. It is a feather in your cap. When you are young you do not think about it, but when you get older, you realize how much work it was.

10. I didn't talk to offensive lineman but if I got the feeling they were tired I just put it up another notch. That motivated me more. It is a team sport, but when you are a defensive tackle against an offensive tackle, it's a personal battle. I liked the challenge of beating the guy that was opposite of me.

11. When I had somebody that was big and athletic that was the biggest challenge for me. I was about 6-2 and 235 lbs. I considered myself as strong as anybody that I played. I was pretty quick for 10 yards so I could beat a lot of people on a pass rush.

12. Defensively from my perspective everybody could just concentrate on doing their job. We always seemed to be able to eventually do the job.

13. Eddie Periard was inspirational for a relatively small guy sitting in middle guard. He was always enthusiastic and had a lot of energy. He always had a motor going.

14. I learned dedication from Coach Kiffin and I learned that being in shape is important. When somebody is driving on you in the 4th quarter. I appreciated his overall enthusiasm and work ethic. He would be there until wee hours of the morning looking at film.

15. I ended up becoming a dentist. I graduated from dental school in 1977. It could not have worked out better for me.

16. Playing for Nebraska helped me in the after football life. I think it was a factor in getting into dental school. People tend to know you no matter how obscure a player you were.

17. Do I feel appreciated by the University for the time I put in? I suppose so, but they do not owe me anything. I gave them what I agreed to. I did not slouch when it came to work on the football field and I got my education and I think we are square.

"I learned dedication from Coach Kiffin... I appreciated his overall enthusiasm and work ethic."

Dave Walline and Willie Harper tackle QB Lynn Dickey.*

anie Westbrook and his son

DONNY WESTBROOK

SLOT BACK AND RUNNING BACK

HUSKER HIGHLIGHTS

1. My best memory is being on the team that elevated to the 1971 National Championship. I came out of high school to a National Championship team and the greatness of the ring.

2. I loved Coach Bob Devaney and always will. Devaney moved me from running back to slot back. Behind Johnny. It was the best move of my life.

3. I fondly remember scoring 4 times against KU in one game.

4. Regarding Nebraska fans, I have never heard of fans like that before or since.

5. I had wonderful relationships with my teammates at NU and still do. They still care at NU.

6. My biggest game was my first game against Oregon. I scored 2 touchdowns and people realized that I could play.

7. I learned about my "center stone", the place where I can start and begin.

8. The best leaders were Johnny Rodgers and Richie Glover led by example on defense. Willie Harper recruited me.

9. My personal goals were education and to go to a National Championship team. And I did it. I wanted everyone to do well and have a good happy life.

10. Coach Devaney instilled hard discipline in everyone. He really cared about you, but on the field he was really stern. Coach Osborne was a totally feeling and caring person.

11. The two most important reasons for the wins were (a) working hard; (b) caring about what happened even after you left. Players still cared.

12. In 1971, we were confident NU would win the National Championship. I saw the talent we had. If we beat Oklahoma, we had it.

13. I did not have to motivate myself because I was in the game. I made my practices. I dreamed about it.

14. One of the most important aspects was that everyone helped me out and advised me. Not only on football but on everything in life.

15. The most outrageous player was Satch, Ralph Powell! It did not get crazier than Ralph.

16. Quarterback Jerry Tagge played hurt the most. The most talented was Johnny Rodgers. People do not believe me when I tell them what Johnny did. Someone hit his legs and he would flip and still land on his feet.

17. The fan support at NU was tremendous. I did not realize it as much until I came back.

18. Running on the field for the first time was a thrill. Everyone was pumped up. I saw everyone in red and yelling and it was so unreal.

19. Playing for Nebraska helped me later. It helped with my future pro career.

20. I feel appreciated by the University for the time I put in. They are the nicest. When I go back, I get total respect. I should have stayed in Lincoln.

21. I know that skill levels have changed, but I don't think you can count the 1971 team out as the best college team of all time.

Daryl and Debbie White

DARYL WHITE

OFFENSIVE TACKLE (CO-CAPTAIN 1973)

HUSKER HIGHLIGHTS

1. When I first came to Lincoln we had people from all different parts of country. It was a great time. It was weird that everyone ended up being real close.

2. Coach Bob Devaney was something else. He would really praise you if you did something right. But if you did something wrong he would definitely let you know and did not care who it was. Everyone got treated the same. You just wanted to play so hard for him. If he asked you to run through a wall you would. He was an unbelievable motivator.

3. Devaney was stern but also funny. He said "You are supposed to come here and play football and go to school. Do not get into any kind of trouble. And if you do, we are going to send you home and we are going to put in your hometown newspaper why we sent you home." That stuck with me. I was not going to get into any type of trouble.

4. Coach Selmer was a stern guy with no nonsense. Coach Fischer was stern but he would also joke around. He would get you laughing. Coach Myles was a good coach. They were all excellent coaches and very technique oriented. They stayed on you and let you know what you were doing wrong. They gave you a lot of pointers on how to improve your game. They were all fair. If you earned a spot you got the spot. They played the people that played the best.

5. Nebraska fans had a tremendous effect. When you see the sea of red and all the noise and support it pumps you up. On the road they were just as vocal as the home team. On game day the whole stadium is red. Anywhere you went in town we were like a celebrity, asking you for autographs. Lincoln is a tremendous college town, and the state is a tremendous state for college football. You cannot ask for a better atmosphere or fan support base. It has to be the best in America.

6. Richie Glover and Johnny Rodgers are still great friends. You can't forget John Dutton. Richie and I were in John's wedding in Sioux Falls South Dakota. Johnny Rodgers used to take me and Richie home and his mom treated us just like we were her sons. And I love his mother for it. It felt just like a big family. Everyone was together to win.

7. Oklahoma did not do a lot of trash talking like most of the teams we played. They played clean football. I have the utmost respect for them and their coaches. The Big 8 was tough. I think Oklahoma respected us just as much as we respected them. Whenever you went to play Oklahoma you knew you had to be on your best and give 120% because they were going to be ready.

8. The fan support was unbelievable. We changed the scope of the campus. There was no African American organization – the football players spearheaded it and we got an African American study center.

9. The most remarkable offensive play I witnessed was the last touchdown in the game of the century with Jeff Kinney (35-31). It was over my side on my block. Jeff stuffed it in the end zone from the 2 yard line.

10. I would not trade my experience at NU for anything. I was an inner city kid going to the Midwest. There was so much camaraderie with the players. No racial conflicts. We all hung together and got along. Tremendous education and support from coaches and from Media Director Don Bryant.

1. We had discipline. We really did not make many mistakes. Very few offside or holding penalties. We were not a penalized team. The lessons that you learn on the football field you can take into your everyday life and you are going to be successful.

2. When I came back home to New Jersey everybody in my community was watching Nebraska games including the Game of The Century (1971). It was amazing. They all watched the game. People that I did not even know would come up to me and say "we watched and saw you on TV.

3. I could relive the Game of The Century in 1971. That last drive. I would say Johnny Rodgers' punt return would be one of the highlights. That last drive and the catch that Johnny made on that 3rd down to keep that drive going and how we just kept plugging away. The one thing I remember about that whole drive was how calm everybody was in the huddle. We knew we were going to get it done. There was no panic in anybody's voice. It was just a calm confidence. We knew we were going to get that ball in that end zone.

4. The best leader on offense was Jerry Tagge. He kept us in line. Johnny led more by example. And he would get us fired up. Richie, Willie, and Jimmy Branch were leaders on defense. They were tremendous athletes. But they all had a confidence and it rubbed off on you. They just said and did the right things at the right time.

5. The defense played their hearts out for Coach Kiffin.

6. My ultimate goal was to get a degree because I was the first one in my family to have a degree.

7. The 3 most important reasons for the wins were (a) discipline (b) coaching (c) personnel.

8. I relate to the lessons that I learned on the field. I take them to work with me in the school system. I try to instill in the kids pride. Give it 110% and just have discipline and self control. I deal with at risk kids who were put out of schools and they come to me with various problems. I instill a confidence in their abilities and in themselves and let them know that anyone can change.

9. It is a tremendous honor to be considered the best. Look at that guys that I played with. I look at college football now and I say to myself we could have beaten them. I actually like college football better than professional football.

20. The scouting report that we got on Sundays motivated me. It let me know who I was going to play against and his size. Just playing at Nebraska motivated me every game. The fans keep you motivated and the tradition keeps you motivated.

21. Quitting never crossed my mind. I got in the weight room and started lifting every day. I worked hard at practice against the Number One guys on defense.

22. The biggest challenge for the team was the OU game in the Game of The Century (1971). One challenge we had was my junior year in the first game against UCLA (1972). We might have been a little bit overconfident. Because we definitely had a better team than UCLA but they beat us (17-20). That really shocked us. I would like to go back and relive that game. Go in there with a lot more confidence and respect for UCLA.

23. The most important aspect that made the team work so well together was a combination of coaches, player's talent, attitude. We had great coaching. Everyone was together. We were all about winning together.

24. Most talented opponent was OU's Leroy Selmon. He ended up being a perennial All-Pro.

25. My most outrageous teammate was Doug Jamail. He was crazy.

26. Playing for Nebraska helped me in the after football life. It opened up some doors for me coaching wise and in education.

27. Do I feel appreciated by the University for the time I put in? Previous years, yes. Now, no. They don't value the tradition as I think they should.

28. Coming back to Lincoln after the Game of The Century, the whole runway was just lined with thousands of people. It seemed like the whole town of Lincoln was there to welcome us back.

30. It was fun going to Hawaii and playing, even though they had a curfew on us. How many people get a chance to go play a game in Hawaii?

WALLY WINTER

OFFENSIVE LINE

HUSKER HIGHLIGHTS

1. Coach Bob Devaney was tough, but he was fair. He could be comical. He was a hell of a storyteller. The thing that impressed me most was the way he talked to every individual. He had something different to motivate each player. When we were getting ready for the National Championship game in the 1971 Orange bowl against LSU. He came up to me and said "I want you to play the way you and I know you can play." I was ready to go through the wall.

2. My position coaches were Carl Selmer and Cletus Fischer. Cletus was fun. In practices, offense and defense did not hang together. You did not step on defense's turf, but we had good rivalries going on. And Cletus would always fire that up.

3. In 1968, we lost three in a row, and the Nebraska fans still applauded us as we came off the field. I could not believe that they did that. We did not deserve it.

4. Bob Newton and I put in that tackle trap for Johnny Rodgers on the wingback inside reverse. We loved coming around there. We crushed a few guys.

5. NU football taught me discipline. It is a team sport. We played as a team.

6. I could go back and relive the 1971 Orange Bowl when we went down the field and scored that final touchdown against LSU (17-12). That was the greatest feeling in the world. Our offensive line was kicking their butt. We just pushed them out of there.

7. We should have beaten Southern Cal. when I was a Junior in 1969. I was playing against Toadie Smith, Bubba Smith's brother. I got him good down in Southern Cal (1970) but he got the best of me when we played in Lincoln (1969). That was a fun match up.

8. One of the greatest victories was Oklahoma in 1969 because they had beaten us in 1969. That was the lowest point of my career(47-0). Steve Owens ran nuts. That was the maddest I had ever seen Coach Devaney. He said basically that "he did not want to see the seniors again and all you underclassmen better have your jockstraps on for Spring ball." That is when things changed. From `68 to `69 in that spring practice we went to those station deals. Going to the racquetball courts helped. That is when the weightlifting really started happening. In 1969 there was an attitude shift in the players and the coaches.

9. Beating Georgia in the 1969 Sun Bowl was one of the most satisfying moments. We were shocked because they were all white and did not speak to anybody. That pissed us off. They wore coats and ties with their heads in the air. We just kicked the hell out of them and had fun doing it.

10. The 1968 season was a rough season. We did not have leadership. Devaney had all those good years before (1962-1966) and

we just thought we could go out there and do it. A lot of changes also came about regarding the offensive line. They did a lot of crab blocking, which is just isolating and getting an angle on a guy. What changed in 1969 was getting more physical.

11. Our best leader on offense was Jerry Tagge. We all stuck together in the offensive line. Donny McGee was a good personal friend of mine and we lockered together and played next to each other for two years and just had a great relationship.

12. The most important reasons for the wins was a change of attitude. I definitely saw a transition from one of the worst to one of the best. I really think the 1970 team was one the best that ever was. It was just a maturity process. We had leadership. We all just did our job. We knew each other's assignments.

13. Playing close to USC in 1969 was the turning point (21-31). After that 1968 season we were a little tentative and we did not think we could hang with USC Our attitude changed and especially the second half. We damn near pulled it out. We were in it at 28-21 with three minutes to go. Then Tags threw an interception. But we got our confidence going.

14. What does it mean to be considered the best? It's a lot of pride. I have traveled quite a bit, and everyone knows Nebraska football.

15. To motivate myself before the game, I got pictures of who I was playing against. I pasted them on the walls. I watched a lot of films and how he used his hands, what type of slant he did, and that type of thing.

16. The NU fans were the motivation. They have always been great. You run out of that tunnel for the first time and you don't even think your feet are on the ground. Kind of floating out there. A great crowd gets you going.

17. My biggest disappointment was my sophomore at that Oklahoma game in 1968. I made second team All Big 8 my senior year. But that is individual and we were more team oriented.

18. You could always say work harder, but we worked pretty hard. I enjoyed every minute of college ball.

19. The most important reason that made the team work so well together was the attitude. We knew what each

other was going to do. We were close on the field. We took a lot of pride in what we were doing. We wanted to be the best. The talent level was way down in `68. The coaches really did a better job at recruiting. They knew that they had let down in recruiting.

20. My most talented teammate was Johnny Rodgers. My most talented opponent was Rocky Wallace from Missouri, a short stocky guy. A very quick defensive tackle.

21. The most inspirational was Rex Lowe who was a good friend of mine. You realize that life is short and you better take advantage of what you have. He had cancer in the back of his neck. I told him to have it looked at.

22. The most outrageous teammate was Eddie Periard. He was a pistol. He was a hyper type guy. He was a hunter and fisherman. He was from Michigan. I took him pheasant hunting a couple times.

23. The hardest worker in practice was Mike Beran ("Red Baron"), but a lot of guys work hard.

24. Bob Newton surprised you the most. He really developed and we became friends. He got in the weight room and did a lot of good things. Dick Rupert was also one of the hardest working guys.

25. Eddie Periard, Doug Jamail and Jeff Hughes kept the locker room the loosest

26. Murtaugh got punished the most. He was constantly in Devaney's doghouse.

27. I credit Cletus Fischer because he had that fire in the belly. That is what I learned. You have to get fired up and Cletus was a little banty rooster type of guy.

28. The fans affected my efforts in the games. You could feel the adrenaline when they started cheering. It picks you up. It was a twelfth man.

29. Playing for Nebraska helped me in the after football life, in various aspects all the way through.

30. I feel appreciated by the University for the time I put in, but not as much since the new regime took over. I am not really fond of how that situation went down. I think they care more about current players than about past players.

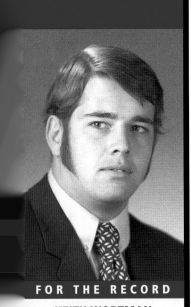

KEITH WORTMAN

OFFENSIVE LINE

HUSKER HIGHLIGHTS

1. I was being recruited by a lot of different teams. I don't know why I chose to go to NU but part of it was (1) the culture in Southern California. I am originally from Montana and my parents wanted to get me out of there. (2) Tom Osborne was honest. Everybody was feeding you stories of grandeur, and Tom never did that.

2. My best memory is the 1970 OU game. I was playing against Lucious Selmon. We called a quick screen pass, and I had to go out there and release quickly. I wound up getting a clipping penalty. Then in the next series I had a holding penalty. And I know that I am going to get Coach Devaney's wrath. So I tried to sneak off the field and go to the other end of the bench. I am looking out the corner of my eye, and Devaney comes storming down there just screaming at me and he says "Did you place a bet on those guys or what?" I played well the rest of the game.

3. The thing that I respect most about Coach Osborne is that Tom had the courage of his convictions – to do things his way and stay the course especially when he became the head coach.

Obviously, over time he changed. When I was playing we ran an offense designed for the Pros. There was a lot of passing Tom also realized that for him to succeed at NU at that particular time period (to beat OU, USC, Penn State and Michigan) we needed to get quarterbacks to run the professional offenses. So he went to the option I saw him adjust to that because he realized that NU did not have the speed to compete at the highest level. They went out and recruited speed and changed that philosophy. Yet he maintained a lot of the traditions and the walk-ons. And I respect that a great deal. Tom and I are polar opposites as human beings. I really personally identified with Coach Devaney but Tom is the reason I went there.

4. In the Oklahoma game in 1971 the most important thing was the blocks that we collectively as an offensive line had to throw for Jeff Kinney to score that last touchdown. Collectively we had a very good offensive line. Most of us played in the pros. We had Doug Dumler, Carl Johnson, Daryl White, all who played professional football, and also Dick Rupert who was a tremendous college football player.

5. I would like to thank Coach Callahan for opening up the facility to the former players. When I do get back there I have been informed about what is going on. You are always welcome to practice. Those are nice things to know that the University does remember you. Two years ago at the spring game they brought us all out there and that was nice. It is also very smart business.

6. I would like to go back and relive Johnny Rodgers spectacular punt return vs. O.U. in `71, except it would be me returning the Oklahoma punt and not Johnny. Obviously, that is not physically possible.

That was one of the top five individual plays in college football history. The instinctiveness of what he showed on that play was incredible. Plus that 27 scissors. What a play.

7. If I could change anything, I would not have had two knee operations. I had one when I first got there in spring ball. The following year I got a terrible staph infection and I think it was 5 or 6 weeks that I was in California and I cut my knee at my summer job and it just blew up on me and I remember calling Coach Osborne and telling him what the problem was and immediately he said "you get on a plane tomorrow morning and get back here." So, I flew back and I spent the rest of the summer in Nebraska and they almost amputated my leg because I had staph so bad. It hurt me in the draft. I was drafted 10th round by the Packers.

8. Any negative memories that I have are far, far outweighed by the fun that I had being a part of the team. A team is about being a part of something. Obviously we had tremendous talent but it was a collective effort. I remember in the Orange Bowl in 1972 at the hotel we were watching the Sugar Bowl and OU was killing Auburn, and Auburn had played Alabama very close. We were getting ready for the Alabama game and it was supposed to be the second "Game of The Century". And I remember us all looking around because OU was laying the wood to them and we said "We will be lucky if we play in the third quarter of this game." That is how confident we were. And we did. We were done midway through the third quarter because Coach Devaney never ran up scores. The game was over almost from the get-go.

One of the great coaching moves of all time happened 3 days before the Alabama game. We were in the team meeting and it was late afternoon meeting. And Coach Devaney says "I understand you guys want to see Ike and his wife." [Ike and Tina Turner]. He had no idea who Ike and Tina Turner were. And Devaney bought a whole section of seats for the entire team. His only comment was to us was "Just don't get too drunk, guys, this is really an important game." We all just went and partied our butts off. But he owned us when he said it was okay for us to go have fun but you better not screw up and be ready January 1st. And we were ready.

A lot of teams will go down to that type of setting and have total lockdown and get so depressed because they cannot do a thing. We had a party the next night after the game and some of the Alabama players were there and they let us know that this was the first time that they had any fun and they are partying with us. That was a great move on Devaney's part. Coach Devaney allowed us to have fun in the process amidst all that pressure. That is a great testimony to a great football coach.

10. In December, 1971 we were playing at Hawaii, and at halftime he comes in and we were playing like crap. It was our game in-between OU and the Orange Bowl. Bob comes in and just chews us out unmercifully. Then he turns around and takes Johnny Rodgers, Jacobson, Glover, and Kinney and they caught a flight for Miami. He left with a bunch of our All-Americans.

"There was no one individual player that was our leader. Our leader was Bob Devaney, and that made us unique as a team."

AN ERA OF GREATNESS: *COACH BOB DEVANEY'S FINAL FOUR SEASONS (1969 - 1972)*

11. There was no one individual player that was our leader. Our leader was Bob Devaney, and that made us unique as a team.

12. I was a country kid. I came from a one room country school in Montana to the Los Angeles school system. Sports was my salvation to blend in from such two different cultures. I was small but fortunately we had good junior colleges. Somehow I played 10 years in the NFL. I played with a tremendous group of guys in St. Louis. It was the best offensive line in the NFL at the time and I was very proud of that group.

13. I had two national championship rings. I gave one of them away to a dear friend in California. The other one I wear every day because I am so proud of it.

14. To motivate myself before a game, I tried to stay away from Bruce Weber. I knew he or Jamail would lead me down the wrong path. My motivation was never to be the weak link where ever I played. You do not want to be the one holding everything back. A lot of motivation to me was peer pressure in sports. I am a real team oriented guy so my concern was not to be the one who let everyone down.

15. My biggest challenges were (a) Overcoming knee surgeries, and (b) overcoming loneliness. It was a hard adjustment for us junior college guys because so many of the players had been together from day one. The year before Nebraska had gone the junior college route because Coach Devaney realized that he needed to plug holes and primarily in the offensive line. Bob Newton was the first one on the offensive line and then Carl out of Arizona. Rupert and I came out of Southern California in `71. Then you had Woody who was an instrumental part of the team. He was out of New Mexico. Bob Terrio was a year older and he was out of Southern California.

16. My biggest disappointment was tying USC in 1970 (21-21). We should have won that game. That was the only blemish in two years.

17. The most important reasons that made the team work so well together were the coaches, players talent, and attitude. All of those things together. There is no one key ingredient for that level of success. We had a selfless attitude. For example, Monte Johnson never started a game at NU, and yet he became the starting linebacker at the Super Bowl for the Oakland Raiders.

There were a lot of talented people coming up through that pipeline. If you don't have the horses, I don't care how good of a wagon you got because you're not going anywhere.

18. My most talented opponent was a guy named Yates at Oklahoma State. He was really a good football player. My most talented teammates were Johnny Rodgers and Willie Harper. The most inspirational was Rex Lowe.

19. The most outrageous players were Jamail and Bruce Weber and Jeff Hughes. I was the MC at a function in Omaha about 2 years ago and Jeff Kinney was there. And he came up to me with his wife, and he says "Keith, dear God, don't tell them anything." I looked at him and said "Jeff, I am telling it all."

20. The Nebraska fans are the best. And that kind of support traveled when we were at away games and Bowl games. Plus, Carl and I had a deal with a local liquor store because we lived at 27th and Vine. We had a clubhouse in the apartment and if we beat the spread, the guys gave us a couple kegs of beer which we would take down to the clubhouse and charge an entry fee. He was an exceptionally good fan.

21. One great story occurred when we were playing Oregon in the opener. It was really hot. We are down on the two yard line and Tagge calls the group together and one of us sees this good looking blonde sitting in the end zone. And there we are starting a season with all these great expectations and we start talking about the blonde in the end zone. We had driven 98 yards, but there was such a relaxed confidence about that group that I don't think it crossed our minds that we couldn't win every game. The only game that any of us played into the 4th quarter was the 1971 Oklahoma game. And they were every bit as talented group as we were. What a great football team OU was. I respected them.

22. I feel more appreciated by the University now than I had felt earlier. I do know that the doors are far more open than they ever were in the past.

SOURCES OF INFORMATION

1) **National Collegiate Athletic Association (NCAA)**
Sports Information Department & Archives
700 West Washington
P.O. Box 6222
Indianapolis, IN 46206

2) Nebraska Sports Information Department
Athletic Department, University of Nebraska
116 South Stadium
P.O. Box 880123
Lincoln, NE 68588

3) **2003 Nebraska Official Media & Recruiting Guide (2003)** (Published by N.U. Athletic Department)

4) The national polling service's ratings of college teams:
(a) **Associated Press Poll** (1936-2004);
(b) **United Press Coaches Poll** (1960-1990);
(c) **USA Today/CNN Coaches Poll** (1991-1996);
USA Today/ESPN Coaches Poll (1997 to present).

5) **Sagarin Computer Rankings** of the best individual teams of all-time.

7) **"When Pride Still Mattered":** A Life of Vince Lombardi, by David Maraniss (1997)

8) **"The Best Season of All-Time";** Article by Tom Shatel, Omaha World-Herald (1/1/06)

9) **The Random House Dictionary of The English Language** (The Unabridged Edition, 1966)

10) The wonderful memories and written comments of fans, former players, coaches, trainers, athletic directors, sports writers and analysts. See attached **interviews** at end of this **book**.

11) **ESPN's Ranking of the Best Teams of All-Time;** (2006)

12) **"Devaney: A Dynasty Remembered"** (1994) (Athlon Sports Communications) edited by Francis J. Fitzgerald and Jerry Tagge.

(13) **"Not the Game But the Glory: A Century of Nebraska Football"** by Jim Rose (2001, Nebraska Book Publishing).

(14) **"The Fans of Memorial Stadium"** (1996, Nebraska Book Publishing Co.) By Joe Starita and Tom Tidball.

(15) **"Tales from The Nebraska Sidelines"** (2002) by Don "Fox" Bryant (Sports Publishing, Champagne, Illinois).

(16) **Spalding Official Foot Ball Guide** (1902-03,1913-15), as provided by the NCAA archives.

(17) **The Billingsley Report** (1996); computerized rankings of early college teams.

(18) **College Football: History, Spectacle, Controversy** (2002) by John S. Watterson

(19) **The National Football Foundation** and **College Football Hall of Fame,** (Sports Information Department), South Bend, Indiana

(20) **"Coach Devaney"**, **The Nebraska Heritage Collection,** The Nebraska ETV Network

(21) **The Elias Sports Bureau** 500 5th Avenue, NYC, NY 10100

(22) **"Heart of a Husker: Tom Osborne's Nebraska Legacy"** Mike Babcock, Sports Publishing L.L.C. (2006).

PHOTO CREDITS

A. **Omaha World-Herald.** All photos marked with an asterisk (*) are the exclusive property of the Omaha World-Herald. They are reprinted in this book with the prior written permission of the World-Herald which retains sole and exclusive copyright interest to all such photos. All rights reserved.

    1.   All photos on the following pages:
       i, 31, 32, 33, 34, 35, 36, 37, 45, 50, 55, 56, 67, 68, 70, 76, 79, 80, 95, 105, 143,
       146, 148, 151, 169, 182, 201, 203, 220, 233, 257, 264

    2.   Photos on part of these pages:
       43 (lower left), 46 (upper right, lower left & right), 53 (middle left & right), 63 (lower),
       69 (upper), 77 (lower), 201 (lower), 211 (lower)

B. **Lincoln Journal Star**
    1.   All photos on the following pages:
       xiv, 11, 54, 55, 57, 62, 68, 77, 160, 185, 195, 210

    2.   Photos on part of these pages:
       25 (bottom), 40 (upper right), 53 (all except left & right middle), 57 (upper), 58 (upper left),
       58 (lower), 69 (lower), 192 (lower), 217 (lower)

C. **UNL Photography Services, University of Nebraska at Lincoln**
    vii, ix, xii, xv, 1, 2, 5, 6, 7, 8, 9, 10, 12, 14, 15, 16, 17, 18, 19, 20, 22, 23, 24, 26, 27, 28, 29,
    40 (upper left, lower left), 42, 46 (upper left), 51, 58 (upper left & right), 59, 62, 64, 65, 69 (lower),
    77 (upper), 78, 85, 86, 87, 89, 93, 96, 100, 102, 104, 106, 111, 115 (right), 116, 132, 139, 268 (all);

    Upper and lower: 163, 170, 178, 183

    Upper: 43, 63, 141, 144, 147, 149, 152, 155, 157, 159, 161, 165, 167, 170, 172, 175, 183, 186, 188, 190,
    192, 195, 196, 198, 200, 202, 204, 208, 211, 213, 216, 217, 221, 223, 226, 229, 231, 234, 236, 237, 239,
    240, 242, 245, 248, 250, 251, 254, 256, 258, 259, 261, 263, inside back cover.

D. **Private Family Photos**
    41, 109, 114, 115 (left), 70 (upper left), 119, 120, 121, 123, 125, 128, 135; 188 (upper & lower),

    Lower: 57, 141, 144, 147, 149, 152, 155, 157, 159, 161, 165, 167, 172, 175, 186, 190, 192, 196, 198,
    200, 204, 208, 213, 217, 221, 223, 226, 228, 229, 231, 234, 236, 237, 240, 242, 245, 248, 251, 254, 256,
    258, 259, 261, 263, lower inside back cover.

E. **Other**
    49, USC Athletic Department;
    91-92, Tampa Bay Buccaneers;
    University of Oklahoma Athletic Department: 124, 126, 129, 130, 131, 137, 138

DEDICATION

This book is Dedicated to The Memory
of the following men who were part of the
NU teams during The Era of Greatness
and who will forever be an important part of
The Husker Tradition:

Coach Bob Devaney    Glen Garson

Coach Mike Corgan    Jerry List

Coach Cletus Fischer    Rex Lowe

Trainer Paul Schneider    Eddie Periard

■

*"Tradition cannot be inherited,
and if you want it you must
obtain it by great labour."*

T.S. Eliot,
"Tradition and the Individual Talent" (1919)

■

*"Competitive sports keep alive in all of us
a spirit of vitality and enterprise.
It teaches the strong to know when
they are weak and the brave to face
themselves when they are afraid.
To be proud and unbending in defeat,
yet humble and gentle in victory.
To master ourselves before
we attempt to master others.
To learn to laugh,
yet never forget to weep,
and it gives predominance of
courage over timidity."*

General Douglas McArthur (1955)
Quoted in "When Pride Still Mattered"
Maraniss, p. 402 (1999)